Far-Right Vanguard

POLITICS AND CULTURE IN MODERN AMERICA

Series Editors: Keisha N. Blain, Margot Canaday,
Matthew Lassiter, Stephen Pitti, Thomas J. Sugrue

Volumes in the series narrate and analyze political and social change in the
broadest dimensions from 1865 to the present, including ideas about the ways
people have sought and wielded power in the public sphere and the language and
institutions of politics at all levels—local, national, and transnational. The series
is motivated by a desire to reverse the fragmentation of modern U.S. history
and to encourage synthetic perspectives on social movements and the state,
on gender, race, and labor, and on intellectual history and popular culture.

Far-Right Vanguard

The Radical Roots
of Modern Conservatism

John S. Huntington

PENN

UNIVERSITY OF PENNSYLVANIA PRESS

PHILADELPHIA

Published by
University of Pennsylvania Press
Philadelphia, Pennsylvania 19104-4112
www.upenn.edu/pennpress

Printed in the United States of America on acid-free paper
10 9 8 7 6 5 4 3 2 1

Library of Congress Cataloging-in-Publication Data
Names: Huntington, John S., author.
Title: Far-right vanguard : the radical roots of modern conservatism / John S. Huntington.
Other titles: Politics and culture in modern America.
Description: 1st edition. | Philadelphia : University of Pennsylvania Press, [2021] |
Series: Politics and culture in modern America | Includes bibliographical references and index.
Identifiers: LCCN 2021005734 | ISBN 9780812253474 (hardcover)
Subjects: LCSH: Conservatism—United States—History—20th century. | Right and left
(Political science)—United States—History—20th century. | Radicalism—
United States—History—20th century. | Right-wing extremists—United States—
History—20th century. | United States—Politics and government—1945–1989. |
United States—Politics and government—1901–1953.
Classification: LCC JC573.2.U6 H86 2021 | DDC 320.520973—dc23
LC record available at https://lccn.loc.gov/2021005734

For Kristen

CONTENTS

INTRODUCTION

The Radical Undercurrent

In early 1967, Louisiana publisher and far-right activist Kent Courtney put out a call to arms. "We cannot dismantle Socialism, or destroy the criminal conspiracy of Communism unless we change the policy of the U.S. government," Courtney told his roughly 25,000 readers. His four-page newsletter detailed the apocalyptic dangers facing America, namely the "pro-Communist and pro-Socialist programs advocated by the Kennedy and Johnson Administrations." Courtney encouraged his fellow conservatives to organize, to join state-level third parties and fight the communist leviathan restricting America's freedoms. The government had become the enemy, Courtney intoned, and neither major party was halting the trend toward communist slavery. The only path forward was a right-wing counterrevolution. Courtney concluded his manifesto with a plea for donations and an ominous warning: "Although education is a preliminary necessity, unless we translate this anti-Communist education into political action, we will end up being the best educated anti-Communists in a Communist concentration camp."[1]

A little over fifty years later, on August 27, 2020, President Donald Trump broke precedent by hosting the Republican National Convention on the White House's spacious South Lawn. Trump shelved his trademark stream-of-conscious surrealism during his keynote address for a staid, teleprompter-guided cadence. Nevertheless, conspiratorial rhetoric rained down from the dais. "This election will decide whether we SAVE the American Dream, or whether we allow a socialist agenda to DEMOLISH our cherished destiny," Trump warned the roughly 1,500 assembled supporters and the 23 million viewers watching from home. Trump meandered through a cornucopia of right-wing talking points—tax cuts, economic deregulation, abortion restrictions, patriotic nationalism—but his fever-pitch fearmongering often took center stage. "If the left gains power, they will demolish the suburbs, confiscate your guns, and appoint justices who will wipe away your Second Amendment and other constitutional freedoms," Trump declared. "[Joe] Biden is a Trojan horse for socialism."[2] According to Trump, any political opposition, including the Democratic Party and its supporters, were un-American subversives.

On the surface, Courtney and Trump had little in common. Courtney was an ultraconservative activist hoping to drum up support for a third-party crusade, a man whose movement was barely respectable, let alone formidable. Conversely, Trump was an incumbent president accepting his party's nomination to run for a second term, quite literally the most powerful politician in the nation. And yet deep ideological roots connected the two men. The conspiracy theories, nativism, white supremacist rhetoric, and radical libertarianism promoted by mid-twentieth century ultraconservatives had metastasized slowly over the course of sixty years until they consumed the Republican Party. During the buildup to the 2020 election, Trump was far from the only conservative voice spreading conspiracies about socialist tyranny, wanton violence, and the erosion of America. "If Biden is elected, there's a good chance you will be dead within the year," wrote cartoonist turned right-wing commentator Scott Adams, before adding an even more apocalyptic declaration: "Republicans will be hunted."[3] An entire conspiratorial subculture known as QAnon emerged during Trump's presidency, adherents of which believed that a cabal of Satan-worshipping Democrats, billionaires, and celebrities ran a clandestine sex-trafficking operation. QAnon hailed Trump as their champion against this "deep state." In turn, Trump embraced QAnon supporters as people who "love our country" and "like me very much."[4] The deluded, conspiratorial language that once marked the far right like a scarlet letter had seeped into the conservative mainstream.

Numerous conservative commentators, out of a concern for respectability, tried to create distance between "conservatism" and Trump. These erstwhile Republicans formed a loose "never-Trump" coalition and condemned him as a "populist," a "big-spending nationalist," a creature of "illiberalism" and "authoritarianism."[5] Mike Madrid, a Republican political consultant and leader of the anti-Trump Lincoln Project, put it bluntly, "[Trump] is not a conservative—he is a cancer on America and her institutions."[6] But this gatekeeping rendered a narrow, misleading definition of modern conservatism. Trump's brand of politics, however off-putting to some of his conservative detractors, represented the apotheosis of conservatism's far-right wing. His conspiratorial mudslinging, casual racism, and authoritarian impulses would have been welcome at a John Birch Society gathering or a Citizens' Council meeting. He was less President Ronald Reagan and more Alabama governor George Wallace, less *National Review* editor William F. Buckley Jr. and more Birch Society founder Robert H. W. Welch Jr. Ultraconservatives spent years out of the limelight, derided as a bunch of irrational kooks, but they nevertheless served as a centrifugal force within the conservative movement. They were looking for a savior, and they found one in Donald Trump. While it is impossible to forecast the direction of conservatism or Trump's Republican Party, one thing remains certain: the far right laid the foundation for the vitriolic politics that pulse throughout twenty-first-century America.

The divide between Trump and his conservative detractors illustrates that conservatism is, and has always been, a contested term. Political scientist Clinton Rossiter once called conservatism "one of the most confusing words in the glossary of political thought and oratory."[7] However, that has not stopped people from trying to define it. Russell Kirk, a traditionalist conservative from the 1950s, once wrote that "for the conservative, custom, convention, constitution, and prescription are the sources of a tolerable civil order."[8] In *National Review*'s mission statement, William Buckley gave this definition a spiritual spin by characterizing conservatives as "disciples of Truth, who defend the organic moral order" and "dissent from the Liberal orthodoxy."[9] In general, American conservatism embodies a distrust of reform, a suspicion of centralized power, and a desire to maintain the sociopolitical status quo. During the Cold War, these tendencies sharpened into libertarian fears of federal encroachment, an anxious defense of social and cultural norms, and an embrace of evangelical anti-communism. A desire for "freedom, virtue, and safety," as scholar George H. Nash put it, undergirded the conservative worldview.[10] Indeed, the conservative tradition contains multitudes, yet political scientist George Hawley's simple but capacious definition portrayed conservatism as any ideology in which equality is not the central pursuit. When viewed as a coherent whole, these contentions form a conservative "big tent." Conservatism is not a monolithic philosophy but rather an ideological map of intersecting ideas. And yet we know much about the conservatism of Reagan and Buckley and far less about the radical foundation upon which they stood.[11]

The American political spectrum resembles a gradient rather than a series of incontrovertible definitions, and conservatism was (and remains) a continuum marked by complex, overlapping relationships. Picture the

American political spectrum as a flat line with definitive end points. On the rightmost edge can be found extreme conservative ideas and groups, such as white power militias and the American Nazi Party, while the farthest left pole houses the American communist movement. The vast majority of Americans can be found somewhere in the middle of the polar extremes. Now, cut the spectrum in half, dividing it into an ideological left and right. Ultraconservatives occupy a broad section of the right-wing continuum, wedged between conservative pragmatists, those willing to moderate their views and work with the political center, and fringe extremists, those who engage in violence to defend their idealized, often racist, vision of American society. When viewed in this light, the far right shifts from the periphery to the core of the conservative typology.

The mid-twentieth century far right was, to use an anachronistic term, the base of the conservative movement, and it left a deep imprint upon the cultural and philosophical bedrock of modern conservatism. Ultraconservatives built a movement as fellow travelers *and* acerbic critics of modern conservatism. They eschewed political politesse, embraced conspiracy theories, manipulated religious anxieties, and exploited fears of government tyranny and racial equality. Their worldview hinged on the belief in an ongoing cultural and political crisis: America was being taken over by communists. Far-right activists smeared liberals as communists and scorned moderates for lacking ideological purity and unknowingly aiding the communist cause. To the far right, the federal government was a destructive leviathan that preyed upon American citizens through oppressive taxation, irksome bureaucracy, and racial leveling. Ultraconservatives went well beyond defending the status quo. They were true reactionaries, dissenters seeking to peel back the advance of the liberal state, hoping to turn one of the major parties, if not a third party, into a bastion of true conservatism. In short, they were the vanguard of modern conservatism.[12]

The ultraconservative movement was also a product of its time. It started off as a small, but influential, group of former politicians and right-wing businessmen fighting against Franklin D. Roosevelt and the New Deal. This origin point at the height of the liberal tide produced one of the far right's guiding principles: an uncompromising hatred and distrust of the liberal state. A malleable philosophy, anti-statism explained and animated ultraconservatives' fears of federal authority, paranoia about communist subversion, and sympathy for states' rights, and the elevation of "free enterprise" rhetoric by the conservative business community. However, the far right's anti-statism doubled as both a deeply held belief and a cynical political strategy. On one hand, ultraconservatives used "small government" philosophies to demonize political opponents, depicting expansive liberal programs as unconstitutional or un-American. But, on the other hand, they eagerly wielded federal power to disrupt left-wing organizing and liberal governance. According to ultraconservatives, liberalism was a liminal, and equally dangerous, stage of communism. State power, when gripped by a firm conservative hand, offered a salve against this existential slippery slope. In this sense the far right portrayed themselves as the heirs of the American Revolution, the true protectors of Americanism.[13]

Ultraconservative ranks grew quickly, especially when the Cold War cast communism as the nation's bête noire. During the 1950s and 1960s, as the threat of global communism vexed American minds, the ultraconservative movement reached its apex. Conspiratorial rhetoric permeated Cold War America; conservatives of all stripes portrayed liberalism as a gateway for, if not outright, state tyranny. While many Americans viewed communism as primarily an external threat, far-right conspiracy theorists believed communism had already poisoned America's institutions. As Welch told his fellow far-right confidants, "Today the process has gone so far that not only our federal government but some of our state governments are to a disturbing extent controlled by Communist sympathizers or political captives of the Communists."[14] To wit, the communists and their liberal comrades-in-arms had pushed America to the brink of authoritarianism and only a conservative insurgency could save the nation.

One of the most potent forms of anti-statism manifested through the far right's defense of states' rights and racial segregation. As the fight for racial equality percolated during the mid-twentieth century, ultraconservatives, especially those in the South, viewed the civil rights movement as a threat to southern tradition. Worse yet, they warned, civil rights activism was actually a front for communism. "Let no one deceive himself," declared pastor Billy James Hargis. "The communist conspirators are interested in using American Negroes only for their own evil purposes."[15] Using anti-communism to denigrate the civil rights movement shielded the far right with a thin veneer of respectability, but outright racism often punctured this façade. When campaigning for Texas governor in 1956, rancher-cum-activist J. Evetts Haley proclaimed that integration would lead to "spiritual degradation" and the "disintegration of the white race!"[16] According to ultraconservatives such as Haley, white America stood poised at the precipice of annihilation. Far-right zealots fused racial resentment, anti-communism, and anti-statism into a political litmus test to purify right-wing ranks and fracture the predominance of liberalism, which ultimately produced an uncompromising mindset and a hyper-partisanship that precipitated and molded the contours of modern conservatism.[17]

The far right formed an indispensable vanguard during the conservative movement's early years. These right-wing shock troops, including leaders such as Courtney, Welch, Haley, Hargis, and Willis E. Stone, established organizations to carry the ultraconservative banner. Their groups—the Conservative Society of America, John Birch Society, Texans For America, Christian Crusade, and Liberty Amendment Committee, respectively—became points of convergence for bellicose activists, right-wing politicians, and conservative businessmen, each one a critical node within the vast ultraconservative network. Their publications, read by thousands of disaffected Americans, preached a gospel of government malfeasance, liberal treachery, and communist subversion. Their members distributed mailing lists, led voter registration drives, and connected with politicians in both major parties. These groups cooperated with other like-minded organizations, such as We the People, the Liberty Lobby, and the Christian Anti-Communism Crusade, to form an extensive institutional galaxy. Other ultraconservatives and their allies—including Buckley, General Edwin A. Walker, Clarence Manion, Democratic congressman Martin Dies Jr. of Texas, minister Gerald B. Winrod, publisher Dan Smoot, Democratic senator Strom Thurmond of South Carolina, George Wallace, and Republican Senator Barry Goldwater of Arizona—collaborated to varying degrees with the far-right network. This vibrant, interconnected web of institutions, activists, and politicians formed the connective tissue of the ultraconservative movement.[18]

The far-right network spanned national, state, and local levels, illustrating how common bonds transcended regional lines while individual chapters still reflected local cultural mores. For example, Courtney's Conservative Society of America, headquartered in the Deep South, wrapped its states' rights ideas in white supremacy and segregation, while Stone's Liberty Amendment Committee, founded on the West Coast, defended states' rights using "colorblind" libertarian economics. Slight differences in rhetorical tone or policy focus did not stifle collaboration; on the contrary, it stimulated the diffusion of far-right ideas. Far-right leaders often assumed positions in each other's institutions—Courtney served as a state chairman for Stone's organization, for example—illustrating the movement's interconnectivity. In particular, the far right experienced tremendous success at the local level by hosting conferences, mass mailer fundraising, and canvassing local municipalities. These efforts disseminated far-right ideas, produced fruitful relationships with conservative politicians, and fostered momentum that ultimately produced watershed moments, such as Goldwater's presidential candidacy in 1964 and Wallace's third-party run in 1968.[19]

Despite their centrality to the conservative movement, the far right was minimized, if not outright mocked, by many contemporary analysts. Senator Thomas H. Kuchel, a California Republican, denounced the far right as "a fanatical, neofascist political cult," while some voters derided ultraconservatives as "a radical clique" full of "nuts."[20] But far-right conservatives were not dupes or crackpots, as critics alleged. Their worldview, which found significant purchase among the conservative grass roots, simply obviated shades of gray. The far right's visibility, if not influence, waned before the conservative movement reached its zenith. Old age caught up to the rabble-rousers by the late twentieth century. The far right did not push the conservative movement across the finish line—Reagan accomplished that in 1980—but they set the very foundation upon which conservatives such as Reagan stood. Ultimately, the far-right movement galvanized millions of Americans disenchanted with the trajectory of U.S. politics, built institutions that served as grassroots training grounds, created media outlets to broadcast right-wing resentment, and, though they often saw themselves as critics of mainstream conservatism, helped lay the groundwork for the later success of the conservative movement.[21]

Nevertheless, the far right has often been undervalued as a political catalyst. Historians held "a rough consensus about the rise of modern American conservatism," read Rick Perlstein's retrospective. "It told a respectable tale." Perlstein, a historian whose oeuvre contributed to this foundational narrative, admitted that this "respectable tale" underestimated "conservative history's political surrealists and intellectual embarrassments, its con artists and tribunes of white rage."[22] Instead, a great deal of scholarship highlighted the growth of conservative suburbs, the decline of outright segregationism and evolution of color-blind rhetoric, and the advocacy of free-market theories. Conservative businessmen, Christian evangelicals, family-values traditionalists, and Cold War anti-communists featured as the loci for this right-wing surge. Conservative intellectuals guarded their ideological flock against the intrusions of far-right crackpots, preserving the movement's respectability, while titanic political figures such as Reagan guided conservatism to electoral victories.[23]

But this "respectable" narrative laundered the history of American conservatism by casting the far right as a bit player or a troubling aberration rather than the base of the movement. The reality was that ideological, tactical, and organizational overlaps blurred the line dividing the far right from the conservative mainstream. The difference between the radicals and the respectables was one of degree, not kind. Two issues ostensibly separated ultraconservatives from their mainstream counterparts: the belief that a vast communist conspiracy subverted and controlled American politics and a black-or-white view dividing the political spectrum into a false binary of pure conservatism versus a communist-dominated enemy, which included liberals and conservative moderates. But these ambiguous dividing lines were porous and blurred to the point of illegibility. As contemporary analysts Benjamin Epstein and Arnold Forster observed, "The two factions are difficult to separate at times, particularly when they sit at the same rallies and applaud the same ideas."[24] In other words, the far-right movement grew out of the same ideological seedbed that nourished the conservative mainstream. Though they experienced few electoral successes, ultraconservatives forced "respectable" conservatives to grapple with their concerns, thereby intensifying right-wing thought and forecasting the trajectory of American politics.[25]

Divining the difference between the radicals and respectables is challenging, but establishing a barometer using 1960s Sunbelt politicians, from mainstream to radical conservatives, helps clarify the political scale. Senator John Tower, a Texas Republican, adhered to the tenets of mainstream conservatism—individual liberty, anti-communism, and limited government—but he cooperated with his party's liberal wing. Senator Barry Goldwater stood a little further to Tower's right, embodying the same principles with greater vehemence and an aversion to pragmatism. Goldwater, an Arizona Republican, referred to liberalism as a "dehumanizing" "leviathan" and contended that anything other than a strict constitutional interpretation amounted to a usurpation of power.[26] If Goldwater epitomized the libertarian conservatism of the western Sunbelt, Senator Strom Thurmond, a South Carolina Democrat, represented the Deep South's segregationist wing. Both men opposed the 1964 Civil Rights Act, but for Goldwater it was a matter of constitutional principle, whereas Thurmond's dissent stemmed from southern traditions of segregationism and racial politics (he was a harbinger of southern political realignment when he switched to the GOP on September 16, 1964). Goldwater and Thurmond, each representing essential far-right factions, helped build a staunch conservative coalition within the GOP.[27]

Spanning the ambiguous space separating the radicals and the respectables were what I call "right-wing translators," conservative politicians and pundits who repackaged ultraconservative ideas for mainstream consumption. The translators straddling that blurred line, such as Goldwater and Buckley, applied a respectable gloss to ideas outside of the political mainstream. As the conservative movement grew, these translators evolved into ideological and partisan gatekeepers, sentries responsible for policing the movement's borders while still siphoning energy from ultraconservative groups and their constituencies. Buckley, for instance, shared numerous ideological touchstones with the far right and networked extensively with their organizations through conferences and grassroots campaigns. He separated himself only after becoming convinced that Welch's conspiracy theories threatened the nascent conservative movement's credibility. This interaction, which will be studied more closely in a later chapter, epitomized how right-wing translators attempted to regulate the porous, shifting border separating the far right from the so-called "responsible Right." These translators elucidated how the ultraconservatives could be both partners and antagonists, propagators and critics, activists and cynics.[28]

Further out on the right-wing continuum, yet not associated with the violent extreme, resided staunch ultraconservatives such as former General Edwin Walker. While serving in the military in 1961, Walker instituted a program called Pro-Blue that fearmongered about communist subversion and outlined voting recommendations to his soldiers. The military relieved Walker of his command for telling soldiers who to vote for, unleashing him to embark on a crusade, including a speaking tour with Hargis, to warn Americans about the imminent threat of communist subversion. Walker portrayed the election of President John F. Kennedy, a Massachusetts Democrat and liberal Catholic, as "evidence that the U.S. government had succumbed to communism."[29] This sort of conspiratorial rhetoric placed Walker slightly to the right of Goldwater on the conservative spectrum. However, Walker found common ground with segregationists such as Thurmond. His actions during the integration of the University of Mississippi, where Walker led a mob of students in revolt against U.S. Marshals, showed both Walker's dedication to defending white supremacy and the permeable boundary separating the far right from violent extremists.[30]

Throughout this book I use multiple terms interchangeably to describe this segment of the conservative spectrum, including ultraconservative, far right, reactionary, and radical right-wing. I employ the term "conservative" in a general fashion to refer to those ideals or individuals that resided on the right half of the political spectrum; however, I take pains to demarcate, as best as possible, conservatism's most extreme elements. Ultraconservatives drew a line between themselves and violent extremists, even though that boundary proved as porous as the separation between the far right and the conservative mainstream. Nevertheless, in my view, groups such as the Ku Klux Klan and Robert DePugh's Minutemen militia exemplified right-wing extremism because they advocated armed aggression and, at times, participated in extrajudicial violence. The far right, in contrast, represented an exaggerated form of mainstream conservatism by expanding anti-statism and anti-communism into the realm of conspiracy. Over time some far-right activists joined forces with mainstream conservatives while others spiraled away from the political center; nevertheless, ultraconservative philosophies and strategies lingered in the political ether, influencing the shape and tenor of the conservative movement.[31]

Far-Right Vanguard documents the history of the ultraconservative movement, its national institutional network, and its centrality to America's rightward turn during the second half of the twentieth century. The first three chapters trace the movement's ideological and organizational origins and partisan complexities, especially the cross-party nature of far-right activism. Chapter 1 examines the historical roots of ultraconservatism, following the thread from the late nineteenth century through the presidency of Franklin Roosevelt. Far-right groups, such as the Jeffersonian Democrats and the American Liberty League, emerged to contest Roosevelt's liberal revolution, which illustrated the movement's bipartisan character and provided a foundation for future far-right activism. Chapter 2 analyzes how the World War II era honed far-right philosophies. Wartime patriotism weakened the far right's anti-interventionist tradition, but the warfare state enabled ultraconservative politicians, ostensibly anti-statists, to employ federal power against liberal opponents. Traditional party loyalties further frayed as angry Democrats mutinied over Roosevelt's fourth-term campaign while far-right businessmen rebelled against wartime economic regulations. Chapter 3 explores the cauldron of early Cold War politics, a critical era for the emergence of ultraconservative institutions. Senator Joseph McCarthy's anti-communist investigations, Dwight D. Eisenhower's "Modern Republicanism," and the nascent civil rights movement convinced far-right activists that the red wolf had breached the door. They responded by creating numerous organizations, including For America and the Christian Crusade, that eventually solidified into a cohesive national movement bent on retrenching the legacies of modern liberalism.

The second half of the book studies the interlacing of the ultraconservative network, the far right's complicated relationship with mainstream conservatives, and the movement's impact on electoral and party politics.

Chapter 4 covers the far right's entry into party politics and the tightening of the far right's institutional network. The third-party campaign of T. Coleman Andrews and the formation of the John Birch Society were pivotal moments when disconnected far-right organizations and activists crystallized into a coherent, unified movement. Chapter 5 analyzes the apex of the ultraconservative movement through the far right's support for Barry Goldwater in 1960 and 1964. Third-party action remained viable, but far-right activists gravitated toward an increasingly conservative Republican Party. However, ultraconservatives came under increased scrutiny from fellow right-wingers in search of mainstream respectability, which led to a boundary-defining conflict over the soul of modern conservatism. Chapter 6 recounts the numerous aftershocks following Goldwater's defeat in 1964. Viewing the radicals as culpable for Goldwater's loss, mainstream conservatives tried to further marginalize the far right. In response, ultraconservatives increased their grassroots organizing and rejected the candidacy of Richard Nixon, a moderate conservative, in favor of George Wallace's third-party crusade in 1968. The book's epilogue discusses the decline of midcentury ultraconservatism while illustrating the movement's profound effect on the ideological, strategic, and rhetorical contours of modern conservatism.

The story of midcentury ultraconservatism, from its New Deal era inception through the turbulent 1960s, reveals that movements without significant electoral victories can still carve deep impressions upon the American polity. It also exposes that the right-wing coalition's more radical elements held widespread influence among the conservative grass roots. The far right's politics of dissent—against racial progress, federal power, and political moderation—laid the foundation for the aggrieved conservatism of the twenty-first century. Far from impotent fringe outliers, ultraconservative activists and institutions formed the vanguard of the conservative movement.

CHAPTER 1

Dissonant Voices

As the crisp stillness of autumn settled into the Midwest, roughly 2,000 people packed into the Concordia Turner Hall auditorium, a few blocks south of downtown St. Louis. It was October 19, 1936, and the upcoming presidential election loomed just two weeks away. Both the Democratic and Republican parties were hosting rallies in the Gateway City to secure last-minute votes, but instead of saddling up with a major party, the assembled citizens at Concordia Turner represented an ultraconservative splinter faction. This particular meeting had been organized by two insurgent far-right organizations, the National Jeffersonian Democrats and the Independent Coalition of American Women. After the crowd settled in, event chairman Isaac H. Lionberger introduced the keynote speaker, former Missouri Senator James A. Reed, the leader of the Jeffersonian Democrats. The crowd whooped and hollered as Reed strode to the stage. When Reed reached the dais, Lionberger praised him as "the greatest Democrat we now have in this country." Reed was seventy-five years old, but he still bore the presence of a man who had spent years thrilling crowds from the stump. He shucked his coat and rolled up his sleeves, ready to denounce the greatest threat to the nation and his beloved Democratic Party: current president, and fellow Democrat, Franklin Delano Roosevelt.[1]

Reed stoked the crowd like a plain-folks preacher, his voice swelling with passion as he condemned Roosevelt for abandoning traditional Democratic tenets. "I'm here fighting the cause of the Democratic Party tonight. What there is left of it," Reed declared. Roosevelt and his liberal cabal had subjugated the Democratic Party, Reed said, and dragged "it over into Red territory." In fact, Reed quipped, "I make the assertion that there isn't a chemist in the world who could analyze a Russian Bolshevist and analyze the New

Deal and tell which was the Bolshevist and which was the New Deal."[2] He impressed upon the audience the importance of saving their party from the clutches of New Deal communism. It was an audacious notion. Retrenching the tidal wave of modern liberalism required putting radical thoughts into action. To Reed's mind, the only path forward entailed supporting the lesser of two evils, which meant convincing these dissident Democrats to spurn their own party and vote Republican in the coming election.

Four years earlier, Roosevelt's election had altered the trajectory of American politics. Roosevelt delivered a liberal revolution that rippled throughout the U.S. polity, a "new deal" that transformed the very relationship between the people and the federal government. He pledged to build America "from the bottom up and not from the top down" and mobilize government resources on behalf of "the forgotten man at the bottom of the economic pyramid."[3] To make good on that promise, Roosevelt called a special session of Congress the day after his inauguration. For one hundred days, Congress was a conveyor belt of New Deal legislation. Bills flew out the door to stabilize the banking industry, establish public works programs, create a safety net for struggling farmers and the unemployed, and implement long-overdue regulations on Wall Street. Roosevelt's New Deal erected a welfare state atop the country's capitalist foundation, a middle path of regulatory liberalism that circumvented both *laissez-faire* economics and state-planned socialism.[4]

Rather than viewing Roosevelt's New Deal as salubrious progressivism, however, the far right spied red-tinged state tyranny. Most ultraconservatives during the 1930s were grassroots activists and former politicians who did not have to satisfy a constituency or maintain a political alliance, which freed them to spread their unvarnished, and at times unpopular, convictions. The far right's disavowal of modern liberalism was not a simple policy disagreement or a prosaic debate over constitutional boundaries. Roosevelt, in their valuation, was a Marxist in sheep's clothing, his New Deal a Trojan horse for communist revolution. Bainbridge Colby, the former secretary of state turned far-right activist, lamented that the Democratic Party was becoming a "thoroughgoing Socialist Party," while Reed took it a step further by calling the New Deal an "unholy combination of Communism, Socialism, and Bolshevism."[5] Reed concluded his St. Louis speech to rapturous applause: "How much further will [Roosevelt] trample upon our Bill of Rights? What wild scheme might be germinating in his brain, or in the brain of some communist advisor? Such a man is not fit to hold the office of president of the United States." Indeed, fears of un-American subversion beset the ultraconservative mind.

The ultraconservative revolt was not simple backlash politics, but a movement with deep roots weaving through both parties and tracing back to the previous century. The nativism, *laissez-faire* economics, and white supremacy that permeated late nineteenth century America formed the far right's ideological heritage. In the early twentieth century, rampant paranoia about cultural decay, communist infiltration, and racial upheaval further directed the ultraconservative political compass. This ideological seedbed bolstered the far right's perception that the New Deal had sparked an existential crisis between a free society and state paternalism. Red-baiting rhetoric, as illustrated by Reed's speech, doubled as both a strategy to encourage political involvement and a cipher for larger structural critiques about the purpose and purview of government. During the lean years of the Great Depression, ultraconservatives occasionally found allies in right-wing Republicans, who held fast to their pro-business conservatism and despised the New Deal's cooperation with labor, corporate tax increases, and mushrooming government programs. The far right also collaborated with conservative Democrats who accused Roosevelt of forsaking Democratic traditions. Though some ultraconservatives maintained their party affiliations, the far right as a whole was less driven by partisan loyalties than by a sense of ideological purity and righteous aggrievement. Ultimately, the far right's ideological blend of economic libertarianism, social traditionalism, anti-statism, white supremacy, and conspiratorial anti-communism catalyzed right-wing action during an era of liberal hegemony.[6]

An interconnected web of ultraconservative reactionaries and organizations coalesced to disrupt Roosevelt's New Deal revolution. Far-right leaders such as Reed, cattleman J. Evetts Haley, and former congressman Jouett Shouse represented the tip of the spear. Their groups served as critical nodes within the far-right network, each a point of convergence for embittered right-wingers. Shouse's American Liberty League, an organization created and funded by wealthy elites, cloaked its illiberalism in a veil of constitutionalism, patriotic fervor, and paeans to individual and economic liberty. Reed's National Jeffersonian Democrats attempted to redeem the Democratic Party through states' rights arguments and conspiracies about federal and communist terror. Southern Jeffersonian chapters, particularly Haley's Jeffersonian Democrats of Texas, peppered their rhetoric with white supremacy and southern agrarianism. While the Jeffersonians teamed up with the Liberty League in 1936, reactionary and quasi-fascist third parties, such as the Union Party and Christian Party, also formed to contest Roosevelt's reelection bid. The breadth of far-right movements illustrated the depth of conservative disillusion during the height of New Deal liberalism. Furthermore, the conspiratorial, anti-statist mindset of 1930s ultraconservatives festered over time, fueling future right-wing activism and shaping the contours of midcentury conservatism.[7]

*   *   *

Mid-twentieth century ultraconservatives did not emerge in a vacuum—they built their movement upon preexisting strains of conservatism. In the late nineteenth century, disparate, and at times paradoxical, right-wing movements and ideologies permeated American society. Conservatism, broadly conceived, crossed party lines. The Democratic Party, especially in the South, was often viewed as the bastion of limited government and states' rights. The Republicans, on the other hand, were divided between the *laissez-faire* impulses of the old guard, the nativist fears of social traditionalists, and the pro-government tendencies of nascent progressives. Conservatism stretched beyond Washington, too. As populist agrarian movements challenged the influence of the business elite, economic titans and their allies developed libertarian arguments to preserve their status, protect their property, and defend against federal economic regulations. These libertarians, such as political economist William Graham Sumner and steel tycoon Andrew Carnegie, disdained social traditions and instead promoted a hierarchical, ruthless capitalism in which inequality fired the engines of progress. But their libertarianism proved situational. Industry magnates often used police power, whether governmental or mercenary, to crack down on union organizing, illustrating that state power in the spirit of "law and order" could be used to bolster the might of capital. On the other hand, social traditionalists distrusted the power of capital and yearned for a return to an idealized past where an entrenched cultural hierarchy commanded deference and civility. Traditionalist conservatives pulled from the ranks of ministers, Republican Mugwumps, and northeastern writers, all of which were groups united by fears of cultural decay, often viewing immigration and direct democracy as a civilizational threat.[8]

In the South, a region dominated by the Democratic Party, traditionalism took the form of white supremacy and an adherence to states' rights. Defeat during the Civil War and the upheaval of Reconstruction produced among southerners a sense of unity as "oppressed" people, struggling under the yoke of northern federal tyranny. A prickly sense of pride and tradition dominated the old Confederacy. Southerners yearned for a return to antebellum social norms. To "redeem" the South, conservatives reduced black Americans to second-class citizens through Jim Crow segregation, and terrorist groups such as the Ku Klux Klan enforced a strict racial hierarchy through extrajudicial violence, all of which extended the nation's legacy of brutal racism well into the twentieth century. While these disparate conser- vatives did not always align ideologically, all three factions—traditionalists, proto-libertarians, and southern conservatives—shared an antipathy for the federal government and a fear of radical change. Looking forward, the mid- century far right emerged from the same ideological waters that nourished the nineteenth century's conservative mainstream. Whether it was anxieties about economic interventionism, militant unionists, or socialist meddlers, anti-statism and anti-radicalism (soon-to-be anti-communism) often served as the bonding elements for the broader conservative movement.[9]

Around the turn of the century, new right-wing ideals and movements intermixed with and built upon Gilded Age conservatism. The patriotic jin- goism of President Theodore "Teddy" Roosevelt and xenophobic nativism of Congressman Martin Dies Sr., a conservative Texas Democrat and father of far-right congressman Martin Dies Jr., promulgated a sense of American superiority and implied that immigration allowed inferior, alien cultures to infiltrate the United States. Though Teddy camped in the progressive wing of the Republican Party and embraced popular democracy, his belief in rule by the elite, his contempt for immigrants, and his glorification of violence in the name of progress denoted a more conservative core. Early twentieth-century conservatism also housed a nationalist wing which opposed international- ism and sought to maintain American neutrality as World War I heated up in Europe. War came anyway, bringing both a more active federal govern- ment and an abrogation of civil rights. When President Woodrow Wilson proposed an international alliance, the League of Nations, to prevent future wars, Republicans such as Massachusetts senator Henry Cabot Lodge argued that the League would trample the Constitution and erode American sover- eignty. Even some of Wilson's fellow Democrats, including Missouri senator James A. Reed, a soon-to-be ultraconservative activist, opposed joining the League. Replacing nationalism with internationalism, they argued, was a key tenet of communism. The tension between foreign policy hawks and anti- interventionists remained unresolved and continued to percolate throughout the twentieth-century conservative movement. Nevertheless, Gilded Age and early twentieth-century right-wing philosophies—nationalism, *laissez-faire* economics, social traditionalism, white supremacy, anti-statism—formed the ideological bedrock for both mainstream conservatives and intransigent ultraconservatives.[10]

As the country sprinted into the postwar era, the sociopolitical environment of the Roaring Twenties provided multiple ideological touchstones for the midcentury far right. The United States emerged relatively unscathed from World War I, but Russia's communist revolution combined with fears of immigration to create a burst of paranoia that rippled throughout postwar society. American journalist John Reed called Russia's October Revolution in 1917 the "ten days that shook the world," an event that paved the way for the First Red Scare, a high tide of xenophobic nationalism, ideological repression, and violence against minorities and labor unionists. The instability born out of the transition to a peacetime society fostered economic unrest. Conservatives viewed the battles between labor and capital as a microcosm of the larger war between socialist-collectivism and capitalism. Previous examples of radical violence, such as President William McKinley's assassination at the hands of an anarchist in 1901, and high-profile events such as the 1919 Boston Police Strike and the 1920 Wall Street bombing heightened the perception that foreign "bolshevism" was invading American shores. The postwar decade, in short, created a petri dish for reactionary conservatism.[11]

The First Red Scare conjured an enemy—communism—that conservatives blamed for socioeconomic problems and exploited for political gain, a red-baiting strategy absorbed and employed by future far-right activists. Mainstream conservatism ascended as right-wing Republicans won the presidency in 1920 on a ticket featuring anti-intellectual, pro-business Senator Warren G. Harding of Ohio and Calvin Coolidge, the union-busting governor of Massachusetts. Xenophobia and anti-communism reverberated throughout Harding's and Coolidge's presidencies. During the 1924 presidential election Coolidge asked "whether America will allow itself to be degraded into a communistic and socialistic state, or whether it will remain American."[12] Coolidge's words hinted at undercurrents of nativist nationalism and highlighted conservative Republicans' willingness to harness anti-communist anxieties for partisan purposes. The language of anti-communism not only defended American institutions that were supposedly under assault from alien ideologies, but also fused together with anti-statism to form the binding agent that melded disparate conservative ideologies into a coherent whole. When red-scare impulses flared again in the mid-twentieth century, ultraconservatives capitalized. Kent Courtney, a third-party agitator and far-right pamphleteer, sent a letter chastising Congress: "Every Congressman should be a militant anti-Communist. In this cold war there is no room for half-hearted Americans."[13] Anti-communism served as a political action strategy for defeating progressive reform while simultaneously congealing into a critical component of modern conservatism's ideological foundation, one that guided the far right's political instincts in particular.[14]

Concern over atrophy at the hands of communist saboteurs or state tyrants extended into the economic realm, leading far-right and mainstream conservatives to develop intellectual defenses of free-market capitalism. Influenced by their *laissez-faire* forebears, conservatives of all stripes viewed free-market economics as a crucial bulwark against the Red Menace. The nation's economy roared after the initial postwar turbulence, bolstering conservatives' faith in free enterprise. Harding and Coolidge initiated policies favored by business leaders, such as high tariffs, low taxes, and deregulation. Herbert Hoover, then serving as commerce secretary, implemented his "associative state," which aligned the interests of government and capital, empowering businessmen while obviating large bureaucracies. Despite the fact that Republicans had their thumb on the scale for capital, many businessmen and wealthy elites viewed federal power as a menace to economic freedom. Albert Jay Nock and H. L. Mencken, both godfathers of the midcentury libertarian movement, took a dim view of government. In his short-lived periodical, *Freeman*, Nock promoted his own radical Jeffersonian vision in which prosperity and progress came only through individual and economic liberty. Though Nock's anti-statism seemed at odds with Hoover's "associative state," each philosophy held an overarching aversion to progressive economic interventionism and a faith in free enterprise. The state, according to Nock, was a destroyer rather than a defender of freedom. This anti-statist language became a staple of far-right thought. According to John Birch Society founder Robert Welch, "The greatest enemy of man is, and always has been, government."[15] Ultraconservative activist Willis E. Stone later helmed a Nockian crusade to abolish the income tax and fight the "bureaucratic domination" and "communistic empires" within the federal government.[16] The midcentury far-right vanguard embodied the fact that libertarianism had crystallized into an ideological staple of the broader conservative movement.[17]

Religious right-wingers also used the Roaring Twenties as a springboard for conservative activism. The culture war between traditionalism and modernism, particularly the teaching of evolution and Darwinism, convinced fundamentalists that American society was in crisis. Driven by a conservative theological philosophy, fundamentalists championed individual conversion experiences, biblical inerrancy, and a broad evangelical mission. Culture wars widened the rifts between liberal modernists and right-wing fundamentalists, dividing major northern denominations, such as the Baptists and Presbyterians; however, modernism failed to penetrate the South's thicket of conservative evangelicalism. Southern evangelicals would soon transport their religious conservatism westward, weaving a fundamentalist thread throughout the Sunbelt. Imbued with faith to purify society, fundamentalists fought against the "one-world, secular" League of Nations and railed against the secularization of public schools. The fundamentalist movement provided a rallying point for ultraconservatives. For example, minister Gerald B. Winrod cut his teeth as an anti-evolution, anti-modernism crusader; he embraced the fundamentalist label, founded the Defenders of the Christian Faith, and eventually became an anti-Semitic fascist during the Great Depression. Thirty years after the culture wars of the 1920s, fundamentalists continued to view the world through a binary lens, though one sharpened by the global communist-capitalist divide rather than the battles over modernism. "There are no two ways about this question," wrote Billy James Hargis, founder of the Christian Crusade. "We are either pro-Christ or pro-Communist."[18] Fundamentalism, like anti-communism and free-market libertarianism, bridged 1920s conservatism to the midcentury radical right and eventually evolved into a critical component of the conservative movement.[19]

The cultural anxieties of the postwar era fueled white supremacy and set off ugly episodes of racial violence throughout the United States. The Red Summer of 1919, part of the broader Red Scare, witnessed dozens of race massacres in major cities such as Chicago and Washington. Roving bands of white vigilantes attacked black citizens, leading to hundreds of deaths, thousands of injuries, and untold amounts of property damage. In 1921, white mobs destroyed the affluent black neighborhood of Greenwood in Tulsa, Oklahoma, killing at least twenty-five black residents and torching thirty-five city blocks. Lynchings plagued the nation, particularly the South. Between the years 1889 and 1924, over 3,000 people, the vast majority of them African American, were lynched. The number of vigilante murders diminished during the 1920s due, in part, to an extensive anti-lynching campaign led by women such as Ida B. Wells and Jessie Daniel Ames. Nevertheless, the turmoil allowed southerners to further entrench racial apartheid in the old Confederate states. Segregation and disenfranchisement thrived. Despite the violence and civil rights abuses, the Southern Agrarians, a group of writers and intellectuals, came together to defend southern culture. Modernity, they cried, threatened the South's traditional social hierarchy. The Agrarians produced a book, *I'll Take My Stand: The South and the Agrarian Tradition*, which contained defenses of segregation and white supremacy, Confederate apologias, and paeans to southern nationalism. Mid-twentieth century conservatives, from far-right agitators such as J. Evetts Haley to pragmatists such as William F. Buckley Jr., embraced Agrarian writers as conservative forebears who valued social order and tradition while opposing communism and the state leviathan.[20]

White supremacy reached a fevered crescendo in the 1920s, which fostered a renascence of the Ku Klux Klan, born again as Protestant defenders of Americanism. Unlike its Reconstruction era predecessor, the 1920s Klan was a mainstream social and political movement. The second Klan spread beyond the confines of the old Confederacy, cultivating a following in the Midwest, Southwest, and West Coast. It established headquarters in major cities such as Houston, Indianapolis, and Portland. Right-wing ministers, including future televangelist Robert Schuller and fundamentalist preacher Bob Jones Sr., lauded the Klan as a bulwark protecting white Protestant America. Through grassroots action and an aggressive membership drive, the Klan gained tangible, and bipartisan, political power. Indiana's Republican governor, Houston's Democratic mayor, Oregon's Republican speaker of the house—all Klansmen. At the height of its influence, the group claimed as many as six million members, though the actual figure is likely closer to one or two million. The Klan's middle-class membership and festive social gatherings resembled the Rotary more than a ragtag cadre of murderous Confederate veterans. Nevertheless, visceral racism and vigilantism lurked close to the surface.[21]

By fusing Protestant morality with preexisting strains of nativism and race hatred, the second Klan created a cocktail of far-right conservatism. Only native-born, Protestant whites were considered "100%" or "true" Americans, according to Klan thinking. Numerous immigrant groups and religious and racial minorities morphed into categorical "others" who represented a latent threat to white American society. Imperial Wizard Hiram Evans demonized Catholics as an "alien" influence spreading discord and sowing a "crop of evils."[22] In 1922, 6,000 people gathered at the Portland Municipal Auditorium to hear Klansman R. H. Sawyer rage, "The negro in whose blood flows the mad desire for race amalgamation is more dangerous than a maddened wild beast."[23] Though the Klan's membership plummeted during the late 1920s, the result of numerous violent scandals, its legacy lived on. Segregationists continued to deploy red-baiting, racist rhetoric as the fight for civil rights challenged the country's racial hierarchy and traditional social norms. The second Klan ultimately reflected a political tradition of white supremacy that stretched from the Reconstruction era through the mid-twentieth century. More broadly, if late nineteenth-century conservatism formed the far right's ideological bedrock, then the conservatism of the 1920s built upon that edifice, laying the groundwork for future generations of far-right activists.[24]

Indeed, the ultraconservative movement grew out of the same ideological soil that nourished mainstream conservatism, germinating a reactionary mass desperate to defend America from perceived subversion. The far right soon got the chance to man the barricades, because by 1934 a sea change had swept through American politics. Republican conservatism declined, humbled by the Great Depression, while Roosevelt's New Deal liberalism ascended. Though the southern conservative wing of the Democratic Party remained entrenched and powerful, Roosevelt's liberal coalition charted a new policy course from Washington. Rather than viewing liberty through the lens of economic freedom, a conservative axiom, Roosevelt defined liberty as economic security for the entire spectrum of American society, from the most vulnerable citizens to banks and industry. The New Deal instituted regulations on the banking sector, committed the government to the welfare of Americans, promised millions of dollars in aid to farmers, and established massive public works relief programs. Additionally, Roosevelt's progressive liberalism created an environment that empowered workers and encouraged average Americans to get more involved in politics.[25]

Yet, where Roosevelt saw a restoration of American promise, conservatives spied looming government oppression. Conservatives, ranging from mainstream politicians to radical activists, distrusted Roosevelt's flexing of state power. Right-wing Republicans bemoaned the erosion of individual and economic liberty and constitutional order, and some, including former President Hoover, spoke to the far right by crowning Roosevelt a socialist bent on wealth redistribution and the destruction of capitalism. Southern Democrats, on the other hand, feared that Roosevelt's reforms would upend the South's exploitative labor system and traditions of white supremacy, so they fought against the New Deal and successfully hampered the benefits extended to minorities and farm laborers. The nascent conservative business movement, led by groups such as the National Association of Manufacturers and Leonard Read's Foundation for Economic Education, believed that New Deal reforms curtailed the autonomy, power, and prestige of business. Right-wing businesspeople criticized the federal expansion and deficit spending of New Deal

liberalism and lifted up free-market economics as a necessary bulwark protecting capitalism from socialist meddling. Mainstream and far-right conservatives alike failed to smother Roosevelt's New Deal, but their arguments
overlapped substantially, establishing the necessary ideological infrastructure
for a broad conservative alliance.[26]

Even though the New Deal served as a buoy, rather than an anchor, for
capitalism, ultraconservatives stoked anti-statist resentment, establishing
themselves as the shock troops for the American Right. Roosevelt's left turn
in 1935, particularly the labor-friendly Wagner Act and proposed tax hikes on
wealthy elites and corporations, spurred a right-wing revolt. Not content to
fight the New Deal within the normal boundaries of polite debate, the far right
proffered conspiracy theories depicting Roosevelt as a communist bent on
destroying America. Such conspiratorial language ran the gamut from overheated accusations of planned state tyranny to bigoted anti-Semitic diatribes
about the "Jew Deal." In his magnum opus, *Our Enemy, the State*, Nock characterized the federal government as "blundering, wasteful, and vicious," a leviathan intent on transforming social power into state despotism.[27] Anti-Semite
James True asserted that his organization, James True Associates, existed to
contest "the Jew Communism which the New Deal is trying to force on America."[28] Most mainstream politicians avoided public anti-Semitic commentary,
but anti-communist conspiracies and libertarian rhetoric flooded the political
discourse.[29]

Rather than solely representing an extremist fringe, conspiratorial anti-
communism had deep roots within the conservative intellectual and political
tradition. Many of Roosevelt's critics, from ultraconservatives to mainstream
right-wingers, utilized the occasional hysterical, red-baiting diatribe for partisan gain. Hoover warned that the New Deal would "enslave" taxpayers. Senator Arthur H. Vandenberg, a Michigan Republican, said Americans were
"living under [a] political dictatorship," and Republican National Committee
(RNC) chairman Henry P. Fletcher compared Roosevelt to Hitler and Mussolini and derided the New Deal as "lettered on the Russian model."[30] This
strategy helped conservatives claw back power, especially when the New Deal
lost steam in the late 1930s. Republican Robert Taft of Ohio, elected to the
U.S. Senate in 1938, warned that the New Deal would "practically abandon
the whole theory of American government, and inaugurate what is in fact
socialism."[31] Anti-communism provided a useful cudgel for portraying New
Deal liberalism as a red tide threatening America. But for some conservatives, particularly the far right, conspiracies alleging communist subversion

served as both strategy and axiom. Ultraconservatives viewed themselves as hardnosed truth-tellers, warning that Roosevelt's New Deal was a veil for communist revolution, and the fact that mainstream conservatives utilized the same anti-communist rhetoric lent legitimacy to far-right crusaders.

James A. Reed, the former Democratic senator from Missouri, was a leader of this ultraconservative vanguard. Known to friends and colleagues as Jim, Reed hailed from a family of midwestern farmers. His father, John Reed, and older brother died during his youth, forcing a young Jim to mature quickly. He helped his mother, Nancy Reed, take care of the farm and attended public school before spending a few semesters at Parsons Seminary (now Coe College). Reed hailed from a family steeped in American politics—one of his ancestors, David Reed, was sued by George Washington over land in Pennsylvania—but Jim turned away from his Republican lineage upon hearing Senator John G. Carlisle, a Kentucky Democrat, bemoan how Republican tariffs hurt farmers. After becoming a lawyer and marrying his wife, Lura Olmstead, Reed moved his family to Kansas City, Missouri, and established a law practice. At the turn of the century Reed ran for and won his first elected office, serving as the Kansas City mayor from 1900 through 1904. Reed's allies viewed him as a "law and order" do-gooder, but opponents caught a whiff of authoritarianism when Reed deployed local police forces and replaced judges to root out perceived municipal corruption.[32]

After winning an open Senate seat in 1910, Reed forged a career as a loyal Democrat so long as the national party dedicated itself to Jeffersonian, small-government ideals. For most of his life, Reed chastised the GOP as "the champion of privilege, the tool of manufacturing and capitalistic interests." He viewed his own party as the protector of "the natural liberties of man," an antagonist toward "every form of special privilege and every kind of tyranny."[33] A staunch reactionary, Reed believed in a particular narrative of American history. For example, he characterized the Reconstruction era as unconstitutional northern oppression. The "blackest pages in our political history," Reconstruction, according to Reed, was a "good example of what happens under a centralized government without states' rights."[34] He saw the federal government as "a pauper" that can only "take from people who possess property" and "give that property to others."[35] To Reed's mind, empowering the government meant eroding individual liberties and traveling the path of communism.

The climax of Reed's political career proved to be his key role in defeating the League of Nations. Despite his Democratic loyalties, Reed joined with

Republicans to criticize the League, issuing standard conservative warnings of an erosion of constitutional principles and a loss of national sovereignty; however, Reed also stooped to the level of race-baiting. "The majority of the nations composing the league do not belong to the white race," Reed declared. "On the contrary, they are a conglomerate of the black, yellow, brown, and red races, frequently so intermixed and commingled as to constitute an unclassified mongrel breed." According to Reed, this "colored League of Nations" would be dominated by "degenerate races" who were "low in the scale of civilization."[36] This type of rhetoric not only reflected the xenophobia of the postwar era, it was also a bigoted appeal to southern Democrats and other white Americans terrified by the prospect of racial equality. President Woodrow Wilson, the League's driving force, scorned Reed for his defiance, calling him a "marplot" and urging Missourians to turn him out in 1922.[37] Instead, Reed won a third term.

Reed defined himself as a defender of individual liberty and states' rights, an heir to the mantle of Thomas Jefferson. Yet, his words and actions occasionally raised questions about his views on race and state power. A few years after stumping against the "colored" League of Nations, Reed supported the Immigration Act of 1924, which implemented severe immigration restrictions, particularly from nonwhite, non-European countries. Three years later, when a Jewish farm organizer sued Henry Ford for libel for his anti-Semitic, conspiratorial columns in the *Dearborn Independent*, Reed helmed Ford's legal defense. Reed disclaimed any sympathies for Ford's anti-Semitism; in fact, back in 1916 Reed gave a speech in which he proclaimed, "To the Jew let me say, the land of America is also your land."[38] But the fact that he joined Ford's defense team, not to mention his racist diatribes during the debate over the League of Nations, cast doubt upon Reed's professions of tolerance. Nevertheless, he remained a popular figure, especially in Missouri. One year after the Ford case, in 1928, Reed ran for the Democratic presidential nomination on, as one writer put it, "the plain, old-fashioned platform of Jackson Democracy."[39] Lee Meriwether—former special ambassador to France and future Jeffersonian Democrat leader—coordinated Reed's campaign and became one of his closest confidants. Reed won two states, Missouri and Wisconsin, but, after losing the nomination to New York's Al Smith, he retired from the Senate and returned to his Kansas City law firm. "To be a fraud is safer and happier in Washington today than it has been since March 4, 1911," wrote H. L. Mencken in *American Mercury*, "For James A. Reed . . . has hung up his sword and gone home to Missouri."[40]

Reed supported Roosevelt's presidential bid in 1932 because he was a loyal Democrat; he even assailed Hoover for establishing "capitalistic social-ism."[41] However, the New Deal's federal experimentation convinced the Missourian that Roosevelt represented a grave threat to America. Much of Reed's hatred of the New Deal stemmed from his strict constitutional inter-pretation and a narrow reading of the Sixteenth Amendment, which gave the federal government the power to levy a national income tax. Reed regarded Roosevelt's tax policies as "robbery perpetrated by the government in defi-ance of the other provisions of the Constitution."[42] At times, Reed's speeches revealed a paranoid mind. "They rush into homes," Reed asserted of New Dealers, "spy upon people, shoot down citizens without warrant and with-out right, inspect the books of partnerships and corporations from the small to the great, and undertake in every imaginable way the supervision and regulation of humanity."[43] Reed never provided any evidence for such state-sponsored violence, but he was less interested in forming a factual critique of the New Deal than fostering anti-government anxieties. "You cannot make socialism and communism democracy by calling them the 'new deal,'" Reed thundered at a Detroit speaking engagement. "Being a Democrat," he con-tinued, "it follows that I am not a Communist, a Socialist, a Bolshevist, or a combination of all three, and that, therefore, I am not a New Dealer." After his address in Detroit, eight Michigan area radio stations carried Reed's message and multiple newspapers, including the *Washington Post* and *Baltimore Sun*, transcribed portions of his speech.[44] The *Kansas City Times* reprinted Reed's address in its entirety. The widespread media coverage convinced Reed that millions of other Americans shared his anti–New Deal animus, a reactionary mass waiting to be awoken by fellow patriots.[45]

Conservatives gravitated to Reed's orbit. Meriwether, then working as an attorney in St. Louis, told Reed, "My own thought is that the thing to do now is to put a brake on the Socialist wheels of Roosevelt's wagon; and the most effective way to apply the brake is to elect Congressmen who will not say Amen to all Roosevelt's demands."[46] James M. Beck, a former Republican con-gressman from Pennsylvania, broached the idea of a new conservative party. Beck believed at least one-third of House Democrats did not sympathize with the New Deal and wondered if "the only way to save our form of govern-ment would be a coalition party which could be called the Constitution Party, which would merge conservative Republicans with conservative Democrats."[47] Enthused, Meriwether wrote back, "I think with you, that in this emergency differences over minor matters should be put aside, and that conservative democrats would join with conservative republicans in trying to prevent any further march in the direction of Moscow."[48] For these right-wingers, the New Deal represented a new type of threat, one that warranted forgetting partisan squabbles in favor of forging a unified conservative front against a despotic, communist-inspired foe. The desire to consolidate conservative factions by redrawing partisan lines increasingly became a central impulse of the modern conservative movement. Reed shared the sentiment. "I do not know what to say about attempting to organize a party to head off what is now going on," Reed wrote, "but if anything is to be done, it ought to be started."[49]

As Reed and his cohort contemplated staging a conservative revolt in 1934, a group of right-wing industrialists formed the American Liberty League to contest New Deal liberalism. The League desired a return to the "employer's paradise" of the Gilded Age, setting an important foundation for the conservative business movement. The organization started with a series of correspondence between John J. Raskob, DuPont vice president and former Democratic chairman, and retired executive R. R. M. Carpenter. Raskob argued that industrialists needed an organization "to protect society from the sufferings which it is bound to endure if we allow communistic elements to lead the people to believe that all businessmen are crooks."[50] He knew that business executives feared the popularity of Roosevelt's New Deal, and he figured, correctly, that their economic anxiety could spark the League's creation. The founding members and financiers of the American Liberty League read like a *Who's Who* of prominent industrialists, including Alfred P. Sloan Jr. of General Motors; the du Pont brothers, Irénée, Lammot, and Pierre; president of Sun Oil J. Howard Pew; Sewell L. Avery of Montgomery Ward; and Weirton Steel executives Ernest T. Weir and Earl F. Reed. On paper the League's board of directors seemed bipartisan, but it was dominated by anti-labor, anti-statist conservatives, including Irénée du Pont, Democrats Al Smith and John W. Davis, Republican congressman James W. Wadsworth of New York, and former New York Republican governor Nathan L. Miller. The former chair of the Democratic Party's executive committee, Jouett Shouse, served as the League's president.[51]

Jouett Shouse was born in rural Woodford County, Kentucky, in 1879 to John Samuel Shouse, a Disciples of Christ minister, and Anna Armstrong. During his youth, the Shouse family moved to neighboring Missouri, where a young Jouett attended the University of Missouri before dropping out at the end of his junior year. Jouett found the newspaper industry more fruitful and soon returned to Kentucky to work as a staff writer and editor of the *Lexington Herald* and the *Kentucky Farmer and Breeder*. After he married his wife, Marion Edwards, the pair relocated to Kansas and Shouse embarked on a political career. In 1912, Jouett aligned himself with the Democratic Party, running for and winning a Kentucky state senate seat. Two years later, he earned a promotion to the U.S. House of Representatives, representing one of Kansas's largest wheat-growing regions, the seventh congressional district. Shouse gained an appointment to the Banking and Currency Committee, where he befriended Chairman Carter Glass, a states' rights Democrat from Virginia. After losing his seat in 1918, Shouse moved into the private sector, serving as a director for various corporations and establishing a tax-counseling partnership with former Kansas congressman Dudley Doolittle.[52]

Despite no longer holding elected office, Shouse remained politically active and grew more conservative as he aged. He became an Assistant Secretary of the Treasury (serving under Secretary Glass), headed Kansas's Democratic National Committee (DNC) delegation in 1920 and 1924, and convinced Kansas delegates to support Al Smith's candidacy in 1928. Shouse served on Smith's Executive and Advisory Committee, working closely with committee chairman and future Liberty Leaguer John Raskob. After Smith's devastating loss to Hoover, Shouse became the chairman of the DNC Executive Committee, where he hammered Hoover and the Republicans for the country's economic turmoil. The year 1932 proved transitional for Shouse. He lost his bid to become the DNC's permanent chairman and give the DNC keynote address, so he turned to political organizing. At the behest of Pierre du Pont, Shouse served as the president of the Association Against the Prohibition Amendment, but he continued to stump for the Democrats and voted for Roosevelt in 1932. It was the last time he ever voted for the Democratic Party. Shouse opposed the New Deal in its entirety and accused Roosevelt's "totalitarian government" of abandoning the Democratic Party's traditional states' rights moorings. His anti-statist inclinations and relationships with industrial giants made him the perfect figure to helm the Liberty League's crusade.[53]

The Liberty League became a vehicle for the capital class to oppose New Deal liberalism. Its founding statement indicated a conservative mission to "defend and uphold the constitution," "teach the necessity and respect for the rights of persons and property," and "foster the right to work, earn, save, and acquire property, and to preserve the ownership and lawful use of property when acquired."[54] In short, the League thought the government existed to protect wealth and privilege. To the far right, the fight for political and economic power was a zero-sum game. Roosevelt's New Deal threatened to diminish their privilege by uplifting exploited groups, including tenant

farmers, factory workers, and racial minorities—an inversion of the existing hierarchy. Any attempt to regulate capital and restrict the hand of the
free market fueled what historian Lawrence B. Glickman called an "elite victimization" complex.[55] Essentially, these industrialists thought *they* were the
"forgotten men" of the Great Depression. Senator Elmer Thomas, an Okla
homa Democrat and staunch New Dealer, saw through the façade, calling the
group an "anti-Roosevelt organization" formed by "die-hards and standpat-
ters who from the start have disagreed with President Roosevelt's New Deal
program."[56] The *Christian Science Monitor* observed that the League united
"the extreme conservative wings of both major parties" and "plainly sets off
its objectives as hostile to those of the New Deal."[57] Nevertheless, immense
funding and appeals to economic freedom earned the League an ephemeral
spurt of fame, propelling the organization's expansion into twenty-two states.
"From the way the letters are coming in," Shouse grinned as he picked up
roughly 1,000 letters from the New York office, "this appears to be the idea of
a lot of people all over the country."[58]

The League's outspoken conservatism caught Reed's attention, and the
former senator united with Shouse against the common enemies of Roosevelt
and the New Deal. In 1935, Reed joined the Liberty League's National Lawyers Committee—a group, also known as the Lawyers' Vigilance Committee,
organized to criticize the New Deal on strict constitutional grounds—and
sent Shouse transcriptions of his speeches.[59] Shouse, for his part, delighted in
Reed's oratory and urged the Missourian to join the League's national advisory board. When Reed sent Shouse one of his addresses he included a message: "It will show you that our minds are traveling along parallel lines."[60]
Certainly the two men occupied similar ideological ground. Both responded
to Roosevelt's attack against "economic royalists" by retorting that communistic New Dealers sought to arouse class warfare. The League declared that
Roosevelt sided with "communists and other radicals, who are deeply igno-
rant of the facts of our industrial life."[61] Reed echoed this sentiment in front
of a crowd of Maine conservatives: "That is the theory of all Communism
and Bolshevism. It is their initial step. They come forward denouncing first
those who have considerable value in property but in the end they destroy
all property and deny all opportunity."[62] Conspiratorial rhetoric fostered
anti-Roosevelt, anti-statist sentiments and lubricated connections within
conservative circles. Indeed, this loose far-right coalition was waiting for
the appropriate moment to awaken the reactionary *vox populi* and kick the
usurper out of the White House.

The 1936 presidential election provided ultraconservatives with the first opportunity to defeat Roosevelt and restore the traditional order. As the election year dawned, the American Liberty League amplified its assault on Roosevelt and the New Deal. The League classified New Deal programs as a "definitive challenge to the American form of government," and wrote, "The progressive tightening and expansion of regulation, inevitably characteristic of economic planning, is a vicious combination of Fascism, socialism and communism."[63] This conflation of political extremes represented an ideological alchemy particular to the far right. In an effort to denigrate the New Deal, Liberty Leaguers derided Roosevelt as a "fascist," "socialist," "communist" "dictator."[64] The most notable critique came from Al Smith, the former New York governor and erstwhile ally of Roosevelt. At a Liberty League function in late January 1936, Smith berated the Roosevelt administration for betraying Democratic principles, ballooning the deficit, enlarging the bureaucracy, and fomenting class warfare. He called Roosevelt an "autocrat" and "socialist" and characterized the New Deal as "communism in disguise." Smith concluded his speech with a shocking, conspiratorial warning: "There can only be one Capitol, Washington or Moscow. There can only be one atmosphere of government, the clear, pure, fresh air of free America, or the foul breath of Communistic Russia. There can only be one flag, the Stars and Stripes, or the red flag of the Godless Union of the Soviet. There can only be one national anthem, 'The Star Spangled Banner' or the 'Internationale.'"[65] Smith's diatribe, presenting an ideological binary pitting liberal communism against conservative Americanism, encapsulated the worldview of the far right. The American Liberty League fired the first shot across the bow, and New Deal Democrats soon found themselves under attack from within their own party.

Just days after Smith's Liberty League address, a group of far-right Democrats challenged Roosevelt for control of the party's future. Texas businessman John Henry Kirby and Georgia's reactionary governor Eugene Talmadge issued a call to all "Jeffersonian Democrats of Southern and border States . . . to repudiate the New Deal."[66] The ensuing "Grass Roots Convention" in Macon, Georgia, provided a platform for ultraconservative Democrats to air grievances against the Roosevelt administration. Liberty League patrons, including Raskob and the du Ponts, funded the gathering, illustrating that wealthy conservatives hedged their bets by backing multiple anti-Roosevelt movements. With racist flyers filtering through the crowd and a huge Confederate flag draped behind the podium, speakers railed against federal tyranny and defended southern tradition. Gerald L. K. Smith denounced Roosevelt as a "communist" and a "cripple" and characterized Eleanor Roosevelt as "the female Rasputin in the White House."[67] Talmadge took the stage after Smith, bellowing, "If the New Dealers can pick their own Supreme Court the wheels of our democracy would catch fire and burn down our freedom." The specter of the Civil War loomed in Talmadge's mind: "States' rights are in the balance today more than they were in the days of 1861."[68] The Macon crowd, composed of thousands of anti-Roosevelt dissidents, whooped and hollered for Smith and Talmadge, but the convention did not spin off into a third party, nor did it unmoor the national Democratic Party from Roosevelt and New Deal liberalism. However, the convention precipitated and emboldened the ultraconservative grassroots movements that coalesced during the 1936 presidential election.[69]

Reed emerged as a prominent leader of the right-wing resistance. As the 1936 primary season got under way, he delivered an inflammatory address in front of the Lawyers Association of Kansas City. Reed's speech, titled "Shall We Have Constitutional Liberty or Dictatorship," portrayed the New Deal as a paternalistic blight on American tradition. "It came like a thief in the night, and has spread with the silence and rapidity of a malignant cancer," Reed thundered. "If it be not speedily cut out, it will soon reach and destroy the heart of American liberty!" Wielding the far right's bipolar ideological alchemy, Reed demonized the New Deal: "They wear the cloak of the Democratic party—but beneath that honest robe are concealed the red garments of bolshevism, communism, socialism, and fascism. Nothing done by Stalin, by Mussolini, by Hitler was more drastic, more brutal, and more destructive of liberty." Near the end of his speech Reed warned his audience against reelecting Roosevelt because they were "facing a crimson tide" that would "sweep over this country."[70] The American Liberty League published Reed's speech as a pamphlet, as did smaller presses such as Kansas City's Martin Printing Company, gaining Reed a fair amount of notoriety within right-wing circles, but the way forward remained unclear as conservatives struggled to shape a national movement within the existing two-party system.

Reed expected Roosevelt to steamroll toward the Democratic Party's nomination, but the GOP lacked a clear front-runner. Conservatives bent on opposing Roosevelt worried that the Republicans would nominate a "me-too" New Dealer, narrowing the ideological spectrum and essentially writing conservatism out of the election. Reed expressed concerns about one particular presidential hopeful, Alfred "Alf" Landon, the moderate Republican governor of Kansas. In a letter to St. Louis attorney Sterling Edmunds, Reed rejected Landon: "If, however, the Republicans nominate a man or adopt a platform leaning over toward the New Deal, there would be nothing left except to vote for the third ticket."[71] Edmunds concurred, "His nomination would give us a choice of evils."[72] Over the course of the Republican primaries, Senator William Borah of Idaho carried numerous states, but, much to Reed's chagrin, Landon emerged from the national convention as the GOP's standard bearer. Landon seemed a savvy choice to party insiders. He was the only GOP governor elected and reelected in 1932 and 1934, and Republican strategists believed he could turn out the vote in the agricultural West. In an attempt to pander to discontented conservatives, the Republican Party platform accused Roosevelt of betraying Democratic principles and proclaimed, "America is in peril."[73] However, the GOP also supported numerous New Deal planks, such as Social Security, labor rights, and economic regulation. Dismayed by Landon's nomination, Reed knew it was too late to organize an effective third party, but he hesitated to support the GOP. While Reed and his inner circle debated Landon's merits, they bore no uncertainty of the political enemy: New Deal liberalism.

After Roosevelt gained the Democratic nomination in the early summer, Reed and Edmunds called for a meeting of conservatives to contest Roosevelt's "collectivist policies" and "discuss what we can and should do in the present campaign."[74] On August 7, 1936, forty delegates from twenty-two states met at Detroit's Book-Cadillac Hotel to lay plans for grassroots action. The hotel's Renaissance-inspired architecture provided an appropriate setting for a group that sought the rebirth of a traditionalist, conservative Democratic Party. The disgruntled attendees, all right-wing Democrats hailing mostly from midwestern and southern states, were united by their desire to defeat Roosevelt. The New Deal was a "betrayal," they declared, an "apostasy to Democratic principles." The conference concluded with a Declaration of Position, which condemned Roosevelt's administration for replacing democracy with a "collectivist state" based on "the tenets and teachings of a blended communism and socialism."[75] Multiple high-profile anti–New Dealers signed the declaration, including Reed; Democrat Joseph B. Ely, the former Massachusetts governor; Colonel Henry Breckinridge, an attorney and former Assistant Secretary of War who briefly challenged Roosevelt for the Democratic nomination; and Bainbridge Colby, a former Progressive Party leader turned Missouri Democrat. Most importantly, the Detroit conference concluded with the formation of the National Jeffersonian Democrats, a group that promoted an idealized version of American democracy that downplayed socioeconomic strife, accentuated individual freedom and states' rights, and viewed U.S. politics through a conspiratorial anti-communist lens. The Jeffersonian Democrats, like the American Liberty League, soon became a critical node in the fledgling far-right network.[76]

The National Jeffersonian Democrats, as the group's name implied, looked to President Thomas Jefferson as their intellectual guiding light. The organization considered Jefferson the true founder of the Democratic Party and cherry-picked anti-statist philosophies from Jefferson's political life to form their ideological core. This perspective had significant purchase among white southerners. In the announcement for the Grass Roots Convention, for example, Kirby and Talmadge wrote that Jefferson "viewed the maintenance of the Constitution and its guarantees of liberties not only as sacred, but as essential to the very existence of the republic." Conversely, they noted, "the present Federal government in Washington has violated the venerated doctrine of States Rights . . . and sought to override and ignore the Constitution." The Jeffersonian Democrats portrayed themselves as the defenders of Democratic principles being uprooted by New Deal liberalism, an ideology they considered "alien, foreign, and inimical to America and Americanism."[77] Additionally, the fact that Thomas Jefferson believed political power should reside in the hands of a "natural aristocracy" appealed to the Jeffersonian Democrats because, like the American Liberty League, many members stemmed from the wealthy, and white, upper crust of southern and midwestern society.[78]

Jefferson represented a convenient, though imperfect, vessel for conservative philosophies. Hopewell L. Rogers, the chairman of the National Jeffersonian Speakers Bureau, boiled the Jeffersonian platform down to four basic principles: "1) economic individualism, 2) political democracy, 3) social classlessness, and 4) local self-government."[79] The call for "social classlessness" was not an egalitarian push for economic and racial equality, but instead represented the group's attempt to define itself against the straw man of Rooseveltian class warfare. They omitted Jefferson's slave-owning and racism—notable, considering his white supremacist views aligned with the those of many ultraconservatives—and skimmed over his expansion of federal power through the Louisiana Purchase. The Jeffersonians even ignored the fact that Roosevelt himself invoked Jefferson to justify the New Deal. Nevertheless, the Jeffersonian Democrats' historical interpretation underscored, according to historian Patrick Allitt, the "elevation of Thomas Jefferson, once dreaded as a dangerous radical, into the hero of anti-government Southern

conservatives in the twentieth century."[80] To the minds of far-right conservatives, Roosevelt and the New Deal were an existential threat to America while
Jefferson's strict constitutionalism, advocacy for states' rights, and defense of
property represented a political panacea for halting liberal progress.[81]

Funding poured in to bolster the Jeffersonian crusade, particularly from
right-wing businessmen. Prominent Liberty League patrons, including Sloan,
the du Ponts, and Raskob, donated to the Jeffersonians. Raskob alone contributed $50,000 to the cause, and Bernard H. Kroger, founder of the Kroger
grocery-store chain, donated $1,000. Louisville entrepreneur Lafon Allen con-
tributed out of fear that Roosevelt intended to "destroy" both national parties
and create his own radical coalition—though, Allen noted, "This might not
be a bad thing, since we would then have a two-party alignment based upon
fundamental differences of political faith, a thing which can hardly be said to
have existed in this country for some years."[82] Perhaps this was the moment,
Jeffersonians thought, to break the current party structure and erect an ideologically polarized system. The Jeffersonian Democrats' modern media strategy helped get the word out. Gleason L. Archer Sr. used his extensive contacts
with major radio networks to schedule broadcasts for the National Jeffersonians. Archer urged the Jeffersonians to purchase evening airtime because he
believed a "silent vote" would be cast by the majority of "fathers and mothers
who sit at their radios and listen to speakers for and against the New Deal."[83]
The archival record does not reveal the total amount of contributions to the
National Jeffersonians, but in just one week, late in October, the organization
spent nearly $100,000. The extensive funding provided a foundation for the
group's movement to depose Roosevelt and, more broadly, revealed an ideological and financial web connecting far-right groups.[84]

The National Jeffersonians established their headquarters in St. Louis and
dedicated themselves to grassroots action. "You, of course, know that it is
extremely difficult to do any organization work from headquarters by letter,"
Edmunds wrote to Reed. "We need organizers in the field."[85] Now serving as
the organization's secretary, Edmunds urged his fellow founders to establish
Jeffersonian state chapters "to which other Democrats may rally and which
will offer a forum for Senator Reed, Governor Ely, Mr. Colby and other speakers who are willing to come into your state."[86] Edmunds became the national
organization's point man; he was responsible for creating an interconnected
network of Jeffersonian state chapters. Colby provided a list of 10,000 individuals in 30 states, to whom Edmunds sent a copy of the Jeffersonian Declaration, an enrollment card, and a form letter imploring fellow Democrats

to spurn Roosevelt in 1936. Edmunds told potential recruits, "There is not a member of the Democratic Party who can read this Declaration without realizing that nothing less than his loyalty to his country is on trial."[87]

Early on the Jeffersonians sought to coordinate a national anti–New Deal resistance rather than support the Republican ticket, a mindset that filtered down to the organization's state branches along with the group's conspiratorial anti-communism. However, the group created no guidelines regarding how to oppose Roosevelt and the Democratic Party, giving individual chapters great tactical latitude. As activists responded to Edmunds's mass mailer, Jeffersonian chapters popped up around the country. The New York Jeffersonians rented space in the Empire State Building, installed long-distance telephone lines, and established connections with local newspapers to promote their ideologies and entice new recruits. California had two Jeffersonian chapters, each called the Jeffersonian Democrats of California, although a dispute over naming rights lingered for years. Right-wingers in Virginia established a Jeffersonian state branch, too. It is difficult to find an accounting of every state that contained a Jeffersonian chapter, but, as evidenced by Talmadge's "Grass Roots Convention," their views found support in conservative pockets throughout country, even if the state lacked an official affiliate. Above all, the most active state chapter was the Jeffersonian Democrats of Texas (JDT).[88]

One of the eight national committee members who signed the Jeffersonian Declaration was J. Evetts Haley, an ultraconservative cattleman who chaired the Texas Jeffersonian chapter. The JDT retained the national organization's free-market idealism and communist conspiracy theories, but Haley's outfit added white supremacism and southern traditionalism to the platform. Haley's upbringing on the isolated plains of West Texas molded his ultraconservative political ideals. Born in Belton, Texas, on July 5, 1901, to John and Julia Haley, "Evetts grew up in an atmosphere of political and educational participation," and he credited his parents for his conservative, traditionalist inclinations.[89] Haley's family tree was drenched in Anglo-Texas tradition; many of his ancestors fought for Texas during the Texas Revolution and joined the Confederacy during the Civil War. The Haley family quickly traded the rolling hills of Belton for the parched climate of West Texas's Llano Estacado, an area that produced a "self-sufficient, lonely, suspicious citizenry, slow to change."[90] Haley cherished the traditionalism of the plains, claiming that he was "bogged deeper in its traditions, and more devoted to its ideals, than to all else besides."[91] This politically charged upbringing in arid West Texas imbued Haley with a belief in rugged individualism, an adherence to white supremacist traditions, and an overarching right-wing bent. A perfect storm of Jeffersonian principles.[92]

During his formative years, Haley made a name for himself regionally as a cowman and historian of the Great Plains before becoming a notable far-right activist. He spent summers developing his cowboy skills by working on his family's land near the Pecos River and on the legendary Long S Ranch. Under pressure from his mother, Haley quit the cow-punching lifestyle to pursue higher education, eventually graduating from the University of Texas in 1926 with a master's degree in history. Haley spent the 1920s and 1930s polishing his promising writing career, which coincided with the First Red Scare and a surge in anti-communist anxieties. Business progressivism—an economic philosophy that valued "public service and efficiency" over state-funded social programs—and the racial violence of the Ku Klux Klan dominated Texas politics during Haley's formative years. This sociopolitical environment fueled Haley's ultra-conservatism, and when Roosevelt instituted the New Deal after his landslide victory in 1932, Haley envisaged the specter of government oppression. His frontier upbringing produced a deep distrust of the federal government; he viewed the state as an alien intruder invading local society. Haley's anti-statism intertwined with the white supremacy that coursed throughout the Deep South. Haley was a Confederate apologist; he lauded the Confederacy's "moral principle" during the "War Between the States."[93] Furthermore, his relative economic privilege further separated him from the plight of racial minorities and immigrants in Texas. In the quagmire of the Great Depression, Haley transformed from a simple cowman-historian into a far-right tribune.[94]

Before the National Jeffersonians' founding meeting, Haley and other right-wing Texans, including John Henry Kirby, founded an organization, the Constitutional Democrats of Texas, to challenge Roosevelt on the Texas ticket. The group soon merged with the Jeffersonian Democrats, rechristened as the Jeffersonian Democrats of Texas. The JDT corporate charter referred to Roosevelt, though not directly, as "some wild political dreamer" who sought to disrupt states' rights and compound "the American people into one common regimented mass."[95] Haley served as the primary JDT organizer and propagandist, and Houston-based judge W. P. Hamblen wrote the Texas Jeffersonians' declaration: "We re-assert our belief in the Constitution, in the rights of the States, and in the Jeffersonian principles. Believing thus, we must condemn the Roosevelt administration."[96]

The Texas Jeffersonians, like the national organization, sought to remove FDR from the Democratic ticket and painted liberalism as a cog in a grand communist conspiracy. Haley spun conspiratorial webs about New Deal welfare spending, communist subversion, and voter manipulation. Liberalism, he warned, would distort Texas's white supremacist traditions. In one pamphlet Haley asserted, "[The] breakdown of color lines and mixture of the races, black, white, and tan, is one of the cardinal principles of the Red philosophy. Already the initial steps have been carefully taken by [the] leading lights of the New Deal."[97] Haley worried that this supposed dissolution of racial barriers threatened the privilege of white southern patricians like himself. Federal relief, he declared, enabled "an army of shiftless negroes and aliens at the expense of all of us," even though farmworkers, many of whom were black or Hispanic, were excluded from New Deal benefits.[98] The Texas Jeffersonians also pandered to the Lone Star State's anti-Catholic anxieties; one pamphlet warned of a Catholic cabal in the postal service that pursued "domination over American politics and [to] wipe out Protestantism."[99] Haley's fearmongering appealed to populist ultraconservatives; however, like the Liberty League, the Texas Jeffersonians' most energetic members stemmed from the upper echelon of Texas society—large landowners, conservative lawyers, and wealthy businessmen. In terms of official numbers, the Texas chapter claimed about 5,000 active members.[100]

Haley used the Jeffersonian network to build a far-right movement through grassroots action. If liberalism threatened the established sociopolitical mores of southern society, as Haley argued, white southerners needed a call to arms. He created mailing and fundraising lists by urging fellow Jeffersonians to provide contact information for like-minded individuals. Thousands of Texans supported the Jeffersonian cause through modest donations, usually between one and ten dollars. Yet the organization's appeal remained limited because Roosevelt's subsidies were popular, especially among Texas farmers, which further bolstered Texans' Democratic loyalties. Lubbock's *Morning Avalanche* newspaper dismissed the Texas Jeffersonians by comparing financial contributions to "pouring sand in a rat hole."[101] Nevertheless, Haley used Jeffersonian funds to distribute anti–New Deal literature across Texas. The organization circulated its self-published newspaper, the *Jeffersonian Democrat*, in every county and made dubious claims that print runs exceeded one million. As historian Keith Volanto noted, "Readers who picked up the *Jeffersonian Democrat* and found no problem with the views expressed, or excitedly experienced a 'Give 'Em Hell!' moment, were safely in the ultraconservative camp."[102] The Jeffersonians also advertised in over three hundred weekly newspapers and at least sixty dailies. One such advertisement declared that the South-oriented

Democratic Party had "passed completely away" because FDR's administration was "flouting the Constitution" and "wooing the Negro vote."[103] Despite tapping into Texas's white supremacist, anti-statist traditions, the Jeffersonians failed to remove Roosevelt from the state ticket because of the Democratic Party's traditional dominance and FDR's popularity.[104]

The Texas Jeffersonians' inability to alter the Texas Democratic ticket or dent Roosevelt's celebrity revealed a major weakness for the National Jeffersonian movement. The only other mainstream option entailed supporting Landon, and right-wingers doubted whether the Kansan could topple a popular incumbent president. "My own belief is that Landon is sunk 10,000 fathoms deep, and that no conceivable salvaging operations will ever bring him to the surface," Mencken wrote to Reed.[105] "Roosevelt might have been beaten by a candidate capable of using an ax," Mencken continued. "Poor Landon is too mild a fellow for the job." Reed, who had already expressed doubts about the Republican candidate, confessed in a letter to Shouse, "I do not think that Landon stands a chance whatever to carry Missouri."[106] These assessments of a milquetoast Landon candidacy notwithstanding, the Jeffersonian Democrats decided that the only way to defeat Roosevelt was by supporting their traditional political enemy. Such a strategic alliance between the far right and the Republican Party was always in the cards.

Rather than allowing Roosevelt to walk away with the election, the Jeffersonians pivoted toward characterizing the Republican Party as the lesser of two evils. Edmunds rushed out letters, warning that the choice between FDR and Landon "will determine whether we are to go on to a condition of greater happiness under a free system of government, or whether we are to ... be subjected to a coercive system of government, under which our rulers will prescribe what we shall and shall not do in every activity of our daily lives."[107] The Jeffersonian Democrats of California purchased radio broadcasts two to three times a day and published hundreds of thousands of pamphlets to promote Landon. Down in Texas, Haley disseminated encouraging form letters predicting a Landon victory: "We are making splendid progress in our movement. The Literary Digest poll indicates that Roosevelt will be defeated, and this has never failed to be correct."[108] Even the office manager of the Houston headquarters, Fannie B. Campbell, got caught up in the frenzy when she wrote to Haley, "I can barely keep my enthusiasm down as the days go by and hundreds of phone calls come in in answer to our various literature we are sending out. I feel so confident at present that we are going to win out."[109] The Texas Jeffersonians deluded themselves into believing that Landon had a chance for victory in the solidly Democratic Lone Star State. A forced pragmatism settled upon the far right as conservative, anti-Roosevelt Democrats talked themselves into supporting Landon.[110]

As the election neared, high-profile Jeffersonians fanned out to multiple states to deliver condemnations of Roosevelt and drum up support for the Republicans. The National Jeffersonians focused on winning over conservatives in the industrial Midwest. Meriwether appeared on St. Louis radio. "I loved my Democratic home," he intoned. "I have moved out of it only because it has been captured by men imbued with Socialistic and Communistic doctrines, by men who would not recognize a Democratic principle were they to meet one in the middle of the road."[111] Colonel Breckinridge spoke at an Indianapolis meeting sponsored by the Independent Coalition of American Women. Reed traveled to multiple cities, including Toledo, Ohio; Cincinnati, Ohio; Cedar Rapids, Iowa; and St. Louis, Missouri. At each stop he took the stage to wild applause and urged his followers to vote against Roosevelt in the coming election. Reed struck familiar conspiratorial chords, accusing Roosevelt of cozying up to Communist Party USA leader Earl Browder, moving the Democratic Party into "Red territory," and, in general, "destroying American civilization."[112] Like a plain-folks preacher, Reed appealed to his constituents' anxieties: "Shall American civilization be preserved or shall it be surrendered into the red hands of the anarchists and socialists?"[113] Reed occasionally stumped for Landon directly, particularly when he coordinated with the American Liberty League in Maine, but more often he praised the Republican Party as the antithesis of New Deal liberalism. Citing "radical changes" in the Republican Party, namely the conservative portions of the GOP's platform, Reed pontificated about saving the nation. "The fact about the matter [is] that all our old party differences that we used to fight over . . . have become almost totally unimportant," Reed declared. "The question is whether we're going to preserve that liberty which our fathers fought for and our boys died for."[114]

The far right's pragmatism, its decision to back an imperfect Landon in order to vanquish Roosevelt, underscored the era's fluid partisan and ideological boundaries. Despite the fact that the Jeffersonians and Liberty League canvassed for Landon across the country, the Kansas governor never passed the ultraconservative litmus test. To the far right, Landon was the lesser of two evils, but an evil nonetheless. However, right-wingers recognized that voting for the Democratic ticket ensured four more years of Roosevelt. The middle path meant stoking anti-liberal anxiety within the Democratic Party while, for the moment, supporting the GOP. At the national and state levels, Jeffersonian Democrats worked with the official GOP machinery during the election. The Republican National Committee printed red-baiting Jeffersonian pamphlets. "What will move [Democrats] to leave is Mr. Roosevelt's repudiation of fundamental American principles," read one such tract by Lee Meriwether, "what no real Democrat can approve or forgive is his adoption of policies imported from Communist Russia."[115] Haley and the Texas Jeffersonians abandoned the Democratic Party and collaborated directly with the GOP and affiliated Landon for President clubs, a move which represented a stark pivot away from the South's Democratic moorings.

The political alliance between the Republican Party and the far right went only so far, however. The southern tradition of white supremacy opened a significant rift in the Jeffersonian-Republican coalition. The Jeffersonians fought for conservative values by stoking racial prejudices and employing conspiratorial, inflammatory language. "The South stands at the cross-roads of destiny," Haley declared in one Jeffersonian pamphlet. "Is it to continue to be a 'white man's country,' or is it to be sunk to the cultural level of the negro, and have the purity of its blood corrupted with mulatto strains?"[116] But the Republicans—Landon, specifically—needed to court voters, and the aggressive tactics of the Jeffersonians alienated African Americans, a key part of the traditional Republican constituency. Landon's campaign refused to embrace race-baiting rhetoric to win southern votes. For example, the Houston GOP branch declined to distribute issues of the *Jeffersonian Democrat* because of Haley's racist demagoguery, illustrating the limitations of Jeffersonian activism. Moreover, Landon struggled to appease both the liberal-internationalist and conservative-nationalist wings that vied for hegemony in the Republican Party. Many right-wingers dismissed Landon as a soft New Dealer, but, at the same time, Landon risked losing moderate Republican support by criticizing popular liberal programs. This conundrum put Landon in an ideological straitjacket—he had little room to maneuver. Regardless, as Election Day approached, Landon pivoted to the right, sputtering about economic regimentation and "attacks on our freedom."[117] Landon nevertheless struggled to gain momentum.[118]

With the National Democratic Party in the hands of New Dealers and the Republican Party toeing a moderate line, multiple third parties emerged to entice disgruntled ultraconservatives. One curious group coalesced under the banner of the Union Party, offering a right-wing alternative to Roosevelt's New Deal. The party included Gerald L. K. Smith, the former organizer of the late

Huey Long's Share Our Wealth program; Francis Townsend, a physician and author of the Townsend Plan, an old-age pension proposal; and Father Charles Coughlin, an anti-Semitic Catholic priest with an incredibly popular, Detroit-based radio show. At the behest of Coughlin, the Union Party drafted North Dakota Congressman William Lemke, an erstwhile Republican, to oppose Roosevelt. The Union Party lobbed blistering attacks at both Roosevelt and his Republican opposition. At a rally attended by 25,000 people, Father Coughlin asserted, "The old corpses of the Democratic and Republican parties are stinking in our nostrils," deriding the New Deal as infested by "atheists" and "red and pink communists."[119] Smith whipped audiences into a frenzy by presenting New Dealers as "as a slimy group of men culled from the pink campuses of America with [a] friendly gaze fixed on Russia."[120] Lemke, a subdued speaker compared to the histrionics of Smith and Coughlin, joined the conspiratorial chorus. "I do not charge that the President of this nation is a Communist," Lemke quipped, "but I do charge that . . . Communist leaders have laid their cuckoo eggs in his Democratic nest and that he is hatching them."[121] Despite paradoxically regarding Roosevelt as a tool of both banking interests and international communism, the Union Party, like the Jeffersonian Democrats, believed anti-communist fearmongering could dent Roosevelt's popularity.[122]

The Union Party faced an uphill battle against a popular president and the historical inefficacy of third-party movements, ultimately fraying apart before the election occurred. The party housed a multitude of zealots but struggled with the day-to-day minutiae of political campaigning. In a party unified solely by an anti-Roosevelt animus, personal and ideological differences proved insurmountable. Lemke was not an inspiring leader; he lacked the public-speaking panache of Smith and Townsend and had a limited political vocabulary. Smith later offered withering criticism, describing Lemke as the "complete composite of unattractiveness. He looked like a hayseed."[123] As the group fractured, Coughlin descended into anti-Semitic attacks on Jewish communism and resented Smith's ability to upstage his own oratory skills. Smith abandoned the shipwreck of Lemke's campaign to build his own revolutionary nationalist movement in order to, as he put it, "seize the government of the United States."[124] In response, Lemke and Townsend denounced Smith's fascist sympathies, which freed Smith to pursue his own far-right ambitions through the Committee of One Million. The Union Party fizzled, making it onto only thirty-four state ballots, six of which did not reflect Lemke as the Union Party candidate.[125]

Another third party emerged when William Dudley Pelley attempted to parlay his notoriety as the leading American fascist into a political career. Pelley took a strange road to the political arena. In 1929, he had a mystical conversion experience, after which he created his own theology combining elements of spiritualism, Christian Science, and anti-Semitism. He sought to create a Christian Commonwealth that would rid the country of banks, unions, currency, and New Deal programs; disenfranchise Jews and force them into ghettos; and classify African Americans as wards of the state. Hitler's rise to the chancellorship of Germany in 1933 inspired Pelley to create an American fascist organization, the Silver Shirts. One year later, the organization boasted 15,000 members. Pelley blamed communists and Jews for destroying American freedoms and considered New Deal liberals complicit partners in this grand conspiracy. During the 1936 election, Pelley suspected Landon had a hidden Jewish ancestry and accused the Union Party of ignoring, and thus enabling, a covert Jewish plot in America. Pelley threw his hat into the ring as a candidate for the Christian Party and used his periodical, *Pelley's Weekly*, as his campaign mouthpiece. However, the Christian Party got on the ballot in only one state, Washington, illustrating that Pelley struggled with political campaigning and appealed to an extreme fringe that lacked the popularity to build a winning coalition.[126]

Despite wealthy patronage, fanatical supporters, and a message of patriotic paranoia, conservatives of all stripes struggled in vain against the tide of Roosevelt's popularity. "As far as the majority of Americans are concerned," a prescient letter-to-the-editor writer surmised, "the real villain today is not Franklin D. Roosevelt but the capitalist system."[127] Roosevelt won the 1936 election in a landslide, receiving over twenty-seven million votes while Landon managed just under a meager seventeen million, a massive ten-million-vote deficit. The electoral disparity was even greater; Landon netted a paltry eight electoral college votes while Roosevelt commanded five hundred twenty-three. The third parties floundered as expected. Lemke and the Union Party received just under 900,000 votes and failed to win a single electoral vote. Pelley's Christian Party registered less than 1,600 total votes. Even the Texas Jeffersonians failed to undermine Roosevelt—FDR won an astounding 87 percent of the popular vote in Texas—which underscored the difficulties of building a successful conservative coalition through the Depression-era southern GOP.[128] In fact, FDR did such a good job demonizing the far right, particularly the Liberty League, that Landon referred to his association with ultraconservatives as the "kiss of death."[129] Roosevelt and the New Deal, it seemed, remained insurmountable.

After the electoral dust had settled, Edmunds sent out letters to the most active Jeffersonians, asking for suggestions about the future of the organization. Most wanted to continue the fight, although "many of them suggested that activities be suspended for the immediate present, in view of the overwhelming character of the vote for Pres. Roosevelt."[130] The Texas Jeffersonians shuttered their Austin headquarters as quickly as the wind dissipated from Landon's sails, but Haley's closing letter to Hamblen summarized the Jeffersonians' self-perception: "This has been a campaign by patriots."[131] Some stalwarts despaired at the turnout for Roosevelt. Meriwether offered the best distillation of Jeffersonian despondence: "What are the Jeffersonian Democrats going to do? What *can* they do?"[132] In a letter to Reed, Edmunds argued that it was best for the Jeffersonians to "avoid publicity" until Roosevelt "again arouses the alarm of the conservative and uncorrupted elements of our citizenship."[133] There was some talk of setting up a headquarters in Washington, D.C., and sending speakers into southern states to promote Republican-endorsed Jeffersonian candidates. Despite FDR's emphatic victory, a feeling that the movement needed to be maintained permeated the far right. After all, Reed noted, "What is to be gained by Jeffersonian Democrats sitting silently on the side line, while men like Roosevelt and [Congress of Industrial Organizations President] John Lewis wreck American institutions?"[134]

During his second inaugural address, Roosevelt soon raised conservative alarms by signaling his intent to pursue a more left-leaning path. Rather than stress the importance of new social programs, FDR used his political capital to target the New Deal's *bête noire*: the Supreme Court. The Court struck down numerous New Deal programs during Roosevelt's first term, notably the National Industrial Recovery Act and Agricultural Adjustment Administration, leading FDR to argue that old age and inefficiency plagued the court. On February 5, 1937, Roosevelt sent his plan to Congress. The proposal would have allowed Roosevelt to appoint up to six new justices for every current justice that had served for at least ten years and waited longer than six months after their seventieth birthday to retire. Six of the nine justices turned seventy in 1937, which meant Roosevelt could have "packed" the court with six New Deal–friendly justices. Additionally, the bill called for appointing more than forty new judges to lower federal courts, thus laying the groundwork to alter the judicial branch for decades. The reaction against Roosevelt's plan was swift. Archconservative Senator Glass condemned the court reorganization plan. Senator Tom Connally, a Texas Democrat and southern conservative but frequent supporter of Roosevelt, added his voice to the opposition, as did Montana Democrat Burton K. Wheeler, a moderate liberal. Even Vice President John Nance Garner took a vacation to Texas to display his displeasure. Perhaps most importantly, more than 50 percent of Americans opposed the court reform plan from its inception.[135]

This political environment seemed ripe for an ultraconservative resurgence, yet grassroots right-wingers stayed out of the limelight. After the debacle of 1936, the far right had become a poisoned chalice. In a letter to former congressman James E. Watson, an Indiana Republican, newspaper editor William Allen White referred to Shouse and the Liberty League as "black beasts" that were "liable to make [Roosevelt] friends instead of enemies."[136] Instead, the Liberty League worked behind the scenes. Fearful that overt criticisms would roust support for Roosevelt's court proposal, Shouse convinced Landon not to mention the plan in his Lincoln Day speech. The Jeffersonians, for their part, made plans to attack the reorganization plan head-on. However, Edmunds revealed to Raskob, "After this plan had been submitted, we were strongly advised by Governor Smith and others to call off our meeting and remain in the background, which we did."[137] Raskob continued funding the Jeffersonians, but the organization remained silent as the court battle roiled and the 1938 midterm elections approached. Ultimately, the Senate rebuked Roosevelt by sending the court bill back to committee in a stunning 70-20 vote, proving to conservative politicians that the far right remained a liability rather than a useful political partner, a lesson adopted by future conservative pragmatists like William F. Buckley Jr. Ultraconservatives had a different interpretation of the court bill's defeat. Raoul Desvernine, the leader of the Liberty League's National Lawyers Committee, regarded the court bill's defeat as a "complete vindication of the teachings of the American Liberty League."[138] Despite getting shunned by the political mainstream during the most important political battle of Roosevelt's first two terms, far-right agitators found solace in the belief that their activism laid the groundwork for future conservative victories.[139]

*   *   *

The revolt against Roosevelt and the New Deal, led by the Jeffersonian Democrats and the American Liberty League, illustrated an undercurrent of disgruntled conservatives within both major parties and among wealthy elites.

Though not all opponents of the New Deal were ultraconservatives, the far right's red-baiting rhetoric honed the anti-communism of the First Red Scare for a new era of preponderant liberalism. Ultraconservatives appealed to the country's latent anti-statism, providing the framework for future critiques of liberalism. The American Liberty League failed to dislodge Roosevelt, but the organization provided a point of convergence for right-wing business-men and professed ideas that permeated the broader conservative movement. Similarly, the rebellious Jeffersonian Democrats highlighted the internecine ideological conflict within the Democratic Party, brought forth a ground-swell of ultraconservative activism, and foreshadowed the South's political reorientation. The Jeffersonian rejection of Democratic liberalism portended and helped initiate the midcentury conservative exodus from the Democratic Party, and their grassroots tactics, especially the mass-mailing techniques, appeared in future conservative campaigns. Both groups constituted critical nodes within the fledgling far-right network, weaving together a patchwork of conservative philosophies, electoral strategies, and right-wing leadership in an era dominated by liberalism.[140]

The Great Depression was a critical inflection point for American politics. Roosevelt and the national Democratic Party forged a sectional coalition that turned into an electoral juggernaut by creating a party wedded to Roosevelt's New Deal liberalism rather than a sense of political aggrievement and south-ern white supremacy. This transformation modulated the power of conser-vatives, particularly those in the South, who were the traditional reactionary force in American politics. After 1936, Roosevelt's congressional opponents solidified within the conservative wings of both major political parties, but each party continued to house liberals and conservatives, stifling resistance to Roosevelt's liberal order. The backlash against Roosevelt's "court-packing" scheme in 1937 resuscitated right-wing opposition, which carried over into the next phase of far-right activism.[141] Even with the threat of World War II on the horizon, New Deal liberalism remained the target for many conservatives, especially those on the far end of the spectrum. As the United States teetered on the brink of war in the early 1940s and Roosevelt's New Deal revolution morphed into a warfare state, the far-right vanguard rejoined the fray.

CHAPTER 2

Radical Patriots

"To hell with the government!" Those were the last words Sewell Avery shouted as two steel-helmeted GIs carried him out of his Chicago office.[1] The confrontation marked the culmination of months of tension between Avery, chairman of the board for mail-order titan Montgomery Ward, and the American government. With the nation focused on World War II and President Franklin Roosevelt keen on keeping the economy humming, Avery's refusal to comply with federal directives to negotiate with a local union put him in Roosevelt's crosshairs. Government officials had arrived around noon that day, April 27, 1944, to serve notice that the federal government was seizing control of Montgomery Ward. Undersecretary of commerce Wayne C. Taylor and Assistant Attorney General Ugo Carusi presented Avery with a certified copy of Roosevelt's order, but Avery refused to budge. Taylor told reporters, "Mr. Avery stated that he does not recognize the legality of my authority and . . . has declined to accede to my demand."[2] A crowd of 1,500 employees, shoppers, and curious bystanders gathered outside as the standoff stretched into its seventh hour. Faced with Avery's intransigence, federal officials called in a fleet of military police. The troops arrived by the truckload, bayonets fixed, and a small squad marched up to Avery's office to carry out Roosevelt's order. When Avery once again refused to leave, Attorney General Francis Biddle, who had flown in from Washington to prevent exactly this type of showdown, ordered his removal. Avery sneered at Biddle, "You New Dealer!" before troops unceremoniously dumped him out on the sidewalk.[3]

The episode became a lightning rod for controversy. Avery's refusal to acquiesce marked the first time a major company stood firm against the federal government's expansive wartime power. Roosevelt later justified the seizure through wartime rationale: "Strikes in wartime cannot be condoned, whether they are strikes by workers against their employers or strikes by employers against their government."[4] Conservatives, however, did not buy Roosevelt's reasoning. A *Los Angeles Times* columnist complained that Montgomery Ward was "NOT a war industry" and raised an alarmist scenario: "Presidential seizure . . . by armed troops are actions bearing an extraordinary resemblance to the Hitlerism we are fighting a war supposedly to destroy."[5] Westbrook Pegler, a labor-antagonizing journalist, also saw the specter of government tyranny in Roosevelt's actions, writing that the seizure boosted "the unioneer, the racketeer, and the Communist" at the expense of "law-abiding citizens."[6] Avery's stand became a symbol of right-wing defiance. The picture of Avery, arms crossed, being thrown out by federal troops made him a martyr of the far right. As a financier of the American Liberty League, Avery had already established himself in the broader right-wing network, and now his battle cry against government oppression recalled the aggrievement felt by Depression-era industrialists. The fact that Roosevelt had used similarly heavy-handed tactics against recalcitrant strikers did not matter; when FDR backed the union over Montgomery Ward, ultraconservatives such as Avery declared that the government had its thumb on the wrong people.

The World War II era marked a pivotal moment for the far right. Fascism stalked Europe, breathing life into similar movements within the United States. The growth of domestic fascist groups such as the German American Bund and the Silver Shirts highlighted conservatism's extremist edge and the overlapping ideologies along the American right wing. Europe's descent into war also sparked foreign policy battles. As the war loomed over American politics, a coalition of old guard conservatives and patriotic nationalists came together to defend neutrality against internationalist hawks. The America First Committee (AFC), a nationalist organization dedicated to nonintervention, sparred against a slow-growing chorus of internationalism, underscoring a dispute over foreign policy neutrality that plagued the conservative movement for years after the war ended.

Furthermore, debates over electoral and organizing strategies continued to divide ultraconservative ranks. Anti-communist conspiracies and grassroots strategies remained far-right staples, but ultraconservatives also discovered how to weaponize state power against liberal opposition. The House Un-American Activities Committee (HUAC), led by Texas Democrat and far-right translator Martin Dies Jr., attacked liberalism as a communist plot and brought ultraconservative conspiracies into the political mainstream, providing a blueprint for using state power to undermine liberalism. The publication of the "Conservative Manifesto" and Roosevelt's failed purge of right-wing Democrats during the 1938 midterms signaled the gradual reorientation of ideological and partisan lines. Two years later, traditionalists sounded the alarm when Roosevelt ran for an unprecedented third term. Disaffected Democrats, notably James A. Reed and the Jeffersonian Democrats, jumped ship to support Republican Wendell Willkie, continuing the pattern of forced pragmatism wherein ultraconservatives viewed Republican candidates, rather than third-party crusades, as the best vehicle for vanquishing Roosevelt and his liberal coalition. Despite Willkie's defeat, the 1940 election further established the far-right's relationship with the GOP, laying the groundwork for the formation of an ultraconservative wing within the Republican Party.[7]

After Japan's attack on Pearl Harbor brought America into the global conflagration, Roosevelt shifted New Deal liberalism toward a more expansive warfare state. Often mythologized as a time of national unity and consensus, the World War II era marked a continuation of substantial social and political divisions. The New Deal's long reach already rankled conservatives, and the fact that the warfare state enlarged the federal government's administrative capacities further stoked right-wing rancor. The regulations of the wartime economy, particularly the federal government's takeover of Montgomery Ward, sharpened the far-right's libertarian, free-market impulses and spawned a new generation of ultraconservative activists. When Roosevelt ran for a fourth term in 1944, a group of conservative Texas Democrats rebelled. The revolt of the Texas Regulars revealed the limits of far-right pragmatism and blazed a trail for future ultraconservative third parties. Ultimately, the maelstrom of World War II forced a maturation of the organizational and ideological contours of midcentury ultraconservatism.[8]

*   *   *

By the late 1930s, the rise of dictators and bellicose nationalism had fractured global relations. After taking an ultranationalist turn in the late 1920s, Japan set out to create its own empire, culminating with the 1937 "China Incident" where Japanese soldiers committed countless atrocities and sacked critical Chinese cities such as Shanghai and Nanking. In Europe, multiple powers fell under authoritarian regimes. Benito Mussolini claimed the premiership of Italy in 1922 by invoking patriotic nationalism and a return to Italian glory. Joseph Stalin maneuvered his way into power after the death of Vladimir

Lenin, relying on fear and oppression to dominate the Soviet Union. During a period known as the Great Purge, Stalin imprisoned much of the nation's military, diplomatic, and intellectual leadership, inoculating himself from political challengers at the expense of national security and civil liberties. The Spanish Civil War broke out in 1936, pitting the Second Spanish Republic against the nationalist (and quasi-fascist) leader General Francisco Franco. The Weimar Republic of Germany struggled under the yoke of the Treaty of Versailles and capitulated when Adolf Hitler assumed the chancellorship in 1933. After the Nazi Party consolidated power, Hitler embarked on his mission to provide *lebensraum* (a homeland) for the people of Germany by invading nearby nations, beginning with the annexation of Austria on March 12, 1938.[9]

Though much of the American public recoiled as Europe descended into turmoil, the rise of fascism and hyper-nationalism abroad stoked similar movements at home. The Great Depression era witnessed an explosion of domestic fascist organizations, notably William Dudley Pelley's Silver Legion of America and the German American Bund. Pelley, a spiritualist writer and admirer of Hitler, formed the Silver Legion, also known as the Silver Shirts, in 1933 in the wake of Hitler's ascension to the chancellorship. A congressional report described the Silver Shirts as a "subversive" organization, "the largest, best financed, and certainly the best publicized."[10] The group capitalized on discontent—whether racial, economic, or cultural—and started with only a few hundred members before peaking just one year later with 15,000. The German American Bund, led by Fritz Kuhn, a naturalized citizen born in Munich, Germany, disseminated Nazi propaganda through its membership and rallies. The American government investigated the Bund and uncovered that the organization sent members to Germany for training and received "its inspiration, program, and direction from the Nazi Government of Germany."[11] Bund leaders estimated that the organization had roughly 20,000 to 25,000 dues-paying members, though a separate Justice Department investigation placed the number much lower—around 6,500. Nevertheless, Kuhn claimed a larger "sympathizer" movement of nearly 100,000. A patchwork of fascist groups coordinated with Kuhn's Bund, including the Christian Mobilizers, Christian Crusaders (not to be confused with Billy James Hargis's ministry), and the Silver Shirt Legion. A number of fascist-adjacent movements also appeared during the World War II era, such as Elizabeth Dilling's Mothers' Movement, Gerald L. K. Smith and the Committee of One Million, and the America First Committee, illustrating that, while most Americans pinned their hopes on Roosevelt's recovery efforts, others turned to the siren song of fascism.[12]

Domestic fascist groups flourished alongside established ultraconserva-tive organizations such as the Jeffersonian Democrats and the American Liberty League, and the two movements shared some ideological touchstones despite holding significant differences. American fascists and ultraconservatives both employed conspiratorial language and considered any opposing ideology illegitimate. For example, the Christian Mobilizers denounced the "growing despotism of the Pinko-Liberal-Internationalist-Communistic-Popular Front in our city state and national governments," a phrase which reflected the far right's ideological alchemy, flattening nonconservative ideologies into shades of communism.[13] A sense of patriotic nationalism also connected fascists and far-right activists. The two movements gained energy from the First Red Scare and notions of "Americanism," both of which marginalized immigrants and left-wing political groups as un-American and magnified the threat of an internal conspiracy. This Manichean mindset fed into the far right and fascist right's belief that America was a white Protestant nation, first and foremost.

Important differences separated ultraconservatives from domestic fascists, however. The fascist right sought to aggressively employ state power and disrupt democratic traditions to defeat their opponents. In their mind, only the creation of an authoritarian white Christian ethnostate could stop the presumed global Jewish conspiracy infecting American government.[14] For example, a reporter for Baltimore's *Sun* wrote that the Silver Shirts "dreamed of and planned an American dictatorship, with William Dudley Pelley as the white king."[15] On the other hand, far-right activists advocated for small government, *laissez-faire* economics, and a minimizing of social strife at the expense of racial minorities. Ultraconservatives claimed to abhor revolutionary upheaval and notions of a dictatorship. Instead, power should be earned through traditional channels. They even used the term "fascist" as a pejorative against liberals, accusing the New Deal of paving the road to authoritarianism.

Nevertheless, the divide between domestic fascists and ultraconservatives was as porous as the separation between the far right and mainstream conservatives. Each faction's view of state power revealed the overlapping circles of the right-wing Venn Diagram. Fascist groups worked to foment a revolution that would end in an authoritarian dictatorship; an all-powerful state that would delineate a hierarchical social structure was the fascists' end goal. The far right, on the other hand, gained power through the republican system and then pulled the levers of power to their advantage. In other words, authoritarian power came through the ballot box instead of revolutionary upheaval. Yet both the far right and domestic fascists approved of state power so long as it matched their political goals or targeted the right kind of people. When the House Un-American Activities Committee leveraged federal authority against liberals, for example, both fascist organizations and far-right groups praised the efforts as necessary for rooting out communism. Many southern conservatives used state power to brutally enforce white supremacy and racial segregation, and right-wing politicians would soon harness the power of congressional investigations to attack liberalism. Ultimately, the professed anti-statism of the far right was a paradox—it was simultaneously a deeply held ideological conviction about the proper role of government *and* a cynical strategy to undermine liberalism while veiling right-wing authoritarianism. Ultraconservatives and domestic fascists occupied adjacent, and at times overlapping, spaces on the political spectrum, but the latter's virulent, revolutionary rhetoric bore the mark of extremism and cast a pall over American politics.

The darkening international scene and growth of domestic fascism alarmed Americans of all stripes, prompting the House of Representatives to create a committee, led by New York Democrat Samuel Dickstein, to investigate subversive activities within the United States. Though the rise of domestic fascism provided the impetus for Dickstein's committee, the anti-communist anxieties of the previous decade had paved the way and would guide the hand of future subversive-hunting committees. In the wake of the Crash of 1929, Congressman Hamilton Fish III, a New York Republican, proposed the creation of a House committee to investigate perceived treacherous organizations, particularly the Communist Party and its affiliated groups. Despite finding that communists held little influence, the Fish Committee recommended, among other things, criminalizing the Communist Party and deporting alien communists. Other right-wing congressmen joined Fish's xenophobic crusade, including a young Texas Democrat, Congressman Martin Dies Jr., who put forth a bill to deport communist immigrants. The Fish Committee set an important precedent of using congressional committees to investigate allegations of communist sabotage; however, by the mid-1930s, the threat of internal fascism replaced communism as the anti-subversive obsession. Alarmed by the rising enthusiasm for Nazi Germany and threats against New York's Jewish community, Dickstein petitioned to convene a new special committee to investigate the prevalence of domestic fascism. The McCormack-Dickstein committee traced a network of financial support stretching from Germany to domestic fascist outlets, which led Dickstein to request another, more expansive, special committee. He hoped to secure $200,000 to combat a subversive "hate campaign" led by 150 far-right groups. Congress tabled Dickstein's request, but the Fish and Dickstein Committees laid the groundwork for future congressmen to use federal investigations as a weapon against partisan enemies.[16]

A couple years later, in the summer of 1938, Congress considered a new proposal to investigate subversive radicalism within the United States. This time Martin Dies Jr. wanted to run the show. Dies hailed from a political family. His father, Martin Dies Sr., had served as the U.S. representative for Texas's second congressional district, a rural and predominantly African American district ensconced within the piney woods of East Texas. The elder Dies campaigned for protective tariffs, old-timey traditionalism, and white supremacy. He told the Republican Party that, to gain votes in the South and West, it needed to "declare for the white man's domination of this Government and integrity of the Caucasian race."[17] Dies Sr. also considered immigrants a threat to America's "free institutions" and supported restrictive immigration policies.[18] Throughout his congressional career, the elder Dies staked out a position as an ultraconservative segregationist and nativist, ideas which presaged his son's future ideological and political palette.

During his formative years, Dies Jr. worked in his father's law office and gleaned many of his father's hard-line conservative platforms. "My father . . . was one of the first men in the United States to denounce against immigration. So you see I was brought up on this doctrine," Dies once wrote.[19] Dies disdained the Texas Ku Klux Klan—exemplifying conservative factionalism, he believed the Klan's violent racism was un-American and "bad for Texas"— but his ultraconservatism nevertheless fused southern racist traditions with anti-statist populism and xenophobic Americanism.[20] Dies excelled on the stump, and he used his family name, oratory skills, and a dash of old-fashioned race-baiting to win a U.S. congressional seat, the same one once held by his father, at the tender age of twenty-nine. He received significant support from John Nance Garner, then the Speaker of the House and a fellow Texas Democrat; Garner ensured that Dies received appointments to numerous congressional committees, where the young Democrat made a name for himself as a nativist firebrand. While serving on the House Committee on Immigration and Naturalization, for example, Dies put forth a bill that would permit "the exclusion and expulsion of alien communists" from the United States; he hoped "to stop all new immigration from every country."[21] To Dies, immigration and political radicalism were inextricably intertwined. "I saw 100,000 Communists march through the streets of New York. I did not see an American in the crowd," he wrote in 1935. "Many of them are aliens that should be deported and others are foreign born who should have their naturalization papers canceled."[22] Though Dies espoused anti-statist philosophies, he frequently urged the use of federal power to enforce anti-immigrant policies, foreshadowing his use of state authority to fight the specter of communist subversion.[23]

Dies originally backed Roosevelt's New Deal, but the gradual support for civil rights among non-southern Democrats and the increasing boldness of labor unions changed his calculus. In 1935 Congress passed the National Labor Relations Act, commonly known as the Wagner Act, which bolstered unions' right to organize and take collective action. But labor unrest during the Great Depression, particularly the General Motors (GM) sit-down strike, alarmed Dies and his fellow conservatives. During a sit-down strike, workers halted production by seizing control of critical plant infrastructure, a radical mutation of the traditional walkout strike. The 1936 GM strike pitted one of the country's largest employers, run by far-right patrons Alfred P. Sloan Jr. and the du Pont family, against its labor force. Strikers took control of at least fifty plants—including GM's crown jewel, the Fisher Body Plant in Flint, Michigan—and demanded that GM recognize the United Auto Workers (UAW) as the exclusive national union for GM laborers. The strike prompted a hard line from GM brass; executive vice president William S. Knudsen scorned the strikers as "trespassers and violators of the law of the land."[24] Violent episodes punctuated the strike, and union leadership—John L. Lewis, founder of the Congress of Industrial Organizations (CIO), and Walter Reuther, leader of UAW Local 174—instructed the strikers to hold out for their demands. After forty-four days and some behind-the-scenes support from President Roosevelt, the strike ended with a massive victory for labor. The UAW now had exclusive representation over all GM employees, and the strike's success inspired others: over 2,000 strikes occurred in 1937 alone.[25]

Labor militancy evolved into an ultraconservative fever dream. Some right-wingers accused the strikers of dooming American democracy by violating the sanctity of property rights. Frank E. Gannett, right-wing publisher and chairman of the National Committee to Uphold Constitutional Government, criticized Michigan governor Frank Murphy and Roosevelt for enabling a slippery slope of "mob rule." "If a group of men can seize Chrysler's plant, they can likewise seize his home," Gannett warned. "If they can seize his home and lock him out of it, they can do the same to you or to anyone else. And if the law ... cannot protect property, our human rights cannot be protected."[26] Matt L. Love, a railroad magnate and constituent of Dies, mirrored Gannett and the aggrievement of the American Liberty League, characterizing unionists as "un-American" and "unlawful." Love implored Dies to do something: "When we have to sit idly by and see property of private individuals just unceremoniously taken away from them without due process of law, I think it is nothing short of a crime and should be dealt with accordingly."[27] Dies agreed, noting that he considered the sit-down strikes a far greater threat than Roosevelt's concurrent attempt to reorganize the court. "If employees can seize other peoples' property with immunity and prevent employers from having access to it or use it, then this Republic is at an end and it is a matter of no importance who is on the court," Dies replied.[28] The workers' seizure of plant property was indeed illegal, but the right wing's retort sought to demonize unions and minimize labor struggles as much as urge a return to law and order.[29]

The conservative response to the strike also bore a familiar conspiratorial anti-communism. Westbrook Pegler called the sit-down tactic a "communist device" that "brings fascism that much closer," even though he acknowledged that most strikers were not actual communists.[30] John Caffrey, a civilian from Aurora, Colorado, urged Dies to deport the "aliens and foreign trouble makers that are giving us all this trouble with sit down strikes, preaching communism and Nazism."[31] Conservatives correctly surmised that communists were involved in the unions and present at the strikes but misplaced the impetus: the union went on strike because of labor grievances, not revolutionary communism. Nevertheless, any communist involvement, not to mention the fact that the sit-down action took over the literal means of production, led ultraconservatives to view the strikes as a communist usurpation. Mistrust of labor stretched across the entire nation during the mid-1930s. One poll indicated that an overwhelming percentage of Americans, 66 to 34, supported GM's non-negotiation stance. Many of Dies's constituents reflected this national majority and encouraged Dies to investigate labor radicalism. Businessmen and white-collar professionals in Dies's district sent letters of support, and even some fraternal labor organizations, such as the local United Brotherhood of Carpenters and Joiners, worried about the events unfolding in Flint. However, one constituent warned Dies not to criticize Roosevelt or the sit-down strikers, believing both shared immense popularity in Dies's Second District. Texans certainly approved of FDR, but a poll revealed that 73 percent of the South, including Texas, favored criminalizing sit-down strikes, making it the most anti-union region of the nation—no surprise considering the South's long history of labor exploitation.[32]

Mistrust of labor became a tool for leveraging conservative gains. Dies demanded that the federal government take action to support GM's management and, more broadly, the rights of property owners. He wanted to fight the strikers using existing antitrust laws and, as a member of the House Committee on Rules, pushed for a new "impartial inquiry," an updated Dickstein committee to investigate the origin of the sit-down strikes.[33] His measure passed the committee but was greeted by laughter in the House after Dies dissembled that this new investigation would "not be directed against labor unions." After a raucous debate and the threat of a fistfight, Congress tabled Dies's measure on April 8, 1937, even though the Senate had voted to condemn the sit-down strikes just one day prior. Dies failed, for now, to create a new investigatory committee, but the Texan's anti-labor stance struck a chord along the conservative spectrum. Through his rhetoric and political stature, Dies became one of the earliest far-right translators, a respectable figure who legitimized ultraconservative beliefs for the political mainstream.[34]

In a twist of irony, it was the proliferation of fascist propaganda, rather than the roiling debate about communist labor saboteurs, that prompted the House to create another special committee to investigate un-American activities. Two months after calling for a renewed investigative committee, Dies viewed an affidavit which alleged that a Bund member advocated assassinating Roosevelt. Dies used it to revive his demand for an anti-subversive investigation, but other congressmen still contended that such an inquiry could lead down dangerous paths. Maury Maverick, a fellow Texas Democrat, worried that the committee would become an "entering wedge to religious persecution," while Nebraska Republican Karl Stefan fretted about provoking anti-German sentiments.[35] Even the previous HUAC chairman, John W. McCormack, acknowledged the committee's potential to devolve into a partisan tool.[36] Nevertheless, on May 26, 1938, a new committee, christened the House Un-American Activities Committee, convened to investigate domestic subversion. McCormack's cautionary words would go unheeded.

Through HUAC, Dies sharpened conspiratorial anti-communism into a state-sanctioned, far-right weapon. The Dies Committee had six members aside from Dies himself: Massachusetts Democrat Arthur D. Healey, Ohio Democrat Harold G. Mosier, New Jersey Republican J. Parnell Thomas, New Mexico Democrat John J. Dempsey, Illinois Republican Noah M. Mason, and

Alabama Democrat Joe Starnes. The group's conservative bent illustrated that, at the time, right-wing ideologies crossed partisan lines. Dempsey and Healey, both dedicated New Dealers who were uncomfortable with Dies's mission, were the odd men out and missed numerous committee meetings. At the inaugural committee gathering Dies laid out his vision: "This special committee was created . . . for the purpose of conducting an investigation of the extent, character, and objects of un-American propaganda activities in the United States; the diffusion within the United States of subversive and un-American propaganda that is instigated from foreign countries or of domestic origin and attacks the principle of the form of government as guaranteed by our Constitution." Dies clarified that the committee was not "after anyone," would be "fair and impartial," and was "more concerned with facts than opinions." However, the Texan failed to enunciate what constituted subversive activities, noting only a need to "distinguish clearly between what is obviously un-American and what is no more or less than an honest difference of opinion with respect to some economic, political, or social question."[37] This ambiguous *modus operandi* allowed Dies to expand HUAC's purview and turn the committee into a right-wing shillelagh—political, cultural, and racial issues were often framed through an ultraconservative prism.[38]

The Dies Committee initiated its investigations by interviewing members of the German American Bund and affiliated Nazi organizations. Dies's investigations were part of a national campaign against domestic fascism led by President Roosevelt and FBI director J. Edgar Hoover. Anti-Semitic fascists attacked Dies and the committee for collaborating with subversive Jews, being Jewish themselves, or ignoring the "real" problems within the United States. For example, Joe McWilliams of the Christian Mobilizers said the Dies Committee was misleading the country because it was "Jew controlled" and blind to the threat of "Jew Communism."[39] Pelley used similar language, calling Roosevelt a "stooge" for East European "kikes" and deriding Dies as "the Jew-lover from Texas."[40] The FBI and Dies Committee produced numerous reports on fascist groups, and the multitiered investigations bore fruit: the government surveilled Gerald L. K. Smith, indicted Winrod, and prosecuted Pelley, resulting in Silver Shirt membership falling to 5,000 members.[41]

After scrutinizing fascist groups—the committee's original focus—Dies soon pivoted to expansive investigations into communism in labor unions and government agencies. FBI leader J. Edgar Hoover similarly widened Roosevelt's mandate into a dragnet that included communist groups, labor unions, and fringe isolationists. This illustrated a pattern in which right-wingers redirected federal power against their ideological opponents. If liberalism was a liminal stage of communism, as many far-right activists believed, then it was wholly appropriate to target liberals as subversives. Dies invited anti-labor advocates to testify and subpoenaed workers involved in the Detroit sit-down strikes. John P. Frey, a leader of the American Federation of Labor, appeared before the committee and proclaimed that communists dominated the CIO. Other CIO opponents levied similar salacious charges, confirming Dies's belief that a cabal of foreign radicals sought to dismantle American capitalism. Communists did control significant portions of the CIO and held positions in the National Labor Relations Board, but witnesses and Dies himself exaggerated their influence. Labor communists did not hold state power and played no policymaking role, as Dies did, and committee witnesses provided scant evidence to support their tales of communist plots. With Dies and his fellow investigators, accusations came first, often without evidence, and dominated the headlines, while denials and corrections were obscured on the back pages.[42]

The Dies Committee amassed files on people accused of subversion and listened to all manner of wild-eyed conspiracies. Witnesses often contorted progressive or liberal beliefs into un-American treason, and investigators accepted hearsay and gossip so long as it fit the correct ideological parameters. In one particularly embarrassing episode, a witness alleged that child movie star Shirley Temple "unwittingly served the interests of the Communist Party."[43] Nevertheless, mainstream media coverage boosted the accusations emanating from committee hearings. "Says Reds Started Sit-Down Strikes," blared one *New York Times* headline; the article relayed that a HUAC investigator believed wives of prominent labor leaders were teaching a nebulous "un-Americanism" in Detroit public schools.[44] In fact, the *New York Times* dedicated five hundred inches of space to the committee within the first two months of its existence, and other outlets provided even more extensive coverage. A cycle of misinformation developed as the Dies Committee gave witnesses a platform and the media promoted the allegations at face value, which fed conspiracies about the size, power, and permeation of internal communist subversion.[45]

Through the committee, Dies and his fellow ultraconservatives used state power to discredit liberalism by portraying it as un-American sabotage. Dies investigated New Deal agencies and many of Roosevelt's closest advisors for communist inclinations. Frequent targets included Secretary of Labor Frances Perkins, Secretary of the Interior Harold Ickes, and Works Progress Administration (WPA) supervisor Harry Hopkins. In a speech before the Boston

Chamber of Commerce, Dies characterized the New Deal bureaucracy as "the intermediate step to dictatorship" and called bureaucrats "wild-eyed monkeys, who know only how to propose some scheme to take away other people's property and other people's rights."[46] At one point, the committee targeted the Federal Theatre and Writers Project—a branch of the WPA that provided jobs to unemployed writers and actors, some of whom were communist activists. Dies Committee member and vehement New Deal critic J. Parnell Thomas roared, "Practically every play presented under the auspices of the Project is sheer propaganda for Communism or the New Deal."[47] The browbeating worked: Congress shuttered the theater project in 1939 in the wake of HUAC's investigation, despite the fact that none of the committee members had viewed any WPA plays. The inquiry illustrated the effectiveness of using state power against liberal programs and laid bare the far right's hypocritical stance regarding federal authority. Despite the occasional Dies Committee highlight, such as the successful dismantling of the German American Bund, HUAC's sloppy procedures, ideological partisanship, and conspiratorial rhetoric cast doubt on the committee's probity.[48]

The tactics and tone of the Dies Committee opened a festering wound within the American polity. Conservatives praised Dies as a hardnosed truthteller. Hamilton Fish proclaimed, "I love the Dies Committee for the enemies it has made."[49] John B. Trevor Sr., a nativist lawyer with significant congressional influence, encouraged Dies's relentless intransigence: "Beware of compromises, Martin, remember they satisfy nobody."[50] Trevor's letter illustrated the far right's worldview in which a stark division separated the American polity into conservative allies and liberal-communist enemies. This mindset diminished pragmatism because compromise meant dealing with the devil. Dies received support from conservative civic organizations, such as the Junior Chamber of Commerce, and many of Dies's local constituents lauded his anti-subversive investigations. One Beaumont man, Paul B. Matlock, wrote to Dies, "The dangerous political groups among us must be not merely checked but eradicated and if in doing so the Government intrude upon some of the beneficent rights we have accorded aliens, at least such barking of shins will be no skin from the citizens of this country."[51] A certain tension permeated far-right conservatism—professed anti-statism often chafed against statist solutions such as investigatory committees or, as Matlock advocated, truncating political rights. Nevertheless, Newton W. Powers, a Texas Civilian Conservation Corps worker, agreed with the use of statist measures to undermine liberalism. Powers wrote to Dies after hearing him on the radio: "Why don't you see that they [the communists] are disposed of . . . are the men in congress a bunch of jelly-fish or are they red blooded Americans who do not want to see this country run by communistic elements."[52]

On the other hand, labor leaders and New Dealers took a dim view of Dies's investigations. Dickstein and other congressmen, including HUAC members Dempsey and Healey, condemned Dies's penchant for partisan bias and enabling of conspiracy theories. Congressman Adolph J. Sabath, an Illinois Democrat, criticized Dies for needlessly investigating the government and withholding evidence that foreign governments sponsored subversive propaganda.[53] Harold Ickes mocked Dies as a cynical opportunist, "hissing through his teeth, rending the air with blood-curdling yelps, freezing the very marrow of our bones with his tales of fearsome, ferocious government clerks who read the *New Republic*."[54] The chairman of Beaumont Typographical Union, A. D. Covin, attempted to change Dies's mind through multiple letters. After failing to make a dent, Covin concluded that the Dies Committee was "a tool in the hands of the corporate interests" bent on unwinding liberal reforms. "Why don't you join the Republican Party and cease being a hypocrite," Covin admonished.[55] Even Dies admitted that at times his committee did an "inadequate and slipshod job," but rather than acknowledging any ideological bias, he cited personnel issues and limited funding, despite receiving roughly $650,000 over the course of the committee's five-year existence.[56]

Conservatives used the Dies Committee to sharpen federal power and anti-communism into an anti-liberal harpoon. During the 1938 midterm elections, the committee went hunting for New Dealers. For example, Michigan governor Frank Murphy had endured intense criticism for his moderation during the 1937 sit-down strikes. In the days leading up to Murphy's tough reelection bid, two witnesses—Paul V. Gadola, a Republican Circuit Court judge, and former Flint city manager John M. Barringer—told the Dies Committee that the governor held a "treasonable attitude" for enabling the sit-down strikes.[57] When Dies inquired whether or not the sit-down strikes would have occurred without communist instigators, Barringer replied, "No, they would not and I'll say further that they would not have progressed so rapidly except for the attitude of the La Follette committee and Governor Murphy."[58] Roosevelt tried to aid Murphy's flagging reelection bid by reminding the nation that the governor's actions prevented bloodshed on the factory floor. Nevertheless, Michigan voters spurned the incumbent and put Republican Frank Fitzgerald into office. Murphy was one of eleven Democratic governors to lose a seat in 1938, underscoring how the conspiratorial anti-communism of the Dies Committee damaged liberal opponents and mainstreamed ultraconservative beliefs.[59]

While Dies laid the foundation for turning state power against liberalism, congressional conservatives moved to consolidate forces during the midterm season. An economic recession hit in 1937, and conservatives hoped to influence Roosevelt's plans for resuscitating the economy. Turner Catledge of the *New York Times* reported that a cabal of conservative senators circulated a ten-point program in order to "establish a basis upon which the moderate and conservative forces of the Senate, Democratic and Republican, could coalesce."[60] The document read like a right-wing wish list: it contained provisions about supply-side economics, capital gains tax reductions, states' rights, an unfettered free market, and an end to federally owned corporations. Though it conceded the legitimacy of "collective bargaining and [labor's] right to organize," rugged individualist and pro-business language permeated the document.[61] Josiah Bailey, a North Carolina Democrat, spearheaded the movement, and he was joined by a bipartisan coterie of other senators, including Virginia Democrats Harry F. Byrd and Carter Glass, New York Democrat Royal S. Copeland, Nebraska Democrat Edward R. Burke, Maryland Democrat Millard Tydings, South Carolina Democrat Ellison D. "Cotton Ed" Smith, Michigan Republican Arthur H. Vandenberg, and Delaware Republican John G. Townsend.[62] This right-wing coalition hoped to gather signatures in support of a drive to, as Bailey later stated, "stop this trend toward collectivism."[63] Dewey L. Fleming of the *Baltimore Sun* recognized Bailey's strategy as an "open bid for a consolidation of conservative forces in Congress."[64]

Yet, the movement struggled to gain momentum, and the soon-to-be-called "Conservative Manifesto" quickly became a flashpoint on the acceptable parameters of right-wing thought during an era of liberal hegemony. Significant portions of the manifesto leaked to the press before Bailey could secure widespread congressional support. The leak put Bailey on the defensive. Interviewers prodded him with uncomfortable questions about whether he hoped to bolster the already formidable anti-Roosevelt, anti–New Deal bloc in Congress. Bailey rejected the term "manifesto" and, despite the fact that the document outlined policy goals in opposition to multiple New Deal platforms, characterized the draft as "entirely non-political and nonpartisan in character."[65] He even suggested that Roosevelt might sign it. Other senators remained wary, however. They remembered Roosevelt's landslide victory in 1936 and how New Dealers caricatured mainstream conservatives by conflating them with far-right groups such as the American Liberty League.

After all, some of the senators associated with the manifesto, notably Byrd and Smith, had ties to the far right. Despite the fact that the manifesto exhibited the significant overlap of right-wing ideologies, mainstream conservatives drew a stark separation between themselves and the ultraconservative right. Charles L. McNary, an Oregon Republican and Senate minority leader, voiced the fears of many who balked at the manifesto by saying, "Anyone who signs that thing is going to have a Liberty League tag put on him."[66]

As the Conservative Manifesto reverberated throughout the political arena, the 1938 midterms proved to be a watershed moment for Roosevelt. One *Baltimore Sun* writer speculated that the manifesto might embolden Congress to contest Roosevelt: "Members [of Congress] now do not bear such striking resemblance to tiny birds in a nest, opening their mouths to receive and swallow whenever they hear a fluttering of wings."[67] Perhaps, as the writer implied, the manifesto marked a turning point, a steeling of the conservative movement against Roosevelt's dominance. With conservative Democrats circling his administration, Roosevelt went on the offensive, attacking numerous anti–New Deal Democrats, including manifesto-approving senators such as "Cotton Ed" Smith and Millard Tydings. Roosevelt eschewed party machinery and appealed straight to voters in support of New Deal candidates, leading high-profile conservative Democrats to sound the alarm about a Roosevelt "purge." Tydings spoke out against Roosevelt on the radio, asserting that the president should be removed from office for election tampering.[68] Dies accused Roosevelt of being guilty of "violating the fundamental principle of Americanism—maintenance of the independence of each branch of Government," high irony considering Dies's congressional crusade against Roosevelt's executive branch.[69] The "purge" made for great copy, and newspapers provided breathless coverage of the theatrics. "Final 'Purge' Showdown at Hand for Roosevelt" blared Turner Catledge's *New York Times* column.[70] Roosevelt occupied a precarious position in 1938, and the electoral drama further fueled the far right's paranoia about state tyranny.

In the end, Roosevelt's "purge" backfired, succeeding only in turning voters away from the Democratic Party. Republicans gained eighty seats in the House of Representatives and eight in the Senate. The Institute of Public Opinion reported that three main issues convinced voters to spurn the Democrats: Roosevelt's court reorganization plan, the attempted purge of conservative Democrats, and the sit-down strikes of 1937. Though Democrats still controlled Congress, the margins were smaller than before. Worse still for Roosevelt, conservative Democrats from southern segregationist states dominated his party's caucus, accounting for more than half of Democratic seats in the House and nearly as many in the Senate. Moreover, the election of Senator Robert A. Taft, an Ohio Republican who chastised the New Deal's predilection for "planned economy and government regulation," signaled a shift in American politics.[71] Taft's election put another far-right translator in the halls of Congress, bolstering the ranks of congressional conservatives and exemplifying the national anti-administration tide. Journalist Mark Sullivan called the results "a visitation of adversity upon Mr. Roosevelt," noting that the "election was a move of the country toward conservatism."[72] For the first time since 1932, Roosevelt's New Deal faction showed signs of cracking.[73]

It seemed that an ascendant bipartisan conservatism might fracture Roosevelt's liberal coalition, but the outbreak of war in Europe in 1939 complicated the political calculus. World War II tested citizens' views of American neutrality. Though a sense of nationalistic neutrality (an essential ingredient in the ultraconservative brew) remained popular with the American public, Hitler's invasion of Poland weakened the noninterventionist wing of the Republican Party and empowered Roosevelt's internationalist inclinations. As the 1940 election loomed, the debate over interventionism and internationalism consumed the nation and dominated the presidential campaign season. Multiple high-profile politicians, including Taft, urged Roosevelt to avoid the European conflict. Right-wing newspapermen, such as Colonel Robert R. McCormick of the *Chicago Daily Tribune*, churned out noninterventionist columns. McCormick's brand of conservatism proved particularly reactionary—he thought Roosevelt's internationalism revealed a would-be dictator bent on destroying American democracy. Nazi Germany's *blitzkrieg* across Europe cast doubt upon America's ability to stay out of the war, but right-wingers refashioned legitimate global concerns into anti-liberal conspiracies. Just days after Germany invaded the Low Countries, Taft declared, "There is a good deal more danger of the infiltration of totalitarian ideas from the New Deal circle in Washington than there will ever be from any activities of the communists or the Nazi bund." Taft further asserted that American entry would be "more likely to destroy American democracy than to destroy German dictatorship."[74] In this moment, Taft was translating far-right ideas for a mainstream audience: New Deal liberalism and war mobilization constituted the nation's greatest threats.[75]

The 1940 presidential election foregrounded the battle over American intervention, but it also represented a pivotal moment for ultraconservatives such as James A. Reed and the Jeffersonian Democrats. As the election year dawned, the Jeffersonians lacked direction, still smarting from their failure in 1936. Multiple Jeffersonian headquarters had shuttered after the 1936 election, which left Reed wondering whether his collaborators had any fight left. He worried about a potential Roosevelt third term and believed that continued New Deal policies would sap grassroots enthusiasm for the Democratic Party. Yet, Reed fretted that the Jeffersonian Democrats lacked the constitution for another political battle, especially with a potential war looming on the horizon. In a letter to Lee Meriwether, Reed complained, "The difficulty appears to be that those who ought to be very earnestly interested and in a fighting mood are on the contrary in a comatose condition."[76]

As the election season heated up, Jeffersonian leaders sent out feelers to gauge the temperament of the most prominent members. The responses revealed a scattershot of opinions and strategies, ranging from rekindling the Jeffersonian grassroots apparatus to joining forces with the Republicans. Meriwether urged aggression; he called for a meeting of the Jeffersonian brass and implored the organization to put out a statement, get "scouts" into vulnerable districts, and promote suitable anti–New Deal candidates.[77] Some members, J. Evetts Haley included, supported Meriwether's thinking, but others favored waiting until both parties had chosen their nominees, hoping that one of the parties would choose a suitably conservative candidate. A few argued that the Jeffersonians should create an alternative, conservative coalition and draft their own candidate—popular choices included Conservative Manifesto supporter Senator Byrd, Vice President John Nance Garner, and publisher Frank Gannett—if the Democrats nominated Roosevelt. W. P. Hamblen, one of the architects of the Texas Jeffersonians, motioned that, if the Democrats selected a New Dealer, the Jeffersonians should "openly espouse the cause of the Republicans." On the other hand, William Ritchie of Omaha, Nebraska, opposed endorsing a Republican "under any circumstances."[78] Uncertainty reigned with the election less than a year away.[79]

After experiencing defeat in 1936 and sitting out the 1938 midterms, the Jeffersonian Democrats struggled to chart a course in 1940. The hegemony of liberalism left little space for far-right ideals. Liberalism still dominated the national Democratic Party, which meant that conservative Democrats, especially in the South, felt alienated in their own party. Even though southern Democrats had already stymied portions of the New Deal and spoke out against Roosevelt, polls indicated that, if Roosevelt ran for a third term, the South would return him to the White House by overwhelming margins. Thus, building a conservative movement within the Democratic Party seemed impossible so long as Roosevelt remained the party's leader. On the other side of the partisan divide, the Republican Party had a growing conservative wing, as evidenced by the emergence of Taft, but it was not yet strong enough to usurp power. That would be a battle left to future far-right activists. The last option, forming a third party, seemed like a feeble vehicle for protest votes. Ultraconservatives knew that a third-party crusade would not dislodge Roosevelt, and thus the utility of third-party action was another argument left to future ultraconservative generations. Ultimately, the far right's political quagmire captured the early moments of shifting party ideologies; in the coming decades, ultraconservatives would form the vanguard of the gradual party realignment and the creation of a conservative, southern-facing Republican Party.[80]

As war ravaged Europe and far-right activists plotted a potential return to politics, the 1940 presidential election illuminated the Democratic Party's perpetual internecine battles. The rift between liberal Democrats and the party's conservative wing, epitomized by Martin Dies's anti-communist investigations and the Jeffersonians' lurking presence, continued to expand. Additionally, the fact that Roosevelt had already served two terms further complicated matters. No president had ever successfully run for a third term after George Washington's decision to step away in 1796, and many Democrats did not support a third term for Roosevelt, including James Farley, the chair of the Democratic National Committee. Though Roosevelt never explained his reasoning, numerous events—Nazi success in Western Europe, a desire to solidify the New Deal's legacy, and his popularity with the public— seemed to compel the president to break tradition. Roosevelt outmaneuvered Democratic challengers, including Vice President Garner, to win an unprecedented third-term nomination. Reed watched the convention from afar. "In a few brief hours, the cruel ravishment will have occurred and the rejuvenated victim will again be able to smilingly greet his friends," he wrote to Al Smith. "It will probably be the most enjoyable and enthusiastic example of cooperative rape yet recorded in history or in the records of the courts."[81] Reed's hideous metaphor underscored his anger—a cabal of subversive liberals had once again desecrated his beloved party.[82]

With Roosevelt's nomination in place, the far right saw a communist consensus taking over American politics. "Here is the great danger. Both parties have been bidding for the votes of the Reds and the Pinks," Reed wrote to Sterling Edmunds. "If, in the next campaign, the Republicans follow their previous course, [we will] simply have a race between two parties traveling on parallel lines and there will be no obstacle to prevent them, either or both, from landing us in the mire of socialism."[83] However, Reed saw a way out. "I am developing a very keen interest in Wendell Willkie," Reed told Edmunds. "If the Republicans could nominate him there would be a clear issue between [the] Roosevelt and anti-Roosevelt philosophy of government."[84] Even though Willkie was not an ultraconservative ideologue, the far right had decided that a centrist was better than a liberal. Reed acknowledged substantial differences between his own ultraconservatism and Willkie's moderation, but he nevertheless believed Willkie stood the best chance of unseating Roosevelt. Reed's interest in Willkie prophesied the direction of the political winds in 1940. As noninterventionism diminished amid the increasing threat of war, the Republican Party needed a candidate who could match Roosevelt's avowed internationalism.

Willkie, a dark horse internationalist who had switched to the Republican Party but two years earlier, seemed like the man for the moment. Born in Indiana and raised by dedicated social reformers, Willkie immersed himself in progressive causes in his younger years. He supported the League of Nations, contested Ku Klux Klan power in Indiana, and even voted for Roosevelt in 1932. However, Willkie's experience in the business world altered his politics. A lawyer by education, Willkie served as legal counsel for Commonwealth & Southern Corporation, a utilities company, where he eventually became president and chief executive officer in 1934. It was from this vantage point as a business executive that Willkie sharpened his critique of Roosevelt's regulatory liberalism. Small wonder why ultraconservatives lined up to support him. Perhaps far-right leaders saw Willkie, the former progressive turned business conservative, as a prodigal son, if not a kindred spirit. During the early New Deal, Willkie supported the idea of a social safety net, but he criticized the Tennessee Valley Authority and coined the term "Big Government" to "demonize the ills of excessive Washington activism." Willkie wove a hawkish foreign policy together with conservative economic platforms, portraying Roosevelt's empowerment of labor and regulatory liberalism as a threat to national security.[85]

Willkie's campaign succeeded in bringing together a cross-party conservative coalition. Eschewing a traditional primary campaign, he instead employed a media strategy to position himself as a political outsider. His opening salvo, a piece in *Fortune* titled "We the People," charged that Roosevelt's New Deal "impeded economic recovery with an antibusiness philosophy."[86] The Indianan's rhetoric of internationalism, property rights, and free markets appealed to a broad swath of conservatives, including moderate-to-liberal Republicans and right-wing newspapermen such as Henry Luce and Ogden Reid. Willkie secured support from corporate executives, such as Pepsi-Cola president Walter Mack Jr. and J. P. Morgan director Thomas Lamont, and inspired legions of grassroots supporters. Oren Root, the grandnephew of Teddy Roosevelt's secretary of state Elihu Root, sent out tens of thousands of copies of Willkie's "We the People" column and helped form the Willkie Clubs, an extra-party organization that collaborated with Republican machinery.[87]

The remnants of the Jeffersonian Democrats weighed aligning with the Willkie forces. Perhaps tired of inaction, many had decided it was better to man the front than sit on the sidelines. Joe Bailey, a leader of the Texas Jeffersonians, suggested that the Jeffersonians should present their platform to the Republican National Committee in the hopes that the GOP would adopt some of their planks.[88] At first, Reed resisted. "I think that is rather a doubtful move," he told Bailey. "It serves to identify us at once with the Republican Party and it might weaken our protest as DEMOCRATS against a third term."[89] However, at the persistence of Meriwether and Bainbridge Colby, Reed consented because, as he saw it, "The concentration of power in our central government has, not gradually but rapidly, deprived the people of the states of their inherent rights."[90] Once again, a forced pragmatism characterized by cross-party cooperation among conservatives trumped four more years of Roosevelt.

Meriwether took the Jeffersonian platform to the GOP. To underscore ideological common ground, he highlighted a section of the 1924 Democratic plank that privileged states' rights over an enlarged federal government and bureaucratic expansion. Meriwether told the RNC, "We are confident" that individual Jeffersonian Democrats "will not support a party with Socialist, and even Communist, leanings, merely because it wears the label 'Democrat.'" Instead, he argued, "These Democrats will support the Republican nominees in the 1940 campaign, once they understand that . . . their major policies in 1940 are based on fundamental American principles." RNC chairman John Hamilton and the Resolutions Committee referred to the Jeffersonian overture as "fine"—not quite a ringing endorsement.[91] Meriwether privately complained that the stunt produced "little publicity," but the tryst hinted that collaborating with the GOP was fast becoming more amenable to disaffected Democrats.[92]

The Jeffersonians' move toward open collaboration with the Republican Party recalled the bolt to Landon in 1936 and illustrated the far-right movement's ideological complexity. Ultraconservatives remained ostracized within

Roosevelt's Democratic Party, which forced them into the political wilderness. The Jeffersonians had crossed partisan lines to support a Republican in 1936 with the sole objective of defeating Roosevelt. In 1940, the group was poised to repeat the effort. Early polls showed Willkie within striking distance of Roosevelt.[93] A few weeks after the Jeffersonian meeting Reed admitted, "I am very favorably impressed by Willkie," revealing an approval he never displayed toward Landon.[94] Indeed, many ultraconservatives viewed Willkie as a far superior candidate to Landon. Despite his penchant for internationalism, Willkie had a business background, raged against "Big Government," and, ultimately, stood a better chance of defeating Roosevelt. The partisan affiliation of the ultraconservative movement was shifting, and the trend line pointed toward the Republican Party, or at least away from the Democrats.

Indeed, the 1940 election was a prelude to the struggle over the contours and direction of the conservative movement. Far-right organizations such as the American Liberty League and Jeffersonian Democrats, because of their hard-line views and visibility in Landon's 1936 defeat, were seen as a threat to conservative hopes in 1940. At Smith's behest, Reed considered shutting down the Jeffersonian apparatus. Rather than staging a third-party insurrection or forging their own grassroots movement, the remaining Jeffersonians decided the group should take a back seat to disgruntled New Dealers such as Lewis Douglas, FDR's former budget director who resigned over concerns of deficit spending and now headed the Democrats for Willkie organization. The Texas Jeffersonians, one of the most active groups in 1936, officially terminated their operations; Bailey confided that some of the Texas Jeffersonians were "ready to turn Republican."[95] Reed, however, remained a defiant Democrat. "Mr. Roosevelt cannot make a Communist or a Socialist out of me by betraying the Democratic flag," Reed declared. "Neither can Mr. Roosevelt make a Republican out of me."[96] Reed never renounced his Democratic loyalties. Instead, by joining the Willkie crusade, Reed sought to redeem his party from Roosevelt's clutches.[97]

The far right used Willkie's status as a former Democrat to illustrate the party's misguided trajectory under Roosevelt and entice disaffected Democrats. Al Smith described Willkie as "a lifelong democrat," while Meriwether observed, "He did not leave the Democratic Party, it left him."[98] The idea that Willkie was the real Democrat, not Roosevelt, appealed to estranged conservatives and influenced the creation of the grassroots Democrats for Willkie organization. Even before the official demise of the Jeffersonian Democrats, Meriwether held a mass rally of 2,000 people under the Willkie Democratic

Club banner, but he and the other organizers found the $600 cost onerous, illustrating the Jeffersonians' weakened state in 1940. As the Jeffersonian apparatus decayed, other groups moved in to feast on the scraps, trying to gain access to the Jeffersonians' mailing lists. Edmunds sent a list of the most foundational Jeffersonians—750 people in thirty-seven states—to Alan Valentine, executive director of the National Committee of Democrats for Willkie. When Valentine's group approached the Jeffersonians about an official organizational merger, Reed saw the potential for a larger movement. Reed issued a statement that Roosevelt's administration had created "a crisis which lays upon all right-thinking persons regardless of party the duty to set aside minor differences and to unite in the protection of democratic and American principles." As a result, he noted, "We have therefore concluded to accept the invitation extended. I believe this will . . . result in the repudiation of the Roosevelt dictatorship and the triumphant election of Wendell Willkie."[99]

The merger marked the official dissolution of the National Jeffersonian Democrats, but multiple issues precipitated the Jeffersonians' decline. The threat of World War II prompted a surge of national security concerns and wartime patriotism, which weakened anti-administration views, boosted Roosevelt's political fortune, and forced a tactical shift from dissident Democrats. Many of the Jeffersonian leaders were elderly and lacked the constitution to continue the toil of grassroots organizing. It is also possible that the 1936 defeat diminished their faith in far-right ideals, but this seems unlikely given the group's ideological intensity. The Democrats for Willkie organization offered a salve to Reed and other conservative Democrats: they could plant far-right ideology within Willkie's campaign, thereby influencing the GOP without abandoning their own party. The new group urged Jeffersonians to "begin the organization of a Democrats for Willkie committee in your community," and Reed encouraged former Jeffersonians to "give their services freely in the furtherance of the state and local organizations of Democrats for Willkie clubs."[100]

As the Jeffersonians disbanded, the American Liberty League met a similar fate. After the disaster of 1936, funding for the organization dried up. Financial backers reneged on their promised donations, and by 1937 the du Ponts were the sole financial string holding the organization together. The Liberty League trimmed its organization down to the bone over the next few years. The League's Executive Committee went into hibernation, holding no meetings between late 1936 and 1940. In 1937, Jouett Shouse's annual salary was slashed from $54,000 to $12,500, and then he served as president without compensation for the next three years. The League's final act, after years of running on a skeleton crew, was to fire its statistician and close its National Press Club office in September 1940. Shouse retreated to his private law practice while the du Ponts, hoping to avoid entanglements with the second Hatch Act, which limited contributions to political campaigns, threw their financial heft behind Willkie. A Senate investigation into campaign finances credited the du Pont family with spending $121,225 on pro-Willkie groups, including Democrats for Willkie. Even though the American Liberty League and Jeffersonian Democrats dissolved during the election, the far right's financial and grassroots network survived and continued to boost conservative causes.[101]

Nevertheless, despite the grassroots outpouring, support from disillusioned Democrats and wealthy financiers, and a handsome, internationalist candidate, the Republicans lost to Franklin Roosevelt for the third election in a row. Willkie received more popular votes than the two previous GOP candidates, Hoover and Landon, but Roosevelt crushed him in the electoral college: 449 to 82. Despite losing a few seats in the Senate, the Democrats retained a stranglehold on both houses of Congress. Roosevelt's allegedly sagging coalition persevered. Conservatives, particularly far-right activists, once again felt the sting of failure. Reed blamed milquetoast conservatives for Willkie's defeat. In a letter to Al Smith, he wrote, "This campaign [for Willkie] began to develop into a real frontal attack. But, even up to the end there were too many mealy-mouthed protestants."[102] The far right's support of Willkie, like their support of Landon, indicated a pattern of forced pragmatism during the early years of the ultraconservative movement. The lack of a true right-wing candidate on a major ticket, combined with a disinterest in third-party activism, compelled ultraconservatives to back imperfect, impure candidates in an effort to defeat liberalism. However, despite the appearance of continued liberal dominance, the 1940 presidential election revealed cracks in the New Deal coalition.[103]

Internationalism won at the ballot box, but the argument over America's global role continued to rage after the election. The controversy intensified on March 11, 1941, when Congress passed Lend-Lease, which gave Roosevelt the power to provide military aid to nations whose defense he considered critical to American security, and extended the tours of duty for men drafted under the Selective Training and Service Act. To noninterventionists, Roosevelt's decision to give military assistance to Great Britain was the opening salvo for American entry into World War II. Hiram Johnson, a Republican senator from California, characterized Lend-Lease as "the wickedest piece of legislation that has ever been presented to the American Congress," while

Montana Democrat Burton Wheeler predicted that the bill would "plow under every fourth American boy."[104] Taft, clinging to the raft of old guard neutrality, lamented, "War is worse even than a German victory."[105] These senators voiced the concerns of many citizens and lent credibility to a surging movement against American involvement.[106]

The America First Committee emerged in the final months of 1940 as a critical node for noninterventionism and patriotic Americanism. A week after the signing of Lend-Lease, the organization rushed out a statement of principles: "Our first duty is to keep America out of foreign wars. Our entry would only destroy democracy, not save it."[107] General Robert E. Wood, chairman of the board for Chicago's Sears, Roebuck and Company, served as America First's national chairman. A man with ultraconservative leanings, Wood went so far as to say that U.S. entry would facilitate "the end of capitalism all over the world."[108] The organization as a whole was not a far-right group—its statement of principles bore no resemblance to the Jeffersonians' overheated ideological screed—but its membership overlapped substantially with the far right. The AFC represented a moment when some ultraconservative ideas, noninterventionist foreign policies in this case, aligned with the political mainstream. Roughly 800,000 people joined the AFC, forming a national network of hundreds of chapters concentrated in and around the Midwest. The organization held rallies, created a research bureau to disseminate policy studies, and engaged in mass-mailer campaigns to convince more Americans to reject the accelerating drift toward war.[109]

Despite promoting mainstream noninterventionist views, the America First Committee became a breeding ground for right-wing extremists. Domestic fascists infiltrated the committee, illustrating the porous borders separating the various shades of conservatism and making the organization an easy target for detractors. Roosevelt denounced committee spokesmen as "unwitting aids of the agents of Nazism" who "preached the gospel of fear."[110] The committee tried to fight this perception by spurning the support of high-profile extremists such as Father Coughlin and the Christian Front, but many Americans still considered Wood's group a front for Nazi Germany. Charles Lindbergh, the famed aviator and one of the committee's primary spokespeople, dealt the AFC an irreparable blow. Appearing before a Des Moines crowd, Lindbergh declared that "the British, the Jewish and the Roosevelt Administration" conspired to assure American entry.[111] Lindbergh's anti-Semitism was beyond the pale, and the outburst of anger toward him was swift and scathing. Willkie spoke for many Americans when he described Lindbergh's speech as "the most un-American talk made in my time by any person of national reputation." "If the American people permit race prejudice to arrive at this critical moment," Willkie averred, "they little deserve to preserve democracy."[112]

The repudiation of Lindbergh's bigotry, while setting an important moral compass for American foreign policy, implicitly provided cover for and revealed the self-perception of the far right. Despite holding white supremacist ideologies, ultraconservatives such as Reed and Haley viewed themselves not as racist bigots, but as defenders of Americanism. Yet, the ultraconservative definition of "Americanism" often excluded various racial categories, religious groups, and political ideologies in order to placate the far right's myopic national vision. This right-wing radicalism threatened to alienate voters, which is why Smith attempted to sideline the Jeffersonians during numerous elections. Regardless, Lindbergh's speech and the surrounding controversy tainted the noninterventionist cause with the stench of bigotry and prejudice. Making matters worse, rather than distancing themselves from Lindbergh's conspiratorial rhetoric, America First leaders signed off on his ideas, further discrediting their own cause.[113]

The linkage to anti-Semitism dealt America First a crippling blow, but the ideological quibbling over neutrality ended when war came to America on December 7, 1941. Japan's assault on Pearl Harbor and Hitler's subsequent declaration of war rendered all noninterventionist arguments irrelevant. One day after the "date which will live in infamy," the United States officially entered World War II. Roosevelt asserted that, in order to win the war, the United States needed to become the "arsenal of democracy," and he created multiple government agencies to facilitate the rise of the warfare state. The War Production Board coordinated the conversion from peacetime commerce to wartime industry. The sprawling Office of War Information produced propaganda by working with Hollywood studios, national and local radio networks, and various publication outlets. Citizens engaged with the warfare state by rationing goods, buying war bonds, supporting labor and consumer rights, and even by paying increased taxes. The transition to a warfare state forced an ideological and societal shift; instead of fretting about social and economic justice, the entire nation bent toward war production and national security concerns.[114]

Though the warfare state facilitated the construction of Roosevelt's "arsenal of democracy," the far right viewed it as proof that liberalism was indeed a red-tinged leviathan. The Great Sedition Trial of 1944, for example, pitted Roosevelt's administration against a coterie of extreme-right activists. The government charged radicals like Pelley and Dilling with conspiring to cause military insubordination. The far right, however, saw the trial as a prelude to political oppression. Perhaps more alarming to ultraconservatives was the government's unprecedented wartime economic interventionism. The government passed a bill allowing for the requisition of war material, created the National War Labor Board (NWLB) to manage labor-capital relations, and permitted Roosevelt to seize industrial plants involved in the war effort. The power to take over specific plants, part of the Smith-Connally Anti-Strike Act, was created to protect industries from labor unrest. There were hundreds of thousands of labor disputes throughout the war but only sixty-four plant seizures. However, Roosevelt's use of this power carried the explosive class antagonisms of the Great Depression and forced Americans to reflect upon the government's expansive economic management.[115]

Within this war-addled regulatory vortex, the Montgomery Ward labor crisis captured the nation's attention and breathed new life into the ultraconservative movement. The local union for Montgomery Ward's Chicago headquarters, the United Retail and Wholesale Employees of America (URWEA), had spent months negotiating against intractable management. An anti-union sentiment coursed throughout Montgomery Ward's leadership. Sewell Avery condemned unions as subversive conspiracies that stripped property owners of their constitutional rights. The situation came to a head when Avery refused to sign a new labor contract. In response, the URWEA local called for a strike on April 12, 1944. Worried about maintaining a well-oiled economy, and perhaps trying to earn labor votes in an election year, Roosevelt instructed Avery to comply with NWLB directives and ordered workers to return to their posts. The union called off its strike, but Avery still refused to negotiate. Instead, the chairman accused Roosevelt of trespassing into the realm of private enterprise and settled in for a prolonged labor dispute by hiring high school–aged scabs. Roosevelt responded by ordering the military to seize Montgomery Ward properties, which culminated in a defiant Avery being hauled out of his office by U.S. troops.[116]

The seizure monopolized newspaper headlines and inflamed conservative anger. "Troops Seize Montgomery Ward Plant," declared the front page of the *Washington Post*.[117] The picture of armed soldiers carting Avery out of Montgomery Ward was emblazoned across the front pages of newspapers across the country.[118] The next day Avery joked, "I've been fired before in my life, but this is the first time they carried me out feet first." Congressional conservatives, however, were not inclined toward humor. Charles S. Dewey, an Illinois

Republican and former banking executive, demanded an investigation and described the seizure as "un-American" and reminiscent of "Gestapo methods."[119] Conservatives of all stripes voiced outrage over Roosevelt's actions. If it could happen to Avery, they surmised, it could happen to anyone. Senator Byrd anointed the event as "an outrageous abuse of power," while General Wood warned, "If the wartime powers of a President can be invoked to virtually confiscate the property and business of Montgomery Ward, then the President can seize the business of any merchant or any other enterprise anywhere and anytime."[120] Avery wrapped himself in the cloak of victimization, proclaiming that "the kind of slavery that is being gradually put into effect now with government help is far worse than anything that ever happened before."[121] Overheated rhetoric, anti-labor conspiracies, and anti-statist rage framed the conservative mindset.[122]

One name was notably absent from the Montgomery Ward controversy: Martin Dies Jr. Considering his anti-labor bona fides, Dies should have been front and center. Yet, while Avery remained locked out of his Montgomery Ward office, Dies fretted about reelection. The patriotic nationalism of World War II dampened the American public's willingness to entertain Dies's conspiratorial investigations. Marquis Childs of the *Washington Post* chided, "Instead of working quietly and efficiently as does the FBI, the Dies Committee wrangles and rants and thereby, in my opinion, damages the lawmaking process."[123] After all, Missouri Democrat John J. Cochran pointed out, "Congress was not intended to be a Muckraking body."[124] Dies claimed that a throat ailment prevented him from running for reelection and threw in the towel. However, columnist Drew Pearson pointed out that Dies faced a tough primary opponent, judge J. M. Combs, and faced damaging allegations of nepotism. A grassroots movement to boost voter rolls in his district further endangered Dies's reelection bid. His decision to step away sealed the fate of the Dies Committee.[125]

Dies's retreat back to private life did not steal attention away from the Montgomery Ward saga, which lingered through 1944 and into 1945. The government returned control of Montgomery Ward to Avery before he signed the union's contract, leading to another Avery holdout and prompting another URWEA strike in December. This time Roosevelt ordered the seizure of the main Chicago plant plus six other Ward locations across the nation, once again forcing Avery from office. The traditional drama of labor versus capital evolved into a referendum on presidential powers during wartime. However, conservatives ignored incidents where Roosevelt used state power against labor—such as the 1944 takeover of the Philadelphia Transportation Company during a racially charged union strike—in favor of portraying the president as an anti-capitalist tyrant. After the second Montgomery Ward seizure, Avery released a statement condemning Roosevelt's action as "a violation of the Constitution." The government did not return control of the Chicago Montgomery Ward to private ownership until after World War II. For workers, Roosevelt's actions throughout the Montgomery Ward crisis indicated a respect for labor rights. However, the seizure fed a growing negative perception of liberal economic regulation and boosted the nascent free-market movement.[126]

The Montgomery Ward saga galvanized an alliance between right-wing businessmen and far-right activists, many of whom viewed the government's actions as tantamount to communist tyranny. Arthur Sears Henning of the *Chicago Daily Tribune* captured this conspiratorial zeitgeist: "The incident has served to focus the spreading feeling in congress and the country at large that President Roosevelt is steadily building a totalitarian dictatorship partaking of a combination of fascism and communism that, if he is successful in his undertaking, will doom democracy in this nation."[127] Avery received over 3,000 letters, many from fellow executives and pro-business organizations, supporting his fight against Roosevelt. Only 172 citizens wrote in to laud Roosevelt's actions.[128] Former Jeffersonian Democrats supported Avery's position, too. Lee Meriwether pondered, "It is possible the Montgomery-Ward affair will awaken people to what's going on in Washington; all with whom I have discussed the matter think the reaction will deal the 'New' Deal a deadly blow."[129] James Reed took a harsher tone. He compared the plant seizure to the upheaval of the Civil War era and evoked the anger of southern whites toward Reconstruction era martial law: "It appears that the rule of law is to be abolished and bayonet rule substituted."[130] For the far right, the Montgomery Ward controversy became a synecdoche explaining communist infiltration, diminishing property rights, and the loss of economic freedom.

Roosevelt's use of executive power catalyzed new activists to join the far-right crusade. Willis E. Stone, a California-based engineer and businessman, viewed Avery as a libertarian martyr, and the Montgomery Ward seizure intensified Stone's conviction that modern liberalism was simply jackbooted communism in disguise. Incensed by wartime economic mandates, Stone drafted a constitutional amendment to limit federal economic incursions. His one-line amendment, published in the pages of the *Sherman Oaks Citizen-Tribune*, read, "The government of the United States of America shall not engage in any business, commercial, or industrial enterprise in competition with its citizens."[131] Stone modified his proposition over time, with the final version aiming to retrench all government economic activity and repeal the Sixteenth Amendment. The proposal was a panacea that would, according to Stone, halt the "growth of this cancer" and "retrieve the ground lost to socialism."[132] His anti-statism aligned with the business-minded conservatism of men such as Avery, Shouse, and Frank Chodorov, a libertarian thinker who contributed to the periodical *Freeman*. Stone's activism continued after World War II; he funded and led multiple organizations to spread his radical libertarianism and his amendment, which he branded the "Proposed 23rd Amendment." The economic interventionism of Roosevelt's warfare state set the foundation for future ultraconservative activism, which would flourish with the beginning of the Cold War.[133]

The presidential election of 1944 occurred amid the battle over Montgomery Ward, providing one final crescendo of far-right action during the Roosevelt era. With the United States embroiled in a two-front war, Roosevelt ran for an unprecedented fourth presidential term. Traditionalists balked at the decision. Many right-wingers, especially in Texas, still resented Roosevelt's replacement of John Nance Garner with labor ally Henry A. Wallace on the 1940 Democratic ticket. The final straw came when Republicans chose a moderate candidate, Thomas E. Dewey, who described himself as a "New Deal Republican." Conservatives had been shut out for the third election in a row. In response, a group of far-right Texas Democrats, who came to be known as the Texas Regulars, separated from the national Democratic Party and formed a third-party outfit. With wealthy Texas businessmen, especially oil tycoons, bankrolling the movement, the revolt resembled a Lone Star version of the American Liberty League. Democratic Senator W. Lee "Pappy" O'Daniel, a folksy ultraconservative who relied on race baiting and conspiratorial anti-communism to drum up white votes, emerged as the movement's leader. The Regulars created a platform that, when examined holistically, called for the redemption of the southern Democratic Party. The platform demanded the "return of states rights" and the "restoration of the supremacy of the white race," both of which the Regulars argued had been "destroyed by the Communist-controlled New Deal."[134] The Regulars created an avenue for aggrieved white conservatives who were still smarting after the *Smith v. Allwright* decision abolished the white primary. Built upon a foundation of libertarianism, conspiratorial anti-communism, and white supremacy, the Texas Regulars' third-party crusade sought to oust Roosevelt and restore the Democratic Party to its Dixieland traditions.[135]

The campaign only materialized in the final months of the election season, so the Regulars and their political allies, such as the Committee for Constitutional Government, hustled to get their message out to voters. Radio stations carried the Texas Regulars' broadcasts during the final two weeks of the campaign, and crowds in the hundreds attended rallies featuring prominent far-right Texans. At the Texas Regulars' first statewide rally, Dies took the stump, deriding liberals as communist dupes and the New Deal as "antidemocratic and un-American." "It is a form of Fascism disguised as a liberal movement to deceive gullible and unthinking people," Dies told the crowd.[136] O'Daniel caterwauled about "smear brigades" and "parasitic government snoopers" and called wartime rationing a "Communistic, totalitarian measure" intended to create "an autocratic, bureaucratic dictatorship."[137] The Regulars followed in the footsteps of the American Liberty League and the Jeffersonian Democrats, raking in donations from wealthy industrialists and portraying the election as an existential, communism-versus-Americanism struggle.

However, the Texas Regulars declined to follow the Jeffersonians down one critical trail: they would not support the Republican Party. The Regulars won over far-right Democrats, but their refusal to cross the partisan divide limited their appeal. Even Dewey's nomination of Ohio governor John W. Bricker, a hard-line conservative who complained that the New Deal was "in the hands of the radicals and communists," for vice president was not enough to sway the Texas Regulars.[138] Furthermore, not all ultraconservatives agreed with the Regulars' third-party strategy. Haley wrote off the Regulars *and* the national Democratic Party, choosing instead to support Dewey by donating to the local Republican apparatus. In a moment of pragmatism, Haley's rancor toward Roosevelt's corruption of the old Democratic Party outweighed Dewey's New Deal leanings. The Regulars captured the Texas Democratic convention and put forth their own slate of electors, but no candidates, which made it all the more difficult for voters to identify with their movement. Their inability to collaborate with the Republican Party and failure to form a broad far-right coalition further narrowed the Regulars' already limited base.[139]

The mutiny of the Texas Regulars failed to temper Roosevelt's popularity. On Election Day, only 135,000 Texans voted for the Texas Regulars' ticket, a smidge under 9 percent of the total vote in Texas. Despite the humbling numbers, the Texas Regulars constituted an important moment for the far right. Not only did the Regulars serve as a predecessor for the 1948 Dixiecrat Revolt, but the debate over third-party organizing versus reforming a mainstream party became an object of ultraconservative obsession in the coming decades.

The GOP experienced similar struggles in shifting voters away from Roosevelt. Dewey got closer to defeating Roosevelt than any other Republican—he lost the popular vote by only 3.5 million votes—but Roosevelt cruised to another landslide electoral victory: 432 to 99. However, less than three months into his fourth term, Roosevelt passed away after years of health problems. It was up to his brand-new vice president, former Kansas senator Harry S. Truman, to bring the war to a close. For Americans, World War II ended twice. The European Theater concluded with the fall of Nazi Germany on May 8, 1945, and the atomic bombing of Japan terminated the Pacific Theater in early August. Six long years of fighting (four for the Americans) left global leaders picking up the pieces of a shattered international order.[140]

*   *   *

The World War II era marked an epochal turning point for American society. Roosevelt continued to dominate national politics, but fissures appeared within the New Deal coalition. During the war, the welfare-state liberalism that marked the Great Depression morphed into an expansive warfare state. This new brand of liberalism protected the existing welfare state—permanent fixtures included Social Security, the Wagner Act, and a vast array of public works projects and regulatory systems—but privileged winning the war above all else. Roosevelt expanded federal power to unforeseen levels, providing far-right activists with more ammunition and new avenues to contest modern liberalism. Ultraconservatives derided Roosevelt's support of labor unions, attacked liberals' perceived hostility toward business, and proffered conspiracy theories that communist cabals propelled federal empowerment. Labor strife and industrial seizures, rather than being viewed as a consequence of the wartime economy, became a referendum on communist subversion and the dangers of state authority. To ultraconservatives, liberalism remained a tyrannical leviathan.[141]

After almost a decade of trying to convince voters of Roosevelt's socialist leanings, the Jeffersonian Democrats met an interminable foe: Father Time. Much of the Jeffersonian leadership was quite old; Reed, Edmunds, and Meriwether were septuagenarians and octogenarians. Sterling E. Edmunds died in the summer of 1944. "He was as sterling as his name," a grieving Meriwether wrote to Reed.[142] A few months later, just weeks before Roosevelt won a fourth term, Reed passed away at the age of eighty-two. Nevertheless, the Jeffersonian Democrats left important legacies for future ultraconservatives.

Cold War far-right groups reflected the Jeffersonian organizational structure, with a national headquarters serving as the tip of the spear while state chapters gathered followers and tailored their messaging for local audiences. They also demonstrated how grassroots activists could collaborate with extra-party organizations, right-wing businessmen, and official party organs. Most important, the Jeffersonians created an avenue for disaffected southern and midwestern Democrats to redeem the party, even if it meant supporting the party of Lincoln. Indeed, the Jeffersonian coalition blurred party lines, foreshadowing the protracted political reorganization of the twentieth century. Haley, a relatively young forty-four years old at the dawn of 1945, would live to see this reorientation come to fruition. The Jeffersonians did not effect an electoral shift and many members died before the Republican Party became synonymous with conservatism, but the organization brought together wealthy businessmen, right-wing politicians, and local radicals, an admixture that fueled the ultraconservative movement and pushed far-right ideas into the political mainstream.

Martin Dies Jr. also straddled the porous separation between mainstream conservatives and the radical right. His anti-labor, anti-subversive investigations left a different, but no less critical, legacy for Cold War ultraconservatives. Dies was an effective right-wing translator—he took the far right's anti-statist, conspiratorial mindset and channeled it into state-sanctioned investigative action against the state itself. He accused liberals of abusing state power while wielding state power against liberal or, as he saw them, communist enemies. Because Dies's investigations also revealed a number of actual domestic communists, he legitimized far-right paranoia and convinced conservatives that New Deal liberalism was in fact a gateway for un-American subversion. Through his committee, Dies bequeathed a strategy for attacking liberalism through a fusion of federal power and conspiratorial accusations. Cold War conservatives inherited Dies's anti-statist blueprint. When anti-communist hysteria gripped America during the early Cold War, HUAC reemerged as a weapon for attacking postwar liberalism and a critical hub for ultraconservative activism.[143]

Ultimately, the World War II era reconfigured the foundations of ultraconservatism. The growing warfare state aggravated far-right anxieties and became the rationale for investigating left-wing subversion, but divergent electoral strategies, especially whether or not to form a third party, would continue to puzzle the ultraconservative movement. World War II restricted the success of some far-right activism—ultraconservatives had been kept at

arm's length during elections, and noninterventionism crumbled amid accusations of bigotry—but it laid the groundwork for Cold War conservatism.
After World War II, the warfare state prioritized the growing rift between
the United States and the Soviet Union rather than returning to welfare-state
liberalism, helping shift the American polity rightward. The ensuing Cold
War provided the perfect environment for ultraconservatism. Though noninterventionists had failed to prevent American entry into World War II,
activists such as Robert McCormick and General Wood carried nativist anti-
internationalism into the Cold War. Republican Senator Joseph McCarthy
inherited the investigatory mantle from Dies and continued stoking anti-
communist hysteria through the mirage of internal subversion. Businessmen
such as Avery and Stone demonized state economic intervention and generated publicity for the blossoming free-market libertarian movement. It would
be up to this new ultraconservative vanguard—one hardened by political
defeat, the Great Depression, and World War II—to bear the far-right banner
forward into the Cold War.

CHAPTER 3

The Cauldron

By July 1952, the Cold War was already in full bloom. The arms race between the Soviet Union and the United States could be measured by hydrogen atoms, nuclear tests, and missile research. Under this atomic cloud, a group of fundamentalist ministers gathered to map out a plan to confront international communism. Instead of relying on the U.S. government's stockpile of nuclear bombs, the ministers believed the best way to fight the communists was to launch the word of God over the Iron Curtain. They crafted a plan to shoot Bibles into Soviet-dominated eastern Europe via long-range balloons, and the International Council of Christian Churches (ICCC), founded by far-right minister and radio host Carl McIntire, agreed to sponsor the effort. McIntire appointed Billy James Hargis, the fiery Oklahoma preacher and leader of the ultraconservative Christian Crusade ministry, as the international chairman of the Bibles by Balloons project. Hargis had already gained a modicum of notoriety within right-wing Christian circles through his traveling revivals and hellfire sermons, which featured provocative titles such as "Communism in America Exposed." With a bellowing voice and a finger jabbing the sky, Hargis levied conspiratorial warnings about "how communism works in [American] government, schools, and churches."[1] Now, by sending Bibles into "Red Russia," he intended to attack communism at the source.[2]

The plan constructed by Hargis and his fellow ultraconservatives built upon previous anti-communist propaganda strategies. Two years earlier, the Crusade for Freedom, a mainstream anti-communist organization, had launched thousands of balloons into the Soviet sphere, each bearing leaflets "carrying the political message of the Western democracies."[3] Hargis's group envisioned an even greater triumph, one that promised to fuse the anti-communist mission of God and country. After all, as Hargis declared, "There is no weapon against communism as powerful as the word of God."[4] West German manufacturers produced thousands of hydrogen-filled, long-distance balloons, each dangling a pocket-sized Bible enclosed in a water-proof envelope. Donations in support of Bibles by Balloons poured in from churches around the world, particularly those in the United States. Hargis urged his followers to donate $2.00 per balloon to jump-start the program, and he then traveled to West Germany to help launch the balloons personally.[5]

However, a political snafu threatened to delay the project. McIntire claimed that the U.S. State Department intervened to prevent the Bibles from being launched, and he wired a telegram to President Eisenhower requesting his "immediate assistance." The State Department denied any obstruction, announcing that it encouraged the sending of "spiritual aid" to "areas deprived of religious freedom."[6] Whether or not the political dustup was manufactured by the ICCC or simply the result of complex international relations, the controversy generated substantial publicity for the project. It also allowed Hargis to vilify a well-worn conservative bogeyman: big government. Hargis later claimed that overzealous liberal bureaucrats had tried to stymie the efforts of anti-communist conservatives: "The State Department had said 'no,' BUT GOD said 'yes.'"[7] After receiving the go-ahead from West German authorities, Hargis unleashed the first salvo from Nuremberg—5,000 Bibles, all printed in Russian. Those few thousand were soon followed by roughly 50,000 Bibles in the fall of 1953. The Christian Crusade published booklets sensationalizing the project, and Hargis rejoiced that the balloons were shaking the communists from their atheistic slumber: "Reports from refugees slipping into West Germany say a wave of religious feeling is now sweeping Poland, Czechoslovakia and the western fringes of Russia itself!"[8]

The project continued for another three years, and the number of balloons launched increased each year. Over 100,000 passed over the Iron Curtain in 1954. In 1955, the total swelled to 250,000. The Bibles floating into Soviet territory were printed in Czech, Slovak, Polish, Russian, and German to ensure that the recipients could read God's good word. While it is difficult to ascertain the spiritual effectiveness of the Bibles by Balloons campaign, it was undoubtedly the event that brought Hargis and the Christian Crusade into American homes. Most major dailies, including the *New York Times* and *Washington Post*, devoted numerous column inches to the balloon project. Not only did Bibles by Balloons increase the national presence of Hargis's Crusade, the project highlighted how the Cold War altered the far right's foreign policy outlook.

Ultraconservative tradition mandated a noninterventionist foreign policy, but some far-right leaders, including Hargis, started promoting interventionism as a mechanism to contain real communist aggression abroad and perceived communist subversion at home. Hargis embodied the intersection of fundamentalist evangelicalism and Cold War interventionism. Ministerial watchmen, according to Hargis, were both the guardians of America's walls and the crusaders peeling back the communist advance.[9]

The cauldron of Cold War politics became a critical inflection point for the midcentury ultraconservative movement. During the early Cold War, far-right leaders laid the foundation for a national activist network and crystallized ultraconservatism into a coherent, if at times paradoxical, ideology. A strong undercurrent of noninterventionism remained—as evidenced by Senator John W. Bricker's proposed constitutional amendment to limit the federal government's treaty powers—but numerous far-right leaders thought the threat of communism demanded a more aggressive foreign policy posture. The Cold War also nurtured ultraconservatives' complicated and inconsistent relationship with state authority. Despite a professed adherence to anti-statist ideas, the far right endorsed the use of government power to retrench liberal gains. Ultraconservatives applauded congressional investigations into communist subversion and roared that federal employees should be forced to sign loyalty oaths, actions which imposed right-wing ideological strictures by flexing state muscles. Liberals, squeezed by Cold War pressures, joined conservatives in a fight against external and internal communism, though right-wingers often failed to differentiate between communist sabotage and honest left-wing dissent. The House Un-American Activities Committee continued hunting for subversives, often catching New Dealers and labor unionists in their crosshairs, while Joseph McCarthy, the Republican senator from Wisconsin, took conspiracy theorizing to new heights, alleging that the taint of communism went deeper than anyone realized. McCarthy's investigations, enabled by a Republican Party yearning for power after years in the political wilderness, helped fuel the Second Red Scare, convincing many Americans that domestic communism represented a clear and present danger.[10]

Though anxiety about communist infiltration existed in previous decades, during the Cold War anti-communism metastasized into a political and cultural imperative, empowering the ultraconservative movement and reflecting its conspiratorial sensibilities. Southern right-wingers rushed to defend white supremacist traditions against the postwar civil rights movement, which they believed evinced red-tinged social upheaval. When the national Democratic Party moved toward supporting civil rights in 1948, southern Democrats launched a third-party revolt rather than supporting the Republicans, illustrating an emphasis on ideological purity and a narrowing fluid ity across party lines. Anti-communism also penetrated the spiritual realm. Right-wing ministers, ranging from fundamentalist hard-liners like Hargis to more moderate preachers like Billy Graham, fused political anti-communism to Protestant evangelism in an effort to save Christian America. The defeat of Ohio senator Robert A. Taft, an old guard Republican and vehement anti-communist, in the 1952 presidential primary was the final straw for many ultraconservatives. America's soul, they argued, needed saving.[11]

New far-right organizations emerged to fight for America's salvation, each building upon the foundation laid by ultraconservative predecessors. Hargis's Christian Crusade stood for Christian nationalism and strict social traditionalism while avoiding overt political organizing. The American Progress Foundation, founded by engineer and businessman Willis Stone, agitated for libertarian solutions to federal economic intervention and the perceived communist influence in government. A coterie of right-wing media activists and businessmen established For America, a descendant of the America First Committee that offered an updated version of anti-internationalism and states' rights ideas. These organizations represented major strands of ultraconservative philosophies, but they did not always mirror each other's goals or strategies. Some organizations were more policy-oriented and less centralized while others coalesced around a cult of personality; however, every group held a binary view of American politics wherein liberalism was a liminal stage (or a clandestine form) of communism, and each group became a critical node within an interconnected far-right network. Ultimately, the cauldron of Cold War politics supercharged the far right's ideological taxonomy and set the foundation for an incipient postwar movement.

*   *   *

While the United States emerged from World War II relatively unscathed, the European belligerents lost millions of lives and experienced unprecedented devastation, leaving the Allied countries to rebuild and tend to a world order that had failed twice in the last thirty years. A tectonic realignment loomed on the horizon. The global Cold War resulted from divergent visions for the world: Soviet premier Joseph Stalin harbored imperialistic ambitions and fostered revolutionary movements in Eastern Europe, while Truman sought to stabilize Western Europe and extend America's global reach. With communism on the rise throughout Europe, Truman fretted about Stalin's totalitarian regime and expansionist goals. The American government created a policy triumvirate—headlined by the Truman Doctrine, Marshall Plan, and an alliance with West Germany—to solidify American influence in Western Europe and stymie Soviet initiatives. Stalin viewed this as an effort to create a western alliance against Soviet interests, and the mutual distrust split Europe into competing blocs. As the Cold War divide calcified, former British prime minister Winston Churchill remarked, "An iron curtain has descended across Europe." Ensuing events such as the Berlin Blockade, the Soviet Union's first nuclear test, China's Maoist revolution, and North Korea's invasion of South Korea fed anxieties about international communism on the march. Ultraconservatives viewed global tensions through an apocalyptic lens. "The Cold War in which we are engaged is certainly no game," John Birch Society founder Robert Welch later wrote. "It is a fatal struggle for freedom against slavery, for existence against destruction."[12]

The conspiratorial dialect particular to the far right permeated the Cold War landscape, lending legitimacy to and fueling the growth of the ultraconservative movement. For the American government, the Cold War became an ideological crusade, one driven by a sense of righteous morality bent on containing communism around the globe. Halting the spread of communism, which was portrayed as the antithesis of western ideals and American capitalism, became the nation's central obsession. The prism of Cold War politics refracted anti-communism onto the entire political spectrum, tainting left-wing politics with a reddish hue, narrowing the acceptable range of left-wing ideas, and forming a petri dish for far-right activism. Prewar strains of noninterventionism remained ensconced within the ultraconservative tradition, but the widespread belief that communist infiltration represented an existential, civilizational struggle sharpened far-right rhetoric and strategies. Through the far right's conspiratorial lens, liberals mutated into outright communists or red-tainted sympathizers. "Our real danger does not come from threats of foreign invasion," warned anti-tax proponent Willis Stone, "it comes from the communistic practices carried on by the bureaucratic empires that have been developed here at home."[13] Cold War anti-communism blended with and amplified preexisting forms of white supremacy, social traditionalism, and radical libertarianism to form the building blocks of the postwar ultraconservative movement.[14]

The hardening of the Cold War reinforced anti-communism as a potent political cudgel, one used by both parties, which helped funnel ultraconservative ideas into the mainstream. In early 1945, John E. Rankin—a Democratic senator from Mississippi and noted racist, anti-Semite, and conspiracy theorist—spearheaded a successful effort to create a standing House Un-American Activities Committee. The now-permanent HUAC continued down the path of its forebear, the Dies Committee, investigating liberal programs and cultural institutions for traces of communism. HUAC plumbed Hollywood for communists, resulting in the infamous Hollywood blacklist and minting the anti-communist credentials of conservative scion, and future president, Ronald Reagan. Conservatives quickly harnessed the power of anti-communism for political gain. Tennessee congressman and RNC chairman B. Carroll Reece reframed the 1946 midterm election into a contest of "Communism vs. Americanism," an ideological binary ripped straight from the ultraconservative playbook. Reece's "Democrats-as-Communists" strategy produced a GOP wave: Republicans gained twelve Senate seats and claimed 55 more in the House, which effectively put Truman's liberal program in a stranglehold. In response to criticisms that the Democratic Party was soft on communism, President Truman initiated a federal employee loyalty program in 1947 which screened over five million men and women, the vast majority of whom were not dangerous subversives. Nevertheless, HUAC's investigations and the GOP's red-baiting strategy, not to mention the explosive spying allegations against State Department employee Alger Hiss, seemed to legitimize far-right assertions that the red wolf had already breached the door.[15]

Indeed, the Cold War created a fearful atmosphere that fueled specious conspiracies, and the fact that prices skyrocketed and labor turmoil churned during war demobilization stirred this paranoid climate. Millions of workers went on strike in 1946, hoping wage increases would cushion postwar inflation. More radical unionists, such as the UAW's Walter Reuther, saw the unrest as an opportunity for economic redistribution. The UAW held a 113-day strike at General Motors to raise pay and improve working-class living standards. In the South, the CIO implemented Operation Dixie, which sought to unionize southern textile workers, many of whom were African American, and break the existing economic oligarchy that profited off of segregation and class-based oppression. The wave of strikes (over 5,000), economic instability, and perceived threats to the traditional racial and social order alarmed conservative businessmen and politicians. Reuther was deemed a "socialist" by GM management and a "violent Red" by Congressman Edward Eugene Cox, a segregationist

Georgia Democrat.[16] Anti-communism squeezed the labor movement. The CIO expelled communists from its membership in the late 1940s, but the stigma of subversive radicalism, particularly the accusations against Reuther, haunted the labor movement well into the Cold War. Hargis's Christian Crusade published a booklet describing Reuther as a "cunning conspirator," "evil genius," and a "Marxist who has been both a Socialist and a pro-Communist."[17] Though the postwar economy paved the way for unprecedented prosperity during the 1950s, conservatives, particularly the far right, continued to view labor unrest through a conspiratorial, anti-communist lens.[18]

Anti-communism became a common motif for right-wingers across the nation, but in the South the burgeoning push for racial equality further inflamed the region's ultraconservative sensibilities. Postwar events highlighting racial inequality and discrimination, such as the maiming of black veteran Isaac Woodard and the Double V campaign, thrust civil rights into the political mainstream. The Cold War heightened the stakes as increased global scrutiny focused on the plight of African Americans. The United States presented itself as the global defender of freedom and democracy, but the Soviet Union pointed to racial segregation and white supremacist violence as evidence of American hypocrisy. Congress wrangled over legislation that would curb lynching and poll taxes, not to mention the legal debate over public school segregation, all of which heaped pressure on southern society to accept, or at least tolerate, racial equality. However, southern Democrats sprinted in the opposite direction. Southern states, by no means homogenous, were prepared to wage war to maintain white supremacy.[19]

When the Democratic Party adopted a robust civil rights platform at its 1948 national convention, far-right southern Democrats (Dixiecrats) rebelled. Every southern delegate voted against the platform. They had no interest in taking Minneapolis mayor Hubert Humphrey's advice "to get out of the shadow of states' rights and walk forthrightly into the bright sunshine of human rights."[20] Instead, Mississippi and Alabama delegates stormed out of the convention in disgust. Two weeks later, white southerners believed President Truman thumbed his nose at them by desegregating the armed forces through executive order. Far-right southerners felt they had no choice but to break away from the Democratic Party in order to defend states' rights and white supremacy.[21]

Five thousand disgruntled Democrats flocked to Birmingham, Alabama, for the Dixiecrat convention. Governor Frank M. Dixon articulated a conservative worldview in stark contrast to Humphrey's progressivism. "This vicious [civil rights] program . . . means to create a melting pot in the South, with whites and Negroes intermingling socially, politically, economically," Dixon raged. "It means to reduce us to the status of a mongrel, inferior race, mixed in blood, our Anglo-Saxon heritage a mockery; to crush with imprisonment our leadership and thereby kill our hopes, our aspirations, our future and the future of our children."[22] South Carolina governor Strom Thurmond echoed Dixon's defense of racial segregation: "We believe that there are not enough troops in the Army to force the southern people to admit the Negroes into our theaters, swimming pools and homes."[23] "If the South should vote for Truman this year," Thurmond continued, "we might as well petition the Government for colonial status." The delegates whooped and hollered for state sovereignty and formed the States' Rights Democratic Party, a third-party vehicle for opposing Truman and modern liberalism in the South. The Dixiecrats nominated Thurmond, and the party's ticket supplanted Truman's national ticket in four Deep South states. The party hoped to cause electoral chaos by pilfering enough southern votes to throw the election to the House of Representatives, a strategy replicated by future far-right campaigns.[24]

The Dixiecrat Revolt illuminated the ideological and regional civil wars roiling the Democratic Party. Propelled by white supremacy and states' rights traditions, southern Democrats pulled away as liberals captured more of the national party machinery. The insurrection also recalled the bolt of the Texas Regulars in 1944. Many southerners still felt a certain loyalty to the Democratic Party, which often rendered working with the Republicans a nonstarter. After all, the South traced its political lineage through southern Democrats such as Andrew Jackson and John C. Calhoun, both racist slaveowners. Conversely, the Republicans were the party of Lincoln, the party of "bayonet rule" and federal "tyranny" during Reconstruction. Between Reconstruction and World War II, the GOP was often synonymous with the northeastern socioeconomic elite and, perhaps most damaging in the South, African American voters. As a result, Republican organizations in Dixieland often resembled desiccated husks, bereft of political potency and largely useless to disaffected Democrats, a lesson the Jeffersonian Democrats learned the hard way. Furthermore, switching parties carried political consequences such as a loss of congressional seniority, which was important for retaining powerful committee positions, so many southern Democrats had stayed despite the shifting character of their party. But the Dixiecrat rebellion drove a wedge into the New Deal coalition, illustrating the growing ultraconservative insurgency within party politics.[25]

The Republicans had their own power struggle occurring behind the scenes. A conflict between liberal and conservative Republicans had divided the party into competing factions. The liberal wing, led by New York governor Thomas Dewey, believed voters would reject a conservative plank. He championed an inclusive platform that would appeal to moderate New Dealers and African Americans while avoiding the anti–New Deal obstinacy of the GOP's old guard. On the other hand, conservatives such as Ohio senator (and far-right favorite) Robert A. Taft argued that Republicans should provide a clear alternative to New Deal liberalism through *laissez-faire* capitalism and limited government. Taft and Dewey tussled for the 1948 Republican nomination, each representing a different vision for the GOP and the country. Dewey outmaneuvered Taft during the primaries, and, instead of choosing a conservative running mate to create a compromise ticket, Dewey alienated the old guard by selecting California governor Earl Warren, a noted Republican liberal. Hoping to take advantage of Truman's unpopularity and siphon away Democratic voters, Dewey crafted a moderate platform that included civil rights provisions, pro-labor policies, and even an equal rights amendment to equalize pay between men and women. Polls suggested a slump in enthusiasm for Truman, who seemed hemmed in by his own ineffectiveness and the Democrats' internal divisions, signaling the potential erosion of the New Deal coalition.[26]

The 1948 presidential race, the first conducted under the Cold War's atomic cloud, not only exemplified how anti-communism dominated American political discourse, but also demonstrated the far right's creeping influence within party politics. Truman's most visceral adversary, the far-right Dixiecrats, purported that a vast communist conspiracy infected his administration. "President Truman and other government officials," Thurmond alleged, "are making a desperate effort to hide the extent to which Communists and Communist sympathizers have honeycombed the Administration and dictated its policies."[27] In fact, ultraconservatives argued that very little separated the two major parties. During a Houston campaign stop, Thurmond declared that communists had infiltrated both parties and threatened to crash America into the "rocks of totalitarianism," giving voice to the both-sides-as-communists notion that became a calling card of future far-right campaigns.[28] The Republican apparatus, particularly the conservative wing, followed Reece's far-right strategy by portraying the election as a fight between "liberty or socialism." At the opening of the 1948 Republican National Convention, Reece proclaimed that the country was divided between two political forces, the Republican

Party and the "Communist Party." Reece told the delegates that the Democratic Party had been tainted by the "Typhoid Marys of communism," otherwise known as New Deal liberals.[29] Dewey did not make anti-communism
a mainstay of his campaign, but he occasionally engaged in a bit of Reece-
esque red-baiting, cautioning Americans that a vote for Truman might aid the
"dead hand of socialism" or the "barbaric hand of communism."[30] All of these
salacious allegations appeared in mainstream newspapers, lending legitimacy
to far-right conspiracies and pressuring Truman to react. Truman reversed
the allegations, arguing that it was actually Republican miscreants who were
inviting communism into America. At a campaign stop in Boston, Truman
declared, "The real threat of communism in this country grows out of the
Republican policies . . . [and] the submission of the Republican party to the
dictates of big business."[31] Regardless of party, the language of conspiratorial
anti-communism framed political debates, which elevated conservatives who
were eager to wield Cold War anxieties as a philosophical truncheon.

Despite Truman's attempt to flip the script, anti-communist conspiracies
levied against his administration landed more often and harder. Polls taken
days before the election showed Dewey leading Truman by five points. To
make matters worse, former vice president Henry A. Wallace, running under
the Progressive Party banner, occupied Truman's left flank. It seemed like
time had run out on the New Deal coalition. Yet, on Election Day, Truman
outperformed the polling to produce a shocking result. The incumbent president bested Dewey by roughly four percentage points in the popular vote
and cruised to victory in the electoral college: 303 to 189. Thurmond carried
the four states where the Dixiecrats had supplanted the national Democratic
ticket (South Carolina, Mississippi, Alabama, and Louisiana), but, mirroring
the failure of the Texas Regulars, southern ultraconservatism failed to percolate beyond the Deep South. The Dixiecrats received roughly the same paltry
total as Henry Wallace and the Progressive Party: just over one million votes.[32]

The Democratic Party maintained its presidential dynasty, but the 1948
election portended numerous changes within American politics. The Dixiecrat mutiny illustrated deep, and ultimately terminal, divisions within the
New Deal coalition. The third-party campaign catapulted Thurmond into the
national spotlight as a segregationist firebrand and harbingered the South's
political realignment. More broadly, the election denoted how ultraconservative philosophies influenced political discourse. Both parties were riven
with internecine conflict between liberal and conservative factions, which
created avenues for far-right activists to infiltrate mainstream politics. The

liberal tilt of the national Democratic Party relegated hard-line conservatives to the party's fringe, but southern conservatives still held immense institutional power. On the other side of the political aisle, the Republican Party's fledgling conservative coalition tilled fertile soil for far-right action, despite Dewey's nomination. Furthermore, the far right's feverish anti-communism found widespread purchase in 1948. Conservatives, ranging from Dixiecrats to old guard Republicans, engaged in red-baiting attacks against liberals within both parties. Even Truman, a liberal himself, dabbled in conspiratorial rhetoric, illustrating that anti-communism had become the political currency of the Cold War. Ultimately, the mainstreaming of conspiratorial anti-communism legitimized and fueled an ultraconservative surge within midcentury American politics.[33]

No politician exploited the fear of communism and the permeation of far-right conspiracies more effectively than Senator Joseph McCarthy. He won a senate seat in 1946 by embellishing his military record—McCarthy called himself "Tail-Gunner Joe" and exaggerated his mission count—and by lobbing anti-communist grenades at his political opponents. In early 1950, with reelection looming in two years, the junior senator from Wisconsin went on a speaking tour to raise his public profile. His incendiary speeches fixated on one issue: the Red Menace. Not only was communism on the march around the world, McCarthy warned, but *agents provocateurs* within America were already poisoning the well of democracy. As part of the Republican Party's Lincoln Day celebrations, McCarthy scheduled a stop in Wheeling, West Virginia. Poised before the Ohio County Republican Women's Club, McCarthy brandished a piece of paper and proclaimed, "I have in my hand 205 cases of individuals who would appear to be either card-carrying members or certainly loyal to the communist party, but who nonetheless are still helping to shape our foreign policy."[34] McCarthy's accusations channeled the same communists-in-government schtick used by far-right conservatives during the 1930s, but the allegations landed harder in a world consumed by existential fears of communist espionage and atomic annihilation. Just a couple of weeks earlier, Alger Hiss, the former State Department official accused of espionage, had been convicted by a grand jury of perjury amid swirling allegations of Soviet treachery. Suddenly, it seemed, the enemy came from within. McCarthy had no proof that the State Department was "thoroughly infested with communists," but the specious accusations harmonized with the Cold War's paranoid melody, setting off a wave of ideological repression that chilled American politics.[35]

McCarthy became the country's leading communist witch-hunter, the symbol of the Second Red Scare and a tribune for ultraconservatism. As an elected official, he found his niche as a far-right translator, promoting and legitimizing ultraconservative conspiracies for the nation at large. He blamed Secretary of State George Marshall, and by virtue the Truman administration, for abandoning Eastern Europe to the Soviets and selling out China to the communists. During a speech on the Senate floor, McCarthy called the Democrats a "party of Communists and crooks" guilty of "protecting Communists in Government."[36] The Senate gallery, swept up in the anti-communist fervor, hung on the senator's every word and gave him a rousing ovation. Democrats were outraged by the accusations. Senator Herbert H. Lehman, a New York Democrat, chastised McCarthy for levying "irresponsible charges of disloyalty against Government officials." Even Republican moderates, such as Maine senator Margaret Chase Smith, questioned the effectiveness and noted the ethical quandary of using "fear, bigotry, ignorance, and intolerance" to win elections.[37] Conservatives, however, sensed the potency of anti-communism and backed McCarthy to the hilt. Senator Taft, despite holding private reservations about McCarthy himself, encouraged the "fighting Marine" to "keep talking and if one case doesn't work out, he should proceed with another one."[38] Eventually McCarthy assumed the chairmanship of the Senate Committee on Government Operations, where he hurled accusations and launched investigations. Allegations of communist sympathies ruined thousands of careers, in both government and the private sector, and disrupted the leftist tradition in the United States. Politicians swerved to the middle-right to avoid being swept up in McCarthy's conspiratorial maw.[39]

Ultraconservatives, always eager to weaponize anti-communism, claimed McCarthy as one of their own. Far-right businessmen lauded the senator's investigations. General Robert E. Wood, the former America First leader, noted, "McCarthy is doing a great job that had to be done to put traitors and spies out of our government. You can't be soft with these people."[40] Dixiecrats such as James O. Eastland, Mississippi senator and chairman of the Senate Subcommittee on Internal Security, tied civil rights activism to communist revolutionaries. Eastland once declared, "Those who would mix little children of both races are following an illegal, immoral, and sinful doctrine."[41] In other words, integration equaled communism, a notion that rang out like a battle cry throughout Dixieland. Furthermore, the trial and subsequent execution of Julius and Ethel Rosenberg, both convicted of passing nuclear secrets to the Soviet Union, seemed to support McCarthy's allegations of a far-reaching conspiracy. The drumbeat of anti-communism—whether sounded through far-right activists or government investigators—provided an important touchstone for ultraconservatives and served as the backdrop for the election of 1952.[42]

The divisions that bubbled to the surface during the 1948 presidential election had hardened by the early 1950s, inflamed by the Second Red Scare and burgeoning civil rights movement. As the 1952 presidential election approached, Democrats put together a compromise ticket featuring Illinois governor Adlai Stevenson and Alabama senator John Sparkman. The ticket highlighted the conflicted composition of the New Deal coalition. Stevenson fit the liberal tradition of Roosevelt and Truman—Republican congressman Richard Nixon smeared him as "Adlai the Appeaser" and McCarthy "mistakenly" dubbed him "Alger" Stevenson—while Sparkman, despite his moderation, represented the enduring influence of conservative southerners.[43] The 1952 Democratic platform pledged support for the New Deal's legacy and featured a section on civil rights, but the civil rights language was so imprecise that the *Wall Street Journal* described it as a "rather flabby combination of clichés."[44] Furthermore, Stevenson struggled to offer firm policy stances and did not cut a commanding figure. Holmes Alexander of the *Los Angeles Times* portrayed him as "slouchy, paunchy, and baldish," a "rather mousy little man" favored by the "middle-roaders and the second choice of the left and right wings."[45] In choosing Stevenson and Sparkman, the Democratic Party tried to paper over its internal ideological fissures.

On the other side of the aisle a similar, and equally bitter, internecine battle raged over the future of the Republican Party. Senator Taft squared off against war hero Dwight D. Eisenhower, who had declined to enter the political scrum in 1948 but felt compelled to run in 1952 against Taft. To Eisenhower's mind, Taft's anti-internationalism threatened the delicate, and still-developing, Cold War balance. Taft turned more hawkish as the Cold War crystallized, but his domestic platforms—fiscal conservatism, strict constitutionalism, free-market economics, limited federal growth, and states' rights—resembled a far-right wish list. Ultraconservatives drew inspiration from Taft's campaign, including businessman and future John Birch Society founder Robert Welch, who delivered twenty-five speeches on behalf of Taft's candidacy and attempted to serve as a Taft-pledged Massachusetts delegate. Taft sought McCarthy's endorsement to deepen his far-right credentials, but McCarthy balked when Taft refused to back his State Department witchhunting. The Ohio senator also turned south in an attempt to siphon the votes of disgruntled conservative Democrats, which might have been a savvy political maneuver had West Coast Republicans not doomed his campaign. California congressman Richard Nixon, who had skyrocketed to fame as a dogged anti-communist investigator, delivered critical votes to Eisenhower at the Republican National Convention, leading to Taft's defeat and Nixon's vice-presidential nod. Incensed, Welch developed a lifelong animus toward Nixon and later characterized Taft's loss as the "dirtiest deal in American political history."[46] Eisenhower and Nixon went on to win a landslide victory over Stevenson, receiving just over 57 percent of the popular vote and an even more commanding 457 electoral votes.[47]

Ultraconservatives viewed Taft's primary defeat and Eisenhower's ascent as the Republican Party's final capitulation to liberalism. The far right despised Eisenhower's "Modern Republicanism," which sought to leaven GOP anti-statism by accepting limited government intervention, and his open disdain for McCarthy's investigations. Taft's convention defeat became a rallying point for enraged far-right agitators. Rather than accepting the result, ultra-conservatives proclaimed that the American government had been captured by a deep-seated, malevolent conspiracy. Welch declared that "Eisenhower's proper political classification was in the red fringes of the Democratic Party," and argued that Taft, had he won the 1952 election, would have led a "grand rout of the Communists in our government."[48] A few years after the election, Kent Courtney, the New Orleans–based far-right publisher, summarized the conservatism-under-siege mentality by casting a pox on both parties: "Both the Democrat and Republican parties have been taken over by ultra-liberals."[49] Colonel Robert R. McCormick, the *Chicago Daily Tribune* editor who stumped for nonintervention during World War II, called for a third-party movement to extract conservative strength from the two national parties. He first tried to create a new American Party before turning to ultraconservative organizing, serving as a founding member of the group For America. During the early 1950s, feelings of resentment and alienation galvanized the far right's political militancy.[50]

The political cauldron of the early Cold War convinced ultraconservative activists that the time had come to repel the liberal tide. In particular, anxieties about social decay at the hands of liberal-communists conjured a revival of right-wing religious activism, a surge which built upon decades of conservative evangelical crusades. During the 1920s, fundamentalists and evangelicals fought against religious modernism and the perceived leftist tilt of some Protestant churches. A few short years and a Great Depression later, right-wing evangelicals politicized further in response to Roosevelt's New Deal and the growth of the welfare state. By midcentury, popular ministers such as Billy Graham were broadcasting a conservative evangelical message into millions of American homes. Though Graham took a moderate position on civil rights, his anti-communism and sermons against big government helped animate the political ambitions of religious conservatives. Government figures, such as FBI director J. Edgar Hoover, further stoked the fires of Christian anti-communism. In 1947 Hoover told a group of Methodist ministers, "Communism is secularism on the march. It is a moral foe of Christianity."[51] In short, Cold War anti-communism synergized with evangelical fundamentalism, crystallizing a worldview wherein a nebulous, atheistic communism menaced Christian America internally and externally.[52]

Billy James Hargis and his ministry, the Christian Crusade, emerged as critical nodes within the ultraconservative movement's evangelical wing.[53] Hargis's early family life and hardscrabble upbringing fostered his religious fundamentalism and ultraconservative political views. Born on August 3, 1925, in Texarkana, a town spanning the Texas-Arkansas border, young Billy James was orphaned by his biological family and adopted by J. E. and Louise Fowler Hargis. The family was too poor to afford a radio, but the boy embraced the Hargis tradition of "daily Bible reading and [singing] weekly community Gospel songs."[54] Thinking back on his youth, Hargis reminisced about a folksy, traditional upbringing: "I can still see my father waiting up for me reading the Bible, sometimes reading aloud while Mother crocheted on the other side of the open gas stove."[55] Hargis received baptism by immersion at the age of nine and later thanked his parents for making him "Christ-conscious."[56] Despite his tender age, Hargis recalled, "I knew what I was doing. I really and truly accepted Christ as my Lord and Saviour at that time."[57]

Undoubtedly Hargis's parents influenced his religious nature, but his family's economic struggles also imparted a respect for hard work and self-reliance. The hardships of the Great Depression required Hargis to work odd jobs while attending public school, though he admitted a disinterest in education because of his "energetic" mind.[58] His family history of bootstrapping and poverty instilled a fierce independence and taught him to value experience over schooling. "I make no pretense of having a great formal education," Hargis proclaimed years later. "What little knowledge I have has come from private study and the college of hard knocks. Many common folks, like me, are familiar with this school."[59] After graduating high school, Hargis spent a couple of years at the unaccredited Ozark Bible College in Bentonville,

Arkansas, but he failed to finish his degree when his money ran short. He returned to Texarkana where he was ordained in 1943 by the pastors and elders of his childhood place of worship, Rose Hill Christian Church. Hargis had a spiritual epiphany when he sought the counsel of an older pastor, A. B. Reynolds. During the meeting Hargis was "awakened to the curse of communism" when Reynolds told the young pastor that he needed to become "God's man to fight this satanic evil that has gotten into our churches!"[60] This pivotal moment transformed Hargis from a rural evangelical pastor to a crusader "concerned about communism and religious apostasy."[61] Hargis called upon his fellow ministers to be society's watchmen, arbiters of faith and politics who guarded against the communist conspiracy and its fellow-traveling liberals.[62] "Ministers must be informed. God expects them to warn people on his behalf," Hargis told his radio audience. "If we fail to do so, the blood of the innocent will be upon the hands of the watchman who failed to inform his people."[63]

To fulfill his watchman duties, Hargis founded Christian Echoes National Ministry, an organization based on Christian fundamentalism and political ultraconservatism. Headquartered in Sapulpa, Oklahoma, Hargis's ministry, more popularly known as the Christian Crusade, vowed to protect America's Christian heritage and "lead God's people out of complacence and apathy."[64] The Crusade served as the umbrella corporation for Hargis's activism—all publications, radio broadcasts, and speaking tours were funded through the ministry. On the stump, Hargis resembled the hellfire-and-brimstone evangelists from the Great Awakening. He employed what Oklahomans called "bawl and jump" preaching, which required "vigorous gestures and a shouting voice to the point of exhaustion and hoarseness."[65] Standing over six feet tall, Hargis cut an imposing figure, but his carnival-barker demeanor gave his ministry the appearance of both legitimacy and spectacle. Opponents of Hargis frequently mocked his "shaking jowls" and "porcine appearance."[66] And, even though he claimed that the Christian Crusade was "a movement of the American homes . . . [and] not a political or denominational movement," his ministry aimed to counter the sociopolitical liberalism of the mid-twentieth century.[67]

Evangelical fundamentalism, anti-communism, and white supremacy formed the pillars of Hargis's political ideology—all other principles filtered through this philosophical sieve. Hargis's fundamentalist worldview projected a black/white binary onto the world. Communism versus anticommunism. Christian America beset by secularism, atheism, and modernity. For Hargis, anti-communism went beyond a Cold War imperative and instead constituted a stringent barometer for judging the spiritual (and political) health of the United States. Hargis considered liberalism, including religious liberalism, an adjunct of communism, and, like other ultraconservatives, he believed that nonconservatives generally fell into one of three categories: "Communists, their sympathizers, and uninformed dupes."[68] This worldview, in which liberals and moderates were redefined as communists, reduced all honest dissent to un-American subversion. In some ways, Hargis was a Cold War manifestation of 1920s fundamentalism. "We are either pro-Christ or pro-Communist," Hargis wrote in a Christian Crusade pamphlet. "All the Liberals in Washington who profess to be Christians must give up their double-faced hypocrisy and take their stand either with Marx or with Jesus Christ."[69] Hargis even wrote a thesis about internal subversion titled "Communism, American Style" in order to earn a bachelor's degree from Burton College and Seminary, a school often derided as a "degree mill" by mainstream educators and theologians.[70] According to his worldview, America was losing the Cold War because communist pied pipers were leading the country down a path of spiritual ennui. The only solution, in the eyes of Hargis, was to mint and muster Christian soldiers.

Another one of Hargis's duties as a ministerial sentry included defending white supremacy. He wrote Biblical defenses of segregation, criticized interracial relationships, stumped for states' rights, and described African nations as "not far advanced from savagery."[71] Hargis called segregation "one of nature's universal laws" and smeared the federal government as "usurpers" attacking the sovereignty of southern states.[72] In one newsletter he wrote that "the evil perpetuated by an all-powerful federal government will outweigh by far the accumulated evils of the governments of the individual states."[73] Despite claiming to have "genuine sympathy for the oppressed," Hargis dismissed the civil rights movement as a communist plot and described media coverage of anti-black discrimination as "extensively exaggerated."[74] Yet Hargis's writings on race often produced ideological contradictions. For example, in one pamphlet he referred to whites as the "dominant race," but in another proclaimed that "there is no such thing as an inferior race."[75] Despite this philosophical paradox, not to mention that the latter statement was simply a ham-fisted attempt to sanitize his own racism, Hargis's racial views reflected the beliefs of vast swaths of white southern conservatives.

Following in the footsteps of right-wing radicals like Father Coughlin and Gerald Winrod, the latter of whom gave Hargis an honorary doctorate from his own Defenders Theological Seminary in Puerto Rico, Hargis created a dictatorial cult of personality within the Christian Crusade. The organization had a strict leadership hierarchy, and Hargis vetted all preproduction publications to prevent any fractures in the Crusade's Hargis-driven ideology. As the Crusade's leader, Hargis "brooked no interference," noted an FBI investigator, and board meetings were reduced to sycophantic events where Hargis quashed any discussion or disagreement.[76] Hargis was an exceptionally paranoid man, striking out at even those close to him. Julian Williams, the Educational Director of the Christian Crusade, gave an interview recounting one of his own brushes with Hargis's instability. At Hargis's request, Williams had fetched some reading material, which the minister read and then absentmindedly placed in his desk. A short while later, Hargis demanded the same material again, insisting that the documents had been refiled. Williams described the scene, remembering how Hargis "stormed about the filing room, tore through the cabinets, and tongue-lashed everyone within range."[77] Upon discovering the files within his own desk, Hargis insisted that someone had planted them there. Williams finished the anecdote by sighing, "He is incapable of admitting a mistake." Such authoritarian characteristics were not without organizational virtues, and in some ways—particularly fundraising, publishing, and broadcasting—Hargis was a cutting-edge proto-evangelist.[78]

Using grassroots tactics to gather a following, Hargis built the Christian Crusade into a central hub within the ultraconservative network. He barnstormed across the nation, visiting conservative hotbeds to give speeches and hobnob with fellow right-wingers. Hargis's goal was political evangelism, and the Crusade formed the fibrous tissue connecting right-wing outposts. For example, a local television station provided coverage of Hargis's three-day campaign in Amarillo, Texas, which resulted in his daily and weekly radio broadcasts being picked up by local stations. Sometimes Hargis blanketed states with rallies. During one of these media blitzes in 1961, dubbed "Operation Mississippi," Hargis traversed the Magnolia State giving speeches at high schools, civic clubs, and public rallies. Many of the events were sponsored by fellow far-right organizations, including the Mississippi Citizens' Council and local John Birch Society chapters. Similar to his visit to Amarillo, Hargis left a standing operation in Mississippi—multiple radio stations and one local television network picked up Hargis's broadcasts. The Christian Crusade also held annual conventions, created a network of anti-communist leadership schools, and established a youth movement called the Torchbearers to foster local involvement. The conventions and the anti-communist leadership schools operated in the same manner: people paid to come listen to a coterie of right-wing luminaries—such as Arkansas governor Orval Faubus, General Edwin Walker, Democratic congressman John R. Rarick of Louisiana, Georgia governor Lester Maddox, and Alabama governor George Wallace—and then published sets of resolutions promoting Christian nationalism and anticommunist conspiracy theories. By the mid-1950s, Hargis had built a grassroots web that stretched from right-wing localities to the national stage.[79]

The Christian Crusade and numerous other far-right groups followed the organizational template created by predecessors, such as the Jeffersonian Democrats, by establishing state chapters, hosting monthly meetings, and founding numerous media outlets. Hargis became a leading right-wing broadcaster—eventually over 200 radio stations carried Christian Crusade programming. The Christian Crusade possessed a massive publishing wing, which produced periodicals and ephemera featuring a menagerie of right-wing authors, including ultraconservative politicians. In one Crusade pamphlet, James B. Utt, a Republican congressman from California, compared welfare liberalism to child molestation: "The child molester always entices a child with candy or some other gift before he performs his evil deed. Likewise, governments promise something for nothing in order to extend their control and dominion over the people whom they are supposed to govern by the consent of the governed."[80] Utt finished his diatribe with an apocalyptic flourish: "This is the short road to slavery." Not only did Hargis agree with such reprehensible dreck—he published it, after all—but his collaboration with Utt demonstrated the gradual intertwining of the ultraconservative movement and the GOP's budding right flank.[81]

Perhaps above all, Hargis excelled at fundraising. Radio broadcasts and Christian Crusade publications encouraged people to pray for America and donate to the Crusade. Hargis emphasized the importance of small donations—a grassroots strategy mirroring the campaigns of other far-right organizations. The vast majority of donations ranged from $1.00 to $10.00, but a few gave $100.00 and there was even a handful of $1,000.00 donations. Hargis occasionally stooped to unscrupulous levels to rake in cash, going so far as urging listeners to "remember [the] Christian Crusade in your will."[82] In a few short years, the Christian Crusade claimed between 75,000 and 100,000 followers and boasted a similar number of subscribers to Hargis's monthly *Christian Crusade* magazine. As contemporary analyst Reese Cleghorn concluded, correctly, Hargis was "the most important of the evangelists on the radical right, and therefore one of the most influential voices in the South."[83]

Not content to level ideological critiques through publications and radio broadcasts, Hargis involved himself in direct actions to fight liberal-communism. Hargis found himself at the epicenter of the Second Red Scare through his relationship with Senator Joseph McCarthy. In 1951, McCarthy attacked Methodist bishop Garfield Bromley Oxnam for ties to communism. Oxnam was a frequent target of right-wing anti-communists because he led an ecumenical ministry in Washington, D.C., and served as one of the presidents for the World Council of Churches. Ecumenical organizations, such as the World Council of Churches, promoted greater cooperation and shared beliefs between Christian sects while simultaneously advocating for liberal platforms such as human rights and redistributive economics. To Hargis, progressive ecumenicalism provided an additional gateway for communist subversion. McCarthy invited Hargis to Washington, where the Oklahoma preacher directed opposition research against Oxnam and the ecumenical movement. HUAC also turned its sights on Oxnam; committee member Donald L. Jackson, a California Republican, condemned Oxnam as a communist double agent whose loyalty to the Lord manifested only on Sundays. Oxnam, who had no ties to subversive organizations, demanded a full hearing to clear his name. He managed to do so, but the entire incident illustrated how the far right used anti-communism, Christian fundamentalism, and political spectacle to slander liberal opponents. Furthermore, it revealed the symbiotic relationship between far-right activists and politicians—ultraconservatives often served as the shock troops for the conservative movement.[84]

While Hargis's evangelical zeal flowed from his own spiritual awakening, Willis E. Stone emerged as the far right's libertarian torchbearer after the 1944 Montgomery Ward seizure. A few years after drafting his anti-taxation amendment, Stone founded a Los Angeles–based organization—first called the National Committee for Economic Freedom and then incorporated in 1949 as the American Progress Foundation (APF)—to spearhead his movement. But Stone had his work cut out for him. The midcentury political consensus stood against libertarian tax reform, and the word "progress" entailed traditional associations with liberal-left reform. Nevertheless, to Stone, "progress" meant retrenching federal authority and stripping away the liberal welfare state. As right-wing author Lucille Cardin Crain explained, "The American Progress Foundation . . . came into being to stem the socialistic tide of government monopoly of enterprise in these United States, choosing to achieve its objective by means of a proposed constitutional amendment, now popularly known as the 23rd Amendment."[85] Stone argued that liberalism constituted a liminal stage of communism, thus positioning his amendment as a key bulwark protecting free-market capitalism and traditional American values.[86]

Stone's personal history and business experience incubated his radical libertarian bent. After a brief military stint during World War I, Stone worked as a salesman, traveling speaker, and industrial engineer. He was a natural marketer. Stone developed new advertising techniques—for example, he created "Color Control" to dramatize Brolite's automobile paint program—and won awards for his salesmanship. His background in industrial sales put him in contact with manufacturing tycoons, and he held positions in conservative, business-oriented organizations, including the Los Angeles Chamber of Commerce. However, Stone struggled to make ends meet and blamed liberal economic policies for his own personal plight. Stone drew from the philosophical tradition of libertarian thinkers such as Albert Jay Nock in accusing the federal government, specifically Franklin Roosevelt and New Deal liberalism, of "invading the sacred realm of private enterprise."[87] Stone's connections to the business world burnished his faith in an unfettered market, which formed the bedrock of his anti-statist critiques and conspiratorial anti-communism.[88]

Defending free-market economics became a Cold War imperative for many conservatives, creating an ideological binary pitting capitalist conservatism against liberal communism. A new generation of right-wing Cold Warriors emerged—including libertarian economists Friedrich Hayek and James McGill Buchanan, *National Review*'s William F. Buckley Jr., and writer-philosopher Ayn Rand—who lamented the decline of free markets and the tyranny of liberalism. Periodicals such as *National Review*, *Human Events*, and *Freeman* combined anti-communist anxieties with libertarian fears of federal encroachment. "The purpose of repealing the income tax law is to reduce the power of the Government," opined Corinne Griffith, the former silent-film starlet turned anti-tax activist, in the pages of *Human Events*. "We are afraid of that centralization of power which has in other countries preceded the introduction of socialism, communism, and fascism."[89] What set Stone apart and distinguished his ultraconservatism were his proposed remedies: repeal of the Sixteenth Amendment, a prohibition on future federal income taxes, and a liquidation of all federally owned economic ventures. Though Stone's radical libertarianism fell well outside of the political center, his paranoid anti-communism reflected a hallmark of Cold War politics, which lent his ideologies a degree of crossover appeal. In fact, Stone's West Coast ultraconservatism overlapped with the Deep South's iteration; he often described states as sovereign entities and used states' rights rhetoric, particularly clarion calls for economic and individual freedom, to market his amendment in the South. Stone veiled his racism with the language of free markets, but his actions nevertheless traced the ideological connections between libertarianism and white supremacy.[90]

The American Progress Foundation transmitted Stone's ideas throughout the ultraconservative network, establishing Stone as a crucial member of modern conservatism's far-right vanguard. Following in the footsteps of other far-right leaders, Stone created an interwoven grassroots structure that contributed to APF's rapid growth. The group's Los Angeles headquarters served as the organizational and messaging hub while state chapters agitated for individual states to adopt Stone's proposed amendment. In 1955 Stone created *American Progress* magazine to broadcast his amendment and serve as his "all-American" amplifier in the "struggle against alien philosophies."[91] *American Progress* distilled and propagated Stone's ultra-libertarian views; indeed, it is impossible to separate Stone from *American Progress* because he served as its publisher, editor, and ideological wellspring. According to Stone, *American Progress* had "the unique distinction of being specifically devoted to the support of the Constitution, of the inalienable rights of the individual, and of the sovereignty of the States which compose our Union."[92] Stone penned editorials for every issue along with writers from a variety of backgrounds and occupations; however, white men, particularly business owners, represented the lion's share of contributions.[93]

Published initially on simple matte newsprint, *American Progress* contained editorials, book reviews, economic studies, condensed speeches from right-wing politicians, and reprinted articles from other like-minded publications, all of which demonized taxation and liberal programs as anti-capitalist or, worse, a pathway to communism. *American Progress*'s first edition set the ultraconservative tone for the periodical's entire print run. Physician James L. Doenges wrote a column castigating Social Security as an "immoral, fraudulent scheme" that would "make everyone a ward of the government [and] destroy personal responsibility and incentive."[94] Stone penned an editorial lauding his proposal to repeal the Sixteenth Amendment as the only bill that would "outlaw the practices of socialism and Communism in America."[95] Numerous writers attacked the Tennessee Valley Authority (TVA), the federally run electric company that originated as a New Deal project to provide jobs and economic development. Congressman Ralph Gwinn, a reactionary New York Republican, derided the TVA as a "vote-getting game" intended "to redistribute the wealth," while George Peck—chairman of the board of the right-wing National Labor-Management Foundation and editor of its magazine, *Partners*—declared that the TVA conspired to "control all the water in the United States."[96] In reality, the TVA's audacious mission of progress and conservation received bipartisan support and reflected the business community's capitalist thinking. Nevertheless, author John K. Crippen summarized the capitalism-under-siege mentality of *American Progress*: "A highly-organized socialist conspiracy . . . has infected every artery of our country."[97]

Over time, Stone became a lodestar for the ultraconservative movement's libertarian wing. Through the American Progress Foundation, he established connections with other far-right organizations and conservative politicians. The leaders of fellow libertarian groups—such as the Los Angeles–based Organization to Repeal Federal Income Taxes and Chicago's We the People— networked with Stone, organized joint conferences, and contributed articles to Stone's publications. Stone formed a fruitful relationship with Hargis's Christian Crusade and later cooperated extensively with Welch's John Birch Society and Kent Courtney's Conservative Society of America. The APF leader even collaborated with local fraternal and social organizations, such as the Kiwanis Club and Lions Club, to spread awareness about the "Proposed 23rd Amendment." Perhaps most critically, Stone's network included right-wing congressmen. For instance, Gwinn wrote for *American Progress* and submitted Stone's proposed amendment numerous times, though the bill never made it to the House floor. By 1953, Stone's movement had blossomed. The Illinois state legislature was the first to adopt a resolution in support of Stone's amendment, while other APF state chapters laid the groundwork for future resolutions. By the mid-1950s, Stone emerged as a herald, one among many, for the strident libertarianism rumbling through the political right wing.[98]

The early Cold War witnessed the inchoate development of modern conservatism, and many right-wingers speculated, even hoped, that the emergence of far-right organizations signaled a coming political shift. Frank Hughes, a journalist from the *Chicago Daily Tribune*, wrote, "Ever since New Dealers, Socialists, and internationalists captured the leadership of both major political parties . . . people of different political beliefs have been seeking a burning issue around which to form a new political realignment."[99] Ultraconservative ideas already filtered throughout the political mainstream; numerous third-party outfits called for an end to foreign aid spending, a liquidation of the TVA, a disavowal of the United Nations, and a return to states' rights. Hughes expended numerous column inches encouraging conservatives to

unify. He even put forth his own two-plank platform which called for supporting Bricker's proposed amendment to limit federal power and repealing
the Sixteenth Amendment. "The wrath of this grass roots upsurge is turned
toward the Republican party that elected [Eisenhower]. People are demanding a political realignment," proclaimed Hughes. "They claim that the Republican and Democratic parties are virtually identical. They want something
else—perhaps a new party lineup which would place Communists, Socialists,
internationalists, and New Dealers in one easily identifiable camp, leaving
the other side of the field to their opponents."[100] This communism-versus-
conservatism mentality permeated the right-wing political sphere, flattening
the ideological spectrum into an us-or-them binary and blurring the line
separating radicals from the mainstream. One letter writer, a Seattle-based
attorney, best summarized this far-right sentiment: "The Republican Party
is dead and should be buried and forgotten with the Federalists and Whigs.
Why not form a new party, get ready for the congressional elections of 1954,
and strike one more blow for Americanism?"[101]

For America, an updated version of the America First Committee,
stormed onto the scene amid these calls for a third-party uprising. A mixture
of civic and business leaders met on May 7, 1954, to resuscitate a movement of
nationalistic Americanism. Colonel McCormick of the *Chicago Daily Tribune*
hosted the meeting, and Hamilton Fish, former Republican congressman and
progenitor of HUAC, served as the group's spokesman. For America's delegates created an organizing committee, featuring Fish; Burton K. Wheeler,
former Democratic senator from Montana; Howard Buffett, former Republican representative from Nebraska; John T. Flynn, a New York journalist
best known for founding America First and peddling Pearl Harbor conspiracy theories; and Clarence Manion, a former dean of Notre Dame's law
school who briefly chaired the Commission on Intergovernmental Relations
under Eisenhower before turning to far-right radio broadcasting. The committee selected Manion and General Wood to co-chair the new organization.
Even though neither man had attended the founding meeting, both accepted
the appointments and vowed to fight Eisenhower's "modern Republicanism."
Manion quipped that his phone was "practically ringing off the wall" with
excited callers.[102]

For America carried the banner of nationalistic nonintervention into
the postwar era, forming a link between the pre-WWII vanguard and Cold
War ultraconservatives. James Morgan of the *Daily Boston Globe* described
McCormick's sponsorship of For America as "a standard revolt against the

[Eisenhower] Administration and its internationalism."[103] Fish wrote For America's Declaration of Principles, which detailed the group's opposition to foreign aid spending, "super-internationalism and interventionism, one-worldism, and communism." On the domestic side, the group advocated for a "return to Americanism, enlightened nationalism," and states' rights while declaring its intention to support the campaigns of conservative purists.[104] For America's platform was steeped in Cold War anti-communism. An "inexorable rising peril" existed within the United States, the group warned, which illustrated the need "to eradicate the Godless evil of Communism."[105] Manion encouraged authoritarian approaches to the supposed danger of internal subversion, urging the Eisenhower administration to "do away with" the Communist Party USA and deport American communists.[106] Noting the group's penchant for conspiracy theories, the *Manchester Guardian* remarked, "The debasement of the standards of public controversy would certainly never be stopped by this group."[107] In short, For America's platform combined traditional ultraconservative tenets, such as free market economics and conspiratorial anti-communism, with an antipathy for the Cold War's internationalist zeitgeist.[108]

The organization rapidly built a national network through the efforts of media activists, grassroots leaders, and libertarian writers. For America's Chicago headquarters ran the national publishing and organizational machinery while state chapters orchestrated local grassroots crusades. Numerous high-profile right-wingers joined the cause, including military men General Bonner Fellers and General Albert C. Wedemeyer; J. Evetts Haley, the former Jeffersonian Democrat who would become a key leader of For America's Texas chapter; Corinne Griffith; libertarian writer Frank Chodorov; George S. Benson, a staunch evangelical and president of Harding College; Richard Lloyd Jones, editor and publisher of the right-wing *Tulsa Tribune* newspaper; and Eugene C. Pulliam, a conservative newspaper mogul. Senator McCarthy described the group as "a good bunch of Americans" and hoped that its founding presaged a political transformation. "I think it would be very healthy some time to get a realignment of parties so there would be no extreme right or left wing in either the Republican or Democratic Party," McCarthy said, apparently oblivious to his own role in driving a conspiratorial, anti-communist wedge into American politics.[109]

For America combined disparate, previously disconnected strands of ultraconservatism into a coherent whole. Griffith and Chodorov represented the libertarian wing, Benson epitomized the rising fundamentalist movement, and Jones and Pulliam illustrated how conservative newspapermen collaborated with and disseminated the views of ultraconservative organizations. For America's states' rights plank also appealed to the far right's segregationist wing. Southern state chapters, such as Haley's Texans For America, injected a dose of white supremacy into the organization. For America portrayed itself as an authentic grassroots uprising rather than a movement mobilized by well-heeled elites. Perhaps wary of the failure of the Depression-era American Liberty League, Fish said the organization would not be a "little business group of rich men" but a mass organization of "little people" who detested the "internationalist viewpoint portrayed by most of the TV, radio, press, commentators, and moneyed groups."[110] This statement obfuscated the truth: For America's core membership, like many far-right organizations, hailed from the upper class, often from the wealthy business community, men and women who were desperate to cloak their gentility with a populist shroud.

For America's star-studded leadership and ties to right-wing publishers heightened the organization's profile, leading multiple national newspapers to broadcast the group's inception. Coverage appeared in multiple dailies, including the *Chicago Tribune, Christian Science Monitor, Boston Globe, Hartford Courant, Los Angeles Times, New York Times,* and *Baltimore Sun.* However, because the group coalesced during the 1954 midterms, many commentators incorrectly portrayed For America as a third-party insurgency. Speculating about a political realignment made for great copy. William H. Stringer of the *Washington Post* ventured that For America aimed "to groom candidates and issues in opposition to the Eisenhower viewpoint."[111] Even foreign outlets viewed For America as a new political party, with the *Manchester Guardian* characterizing the group as a "third national party which would unite under one banner the isolationists, the opponents of economic reform, the supporters of segregation in the South, and the defenders of state rights."[112] The *Guardian* got the coalition right, but the organizational impetus wrong. Fish denied any intention to form a conservative third party; instead, For America defined itself as a nonpartisan political action group dedicated to fighting within the two-party system. The organization pledged to support right-wing politicians, regardless of party, illustrating the residual ideological fluidity across party lines. Fish, banking on a conservative silent majority, estimated that the group would accumulate "five million members in no time and sweep the country like a prairie fire."[113]

To foster this growth, For America submitted an application with the Internal Revenue Service to be classified as a nonprofit "educational trust."

This designation was highly prized because it exempted organizations from taxation and allowed patrons to subtract donations from their income on annual tax returns through IRS code 501(c)(3). The Associated Press described the designation as a "big help in obtaining contributions."[114] In effect, "educational trusts" served as tax havens for wealthy activists, funneling money away from the state and toward political causes. Despite the group's stated commitment to aiding right-wing candidates, For America tried to hide its political ambition by writing bylaws that privileged political "education" over action. The emphasis on education angered Fish, who fulminated that the bylaws rendered For America "utterly, totally useless." Fish declared that the focus on education nullified For America's Declaration of Principles and only served "to have a few rich men contribute large sums of tax-exempt money to finance this educational organization."[115] Believing For America had abandoned its mission, Fish resigned and founded his own organization, the American Political Action Committee, which did not apply for tax-exempt status.[116]

Despite the internal discord, For America helped push ultraconservatism into the political mainstream. In early 1955, General Wood sponsored a gathering of prominent right-wing Republicans—including Eisenhower's secretary of labor James P. Mitchell, Senator Everett Dirksen of Illinois, Senator McCarthy, Illinois governor William G. Stratton, and Utah governor J. Bracken Lee—to discuss a rightward turn for the GOP. Russell Baker of the *New York Times* observed, "The hard core of the Republican Old Guard convened here [in Chicago] today to cheer verbal assaults on the United Nations, the State Department and the Eisenhower Administration."[117] The crowd of roughly 2,000 whooped and hollered when Senator McCarthy took the stage and roared its approval of the Bricker Amendment. Next up, Wood spoke briefly to introduce Dirksen, stating that "since the death of Taft, he [Dirksen] is the man in the middle west we depend upon to carry on for us."[118] Dirksen struck a middle path, lauding Eisenhower for backing Formosa (Taiwan) against China's oppression but voicing support for the Bricker Amendment. Lee, who later became a fixture in Willis Stone's organizations, gave the most inflammatory speech of the night. He voiced the possibility of a third-party bolt, excoriated federal taxation, alleged that the United Nations sought to subvert American sovereignty by forming a world government, and even questioned Eisenhower's loyalty to Republican ideals. "We have gone farther to the left in the last two years than in any other period in our history," Lee remonstrated.[119] Indeed, far-right Republicans like Lee felt a certain sense of alienation and disillusion, an estrangement from the liberal elements within the GOP. This schism became all the more discernable because the official Republican organ did not recognize the meeting and held its own Lincoln Day celebration.[120]

Nevertheless, the rally, and Wood's sponsorship of it, illustrated the growing symbiosis between ultraconservatives and their mainstream counterparts. The meeting brought Republican politicians together with ultraconservative activists, allowing Wood, and For America itself, to network and promote far-right ideals without stumping for particular candidates. Wood tried to temper Lee's third-party talk: "While a lot of us get irritated with Eisenhower out here [in the Midwest], we still figure he's a lot better than anybody the Democrats can put in there." However, as Baker reported, the ideologies presented at the rally "appeared to differ little from those of For America," and many of the attendees viewed Eisenhower's political philosophy as "dangerously leftist, particularly in social welfare programs."[121] This axiom—that the Democratic Party had turned hopelessly left-wing, despite still boasting a significant number of conservatives, and that the Republican Party was following the same path—permeated right-wing circles. Corinne Griffith encouraged For America to form a legitimate third party to back the Bricker Amendment, repeal the Sixteenth Amendment, and rebuke the United Nations. She was convinced such a party could win over California conservatives. For the moment, however, For America rejected third-party ambitions in favor of its purported educational mission. Griffith, like Fish before her, failed to recognize that, to ultraconservatives, education *was* political activism.[122]

For America's strategic sleight of hand did not fool the IRS. The IRS recognized that For America's tactics crossed into the realm of political action and rejected the group's request for tax-exempt status. The group's support for the Bricker Amendment factored into the IRS's decision, though the third-party murmurs probably did not help either. Instead of defining For America as an "educational trust," the IRS categorized the group as a "social welfare" trust, section 501(c)(4) of the IRS code, which meant that the organization's income was tax exempt but contributions were not. Similar decisions had occurred before—Henry Regnery's conservative publishing company had its application rejected in the 1940s—but this ruling was a significant blow to For America's fundraising hopes. Wood fumed that the IRS's decision threatened to "destroy the effectiveness of For America as a nation-wide educational organization" and raged that "left-wing, internationalist, and un-American" groups—he listed the Atlantic Union Committee, the Fund for the Republic, and the American Institute of Pacific Relations—claimed tax exemptions.[123] Right-wingers circulated conspiracy theories that the IRS favored left-wing organizations and stifled conservative groups, accusations which boiled over into the next decade when the IRS denied a similar application from Hargis's Christian Crusade.[124]

After failing to hoodwink the IRS, For America reorganized into an overt political action group. The policy committee elevated Wood to honorary chairman status and appointed Dan Smoot, the Dallas-based ultraconservative publisher, to serve as co-chairman with Clarence Manion. Now unencumbered by the need to appear neutral and nonpartisan, For America produced a political platform that became a rubric for the noninterventionist far right. Self-identifying as a group of "strict constitutionalists," For America promoted "states' rights, competitive enterprise, private property and individual liberty" and opposed "all concessions to internationalism, socialism, or collectivism under any name."[125] The organization supported Stone's movement to repeal the Sixteenth Amendment provided that adequate budgetary safeguards were implemented. On the other hand, the platform opposed global alliances and military interventionism. One passage best exemplified For America's ultraconservative mission objective: "We oppose all moves toward internationalism, fascism, socialism, and godless communism. We will tolerate no surrender of American independence. For America seeks to provide all citizens, regardless of party affiliation, a vehicle by which they can make their influence felt in each party."[126] With a firm platform and goal in place, For America's leadership started laying plans to foment an ultraconservative revival through a network of state chapters and grassroots activists.

*   *   *

The cauldron of Cold War politics inflamed and legitimized far-right beliefs, catalyzing the creation of multiple organizations and highlighting how various ideological strands intertwined to create the ultraconservative movement. The Christian Crusade exemplified the evangelical far right, and Billy James Hargis's relationships with right-wing politicians, such as Senator McCarthy, catapulted him into a leadership position within the ultraconservative network. Through the American Progress Foundation, Willis Stone forged a nexus of libertarian organizations and built momentum for a showdown over federal taxation. For America and its leadership stood for states' rights and anti-internationalism, and its organizational web highlighted the burgeoning alliance between conservative media outlets, right-wing Republicans, and ultraconservative activists. The group also laid an important foundation for T. Coleman Andrews's third-party run in 1956, an event that hinted at an eventual political realignment. All of these groups, on some level, adhered to tenets of white supremacy, whether through overt racism or paeans to states' rights. While these organizations differed on goals and strategies, they each promoted communist conspiracy theories to drum up support for their platforms and forged relationships with right-wing politicians, media activists, and businessmen to initiate a rightward shift in American politics. These organizations, in short, became critical nodes in the far-right network. More broadly, the Cold War's ideological crucible, which privileged conspiratorial accusations against the government and stoked anxieties about communist infiltration, molded ultraconservatism into a cohesive philosophy and nourished the blossoming movement.[127]

As ultraconservatives looked toward the second half of the decade, two events occurred in 1954 which solidified their communists-in-government outlook: the censure of Senator Joseph McCarthy and the *Brown v. Board of Education* decision. Though McCarthy rose to power by smearing the Democrats as the party of communism, he targeted his own party after Republicans took power in 1953. McCarthy alleged that Eisenhower's administration was stained by communism as much as Truman's, translating the far right's overheated conspiracies for a national audience. However, many Republicans quickly distanced themselves from McCarthy. Eisenhower tried to mollify the issue by strengthening Truman's loyalty program and ignoring, or at least not speaking out against, McCarthy's more hysterical accusations. The Wisconsin senator persisted and eventually dug his own grave by accusing the Army Signal Corps of covering up communist infiltration. The televised Army-McCarthy trial captured the nation's attention and unveiled McCarthy's dishonest bullying. In late 1954, the Senate censured McCarthy for flouting congressional norms, though notably many old guard Republicans voted against the censure. Humiliated, McCarthy lost numerous political allies and friends—he was now a cast-off misfit in an ideologically divided party.[128]

Anti-communism remained a powerful political force, however, and far-right activists laundered McCarthy's indiscretions. Robert Welch, for example, found "nothing wrong with McCarthy's methods from the point of view of the patriotic American."[129] Hargis defended McCarthy by erroneously arguing that "every single person exposed by Sen. McCarthy as a communist and subversive was guilty according to the evidence."[130] Kent Courtney considered Taft and McCarthy "great Americans sacrificed on the altar of political expediency by demagogic Socialists within their own party."[131] Even mainstream-facing right-wingers, such as conservative scion William F. Buckley Jr., defended McCarthy. Buckley and his brother-in-law, L. Brent Bozell, penned *McCarthy and His Enemies*, in which Buckley hailed the senator as part of a decades-long "American Resistance," "a handful of prophets" who had "tried to alert the nation to the communist threat."[132] McCarthy's censure, coming on the heels of Taft's primary defeat in 1952, emboldened the right-wing precept that communists, often disguised as liberals, controlled the government and continued to sabotage American society.

In a similar vein, far-right activists viewed the nascent civil rights movement as a conduit for communism and social upheaval. On May 17, 1954, former vice-presidential candidate Earl Warren, now the chief justice of the Supreme Court, delivered the court's unanimous *Brown v. Board* decision, mandating the desegregation of America's public-school system. The *Brown* decision overturned long-standing racial norms, and southerners formed a "massive resistance" campaign to defend southern apartheid. They resuscitated the political theory of interposition, which postulated that individual states could interpose their sovereignty against the national government and nullify federal laws.[133] Southern reactionaries disparaged the *Brown* decision as "Black Monday" and formed White Citizens' Councils to protect the South's economic and racial hierarchy.[134] Welch called the *Brown* decision "the most brazen and flagrant usurpation of power that has been seen in three hundred years," and contended that Warren's "unconstitutional" decisions necessitated the justice's removal.[135] Two years after *Brown*, Haley fought integration in Texas by running a segregationist gubernatorial campaign. In Oklahoma, Hargis linked the fight for racial equality to Cold War anti-communism and white southerners' long-standing fear of state power: "The communists have been urging their followers to bring pressure upon the federal government to force Reconstruction days upon the Southern states again."[136] The allegations leveled by ultraconservatives were ultimately false: communists aided the fight for civil rights, but neither communism, individual communists, nor the Communist Party were the movement's driving force. However, deploying anti-communism as a weapon against the civil rights movement concealed the far right's underlying racism with a thin veneer of respectability. For ultra-conservative activists, especially those in the South, the civil rights movement not only threatened traditional social mores, it also represented a pathway for communist subversion. The cauldron of early Cold War politics, capped by McCarthy's censure and the *Brown* decision, set the stage for the maturation of the ultraconservative movement.[137]

CHAPTER 4

Tightening Networks

"How many stay-at-home voters will there be in the 1956 Presidential election?" New Orleans publisher Kent Courtney thundered in a letter to the *Hartford Courant*. "They may number in tens of millions who cannot in good conscience vote for either a New Deal Democrat or a New Deal Republican." During the summer of 1955, Courtney worked as the executive secretary and main propagandist for the Interim Committee for a New Party, which sought to provide Americans with a right-wing alternative to the two major parties. Courtney envisioned establishing a party of conservative purists that would stop America from becoming a "one-party socialist nation." To Courtney's mind, President Dwight Eisenhower and the Republican Party were just as complicit in putting America on the path to communism as the Democrats. "We believe the American people have a right to have a choice," Courtney fulminated. "Americans should have the opportunity to vote for a man who stands for the principles set forth in our Constitution and Bill of Rights."[1]

By the mid-1950s, numerous ultraconservative organizations declared that the liberal hegemony in American politics necessitated radical action, a fracturing of the two-party system. These organizations included For America, the Christian Crusade, the American Progress Foundation, and other affiliated groups, a growing network that snaked from the Northeast through the industrial Midwest and the South before terminating on the West Coast. Not every far-right group stumped for political candidates, but the trend line showed ultraconservatives moving toward party politics. Courtney's Interim Committee, for example, argued that conservatives were "the numerical majority" and contended that a right-wing party would stymie "the socialism that is taking over the country." The group's slogan, "Get the change in '56 you voted for in '52," spoke to Eisenhower's perceived betrayal of right-wing values.[2] The Interim Committee soon morphed into the National Committee for a New Party (NCNP)—Courtney maintained his position as executive secretary—and set up a headquarters in Chicago. Conservative posters adorned its walls. "Get government out of private enterprise." "Release American soldiers from Red Chinese prisons." "Federal aid means federal control." "Foreign aid aids Reds."[3]

The NCNP helped establish the Constitution Party in 1956 on a far-right foundation. The new party exemplified the ultraconservative movement up to that point: a fringe caucus agitating for a strict interpretation of the Tenth Amendment, a repeal of the Sixteenth Amendment, withdrawal from the United Nations, and a coded white supremacist recognition that "each State is an independent and sovereign republic."[4] Though the Constitution Party represented a small band of diehards, the group forged alliances with other ultraconservative outfits, including For America and the Federation for Constitutional Government. The *Chicago Daily Tribune* described the Constitution Party as "a collection of splinter parties" attempting to "bind themselves into a big political stick."[5] The stick's target: Dwight Eisenhower and his liberal allies.

The political environment of the mid-to-late 1950s fueled ultraconservative organizing and tightened far-right networks. The continued dominance of modern liberalism and the burgeoning civil rights movement stoked a conservative backlash and, to radical right-wingers, evinced communist influence in government and society. Ultraconservatives saw their country being dominated by a statist cabal that was dedicated to collectivization and egalitarian leveling. During Eisenhower's 1956 reelection bid, a revanchist right-wing coalition united to stem the liberal tide. New activists and organizations, including Courtney and the Constitution Party, joined forces with old hands such as J. Evetts Haley and Clarence Manion to sunder the two-party duopoly through third-party organizing.[6]

The third-party candidacy of former IRS chairman T. Coleman Andrews in 1956 served as a central nexus for disgruntled conservatives and galvanized far-right mobilization. Willis Stone and the American Progress Foundation capitalized on Andrews's anti-taxation messaging to cultivate support for Stone's "Proposed 23rd Amendment." During the late 1950s, Stone's proposal received backing from right-wing politicians and far-right allies, enabling its passage in multiple state legislatures. After spearheading Andrews's candidacy, For America extended its activism through state chapters, particularly Haley's Texans For America affiliate. Then, in 1958, an Indianapolis meeting led to the creation of the most infamous midcentury far-right group: the John Birch Society. Robert H. W. Welch Jr., the self-styled founder of the society, believed liberal politicians conspired to conceal a communist leviathan. "This octopus is so large," Welch declared, "that its tentacles now reach into all of the legislative halls, all of the union labor meetings, a majority of the religious gatherings, and most of the schools *of the whole world*."[7] Welch established an ultraconservative empire by stoking anxieties about internal subversion and the erosion of sociocultural traditions—the Birch Society became a critical node within the burgeoning network of far-right institutions and activists. Throughout the late 1950s, ultraconservatives put their stamp on the political landscape by invading party politics, laying the groundwork for an eventual coup within the two-party system.

*   *   *

Dwight Eisenhower's Modern Republicanism convinced ultraconservatives that the GOP had given over to liberalism, if not communism. Eisenhower described his political beliefs as a "middle way," a moderate philosophy which sought to curb the anti-statist impulses of old guard conservatives while reducing the "big government" imprint of modern liberalism. According to Eisenhower, the government was, in some respects, responsible for the general welfare of the country; he notably called the military-industrial complex "a theft from those who hunger and are not fed."[8] Despite his own conservative convictions, Eisenhower followed in the popular liberal footsteps of Roosevelt and Truman. He expanded Social Security coverage; created the Department of Health, Education, and Welfare; and initiated the building of a vast federal highway system. To fund all of these enterprises, and to rein in debt from World War II, a bipartisan coalition of Republicans and Democrats hiked taxes. Rates soared for the wealthiest Americans, and the trimming of corporate tax rates failed to mollify the rancor of business executives.[9]

To far-right conservatives, Eisenhower was a New Deal wolf in sheep's clothing. Clarence Manion, For America's co-chairman, analyzed Eisenhower's presidency in stark terms: "The solvency and sovereignty of the United States are threatened by the growing centralization of socialistic despotism."[10] As the 1956 campaign season approached, a right-wing rallying cry came from an unlikely source: T. Coleman Andrews. A former Democrat who bolted to support Eisenhower in 1952, Andrews served as Ike's IRS commissioner from 1953 through 1955; ironically, he was the man responsible for denying For

America's tax exemption. He then returned to the private sector, where he worked as the board chairman for American Fidelity and Casualty Company. After resigning his post as the country's primary taxman, Andrews published a scathing anti-taxation screed in the *Washington Post*. Andrews did not have a change of heart—he equivocated that no one bothered to ask his opinion on taxation during his IRS stint. Now, Andrews described taxation as an "intolerable threat to the unfettered freedom of enterprise," "legalized confiscation," and a Marxist plot to "bring capitalism to its knees." Progressive taxation was anti–middle class, he claimed, and any "advocate of statism" was "either a dupe or, at heart, a dictator." Andrews foreshadowed the language of future tax-reductionists, calling the tax code "bewildering, confusing, and frustrating." Reflecting the ideals of the business conservative movement, especially Willis Stone's critiques, Andrews excoriated "the government's engagement in business activities that compete with private enterprise." As with many right-wing businessmen, Andrews's anti-tax agenda doubled as a medium for his own economic self-interest. Nevertheless, Andrews warned, "Time's a-wasting, and the enemies of the way of life that we cherish rejoice as we are obligingly led closer and closer to national suicide."[11]

Suddenly Andrews's name was on the lips of ultraconservatives around the country. In *American Progress* Willis Stone crowed that Andrews had "joined the resistance" against "the piracy we call income taxes" and the "evil of bureaucratic competition with private enterprise."[12] Andrews's rapid ascent in right-wing circles sparked rumblings of a new challenge to the liberal order. In mid-August, Charles Edison, the former Democratic governor of New Jersey, threw together a conference to convince Andrews to run as a third-party candidate in 1956. States' rights advocates from around the country flocked to meet with Andrews. Manion went with For America's national director Bonner Fellers, a former Brigadier General and Republican who defected from the RNC after Eisenhower's nomination. Also present were John U. Barr and Zack R. Cecil. Barr was a New Orleans industrialist and chairman of the Federation for Constitutional Government (a "coordinating body for the pro-segragation [sic] citizens councils in 11 southern states"), while Cecil directed the monetary research division of the libertarian American Economic Foundation.[13] Frank Chodorov, author of *The Income Tax—Root of All Evil*, lent his libertarian heft to the cause. The meeting's ideological heterodoxy illustrated the intertwining of southern segregationism, free-market theories, noninterventionist philosophies, reactionary traditionalism, and conspiratorial anti-communism.[14]

For America played a key role in the movement to draft Andrews. Manion served as the coalition's spokesman, remarking, "Andrews would give millions of Americans a chance to vote against socialism, to which both the Democratic and Republican parties have now officially surrendered." For America devoted increased attention to tax policy, the issue that made Andrews a star. Manion referred to the income tax as "the root cause of this evil," "confiscatory," "class-conscious," and "discriminatory."[15] Dan Smoot, For America's other co-chairman, said his organization supported Andrews because he was the "foremost enemy of our iniquitous Federal income tax laws."[16] Andrews's running mate, Thomas Werdel, was a darling of states' rights advocates because he had run against Earl Warren in the 1952 California gubernatorial primary. For America produced pamphlets lambasting the two-party system. "Remember!" urged one pamphlet. "When you vote for the lesser of two evils you are still voting for evil!"[17] Manion proposed to "draft" Andrews by putting independent electors on individual state ballots—electors who could have voted for Andrews if no other candidate won a majority—which wooed Andrews into giving For America's proposal "serious consideration."[18]

However, For America was not the only group eyeing Andrews as a potential third-party challenger. In late August, the Constitution Party held its national convention in Fort Worth, Texas. Rather than selecting a candidate—in many states the date had already passed to put a candidate on official ballots—the seventy-five delegates representing seventeen states recommended that state-level organizations "draft" Andrews as the candidate. Neither Andrews nor Werdel attended the convention, foreshadowing that the third-party movement would be led by grassroots activists rather than a centralized campaign. In fact, Andrews admitted that he could not devote time to a presidential contest. Nevertheless, the Constitution Party planned a mid-September National States' Rights Conference in Memphis, hoping to unify the ultraconservative movement under a permanent third-party banner. Robert Bent Taft, a Chicago industrialist and cousin of the late senator Robert A. Taft, and Marion R. Cleveland, the director of the Independent Elector Plan association, pledged to attend on behalf of the Illinois States' Rights Party. The leadership of For America and the Federation for Constitutional Government also answered the call. The man coordinating this broad far-right alliance was the Constitution Party's executive secretary, Kent Courtney.[19]

Courtney used the 1956 election as a launch pad for his extensive career in far-right activism. Born in St. Paul on October 23, 1918, Kent was raised in a conservative, Catholic household by Joseph Frank Courtney, a production engineer, and artist Zella Edana Smith. The Courtneys moved to New Orleans during Kent's childhood, and the Big Easy later served as his home and activist headquarters. A young Courtney joined the U.S. Navy as an aviator on September 12, 1941, but was honorably discharged less than a year later on August 19, 1942. Archival documents do not reveal the reason behind Courtney's abrupt discharge, but he continued to work with the U.S. military by transporting troops overseas as a pilot for Pan American Airways. Afterward he attended the University of Idaho and Tulane University, receiving a business degree from the latter in 1950.[20]

Courtney's formative years fostered his ultraconservative zeal. His radicalization started with positions in the American Legion, the Chamber of Commerce, and the New Orleans Citizens' Council. While working as the counter subversive chairman for the New Orleans area American Legion, Courtney honed his right-wing rhetoric. He also spent two years as the membership director for the New Orleans Chamber of Commerce, where he gained valuable marketing experience by promoting the organization's business and civic affairs. Kent married Phoebe Green Courtney and the pair started a self-publishing business in 1954 that evolved into the foundation for their activism. Phoebe sharpened Kent's writing, often serving as the editor of the duo's newspaper, *Free Men Speak*. She reminded contemporaries of fire-breathing women such as Elizabeth Dilling; Kent dubbed Phoebe the "tigress of the Right."[21] Phoebe accomplished a great deal behind the scenes as a writer and editor while Kent endeavored as the organization's primary spokesperson.[22]

Kent Courtney's political philosophies ticked all of the ultraconservative boxes. He viewed the civil rights movement as a communist usurpation of property rights and called for an unfettered free market, the nullification of union power, and severe spending cuts. He opposed federal taxation and became the Louisiana state chairman in Stone's organization. "You have no moral right to pay taxes which support the hundreds of government activities which are in direct competition with private enterprise," Courtney wrote in a *Los Angeles Times* letter to the editor, concluding, "In effect they are buying you off with your own money."[23] Not only did Courtney view taxation as a moral issue, he equated liberal economic platforms with communist planning. "It matters very little if . . . [Franklin] Roosevelt or Eisenhower is a Communist or not," Courtney proclaimed. "What does matter is that they have advanced the Communist cause and American Liberals, by participating in the advance of the cause of Communism are unwitting dupes of the International Communist Conspiracy."[24] The combination of anti-communist conspiracies, states' rights segregationism, and fiscal conservatism placed Courtney well within the ultraconservative vanguard. Phoebe proved just as radical as Kent, but the Courtneys avoided anti-Semitism and violent rhetoric out of a concern for respectability.[25]

Kent's far-right philosophies and lack of faith in the two major parties catalyzed his political activism, starting with the Constitution Party's 1956 campaign. Throughout his life Courtney identified as a political outsider, oscillating between third-party activism and supporting right-wingers in both major parties. He feared the American republic would "disappear into some sort of One-World Government" without the emergence of a truly conservative party.[26] However, Courtney's call to create a permanent third party, not just an ephemeral election-year challenge, revealed a strategic fault line within the ultraconservative movement. Some activists, like Courtney, believed that political change would happen only by forming a brand-new party of conservative purists. On the other hand, leaders like Manion hedged against forming a permanent alternative party. Manion believed his independent electors initiative could form a conservative firewall while obviating any sticky third-party affiliations. William F. Buckley Jr., editor and founder of *National Review*, supported Manion's gambit, emphasizing that the independent elector strategy might enable conservatives to "defeat [the] international Socialism which has captured both political parties."[27]

This strategic disagreement—of whether to form an official third party or to work within the traditional two-party channels—underscored the larger debate over party politics dividing the ultraconservative movement. The debate pitted political pragmatism against ideological purity. The goal was to sunder the liberal two-party duopoly and carve out a right-wing party. One strategy involved a pragmatic, gradualist approach, building a conservative movement within, and then eventually taking over, one of the major parties. On the other hand, far-right puritans like Courtney obsessed over third-party action—they had no interest in reforming one of the existing parties because it required a longer timeline and necessitated working with moderates. During the late 1950s, ultraconservatism crossed party lines, which made calls for a cross-party ideological alliance, a conservative third party, seem reasonable. As liberalism increasingly dominated the Democratic Party and reduced southern conservatives to a rump faction, this idea seemed even more plausible. However, the Republican Party provided fertile soil for conservatives, and far-right activists eventually came to believe that infiltrating the GOP provided the best avenue for creating a conservative party. This protracted debate played out over the next couple of decades as ultraconservatives vacillated between forming third parties and collaborating with the Republicans.

Courtney hoped his National States' Rights Conference would convince other activists to join his third-party crusade and, thus, unify the ultraconservative movement. In mid-September, over 300 delegates representing 25 states, plus around 150 spectators, most of whom were die-hard states' rightists, traveled to Memphis. Conference leaders believed the gathering evinced a thriving "national conservative movement" and crafted a platform featuring familiar right-wing demands such as limiting federal power, eliminating the Sixteenth Amendment, restraining presidential power through the Bricker Amendment, restricting the Supreme Court to "only its constitutional duties," and urging Congress to "repeal all illegal, anti-states rights acts enacted by the Supreme Court under the guise of judicial decisions."[28] As the last two planks indicated, the platform veiled the attendees' anti–civil rights impulses behind the mask of states' rights and strict constitutionalism. Neither Andrews nor Werdel attended the conference, but both agreed to be placed on state ballots where possible. The meeting appeared to portend a viable third-party movement and the issue was put up to a vote, but Courtney's dream of a permanent conservative coalition crashed against the same partisan rocks that stymied the Dixiecrats in 1948. According to *New York Times* writer John N. Popham, numerous far-right leaders worried that a permanent third party "would constitute a barrier for independent electors in southern states where voters traditionally adhere to the Democratic Party and usually frown on giving support to any other group with a party label."[29] Conference leaders voted down Courtney's third-party ambitions. Defeated, Courtney settled for promoting Andrews in 1956, but he never abandoned his dream of forming a permanent conservative third party.

The 1956 election marked the first presidential contest since the development of a national right-wing media sphere, headlined by Buckley's *National Review*. In its early days, *National Review* overlapped significantly with the ultraconservative movement. Robert Welch purchased $2,000 of privately issued stock to aid the inchoate magazine. Buckley, the periodical's intellectual doyen, promised Welch that *National Review* would provide a medium for conservatism's "desperately isolated voices."[30] On the other hand, John Fischer of *Harper's* denounced *National Review* as "an organ, not of conservatism, but of radicalism," the readership of which formed "the hard core of many religious, nationalist and revolutionary movements."[31] Fischer's words seem hyperbolic, but in its infancy *National Review* reflected, or at least pandered to, the more radical elements of the conservative movement. Buckley opposed Eisenhower's reelection and declared the GOP platform "essentially one of measured socialism," which he admitted was preferable to the unmeasured version proffered by the Democrats.[32] Buckley's socialism-in-both-parties rhetoric bore a strong resemblance to the far right's conspiratorial language; however, the *National Review* founder took a moderate position by not endorsing Andrews's ticket, setting himself up as a future right-wing gatekeeper and translator. By and large, conservatives had to forge their own path outside of the political mainstream in 1956.

The movement to draft an alternative ticket did not gain steam until October, far too late to make any discernable impact on the upcoming election; however, the National Committee for Andrews-Werdel brought together a coterie of hard-line right-wingers. Manion, Smoot, Fellers, and J. Evetts Haley all served on the committee, illustrating For America's centrality within the ultraconservative network. In fact, For America housed the Andrews-Werdel headquarters in Washington, D.C., and acted as the ticket's public relations firm. Vivien Kellems, the leader of the anti-tax Liberty Belles, and General George E. Stratemeyer, the McCarthy-supporting chairman of the "Committee for Ten Million Americans," also joined the National Committee. Augereau Gray (A. G.) Heinsohn—the APF Tennessee state chairman, For America committeeman, future Birch member, and owner of Spindale Textile Mills—connected the Andrews campaign to Willis Stone's anti-tax movement. Other notable members included retired New York broker Robert M. Harriss, former Democratic congressman Samuel B. Pettengill, and Ruth McCormick Tankersley, the former editor of the *Washington Times Herald* and niece of the late Colonel McCormick. Notably, Courtney did not hold a position on the National Committee. Courtney's hard-line third-party demands rendered him an outcast, for the moment, highlighting the ultraconservative movement's strategic and ideological fault lines.[33]

Less than one month before the election, the official National States' Rights Party convention took place in Richmond, Virginia. Andrews took the Mosque auditorium's stage to a cacophony of 2,200 rabid supporters, and his diatribe did not disappoint. "Yes, my friends," intoned the 57-year-old former Democrat, "the income tax has been the bonanza that has financed every boondoggling usurpation of the rights of States and every something-for-nothing fraud against the people that the perverted mind of the New Dealers, Fair Dealers and raw dealers have conceived and foisted upon us since we started down the road to Socialistic ruin in 1933." Andrews bellowed that both major parties had "converged onto a common highway to one-doctrine, one-party dictatorship under which, as in Russia and her satellite countries, the people are permitted only a choice of men, never a choice of political philosophies."[34] Appealing to his southern audience, Andrews condemned Supreme Court chief justice Earl Warren as an "integrationist" who had usurped state control over public schooling. During the proceedings, an 80-year-old widow even serenaded the audience with an original states' rights hymn:

> Every star with equal light . . . Not one State a satellite
> O Lord from rash dictator's might . . . Defend our Statehood's glory.
>
> Let no thoughtless court decree . . . What our way of life shall be
> O keep us safe from tyranny . . . And all who would divide us.

Unsurprisingly, Andrews's overt states' rights appeal struck a chord in the old Confederacy. By late September the Andrews-Werdel ticket had made it onto the ballot in eight former Confederate states and fourteen states overall: Arkansas, Alabama, Connecticut, Iowa, Kentucky, Louisiana, Mississippi, New Jersey, New Mexico, South Carolina, Tennessee, Texas, Virginia, and Wisconsin. Numerous other states had a slate of independent electors who could have chosen Andrews in the unlikely absence of a clear winner. In theory, Andrews's strategy was to siphon enough electoral votes to throw the election to the House of Representatives. However, the National Committee for Andrews-Werdel knew this was a pipe dream, so they portrayed the Andrews movement as a protest vehicle against the two major parties. Rather than turning into a permanent third party, Andrews's ticket became an experiment to gauge the strength of ultraconservatism with an eye toward 1960.[35]

On Election Day, the Andrews-Werdel ticket encountered numerous difficulties. Ballot naming conventions reflected the slapdash nature of the far right's third-party effort. Andrews's party, officially called the Independent States' Rights Party, appeared under a variety of names, including the States Rights Party, the Constitution Party, For America, the Conservative Party, and the New Party. Even the "States' Rights Party" ticket was not identical on every state ballot. In South Carolina and Mississippi, the States' Rights ticket featured a pair of southerners aligned with the Democratic Party's Dixiecrat wing, Virginia senator Harry F. Byrd and Mississippi congressman John Bell Williams. In Kentucky, Byrd was listed under the States' Rights banner alongside Senator William E. Jenner, an Indiana Republican. Additionally, some states did not provide a full count of third-party votes. In Arkansas, for example, the Andrews-Werdel ticket received an estimated 5,000 votes, but numerous counties failed to include the ticket in their final tallies, so the actual total remained a mystery. Even though Andrews's campaign had zero chance of winning, these technical difficulties further diluted the power of Andrews's third-party protest.[36]

Eisenhower skated to a blowout landslide in 1956. The two major parties accrued over 60 million votes, with Eisenhower netting over 35 million votes to Democrat Adlai Stevenson's 26 million. The Andrews-Werdel ticket earned a paltry 111,178 votes, with four old Confederate states, Texas, Tennessee, Louisiana, and Virginia, tallying the most votes. The party notched zero electoral votes. But the national humiliation did not diminish ultraconservative ambitions. On the contrary, the defeat galvanized the far right's resolve to challenge Eisenhower's Modern Republicanism and the liberal consensus. Andrews remained defiant. "If we were an old established party, I would feel discouraged but we are just starting," he asserted. "We are here to stay."[37]

The 1956 election revealed an ultraconservatism in flux. One year earlier, the historian Richard Hofstadter wrote, "Third parties are like bees; once they have stung, they die," the general assumption being that a successful third-party movement will be co-opted by a major party.[38] However, the Independent States' Rights Party did not earn enough votes to sting either side in the election; 100,000 ballots were not going to threaten the behemoths. Yet, Andrews's candidacy left a substantial legacy. It forced right-wingers to wrangle with strategic choices: whether to pursue a permanent third party or stage a coup within an existing major party. Most importantly, Andrews's campaign marked the first time ultraconservatives united under one banner. It served as a rallying point and harbinger of further far-right action. George Peck, the distribution point man for Stone's *American Progress*, spoke for many ultraconservatives who viewed the grassroots fervor surrounding Andrews's candidacy as a predictor of future success: "There are millions of conservatives who for the past five national elections have voted for the lesser of two evils—or did not vote at all. In 1960 they'll find a haven of refuge in the States Rights Party."[39] The 1948 Dixiecrats provided a regional spark, but Andrews's candidacy solidified a national web connecting a heretofore disparate far-right patchwork.

It was no coincidence that ultraconservatives rallied around states' rights ideologies at the exact moment the civil rights movement blossomed into a national phenomenon. Numerous events during Eisenhower's presidency galvanized civil rights activism and illuminated the deep-seated racism in southern states. In the summer of 1955, 14-year-old Emmett Till was kidnapped and brutally murdered in Mississippi for allegedly offending a white woman. Later that same year, Rosa Parks was arrested in Montgomery, Alabama, for violating a city segregation ordinance, initiating the Montgomery Bus Boycott and the meteoric rise of Martin Luther King Jr. Public schools in a post-*Brown* world became the brightest flash points. In early 1956, Autherine Lucy broke the color line by enrolling in the University of Alabama, but rioting whites, including Alabama Klansmen, screaming "Kill her!" convinced the school's leadership to expel Lucy and restore segregation. The very next year a high-profile standoff occurred in Arkansas when nine black teenagers enrolled in the all-white Little Rock Central High School. Arkansas governor Orval Faubus used the National Guard to keep them out while angry white mobs stalked the streets. Eisenhower sent in the military, under the leadership of future far-right firebrand Edwin Walker, to integrate the school by force. The global Cold War put these events under a microscope, paving the way for slow, incremental civil rights successes.[40]

Right-wing outrage smoldered over federal intervention. Congressman Williams adopted the rhetoric of the Confederacy's "Lost Cause," arguing that favorable civil rights laws and court decisions constituted "the most serious constitutional crisis . . . since the war for southern independence."[41] Overt racism and distrust of civil rights and federal action was not limited to the South or the Democratic Party. Buckley wrote a *National Review* column admitting his belief that the "White community" should dominate southern culture because it was the "advanced race."[42] Congressman Noah M. Mason, an Illinois Republican, lambasted Eisenhower for disregarding states' rights. "I think he not only exceeded his authority but went entirely contrary to the constitution of the United States," Mason argued on a Citizens' Council radio show.[43] However, the South, ever the poster child of segregation and racism, lobbied the hardest against civil rights. Over one hundred congressmen, including Martin Dies Jr. of Texas, signed the "Southern Manifesto," a bold defense of segregation and states' rights penned by senators Strom Thurmond and Richard Russell. Many reactionaries, especially those from the South, viewed Eisenhower's actions, and the civil rights movement more broadly, as proof of liberalism's red-tinted tyranny. In the wake of Little Rock, radical agrarian Richard M. Weaver wrote in the pages of *National Review*, "Integration is Communization."[44] Southern politicians and far-right activists developed "massive resistance" to civil rights by harmonizing the conspiratorial anti-communism of the Cold War with states' rights philosophies.[45]

The *Brown* decision, combined with Cold War anti-communism and lingering white supremacy, produced outbursts of reactionary violence, notably from the specter of the Old South, the Ku Klux Klan. After its zenith in the 1920s, the Klan experienced lean years during the Great Depression and held marginal influence during World War II through collaborative efforts with extremist groups such as the German-American Bund. The Klan nevertheless carried its extensive list of hatreds into the Cold War—a list that included blacks, Catholics, Jews, unionists, moral trespassers, and "radicals" of all stripes—and when the push for racial equality stoked a southern backlash, the Klan stood ready to capitalize. Atlanta-based obstetrician Samuel Green organized the first Stone Mountain cross burning of the Cold War era in October of 1946. Green hoped to restore the "Invisible Empire" to its 1920s glory days, and in some ways he succeeded: the Klan intimidated black voters and helped segregationist Eugene Talmadge win the Georgia governorship. However, pressure from federal, state, and local governments impeded his efforts. In 1947, the Klan found itself next to the Communist Party on the Attorney General's list of subversive organizations, and numerous states passed anti-mask laws and prohibited cross burnings. When Green unexpectedly passed away in 1949, the delicate centralized structure of the Klan splintered. Numerous competing Klans popped up throughout the South, including the Knights of the Ku Klux Klan (or the U.S. Klan) in Georgia, North Carolina's United Klans of America, and Alabama's Ku Klux Klan of the Confederacy.[46]

Despite the factionalism, the Klan remained active, and violent. Groups of hooded Klansmen went on "night rides," carrying out harassment, threats, floggings, and even murders. At least 145 Klan-inspired bombings took place throughout the South between 1956 and 1963, many of which targeted civil rights leadership. Martin Luther King Jr. and Fred L. Shuttlesworth, the co-founders of the Southern Christian Leadership Conference, both survived bombings at the hands of local Klansmen in 1956. Asa Earl "Ace" Carter's Klan of the Confederacy proved particularly violent, gaining national notoriety when seven Klansmen stormed a Birmingham stage and assaulted popular black singer Nat King Cole. The Klan also targeted white integrationists, union leaders, Jews, and black homeowners in white neighborhoods—anyone deemed a threat to the South's racial, religious, and social tradition. Unlike the 1920s, however, the Klan struggled to gain respectability during the Cold War, a phenomenon explained by the nation's growing discomfort with the group's wanton violence. The largest group, the U.S. Klan, led by Eldon Edwards, credibly claimed between 12,000 and 15,000 followers while other Klans garnered only a few thousand members. The Klan flourished in states where white citizens viewed their state government as insufficiently dedicated to resisting racial integration, such as North Carolina, but violence generally relegated the organization to the political fringe.[47]

Instead of risking credibility by joining the Klan, many of the South's more "respectable" citizens formed a new organization to maintain white supremacy: the Citizens' Council. The original Citizens' Council formed in the summer of 1954 in Indianola, Mississippi. The seat of rural Sunflower County, Indianola was a sleepy town of roughly 5,000 nestled along the banks of a thin tendril of the Mississippi Delta. The fact that arch-segregationist Senator James O. Eastland maintained his vast cotton plantation in Indianola betrayed the region's conservative bent. Voter suppression was rampant. Black citizens comprised a majority of Sunflower County's population but only 0.03 percent of its registered voters. After the *Brown* decision threatened seg-regationist tradition, a cadre of Indianola's civic and economic elite, including the town's mayor and city attorney, founded the first Citizens' Council. The group had been inspired by Mississippi Circuit Court judge Tom P. Brady's speech-turned-booklet titled *Black Monday*. Rife with white supremacist and anti-statist language, Brady's book blared, "Segregation or Amalgamation . . . America has its Choice."[48] "Black Monday" became a pejorative for the *Brown* decision, and Brady's book served as a populist rallying cry for white south-erners. Indianola lit the torch, and Citizens' Councils started spreading across Dixieland like wildfire.[49]

The Citizens' Council became the most powerful, well-known group in a constellation of "protective societies" dedicated to preserving states' rights and white supremacy. Roughly 90 Citizens' Councils and council-affiliated groups dotted the South, a network which credibly claimed over a quarter of a million members by 1956. The organization had a much more main-stream footprint than Klan. Leadership often stemmed from the South's eco-nomic and social elite, but the councils employed grassroots populism to appeal to working-class whites. Though at first excluded from membership, white women joined the Citizens' Council in droves, energizing the council by recruiting, organizing, and serving in leadership positions. The Citizens' Council blanketed the South with segregationist propaganda, including a radio show, weekly telecasts, newspapers, pamphlets, reprinted speeches, and broadsides. Publications ranged from lowest-common-denominator racist screeds to more sophisticated appeals to southern whites who were wary of publicly supporting "massive resistance." Council messaging, particularly the more refined variety, often stretched beyond Dixieland's borders and landed in the working-class communities of the Midwest and Northeast.[50]

Distancing the council from extremists was critical to the organization's success. Brady urged the Indianola Citizens' Council to "pitch our battle on a high plane" and avoid the "demagogue, the renegade, the lawless and the violent."[51] The Citizens' Council rejected Klan-style terror, instead using economic sanctions to maintain racial segregation. The councils supported right-wing candidates, stymied civil rights progress, and suppressed dissenting opinions, even from fellow white southerners. Council activity often intertwined with state and local power structures. Famous segregationists, such as Georgia governor Eugene Talmadge and Senator Eastland, frequented council gatherings as invited speakers, lending the organization a degree of legitimacy. However, many contemporary critics saw little difference between the Citizens' Council and extremist groups such as the Ku Klux Klan. Writers derided the council as a "white-collar Klan," an "uptown Klan," and a "country club Klan." At times the line demarcating the council from the extreme right blurred when individual council members were linked to violent terrorism, the most famous example of which was the trial and acquittal of Byron De La Beckwith for the assassination of civil rights activist Medgar Evers. Nevertheless, despite the organization's acidic racism, open defiance of federal mandates, and links to right-wing extremism, the Citizens' Council provided a respectable alternative to the Klan's night-riding vigilantes.[52]

The council's complicated, overlapping relationship with extremism and respectability was a microcosm of the far right's political reality. Indeed, the Citizens' Council constituted a thick branch of the ultraconservative family tree, and a great deal of connectivity existed between the council and other far-right organizations. Kent Courtney joined the New Orleans Citizens' Council, while Texas council members supported J. Evetts Haley's gubernatorial bid in 1956. In multiple states the Citizens' Council formulated independent elector initiatives similar to the Texas Regulars revolt and Andrews's campaign to try and deadlock elections. Even though visceral racism constituted the "nucleus" of Citizens' Council thought, the councils shared the far right's philosophical framework of anti-communism and anti-statism. Medford Evans—a southern journalist, future John Birch Society member, and father to *National Review*'s M. Stanton Evans—roared in the council's publication, *The Citizen*: "Forced Integration is Communism in Action."[53] The Citizens'

Council portrayed integrated union campaigns as efforts to empower blacks and communists. Anti-communism never eclipsed the council's focus on defending racial segregation, but it provided a strategy for building grassroots coalitions and a link to the broader conservative movement.[54]

Ultraconservative leaders eagerly defended the social substructure of white supremacy, states' rights, and anti-communism. Billy James Hargis employed a biblical justification for segregation and saw interracial relationships ("mongrelization," according to Hargis) as a communist plot to "build a world race, by gradually wearing down the resistance between the races."[55] Courtney accused both political parties of trying to "establish tyrannical rule over the sovereign states."[56] Haley and For America derided Eisenhower's forceful integration of Little Rock Central High as "one of the worst depravities of political history" because it reduced "the once sovereign states to iron-curtain satellites."[57] Stone, a California radical, did not wield the racist, segregationist language of his southern brethren, but he employed the language of states' rights and contorted civil rights philosophies into diatribes against federal overreach. In the wake of the *Brown* decision, for example, Stone argued that his proposed amendment would "prevent this new invasion of the states."[58] Former America First leader John T. Flynn wrote the only article in Stone's *American Progress* to mention "civil rights" in the title—"What About This Civil Right?"—in which he argued a citizen should possess "the great civil right to spend his own money."[59] Refusing to acknowledge the reality of racism and discrimination, ultraconservatives instead refracted rights-based rhetoric onto the language of states' rights, property rights, free markets, and societal traditionalism.[60]

J. Evetts Haley joined this "massive resistance" by running an ill-fated campaign for Texas governor in 1956. If elected, Haley promised to deploy the Texas Rangers to stop the federal government from enforcing the *Brown* decision in Texas. He peppered his segregationist rhetoric with anti-communist conspiracies: "I am for [the use of interposition] to stop this mixing, by coercion and immoral force, of white and Negro children in public schools, with its consequent destruction of our race and our way of life."[61] Letters from Haley's supporters revealed anxieties about "the destruction of the white race," "red-tinged judicial tyranny," and "the conspiracy to change our form of gov't."[62] Smoot, a fellow Texan, supported Haley's crusade: "For years conservatives have belly-ached—with just cause—that we didn't have a real choice to vote for. In Texas this year we do have a choice—and I hope that every Texan who calls himself a conservative will work for J. Evetts Haley."[63] Haley ultimately placed fourth in the Democratic primary; W. Lee "Pappy"

O'Daniel, the former senator, governor, and leader of the Texas Regulars, split the segregationist vote with Haley. Moderate Democrat Price Daniel won the ensuing runoff and general election with ease. Nevertheless, Haley's campaign exemplified how "massive resistance" served as a gateway for ultraconservative activism and fueled the "Southern Red Scare," wherein southerners sought to stymie the push for racial equality by associating the civil rights movement with communism.[64]

Following the 1956 election, Haley poured his energy into For America and its state affiliate, Texans For America (TFA). After leading the third-party charge in 1956, For America emerged as a central player in the far-right movement. The organization received $73,000 during the election from around 7,000 individual contributors, and by the end of 1956 For America had 33,000 members and chapters in all fifty states. Manion described For America's support in the South as "more vehement than anywhere else in the nation," a result of the group's dedication to states' rights and social traditionalism.[65] In fact, Manion thought the South's growing discontent was the key to unlocking a conservative Republican Party in the future. The 1956 election marked For America's transition into an action group hell-bent on reorienting national politics, but the organization's influence extended well beyond the confines of presidential contests. Similar to far-right predecessors such as the Jeffersonian Democrats, For America's state chapters marshaled the ultraconservative vanguard at the ground level, and (again like the Jeffersonians) the Lone Star State boasted one of the most active branches.[66]

Haley joined For America prior to his gubernatorial campaign—he helped establish TFA in 1954 and served as the state chairman—but he accelerated his efforts after losing the primary. Haley infused TFA with his combination of states' rights, conspiratorial anti-communism, and anti-statist libertarianism. Speaking before the American National Cattlemen's Association, Haley inverted Franklin Roosevelt's pledge to privilege economic security over economic freedom, arguing that "the communistic goal of material security, aided and abetted by public education, sometimes by the churches, and especially by the government, is taking the place of the adventurous appeal of liberty."[67] He stumped for "individual liberties and sound government," implying that liberals discarded both, and warned about the power of "socialists and communists . . . to divide and conquer."[68] Haley and TFA's primary objective was to promote far-right ideals with the intent of transforming one of the major political parties—the focus eventually became the GOP—into a bastion of conservatism.

Texans For America promoted its brand of far-right conservatism by blanketing the state with propaganda ranging from polemical educational materials and films to traveling speakers and radio/television programs. Most importantly, Haley established TFA's Committees of Correspondence, which were modeled after the Revolutionary-era committees of correspondence, wherein patriots would disseminate revolutionary propaganda and news throughout the colonies. The committee's mass-mailing campaigns represented the bulk of TFA's grassroots action in the Lone Star State. Haley argued that the "*concentration of firepower* on the *proper target* at the *right moment* will amplify, in geometric proportions, our strength and effectiveness."[69] He and Kara Hart, a fellow conspiracy theorist and chair of TFA's correspondence committees, recruited letter writers by surveying Texas newspapers for conservative editorials and letters to the editor. By late 1959, TFA had over 250 correspondence committee members. Many of the letter writers enlisted by Haley and Hart saw the specter of socialism around every corner, especially concerning federal economic regulations. The committees promoted conservative platforms through fearmongering, ranging from allegations of communist infiltration to diatribes against integration and increased taxation. For example, Haley derided Governor Daniel's plan to increase teachers' salaries as the "teacher tenure" bill and called it a clandestine scheme to increase taxes. TFA's committees followed Haley's lead, writing hundreds of letters criticizing the bill and urging Daniel to slash the budget instead. The debate over teacher salaries raged for two years, but Daniel's teacher pay bill passed in 1961 despite far-right acrimony. Nevertheless, the Committees of Correspondence helped build the grassroots coalition that Haley envisioned would transform conservatism in Texas by pressuring politicians to address right-wing concerns. Furthermore, Haley's ability to cultivate a politically engaged constituency illustrated his gradual maturation as a far-right leader.[70]

In order to support the broader ultraconservative movement, Haley connected TFA with other far-right leaders and organizations. Texans For America teamed up with Hargis's Christian Crusade to fight the Forand Bill, formally titled the "Social Security Amendments of 1958," which tried to extend Social Security hospital insurance benefits to elderly citizens. Haley decried the Forand Bill as "communizing medical treatment," while Hargis prevaricated that "left-wingers" devised the legislation to implement "a fully socialized medical system in America."[71] Ultimately, the Forand Bill failed to pass the House Ways and Means Committee; Secretary of Health Arthur S. Flemming argued that the legislation failed to address Social Security's problems. Haley and TFA also accused Earl Warren of "usurping" power through civil rights decisions. A TFA petition demanding the impeachment of the entire Supreme Court contained around 12,000 signatures by January 1959. The signature count by no means indicated an ultraconservative mandate, but TFA's anti-Warren campaign provided a grassroots foundation for the Birch Society's future battle against the Supreme Court. Through these coordinated efforts, Haley bolstered the institutional connections within the ultraconservative network.[72]

Haley attempted to establish a similar relationship with the business community. Big business, especially the oil industry, played a crucial role in Texas politics, and Haley recognized that recruiting high-profile entrepreneurs would legitimize TFA as a mainstream conservative outlet. Haley told his constituents, "We cannot succeed without the support of business," citing "the deadly threat to free enterprise" as "an opportunity to enlist strong financial support."[73] Though Haley's ideologies intersected with the free-market ideals of the business conservative movement, TFA's financial statements revealed that the organization struggled for funding and often operated on a shoestring budget. TFA failed to obtain corporate backing and relied on small, individual donations, indicating that Haley's racially charged rhetoric might have disaffected commercial benefactors. In fact, Texas politics was experiencing an important transformation during the late 1950s as politicians softened their white-supremacist rhetoric. Southerners were alarmed by the rapidly changing racial mores of southern society, but, in general, Texans had greater tolerance for racial inclusion than the rest of the Deep South. Nevertheless, Haley tapped into an ultraconservative constituency that viewed liberalism as anathema to traditional sociopolitical norms, and TFA's mass letter-writing campaigns indicated an eagerness to amplify conservative demands through local activism and organizational networks. Ultimately, Haley and TFA galvanized grassroots right-wingers and established connections with other ultraconservative groups, underscoring the broader right-wing surge happening across the country.[74]

Out on the West Coast, Willis Stone's crusade to pass the "Proposed 23rd Amendment" continued to gain steam during the late 1950s. In 1957, Republican congressman Clare E. Hoffman of Michigan, a former America Firster with fascist sympathies, introduced a bill to repeal the Sixteenth Amendment. Stone quickly adapted Hoffman's idea to his own proposal. The final form of Stone's bill sought to retrench all government economic activity and strike down the Sixteenth Amendment. That same year, Congressman Ralph

Gwinn, a right-wing Republican from New York, submitted Stone's "Proposed 23rd Amendment" twice, once without a section about dismantling income taxes, and then again, just a few months later, with an updated section calling for the Sixteenth's repeal. Though Congress tabled both of Gwinn's proposals, the support of far-right congressmen helped Stone gain traction. The House Ways and Means Committee invited Stone to speak in 1958, where he argued that his amendment's economic alchemy would turn a massive debt into a surplus. Stone told the committee members, "Instead of the violent conflict between government and people regarding which shall own and operate the enterprises created by the people, we will have a government devoted to protecting our lives and properties."[75] Of course, Stone's proposal necessitated unwinding the lingering welfare state, an action he viewed as an appropriate "return to the basic concept which we all regard as truly American."[76] A mythologized free market, in other words. Three days after Stone's appearance before Ways and Means, Congressman Edgar Hiestand, a California Republican and future Birch Society member, put forth a bill to create a select committee to investigate the "scope of and justification for activities of the United States that compete with private enterprise."[77] Hiestand's language seemed to come straight from Stone's presentation.[78]

Stone's ideas percolated throughout Washington's right-wing circles. Later that summer, Congressman James B. Utt, an ultraconservative Republican from Orange County, California, appeared on Courtney's radio show. Utt had sailed into office during the Eisenhower electoral wave in 1952 and received an immediate appointment to the Ways and Means Committee—a rare privilege for a freshman congressman.[79] During the interview, Courtney quizzed Utt: "Are you familiar with Stone's proposed constitutional amendment?" "Yes, I am," Utt enthused. "I am a hundred percent in support of it."[80] One year after Stone appeared before the Ways and Means Committee, Utt introduced Stone's amendment as House Joint Resolution 23. Then, fifteen days after Utt's proposal, Hiestand submitted numerous bills to reduce capital gains taxes and lower taxes on business owners. Hiestand sent copies of the bills to Stone, who wrote an encouraging note back: "You are doing a great job in these efforts, and I hope they materialize."[81] The fact that Hiestand, Utt, and Gwinn advocated Stone's ideas illustrated that ultraconservative positions were gradually seeping into the GOP. Stone had become a confidant and ideological wellspring for the Republican Party's right-wing vanguard.[82]

The excitement surrounding Stone's amendment extended to the grass roots. In 1959, activists pushed resolutions in favor of the "Proposed 23rd

Amendment" through the state governments of Wyoming and Texas. They were joined one year later by successful resolutions in Nevada and Louisiana. *American Progress* served as APF's organizational nerve center and information clearinghouse, promoting state-level activism and providing in-depth coverage each time Stone's amendment passed a state legislature. For example, Ernest E. Anthony Jr., APF's Texas state chairman, wrote an ebullient editorial after Texas passed an affirmative resolution. Anthony lauded the efforts of State Representative Jerry Sadler, a segregationist southern Democrat, and grassroots activists, including Haley and Texans For America, for their role in spearheading the movement. Anthony regaled readers with stories of "telegrams, phone calls, letters, [and] cards from across the state flooding the Texas capital."[83] Reverend Gordon Winrod—an anti-Semitic extremist and son of radical preacher Gerald B. Winrod—also received praise from Anthony and Stone, highlighting the intersection of Protestant fundamentalism and political ultraconservatism. More propaganda appeared in *American Progress* as Stone's movement gained momentum, recounting the patriotic efforts of activists in early-adopter states.[84]

Stone leaned on his business acumen and marketing experience to build upon his movement's early success. Selling advertisements in *American Progress* kept the periodical afloat and provided an opportunity for business owners to contribute to the cause while simultaneously advertising to like-minded customers. To right-wing thinking, soliciting the support of conservative businessmen offered a powerful counter to liberal politicians and union leaders. "Frankly," Hiestand wrote to Stone, "we can't ever recover the control of Congress unless we adopt and develop more hard business-like political management techniques."[85] Stone targeted the economic self-interest and libertarian lean of right-wing business owners; he boasted that *American Progress* was "a highly effective media for advertisers seeking to preserve American ideals as well as promote their products and services." Advertising in *American Progress*, Stone declared, proved that patron companies were "in favor of FREE ENTERPRISE."[86] Stone sold advertisements—ranging from $50 for partial-page to $500 for back-cover ads—to a wide range of firms, and his relationship with business owners produced a cozy environment where commercial and editorial interests intertwined. In short, ads often doubled as right-wing propaganda.[87]

Owners of small and medium-sized businesses lined up to purchase space in *American Progress*, a periodical that reflected their libertarian values. One alarmist advertisement, paid for by businessman and future Birch Society councilman F. Gano Chance, castigated liberalism as a grand plot to destroy capitalism. "This is a process that must be stopped, for it can only destroy our free, competitive private enterprise system," blared Chance's full-page advertisement. "And it must be stopped soon, for anyone who has watched the tidal wave of governmental control over private business knows—IT IS LATER THAN YOU THINK!"[88] Other ads professed support for Stone's amendment. Joseph S. Kimmel Sr., President of Republic Electric Company, disguised a full-page advertisement as an open letter to taxpayers. "The worst self-inflicted thing that ever happened to the American people was the adoption of the 16th Amendment," read Kimmel's letter.[89] Such propagandistic messaging laid bare any notion of ideological impartiality, but to Stone that was the whole point: advertisements funded *American Progress*, amplified its right-wing philosophies, and burnished the relationships between business interests and far-right activists.

Broadcasting ideological values through advertisements highlighted the collision between sociopolitical activism and American consumer culture. Stone's advertising ethos mirrored that of the Advertising Council, a conglomerate of ad agencies and corporations that promoted free-market capitalism and fretted about Americans turning into "pawns of a master state."[90] Politically charged ads appeared throughout right-wing publications, from Buckley's *National Review* to Hargis's *Christian Crusade*. Ads in *National Review* for industrial companies such as Kennametal—owned by Philip McKenna, an *American Progress* advertiser who doubled as an APF state chairman—and Timken Roller Bearing Company featured conservative talking points about returning to the gold standard and reducing taxes. Stone also provided space, free of charge, for *National Review* ads. Right-wing periodicals cultivated an incestuous community—they advertised each other's magazines, received funding from the same sources, and bore similar ideological overtones, all of which revealed a significant overlap between mainstream conservative outlets and far-right publications. Furthermore, the corporate support for Stone's crusade indicated that businessmen identified more with Stone's "colorblind" libertarianism than Haley's fire-breathing segregationism.[91]

The emphasis on advertising facilitated *American Progress*'s slow, fitful growth. By 1957 each issue raked in roughly $2,000, keeping annual subscriptions at the low cost of three dollars and facilitating the introduction of bicolor gloss covers by the end of the year. The gradual aesthetic improvements signified the maturation of Stone's movement. In 1959 Stone sent only 8,000 copies of *American Progress* to a select few states: Washington,

Massachusetts, Texas, Illinois, Wyoming, California, and Oregon. By the early 1960s, however, Stone and APF distributed over 16,000 copies of *American Progress* throughout twenty-eight states in all regions of the country. Local social organizations, such as the Kiwanis Club in Glendale, California, helped APF hand out copies of *American Progress* (the Glendale Kiwanis Club dissembled that it was taking not a political stance, but rather "an active interest in the principles upon which the conduct of government depends").[92] Stone claimed that subscribers circulated the magazine to friends and colleagues, estimating that over 50,000 "business, labor, civic, professional, and industrial leaders of the 48 sovereign states" read *American Progress*.[93] Even if Stone exaggerated the numbers, *American Progress*, and APF by extension, nevertheless served as a binding agent, intertwining the philosophies and actions of right-wing businesspeople, activists, and institutions.[94]

Not all of Stone's organizational maneuvering went according to plan, however. Stone attempted to expand the anti-tax movement in 1957 by merging APF with another Los Angeles–based libertarian organization, the Organization to Repeal Federal Income Taxes (ORFIT). He hoped the unification would create a well-organized anti-tax program in every state and strengthen the lines of communication between local activists. *American Progress* became the merger's de facto periodical, and Stone provided editorial space for ORFIT's leadership. The organizations created a Joint Operating Committee (JOC) to manage the merger, but the union was fraught from the beginning. Funding and membership were meddlesome problems; ORFIT and APF brought in only a few dozen members every month and operated on meager budgets, rarely carrying over more than a few hundred dollars a month. The turmoil escalated when Stone accused the Joint Committee of neglecting fundraising and charged JOC vice president and general manager Paul K. Morganthaler with shutting him out of the decision-making process. Stone believed the merger was sabotaging the central mission of promoting the "Proposed 23rd Amendment." The arguments over money and authority turned personal, and by 1958 Stone found himself ostracized as the merger imploded. In a private letter to F. Gano Chance, Stone claimed that he and the other APF board members had been ousted by a "willful few who grabbed control of the machinery."[95]

Though Stone lost access to APF's subscription lists, he retained ownership of *American Progress* and created a new organization, the National Committee for Economic Freedom (NCEF), to continue his anti-taxation crusade. Most APF state chairmen followed Stone to NCEF, and Stone recruited other key ultraconservative figures, such as Kent Courtney, to bolster the new organization's reputation. Courtney served as the national vice chairman and Louisiana state chairman while businessman Walter Knott—a longtime advertiser in *American Progress*, future Birch Society member, and owner of Knott's Berry Farm, a theme park featuring an idealized, right-wing version of the American frontier—worked as treasurer. By the end of the 1950s, Stone could boast that he led the preeminent anti-tax organization and that four states had adopted resolutions in favor of his amendment.[96]

As the decade drew to a close, the far right's disjointed patchwork was starting to resemble a coherent, interconnected web, but the ultraconservative movement still lacked a flagship organization. Robert Welch decided to create one. In late 1958, Welch summoned eleven fellow ultraconservatives to a mysterious meeting in Indianapolis. Welch's invitations provided no information about the gathering, but his guests were about to be treated to a two-day seminar on the growing communist threat in America. After the men settled in, Welch got to the heart of the issue: "Gentlemen, we are losing, rapidly losing, a cold war in which our freedom, our country, and our very existence are at stake."[97] On the first day, Welch spent seven hours detailing his conspiratorial theories while his guests took copious notes. The attendees included T. Coleman Andrews; industrialists Fred C. Koch, William J. Grede, Ernest G. Swigert, and Louis Ruthenberg; and anti-Semitic professor Revilo P. Oliver. Welch told them that conservatives needed to organize, to fight the existential threat of communism by adopting communist tactics.[98]

On the second day, Welch proposed the creation of the John Birch Society, a new far-right organization to lead the charge against the communist conspiracy. Named after a Christian evangelist whose death at the hands of Chinese communists made him the first casualty of the Cold War—according to Welch, at least—the John Birch Society promoted an apocalyptic vision of Christian conservatives under siege by atheistic communists. The time to organize was now, Welch informed his confidants, because "both internationally, and within the United States, the Communists are much further advanced and more deeply entrenched than is realized by even most of the serious students of the danger among the anti-Communists."[99] To Welch, the war against communism represented a civilizational crisis, and losing meant ushering in "long and feudal Dark Ages after we have been killed, our children have been enslaved, and all that we value has been destroyed."[100] Spurred into action, ten of the eleven attendees became the first Birch Society members, and nine, including Andrews, formed the organization's inaugural National

Council. Welch installed himself as the "Founder" atop an organizational hierarchy because, as he told his fellow conspirators, "Communist infiltrators could bog us down in interminable disagreements, schisms, and feuds."[101] He turned his meeting notes into the group's ideological blueprint and recruiting tool, *The Blue Book of the John Birch Society*, and the society soon became a far-right nexus, one that came to define the shape of the mid-twentieth century ultraconservative movement. [102]

Robert Henry Winborne Welch Jr. was born on December 1, 1899, to a landowning family in North Carolina, and during his formative years he developed the ideologies that shaped the John Birch Society. Welch grew up in a wealthy household. His parents, Robert and Lina Welch, hired seasonal farmhands, which afforded young Robert the opportunity to focus on education. A precocious youth, Welch excelled in academics. He finished high school by age twelve and then graduated from the University of North Carolina four years later at the age of sixteen. During World War I, Welch briefly attended the United States Naval Academy before transferring to Harvard Law School in 1919. Welch's time at Harvard coincided with the onset of the First Red Scare, which incubated his anti-communist, conspiratorial mindset. The federal government passed anti-sedition legislation and deported supposed radical immigrants while Welch attended classes in Cambridge. Accusations of communism punctuated the battles between labor and capital. One of Welch's Harvard professors, Felix Frankfurter, a future Supreme Court justice, sympathized with immigrants and labor unions. After enrolling in Frankfurter's class on labor law, Welch accused the professor of harboring Marxist sympathies. Welch's characterization of Frankfurter distorted reality. Frankfurter openly disavowed Bolshevik communism and instead adhered to the reformist mindset of the Progressive era. Regardless, Welch believed Frankfurter's (and the broader academy's) progressive tendencies suggested communist underpinnings. Welch's perception of Frankfurter highlighted his own Manichean worldview—a person was either a conservative, representing true American values, or a dangerous subversive with communist sympathies. The anti-communist, anti-intellectual anxieties Welch developed during the First Red Scare shaped his political philosophies for the rest of his life.[103]

Welch soon left Harvard to join the ranks of entrepreneurial Americans, which put him in contact with right-wing businessmen and nurtured his ultraconservatism. Welch had a briefly successful venture with the Oxford Candy Company before leaving in 1935 to work as a sales manager for his brother's company, the James O. Welch Company. Welch's enterprising nature led him into political activism; he joined the Boston Chamber of Commerce and the National Association of Manufacturers (NAM) during the 1930s and 1940s. The National Association of Manufacturers originally formed in the late nineteenth century to fight industrial labor unions, and during the 1930s it expanded its mission by attacking Rooseveltian liberalism. Through NAM, Welch joined the angry chorus of anti–New Deal industrialists and imbibed the group's message of free-market capitalism, managerial and property rights, and enmity toward organized labor. The presidential election of 1952, particularly Senator Robert Taft's primary defeat, convinced Welch that a vast conspiracy controlled the government, thereby preventing conservatives from gaining tangible political power.[104]

Anti-communism jaundiced Welch's entire worldview. Welch blamed liberalism for abetting communist infiltration and conflated liberal policies with the Soviet Union's state-dominated economy and political repression. He alleged that Woodrow Wilson and Franklin Roosevelt implemented a "Marxian program" through progressive income taxes, and argued that any expansion of the welfare state paved the way for an "all-powerful completely socialistic central government."[105] An FBI official aptly described Welch as a "disillusioned" "Republican of the extreme Right-Wing" who was "frustrated by the preponderance of Moderate Republicans in the present administration."[106] Welch's delusions occasionally surpassed even those of his fellow ultraconservatives. For example, not only did Welch believe Eisenhower intended to destroy the Republican Party's anti-communist impetus, he argued that "communist bosses" controlled Eisenhower because the president refused to break up or sell the Tennessee Valley Authority.[107]

Welch's conspiratorial anti-communism inflamed his antipathy toward civil rights. A native-born southerner, Welch resembled the white antebellum patricians who believed only they understood the realities of race relations. Instead of viewing the lingering impact of economic exploitation and segregation as the catalyst for civil rights activism, Welch held communists responsible for disturbing the South's "peaceful" race relations.[108] Communists intended "to stir up such bitterness between whites and blacks in the South that small flames of civil disorder would inevitably result," he declared.[109] Welch even referred to the civil rights movement as the "Negro Revolutionary Movement," which he believed was intent on setting up a "Negro Soviet Republic" in the South, even though the already minuscule number of black communists dwindled steadily during the Cold War.[110] The insistence that the push for racial equality was communist-inspired explained

Welch's adherence to states' rights ideologies and the intense support he garnered from white southerners.[111]

Welch also attributed a decline in social traditionalism to communist infiltration. During his youth Welch attended a fundamentalist Baptist church,
but he rejected the tenets of strict fundamentalism as an adult. Nevertheless,
Welch understood that his anti-communist movement needed the support
of conservative Christians. By depicting deceased missionary John Birch as
a martyr for conservatism and appropriating his name, Welch's organization
became a defender of Christian America. Welch argued that "family units
[were] the very bricks out of which a stable and happy society is built," illustrating an inchoate form of the anti-welfare, "family values" ideas that would
later dominate American conservatism.[112] Furthermore, he pushed an inclusive version of Christianity to broaden his appeal. Using a phrase coined by
poet Harry Kemp, Welch tried to unify religious conservatives by noting
that all denominations preached an "upward reach in the hearts of man."[113]
Though Welch's moralism ironically resembled a form of religious collectivism, it served as a politically motivated proxy to aid his far-right crusade and
connected him with anti-communist ministers such as Billy James Hargis
and Fred Schwarz.[114]

The Birch Society became Welch's vessel for thrusting his conspiratorial
ultraconservatism into the political arena, and the founder used numerous
platforms to amplify the Birch Society's outreach. Periodicals served as both
recruitment tools and a method of ideological indoctrination, or, as Birchers
saw it, anti-communist education. Welch started a self-publishing operation
in 1956 with the creation of *One Man's Opinion*, which eventually transformed
into *American Opinion*, the official Bircher publication. *American Opinion*
amounted to a far-right review of current affairs with editorial contributions
from fellow ultraconservatives, including former HUAC chairman Martin
Dies Jr., Revilo Oliver, Dan Smoot, and General Albert C. Wedemeyer, a U.S.
Army general and member of For America's National Policy Committee. Analysts from the Anti-Defamation League called *American Opinion* "a molder of
'Americanist' thinking" that imparted "a profound consciousness of the all-
pervading Communist conspiracy."[115] The organization's other major periodical, the monthly *John Birch Society Bulletin*, disseminated Welch's marching
orders to the Bircher faithful. In this respect, the *Bulletin* was the Society's core
publication. The *Bulletin* contained Welch's short- and long-term goals for
the organization, promoted Society-approved books for purchase, and listed
the "Agenda of the Month," which detailed the Society-sponsored political

activism expected of each member. Illustrating a similarity to Haley's Texans For America, one member noted that Welch expected individual Birchers "to conduct a massive one-man letter-writing campaign, directed at our congressmen, state senators and representatives and other public officials."[116] On a national level, Birch Society activism took place through front groups—a political action strategy pioneered by communist groups which produced high levels of grassroots participation while providing the parent organization with a certain amount of plausible deniability.[117]

Despite his organization's overt political goals, Welch attempted to maintain a façade of impartiality by forbidding the Birch Society, but not individual Birchers, from supporting or funding specific politicians or their campaigns. He used indirect language—"urging" or "expecting," rather than ordering—to avoid accusations of partisanship. This curated language, to Welch's mind, defined the Birch Society as an educational, not political, organization. However, this description did not match reality. Newspaper editor Leonard Finder thought only "apologists" believed that the Birch Society, a group driven by "fanatical" conservatives, was a strictly educational, apolitical organization.[118] The society supported conservative politicians rather than a single political party, but Birchers infiltrated the Republican apparatus, especially in California, in order to push the party rightward. Welch believed the GOP needed Bircher help doing "the thorough and painstaking organization and work at the precinct levels, which wins elections."[119] Bircher activism also included the legion of Birch-fronted bookstores that sold *American Opinion* pamphlets and various conservative books and magazines. Other far-right periodicals, such as Hargis's *Christian Crusade*, advertised Birch Society books, which lubricated the relationships between ultraconservative organizations.[120]

In fact, the Birch Society bridged many of the regional and ideological divisions separating ultraconservative groups. Welch discouraged John Birch Society chapters from inviting outside speakers, so the organization created the American Opinion Speakers Bureau, featuring high-profile ultraconservatives such as Willis Stone, to cement ideological standardization and speak for the "entire Conservative movement."[121] Stone wrote for *American Opinion* and traveled to conferences with Welch. Such was the trust between the two men that Welch sent Stone an advance copy of *The Politician*—Welch's inflammatory manuscript in which he accused numerous government officials, including President Eisenhower, of being communist agents. A significant amount of symbiosis existed between the Birch Society and Stone's organization. Retired brigadier general W. C. Lemly, who served as both a

Birch chapter leader and one of Stone's national vice chairmen, noted this phenomenon to Welch: "I am fully aware of the dedicated work of very many Birchers for [Stone's proposed] Liberty Amendment, and I know a lot of Birchers who were recruited into the JBS through their participation in the Liberty Amendment movement."[122] Courtney, also an NCEF chapter leader, joined the Birch Society in 1960 and soon became the chairman of Chapter 246 in New Orleans. Welch described Courtney's efforts as "parallel to my own."[123] Seven members of the Birch Society's National Council, including future California congressman John Rousselot and Clarence Manion, served on the Christian Crusade's National Advisory Committee. In return, Hargis served on the Birch Society's advisory board, and Martin Dies Jr. worked as a contributing editor for *American Opinion*. Not only did the Birch Society serve as a central hub for the far-right movement, its political activism sparked increased far-right collaboration.[124]

The creation of the first Bircher front group, the Committee Against Summit Entanglements (CASE), marked the society's initial foray into national politics. CASE was a reaction to a proposed summit between Soviet premier Nikita Khrushchev and President Dwight Eisenhower in July 1959. The thought of a Soviet leader stepping foot on American soil horrified Welch. Just a year prior Welch had published an acerbic, delusional open letter to Khrushchev, accusing the premier of being a "front" for the real Soviet dictator— Welch suspected Communist Party leader Georgy Malenkov—operating behind the scenes.[125] Months before the scheduled summit, President Eisenhower announced that he and Khrushchev were going to take good-will visits to each other's countries. The Birch Society, in response, circulated 70,000 petitions to protest both Khrushchev's visit and the summit meeting. Bircher handbills screamed "Please, Mr. President, Don't Go!," and full-page Society-sponsored advertisements in the *New York Herald Tribune* and the *New York Times* called Khrushchev's planned visit a "crime against humanity."[126] Welch estimated that the petitions gathered one million signatures total, a number which seems exaggerated and is impossible to verify. CASE grew into the largest national Bircher front organization and provided an outlet for non-Birch conservatives to protest Eisenhower's Modern Republicanism.[127]

The CASE campaign knit together a broad right-wing coalition. Welch served as the chairman, and right-wing Republicans, including Arizona senator Barry Goldwater, New York congressman Norman J. Gould, and former Utah governor J. Bracken Lee, joined CASE's executive committee and national board. The front group featured numerous industrialists, including

Roger Milliken, Pierre S. du Pont III, and Fred C. Koch. For America was well-represented: Manion and Wedemeyer served as vice chairmen and Fellers occupied a spot on the executive committee. CASE featured numerous Willis Stone associates, such as Courtney, Chance, Heinsohn, and Kimmel. The CASE national board also housed a wide range of conservative thinkers, including Andrews, Buckley, Ludwig Von Mises, and L. Brent Bozell. Elizabeth Churchill Brown, a right-wing journalist, tentatively agreed to serve on the board, but she sent a letter cautioning Welch against collaborating with open anti-Semites. Though Brown did not name the individual, she most likely meant Revilo P. Oliver, the classics professor, founding Birch Society member, and CASE board member. As the far-right movement gradually penetrated the political mainstream, Brown did not want to see the ultraconservative cause delegitimized over associations with fringe extremists.[128]

Numerous nodes within the far-right network promoted CASE's crusade. TFA's Kara Hart thought Soviet premier Nikita Khrushchev's proposed visit constituted an "abject surrender to the communist conception of coexistence." She sent instructions to TFA's committees of correspondence: "Register your opposition."[129] Stone published articles condemning the summit. Tom Anderson—CASE executive committee member, publisher of the right-wing *Farm and Ranch* magazine, and Christian Crusade advisory board member—wrote in *American Progress*, "The only way to coexist peacefully with the Communists is to surrender."[130] Fellers went on Manion's radio show, *The Manion Forum*, and wondered if the summit was laying the groundwork for total disarmament and a new "world order."[131] Wedemeyer also appeared on Manion's broadcast, questioning Eisenhower's judgment for engaging with "fanatically mad, atheistic materialists" and warning that the summit might sound "the death knell for this Republic and in fact for all free nations."[132] Manion himself finished one broadcast with a conspiratorial flourish: "My friends, since 1945, we have sold hundreds of millions of people into Soviet slavery for the counterfeit coin of Communist promises. This time the Red tiger is demanding that we feed him with our own flesh. It's your slavery that is at stake now."[133]

Ultimately, Khrushchev's trip to the United States occurred as planned, but Eisenhower did not make the return trip to the Soviet Union. Ultraconservatives believed their outcry influenced Eisenhower's decision. In reality, the U-2 Incident—a scandal involving the downing of a U.S. spy plane by the Soviet Union in May 1959—bred mistrust between the two superpowers and scuttled Eisenhower's trip and the summit meeting. Nevertheless, from the perspective of the Birch Society, CASE was a resounding success. Not only did the Birchers feel that their pleas were heard by national politicians, but the campaign galvanized their constituency and further reinforced the far-right network. By decade's end, the Birch Society had built upon the movement's foundations to become the apotheosis of the midcentury far right. The question for the next decade was how to turn that grassroots zealotry into tangible political victories.[134]

*   *   *

In the fall of 1959, hundreds of ultraconservatives gathered for a rally at Chicago's Morrison Hotel. The New Party Rally, sponsored by Courtney's *Independent American* newspaper and Stone's National Committee for Economic Freedom, sought to continue the fight started by Andrews's third-party run in 1956. The conference illustrated the growth of far-right conservatism during Eisenhower's presidency. Over five hundred people from thirty-five states flocked to Chicago, impressive growth considering the Constitution Party's 1956 convention attracted a meager seventy-five delegates. Numerous right-wing luminaries appeared on the speaking schedule. Buckley addressed a dinner preceding the rally, while Smoot, Welch, Haley, Anderson, Courtney, Lee, and Medford Evans each took a turn on the convention stump. According to a *Chicago Daily Tribune* reporter, the conference's central message was that "both national parties are practicing socialism today, so a new party is the answer."[135] Or, as Tom Anderson quipped, "changing from Eisenhower to Rockefeller, Nixon, Symington, or Kennedy is like leaving the diaper on the baby and just changing the pin."[136]

The conference issued a For America–inspired statement of principles, and Courtney hoped to consolidate the third-party forces around the country into a collaborative federation, the Independent American Federation of State Parties, before the election of 1960. Rather than resuscitating the Dixiecrat or States' Rights parties, under Courtney's plan state-level third parties would retain their independence while working together to boost national candidates and put independent electors on state ballots. This strategy would obviate the problem of needing to create, as Courtney put it, "a national platform that will appeal to all sections of the country and a candidate who will personify those things."[137] The federation intended to bring isolated third-party outfits, such as New Jersey's Conservative Party, Louisiana's States' Rights Party, and Washington's Constitution Party, into a cooperative third-party confederation. This was Courtney's answer to losing the strategic argument in 1956. Texans For America lauded the creation of the federation as an important strike against the "Republican-Democrat, socialistic coalition."[138]

In an interesting twist of fate, the Lincoln National Republican Club held its own conference at the exact same time and place. Led by Southern Baptist minister and former Air Force major Edgar C. Bundy, the Lincoln Club advocated "corrective measures" to ensure a more conservative Republican Party. Senator Styles Bridges, a New Hampshire Republican, told the club's audience, "All over the world, and in this country, there is a political upsurge in the conservative direction."[139] Bridges pointed to recent conservative congressional victories, including a "strong labor bill" and opposition to "free spending," as evidence of this right-wing groundswell. The Lincoln Club's message seemed simple enough—keep proposing reasonable conservative legislation and the voters will follow—but it hinted at a significant shift in Republican strategy. Despite the continued influence of liberalism during the mid-1950s, more Republicans were beginning to view conservatism as the party's future. The GOP was gradually pivoting toward its right-wing vanguard.[140]

Nevertheless, the two meetings illustrated the variance in conservative strategies. Lincoln Club leaders believed America leaned conservative and thus pushed for reform, hoping to nudge the Republican Party further to the right. The New Party Rally, on the other hand, pursued a political revolution. Courtney and his collaborators yearned to throw off the shackles of the two-party duopoly and consolidate conservatives within a new party. When asked about the fortuitous scheduling, Courtney noted that the rallies' concurrence was "very much of a coincidence."[141] He wanted nothing to do with the Lincoln Club's gradualist approach. However, the ultraconservative coalition remained divided. Courtney's bid for a permanent third party went down in flames in 1956, and now, heading into the election year 1960, conservative Republicans had a promising standard bearer: Senator Barry Goldwater. Goldwater's unabashed right-wing platforms and participation in CASE led ultraconservatives to view him as one of their own. During the early 1960s, the far-right movement burst into the political mainstream as activists mobilized behind Goldwater and the Republican Party.

CHAPTER 5

The Apex

In the wake of the early civil rights movement, radios around the country crackled to life with a stirring rendition of "I Wish I Was in Dixie." The song served as the introduction to the Citizens' Council of America's Radio Forum, a broadcast recorded in the nation's capital that promoted the reactionary politics of the Deep South. The program, much like the Citizens' Councils themselves, proclaimed a dedication to "states' rights and racial integrity. To individual liberty and race relations based on common sense, not on the power politics of left-wing pressure groups." Or, to quote the show's slogan, "The American viewpoint with a southern accent." Far-right grandees from arch-segregationist Strom Thurmond to Birch Society and Citizens' Council member Medford Evans came on the show to spread ultraconservative values, particularly a legitimized version of Old South white supremacy vis-à-vis states' rights ideals.

Senator Barry Goldwater, the right-wing Arizona Republican, appeared on the program in 1959. In years past, a Republican senator would have been persona non grata in the South, but the longtime Democratic bastion was starting to fracture. Many southerners rejected the liberal trajectory of the national Democratic Party. On the precipice of a new decade, and amid waves of civil rights activism, Goldwater's states' rights libertarianism harmonized with the Deep South's sociopolitical traditions. Goldwater's conversation with Forum host Dick Morphew meandered through right-wing concerns about organized labor before settling on the broader issue of federal power. Morphew asked Goldwater about the recent dispute over water rights in western states, to which Goldwater responded, "That's a states' rights problem, the federal government has no business in it, like they have no business in most of our affairs in the states." Morphew pushed him on this point: "Does this seem to be part of an overall trend toward big government?" "Oh certainly," Goldwater replied, "it's been going on now since 1932."[1]

Goldwater saw Franklin Roosevelt's New Deal as America's original sin. He noted with pride that conservative Republicans were contesting liberal policies on every front. The key to this battle, Goldwater told Forum listeners, was empowering the states. "I'm one person that believes that states' rights is the cornerstone, the keystone, of our whole constitutional republic."[2] It is unclear whether or not Goldwater intended to reference Confederate vice president Alexander Stephens's 1861 "Cornerstone Address," wherein Stephens asserted that white supremacy was the foundation of the Confederacy, but the senator certainly hit similar notes. Goldwater's western libertarianism shared a deep ideological tradition with southern states' rights ideologies, particularly a distrust of federal power. This philosophical intersection—plus a vehement, bordering on paranoid, anti-communism—positioned Goldwater as a key tribune of midcentury ultraconservatism. During the early 1960s, a symbiosis developed between Goldwater and far-right activists; indeed, ultraconservatives played a critical role in Goldwater's ascent.

The 1960s was a decade of profound political turmoil and change, and Goldwater occupied a central position in the partisan pageantry. At the beginning of the decade, his ideologies were on the fringe of mainstream politics, which made him a perfect conduit for far-right activists. Goldwater chatted, brainstormed, and organized with ultraconservatives, and to the far right he seemed like one of them. Right-wingers backed Goldwater as a presidential candidate twice, once in 1960 and again in 1964. More than any other figure of the era, Goldwater emerged as the premier right-wing translator, a person who legitimized ultraconservatism and established credibility within Washington *and* far-right circles outside the Beltway.

The early 1960s marked the apex of midcentury ultraconservatism. In the nation's popular conscience, the 1960s are often remembered as a progressive decade, one headlined by civil rights action, heady liberalism, and counterculture undercurrents. Even the electoral results, particularly Lyndon B. Johnson's landslide victory in 1964, seemed to confirm the preponderant power of liberalism. Yet, the 1960s also witnessed the equally vibrant zenith of the far-right movement, a phenomenon which undergirded the broader conservative coalescence. In fact, the far right served as the shock troops of modern conservatism. Groups such as the Birch Society and Christian Crusade reached heretofore unthinkable levels of political influence. New

political action organizations cropped up, such as Kent Courtney's Conservative Society of America, which were eager to continue building a movement
of conservative purists. Yet support from radicals damaged Goldwater's mainstream bona fides, which sparked a heated debate in right-wing circles about
respectability, ideological boundaries, and the movement's future. This era of
ultraconservative activism, particularly Goldwater's presidential campaigns
and the tension between the far-right vanguard and "responsible" conservatives, helped lay the foundation for the nation's gradual political realignment.[3]

*   *   *

Barry Goldwater seemed like a hero from western folklore. The tall Arizona
senator boasted a southwestern drawl, square chin, and black horn-rimmed
glasses. During a photo shoot for *Life* magazine, Goldwater cradled his mare
(a white-and-tan palomino named Sunny) while clad in a cowboy hat, cham-
bray button-down, and dark blue jeans cinched together with a silver belt
buckle. However, Goldwater's swaggering cowboy caricature was not solely
an effort to pander to Arizona voters—the Goldwater family had deep roots
in the southwestern frontier. His grandfather, Michel "Big Mike" Goldwater, a
Jew born in Russian Poland, traversed through California boomtowns before
finding success as a financier to dusty Arizona settlers. This origin story of a
hardscrabble, self-made patriarch became the Goldwater family legend, often
eliding the fact that, as the U.S. military moved in to quell Native American populations, the Goldwaters benefited from federal spending in western states. The family opened a series of successful businesses, and Morris
Goldwater, Mike's eldest son and Barry's uncle, became the mayor of Prescott,
Arizona. Morris described himself as a Jeffersonian Democrat dedicated to
limited government and rugged individualism, the same ideological wellspring that birthed the movement led by James A. Reed and J. Evetts Haley
some fifty years later. Baron Goldwater, Mike's youngest son, ran the family's
branch store in Phoenix. There Baron married Josephine "JoJo" Williams,
a "lunger" who had moved to Arizona to escape the grips of tuberculosis.
This family history of bootstrapping, local politics, and boomtown capitalism
formed Barry Goldwater's ideological bedrock.[4]

    Barry, the first of three children born to Baron and JoJo, was raised in a
conservative household. Estranged from his Jewish ancestry, Baron had his
children baptized in the Episcopal Church, which insulated young Barry—
he never felt alienated by Protestant-dominated America despite being half

Jewish. JoJo raised her children in a religious household, though religion entailed less church attendance and more of a nebulous ethical conviction. Goldwater later credited his parents for instilling a sense of "honesty, loyalty to America, respect for the flag, understanding the responsibilities of citizenship."[5] During his formative years, Morris, the self-styled Jeffersonian Democrat, became Barry's ideological mentor, imparting a deep distrust toward the federal government upon the young Goldwater.

A precocious but mischievous youth, Barry was shunted off to Staunton Military Academy in Virginia. There, Barry excelled, emerging from the academy an improved student, leader, and hardened patriot. After a brief stint at the University of Arizona, Barry went into the family business, became a second lieutenant in the Army Reserve, and married Peggy Johnson, a woman from an affluent family. Up to this point, politics held little interest for Barry, but his political awakening came during the Great Depression. Influenced by his mother's partisan affiliation and his own independent streak, Barry registered as a Republican in a Democrat-dominated state. As the economy wilted, Franklin Roosevelt and various New Deal agencies poured money into western states, including Arizona. At first, Goldwater supported the New Deal, but he soon soured on Roosevelt's regulatory liberalism and enabling of labor unions and instead lauded the free-enterprise philosophies of Herbert Hoover. Goldwater later wrote in his autobiography, "I think the foundations of my political philosophy were rooted in my resentment against the New Deal."[6]

When World War II broke out, Goldwater stood against Roosevelt's plan to arm western Europe against Hitler's Nazi Germany, but after Pearl Harbor Goldwater threw himself into the war effort as a support pilot for the Army Air Corps. The war boosted Goldwater's belief in military spending, but, paradoxically, he argued for the primacy of free-market capitalism in the postwar era, even while the burgeoning Cold War defense industry spread affluence into Sunbelt states. Goldwater parlayed his family's business connections into a Phoenix city council position, which served as a springboard for his 1952 senate campaign against incumbent Democrat Ernest McFarland. During the campaign Goldwater red-baited McFarland, tarring the liberal Democrat as a soft-on-communism spendthrift. Eisenhower endorsed Goldwater in a visit to Arizona, and Senator Joseph McCarthy made McFarland a personal target for his anti-communist ire. Eisenhower's electoral wave swept Goldwater into the nation's capital.[7]

Goldwater established himself as a conservative warhorse, an ideological heir to Taft and Hoover—though Taft was more flexible on government spending and both were less hawkish in foreign policy. His hard-nosed opposition to labor unions, federal interventionism, and civil rights legislation endeared him to both southern segregationists and western libertarians. Goldwater viewed the *Brown* decision as unconstitutional judicial activism and rejected federal integration mandates. Like many western ultraconservatives, Goldwater glossed over the oppression of black Americans in the South, arguing that civil rights issues were best left up to local communities. Goldwater sowed seeds with the far-right vanguard by voting against the censure of Senator McCarthy (even though he disapproved of the senator's witch hunting), appearing on Clarence Manion's broadcasts, and joining Morphew on the Citizens' Council Radio Forum. Birch Society founder Robert Welch viewed Goldwater as a potential ally and sent the senator an early copy of his unpublished manuscript, *The Politician*. Goldwater rejected Welch's overtures and conspiracy theories, illustrating the thin degree of separation that would allow Goldwater to translate far-right values while preserving mainstream credibility. Nevertheless, Welch donated $2,000 to Goldwater during his 1958 senate run and lauded the senator in the *Blue Book*. "I'd love to see him president of the United States," Welch wrote, "and maybe some day we will."[8]

Far-right activists had spent years stumbling between third-party failures and convention defeats, but Goldwater represented the type of red-blooded conservative behind which right-wing forces could unify. In the spring of 1959, Goldwater met with For America's vice chairman Clarence Manion and a cabal of conservatives to discuss the 1960 presidential election. Some far-right activists, particularly Kent Courtney, hoped to draft Goldwater as a third-party candidate (Courtney had even floated the idea of running Senator Strom Thurmond or even Manion himself on a third-party ticket to counter the "socialism" of the major parties). Goldwater ruled out a third-party candidacy—he was a loyal Republican—but he had a firm read on the conservative base. A "me-too" Republican, a liberal in sheep's clothing, would not energize the diehards. Vice President Richard Nixon, the overwhelming front-runner for the Republican nomination, did not pass the far right's ideological litmus test. However, convincing the rest of America that Goldwater was the man for the moment would take a great deal of effort. As the election year dawned, a poll indicated that a paltry 1 percent of Republicans favored Goldwater as the candidate. Campaign chronicler Theodore White characterized Goldwater as "an odd one, out there on the extreme, no menace to anyone for the 1960 season."[9] Nevertheless, the far right marshaled a two-stage push to raise Goldwater's profile, hoping to nip the Republican nomination through sheer grassroots force.[10]

Ultraconservatives tapped into the far-right network to animate Goldwater's movement. Compared to the youthful exuberance of John F. Kennedy, conservatism seemed antiquated and stale. A rechristening was in order. Manion gathered shock troops to support this mission, including Welch, J. Bracken Lee, and Phyllis Schlafly, an ultraconservative moralist and organizer. Then, Manion encouraged Goldwater to produce an ideological blueprint that would rebrand conservatism, raise the senator's national profile, and build momentum for a right-wing Republican insurgency. Goldwater could not dedicate himself to writing a book, so Manion recruited L. Brent Bozell—Buckley's brother-in-law, a *National Review* editor, and co-author of the McCarthy apologia *McCarthy and His Enemies*—to ghostwrite Goldwater's manifesto. The book he produced, *The Conscience of a Conservative*, bore Goldwater's name and set the conservative movement ablaze.[11]

Conscience put Goldwater on the map as the nation's foremost right-winger—he eventually earned the moniker "Mr. Conservative." In the book, Goldwater straddled right-wing foreign policies, advocating escalation against global communism while simultaneously appealing to the isolationist tradition by criticizing involvement in the United Nations as "an unconstitutional surrender of American sovereignty."[12] As in his interview with Morphew, Goldwater mapped out a strident states' rights argument: "Thus the cornerstone of the Republic, our chief bulwark against the encroachment of individual freedom by Big Government, is fast disappearing under the piling sands of absolutism."[13] This defense of states' rights was part of the book's broader anti-statist bent. Hearkening back to the ideals of libertarian thinker Albert Jay Nock, Goldwater wrote, "Throughout history, government has proved to be the chief instrument for thwarting man's liberty."[14] The state, in Goldwater's eyes, was a leviathan that ruled by "threats," "coercion," "blackmail," and "bribery."[15] He also harped against unions, income taxation, economic intervention, and the Supreme Court's *Brown* decision. Goldwater did not ascribe the state of America to a vast communist plot, but his anti-statism sounded a dog whistle to ultraconservatives long convinced of nefarious government cabals. "Socialism-through-Welfarism," Goldwater argued, was even more insidious than nationalizing industry.[16] *Conscience* did not break new ideological ground, but the book synthesized diverse, and sometimes discordant, right-wing traditions into a modern conservative blend.[17]

Indeed, Goldwater's *Conscience* became the blueprint for midcentury conservatism. Manion published the 123-page book—adorned with a red, white, and blue cover—through Victor Publishing, a nonprofit imprint he created in Kentucky. When Manion brought the book to a Birch Society meeting, Fred Koch, the industrialist and society National Council member, bought 2,500 copies for distribution throughout his home state of Kansas. The book received praise in mainstream outlets such as the *Washington Post, Chicago Tribune,* and *Wall Street Journal.* Right-wing periodicals such as *Human Events* went a step further by urging readers to purchase, read, and circulate Goldwater's book. The slim volume sold 85,000 copies within the first month, and by Election Day Manion had moved over half a million. *Conscience of a Conservative* made the *New York Times* and *Time* magazine best-seller lists and was reprinted twenty times in four years, eventually selling over three million copies. Industrialist Roger Milliken thought Goldwater captured the "thinking of conservative people in South Carolina and, indeed, the nation."[18] In short, *Conscience* elevated Goldwater's public stature. He was now the spokesman of the conservative movement, bridging the gap between the ultraconservative right and mainstream acceptability.[19]

Conscience accomplished Manion's first goal, rebranding conservatism, which paved the way for the second phase: building a Goldwater insurgency during the 1960 election. Before the movement could lift off, however, far-right leaders had to tamp down the third-party agitations occurring on the fringe. In particular, Manion worried about Courtney setting conservatism back decades by "going off half-cocked."[20] Manion tried to convince Courtney to call off his crusade by visiting him down in New Orleans. Welch chimed in, writing to Courtney that he saw Goldwater as a "rallying point, as offering a somewhat better prospect of real progress."[21] After realizing that Goldwater was the conservative movement's best hope, Courtney threw himself into the unofficial Americans for Goldwater movement. Courtney worried that liberal Republicans might drown out conservative voices at the GOP convention, so he encouraged right-wingers to draw strength from the lingering resentment over Taft's defeat in 1952. For the moment, and for the first time since its inception, the ultraconservative movement unified behind a major party candidate, a Republican no less.[22]

The unofficial "Goldwater clubs" spread like wildfire, thanks in part to the efforts of ultraconservative activists. For America's General Wedemeyer signed on as the chairman of Americans for Goldwater. Just a year earlier, at a Texans For America soiree in Houston, Wedemeyer had proclaimed, "What can be done to save America? There must be a political realignment in both parties!"[23] Wedemeyer, along with the rest of the far right, hoped the Arizona senator could catalyze such a transformation. Within a couple of months, Americans for Goldwater had spread into Washington, D.C., and thirty-one states. Manion opened an Americans for Goldwater headquarters in Chicago on July 7, and one week later took out a promotional advertisement in the *Chicago Daily Tribune*. All told, over four hundred Goldwater clubs, plus a host of affiliated organizations such as Youth for Goldwater and the Goldwater Coordinating Committee, were in operation by the end of the summer.[24]

The grassroots fervor convinced far-right activists that their candidate had arrived. Elizabeth Churchill Brown wrote to Goldwater, "Dear Barry: Do you know you are the FIRST American political leader who has recognized the fact that you are waging a war against a conspiracy and not an old fashioned political campaign?"[25] She forwarded Goldwater and Strom Thurmond information she had been "studying" regarding the conspiracy "to destroy state lines and local governments." Down in the Lone Star State, Haley and Texans For America lauded Goldwater's defense of the Connally Reservation, a legislative clause restricting the World Court's authority over domestic issues. Courtney invited Willis Stone to join the Goldwater movement, but Stone declined, still struggling in the wake of his ruptured organizational merger. Nevertheless, Courtney launched a petition campaign to convince Republicans to put Goldwater on the ticket, opened a "Goldwater for President" headquarters in Chicago's Morrison Hotel, and hosted a rally for Goldwater before the GOP convention. Welch threw the heft of the John Birch Society behind Goldwater, too—a Birch-driven mass-mailer campaign sent postcards reading "Nominate anybody you please, I'm voting for Goldwater" to Republican convention delegates.[26] At a Goldwater rally the night before the Chicago convention, Welch took apart presumptive favorite Richard Nixon "bone by bone," according to Brown, and urged conservatives to "write in Goldwater for President."[27]

Goldwater traveled to the Republican National Convention riding a grassroots wave, but he lacked any tangible electoral heft. The only Goldwater-pledged delegates came from his home state of Arizona. Ignoring the cacophony of grassroots conservatives, Nixon instead solidified his lead by brokering a peace with Republican liberals. Nixon visited Governor Nelson Rockefeller, the liberal leader of the urban, eastern establishment, in his New York high-rise, and rumors swirled that Nixon offered him the vice-presidential post.

Conservatives were apoplectic. Goldwater characterized Nixon's actions as the "Munich of the Republican Party," directly comparing Nixon's kowtowing to Neville Chamberlain's appeasement of Hitler in 1938. The fact that the Republican brass willfully ignored the conservative groundswell further convinced ultraconservatives of the need to mobilize. The internecine battle extended into the convention. Goldwaterites lined the streets and staged a raucous demonstration on the convention floor, singing and marching along to an orchestral rendition of "Dixie." Yet, Nixon appeared unbeatable, so Goldwater opted for unity over division. After taking the rostrum he released his delegates (much to the chagrin of the floor agitators), told conservatives to unite behind Nixon, and thundered against a Kennedy-led "Armageddon." But, he also chastised his fellow right-wingers. "We have been losing elections because conservatives too often fail to vote. . . . Let's grow up, conservatives," Goldwater intoned. "If we want to take this Party back, and I think we can someday, let's get to work."[28]

The election of 1960 marked the first time that conservatives mounted a significant challenge to the GOP's dominant liberal-moderate coalition. Goldwater had, in effect, sounded a call to arms, but his mandate to "grow up and get to work" highlighted the uneasy relationship between the far right and the "respectable" right. For example, when Welch printed and distributed copies of his preconvention pro-Goldwater speech, Brown feared that Birch Society support might damage Nixon's electability and chastised Welch as "politically naïve."[29] Goldwater owed a great deal of his traction to far-right activism, but he agreed that Welch was "politically naïve to a marked degree." Perhaps "his dedication and his intelligence could be put to much better use if he didn't inject them into the political stream directly but by the circuitous route of candidates," Goldwater mused.[30] Goldwater later said that many of the unofficial Goldwater clubs caused him "deep embarrassment," but he still hoped to transmute far-right zealots into conservative Republican voters.[31] Goldwater's speechwriter Steve Shadegg offered a more damning indictment, arguing that right-wing extremists "twisted and distorted" the "Goldwater image."[32]

Yet, while Shadegg cast Goldwater as a "sober, reasonable, forward-looking" conservative, the far right thought that Goldwater represented *their* values.[33] Ultraconservatives had marshaled the right-wing vanguard and claimed Goldwater as one of their own. The reality was that Goldwater straddled the porous ideological boundary separating the far right from the mainstream. Goldwater's language during the campaign often mirrored that of ultraconservatives. At the convention Goldwater described Kennedy's platform as a "blueprint for socialism," and just one year later Courtney deemed Kennedy's "New Frontier" a "front for socialism."[34] The relationship between Goldwater and ultraconservatives proved symbiotic—they each drew strength from and reflected the values of the other—and the senator often translated far-right ideals for a mainstream audience. Elizabeth Brown spoke for conservatives of all stripes in noting, "Whatever the outcome of the election, Barry has given us hope for America's future."[35]

In the immediate sense, Kennedy dashed Republican hopes by squeaking out a victory over Richard Nixon, initiating a period of conservative soul-searching. The Massachusetts scion overcame significant barriers—age, anti-Catholic bigotry, southern discontent with liberalism and civil rights activism—to win the presidency. Conservatives, especially the far right, considered Kennedy's victory a disaster. Not only did liberalism maintain its grip on the executive branch, but Nixon's alliance with moderates looked worse in hindsight. Angry ultraconservatives even accused Goldwater of betraying the cause. After the election Courtney seethed that, by supporting Nixon, Goldwater had "compromised his own conservative principles" and "tainted himself with socialism."[36] Over the next couple of years, Courtney returned to crusading for a third party, but, despite hosting conferences with hundreds of attendees, he struggled to gain traction. Congressman Edgar Hiestand, the Republican Bircher from California, spied a more promising solution. "It makes better sense to revamp a going business like the Republican Party than set up a new one," Hiestand observed.[37] Like Goldwater, Hiestand saw potential in the current direction of the conservative movement—after all, he was a Republican Bircher serving in the U.S. Congress!—and forming a third party risked splitting the nascent movement. Indeed, the GOP's rightward list rendered Courtney's third-party desires an outlier, a nonstarter. Over the next four years, ultraconservative activists rallied around the promise of a future Goldwater nomination and, more broadly, a Republican shift to the right.[38]

While Goldwater's emergence intensified the conversation over partisan affiliation, the burgeoning civil rights movement provided another significant catalyst for far-right mobilization. School segregation remained a critical flash point—white mobs rioted over the integration of the University of Alabama, for example—and southern pulses quickened as civil rights activists employed increasingly confrontational tactics. The fight for racial equality evolved from court battles and boycotts into mass public protests. The opening shot of this new phase occurred in North Carolina on February 1, 1960, when four black students ordered a coffee at a "whites only"

Woolworth lunch counter in Greensboro. Management refused to serve them, and in turn the students refused to give up their seats until the store closed for the day. The "sit-in" protests spread across the nation and inspired additional nonviolent direct action. In 1961, the Congress for Racial Equality and the Student Non-Violent Coordinating Committee sponsored an integrated Freedom Ride from Washington, D.C., to New Orleans, hoping to test the South's adherence to integration laws. The ensuing violence in Alabama—one bus was firebombed in Anniston and Klansmen attacked and hospitalized numerous passengers in Birmingham—illustrated the South's bellicose defiance of federal laws and civil rights demands. In the spring of 1963, Martin Luther King Jr. and the Southern Christian Leadership Conference called for mass protests in Birmingham, a city notorious for Klan violence and racism. Thousands of nonviolent demonstrators flooded the streets, and police commissioner Eugene "Bull" Connor responded with fire hoses, billy clubs, and police dogs. The street conflicts, particularly the sight of black bodies getting beaten by white badges, dominated headlines and helped convince more Americans, including President John F. Kennedy, to support audacious civil rights solutions.[39]

White supremacy and conspiratorial anti-communism fueled animosity toward the civil rights movement. States' rights language often served as a veil for southern apartheid. Strom Thurmond, the man who filibustered the 1957 Civil Rights Act for over twenty-four hours, combined states' rights rhetoric with the business conservative movement's language of property rights. "When the government steps in and directs the use of property, controls property, that is the beginning of a dictatorship," Thurmond warned Citizens' Council Radio Forum listeners.[40] White anxieties of racial upheaval bred conspiracy theories. Thurmond believed civil rights legislation promoted "discrimination against the white man," while Hargis's *Christian Crusade* published unhinged editorials characterizing civil rights as "a communist plot to enslave the South and our entire nation."[41] Communists *had* to catalyze the movement, argued Julian Williams, the Christian Crusade's director of research, because "the Southern white man has done more for the Negro than the Negro was able to do for himself."[42] Despite the fact that communists merely cooperated with, but were not the inspiration for, the push for racial equality, many conservatives characterized the civil rights movement as a communist insurrection. Mirroring Welch's language, Brown and Goldwater both called the civil rights movement a "revolution," but Goldwater also admitted that discrimination was "the major obstacle in front of world peace and the ultimate brotherhood of man."[43]

The paradox was that Goldwater's states' rights philosophies undergirded the very discrimination he disavowed.[44]

The militancy of civil rights activists, boldness of proposed legislation, and fear of federal tyranny galvanized ultraconservatives, Kent and Phoebe Courtney in particular. After multiple forays into national politics—the defeat of the 1956 States' Rights Party, the aborted 1960 Goldwater candidacy, the numerous attempts to form a third party—had failed to cause a right-wing counterrevolution, the Courtneys turned to grassroots organizing. The Courtneys founded the Conservative Society of America (the acronym of which was a not-so-subtle nod to the Confederacy) to serve as the tip of the right-wing spear. As the national chairman, Kent Courtney steered the organization. "The [CSA] was founded on the bedrock of Constitutional principles," he wrote to CSA members, which meant states' rights, strict constitutionalism, free-market economics, and an end to communist "appeasement."[45] Courtney sought "to restore the two-party system" by giving voters "a choice between a) Liberal-New Deal-Socialism and b) Conservatism."[46] Their unabashed political purpose, Courtney told CSA members, was "to elect Patriotic Americans—conservatives—to office."[47] The CSA invigorated Courtney's third-party ambitions while allowing him to support right-wing candidates, regardless of party affiliation.

Through the CSA, Kent and Phoebe Courtney established one of the largest publishing empires within the far-right network. The pair's original periodical *Free Men Speak* evolved into the *Independent American* and became the centerpiece of their press. Circulation of the *Independent American* stood at 9,000 in 1961, but by 1965 that number had ballooned to 20,000 subscribers thanks to membership-list swapping among conservative organizations. The society funded a radio broadcast, the "Radio Edition of *The Independent American*," and produced countless fearmongering pamphlets featuring titles such as "Communist Agitation and Racial Turmoil" and "How the U.S. Is Being Communized." The couple published small, tabloid-style periodicals called *CSA Info Memos* that aggregated conservative newspaper columns, radio broadcasts, and speeches from notable right-wing politicians. Members received information about upcoming local actions through the biweekly *CSA Newsletter*, which eventually turned into a major source of right-wing propaganda during George Wallace's 1968 presidential run. The Courtneys also published numerous conspiratorial books and created "CSA Voting Indexes," which served as right-wing voter guides by grading individual congressmen's votes based upon the Courtneys' own stringent political scale. Book sales, membership dues, and individual contributions supplemented their publishing empire, which, in turn, became a conduit for grassroots activism.[48]

To effect their desired right-wing revolution, the Courtneys established Political Action Units across the United States to target local and state races. They hired Ward Poag, a former Birch Society organizer in Tennessee and Arkansas, as the CSA's national field organizer responsible for developing and coordinating the action units. Poag wrote significant portions of the *CSA Political Action Bulletin*, an instruction manual for creating conservative enclaves through door-to-door canvassing and voter censuses. Members received a *CSA Action Handbook*, a personal ledger containing everything from local newspaper clippings to instructional memos such as "How to Write Your Congressman" and "How to Write Letters-to-the-Editor." In stark contrast with Welch's hierarchical Birch Society, CSA action units were fairly autonomous as long as they adhered to Courtney's strict definition of conservatism, pursued "the right kind of people" for leadership positions, and actively engaged the local political scene. However, CSA pursued conspiratorial, borderline authoritarian outcomes. Courtney urged action units to dominate local elections in order to create what he called a far-right "shadow government." "The office of sheriff has a potential for juvenile education and other activities which in many cases has not been sufficiently exploited," Courtney theorized. "Just imagine the amount of anti-communist education which could be carried out by a Conservative sheriff who would establish a junior sheriff's posse." Courtney envisioned a school board that would use auditoriums for "patriotic gatherings," host "adult education seminars concerning national and international affairs," and compel "the adoption of pro-American and anti-Communist study courses."[49] "The whole idea," Courtney wrote to a CSA leader in Columbus, Georgia, "is to saturate your Congressional district with the Conservative viewpoint."[50]

The aggressive, localized strategy targeted particularly right-leaning areas and plugged CSA into the national far-right network. For example, CSA focused on cities in West Texas—Midland, Odessa, and Lubbock—that had a history of anti-statism and "frontier individualism." Poag traveled throughout California, linking CSA units to preexisting conservative groups, including John Birch Society chapters. The local canvassing succeeded in building an active national constituency. By the end of 1962, official membership numbered in the low thousands and spanned forty-five states, and CSA action units permeated the Sunbelt with numerous branches in key battlegrounds such as Texas and California.

However, CSA's far-right philosophies occasionally attracted unwanted attention from extreme white nationalist groups. The American fascist movement had surged back into the public eye by the 1960s. Building upon the foundation left by the German American Bund and Silver Shirts, the American Nazi Party (ANP) formed in 1959. Its founder, George Lincoln Rockwell, an admirer of the late Senator Joseph McCarthy and Adolf Hitler, got his start in right-wing activism by hawking copies of *National Review* and writing columns for *American Mercury*. As the leader of the ANP, he became the poster boy for right-wing extremism. Rockwell promoted strict white nationalism, including sending black Americans "back to Africa," rather than segregation. The fight for racial equality threatened to destroy western civilization because, according to Rockwell, blacks were "a less advanced branch" of humanity while whites were "the Master Race." Furthermore, he insisted that communist Jews controlled the civil rights movement and were sending "black armies" to destroy white nations.[51] To Rockwell's mind, Jews were the puppet masters of global upheaval. He promised to gas all of the "Jew traitors," which he once told a reporter included roughly 80 percent of all Jews.[52] The only way to unify aggrieved whites, Rockwell maintained, was through a well-oiled fascist movement, because other conservative organizations, including extremist groups such as the Klan, lacked the fortitude to take action against the Jewish threat.[53]

A narrow ideological and substantial strategic divide existed between the fascist and far right, but overlaps remained. Rockwell's racism and conspiratorial overtones resembled far-right diatribes, and, as the ultraconservative movement expanded, anti-Semitic extremists filtered into ultraconservative groups, held leadership positions, and wrote for their periodicals. Revilo P. Oliver, a book reviewer for *National Review* and founding member of the Birch Society, remained welcome in the far-right movement for years until his virulent anti-Semitism and outlandish conspiracy theories rendered him an outcast. However, some ultraconservatives had a more limited tolerance for anti-Semitism and violent extremism. Courtney liquidated a Pennsylvania action unit after he discovered that members of the Nationalist Action League, an organization with ties to the American Nazi movement, held prominent positions. He then installed rigid organizational uniformity, insisting that CSA leadership sign loyalty oaths that stated opposition to "all forms of totalitarian government" and disclaimed links to subversive groups.[54] Similar to how Brown urged Welch to disavow anti-Semitism in CASE, Courtney feared that overt linkages to white nationalism would damage the far right's credibility, even though their ideologies and rhetoric often overlapped. Certain lines of propriety existed that even Courtney was reluctant to cross, illustrating a key difference between the fascist and far right: ultraconservative groups yearned for mainstream respectability and policed their boundaries to avoid being tarred as extremists. Soon, that same concern for respectability would consume the conservative movement and lead to renunciations of the far right.[55]

As CSA grew into a critical ultraconservative hub, the Courtneys' prominence within the far-right movement flourished. Because he served as the chairman of CSA and the New Orleans Birch Society chapter, Kent encouraged CSA members and Birchers to sign up for both organizations. He lubricated the CSA-Bircher relationship by advertising in *American Opinion* and giving the society a 50 percent discount on all CSA-published books, which prompted Bircher-fronted bookstores to stock the Courtneys' books. Kent maintained a close relationship with Welch throughout the years—the two organizations even shared mailing lists. The Christian Crusade also received a CSA book discount to help Hargis make a larger profit. Courtney served as a faculty member—a glorified title for giving speeches—in the Christian Crusade's Anti-Communist Leadership School in Shreveport, Louisiana. Hargis and Courtney networked through far-right conferences and planned a future speaking tour together. Kent also served as the Louisiana state co-chairman for the National Committee for Economic Freedom, published Willis Stone's speeches and amendment proposals in CSA media, and assisted in the passage of a resolution in favor of Stone's proposed amendment through the Louisiana state legislature. Through Kent Courtney's intense networking, the CSA became a key lodestar within the far-right constellation.[56]

The creation of CSA coincided with, and allowed the Courtneys to get involved in, the Birch Society's second major campaign: the drive to impeach Earl Warren. The "Impeach Earl Warren" movement was grounded in white aggrievement, far-right conspiracy theories, and states' rights ideals. Welch called the Warren Court's *Brown* decision "unconstitutional" and "pro-Communist."[57] Failure to remove the chief justice, Welch argued, would transform America "into a province of the world-wide Soviet system."[58] The Birch Society designed the Impeach Earl Warren campaign to resemble CASE. Many tactics carried over, including mass letter campaigns to Congress, petitions for impeachment, local-level organizing, and promotional materials (such as the "Warren Impeachment Packet") appearing in the Birch Society *Bulletin*. However, in a significant departure from CASE, Welch targeted college students through an essay contest: $2,300 for the best essay describing the "grounds for impeachment" of Warren. Welch intended "to stir up a great deal of interest among conservatives on the campuses," hoping that the campaign would appeal to burgeoning right-wing youth organizations, such as Young Americans for Freedom.[59]

The Impeach Earl Warren campaign tapped into white anxieties about civil rights and the erosion of traditional society. Despite the fact that communism had no impact on Warren's decision in the *Brown* case (Warren argued access to education was a "fundamental right"), Welch's conspiratorial rhetoric mirrored the language of "massive resistance." Senator Olin Johnston, a South Carolina Democrat, alleged that "communist sources" dictated the Warren Court, while Senator James O. Eastland, a Mississippi Dixiecrat, derided the *Brown* decision as a "pro-communist" threat to the South's "racial harmony."[60] "The states of this country have got to assert their sovereignty against the Supreme Court," Eastland told Citizens' Council Radio Forum listeners.[61] One of Eastland's Senate speeches, titled "Is the Supreme Court Communist?," was included in the Birch Society's "Impeach Earl Warren" packets. Birch-sponsored billboards featuring Confederate flags and urging local voters to join the impeachment movement dotted the South. However, antipathy toward the Supreme Court was not limited to white southerners. Congressman Noah M. Mason, an Illinois Republican, told Forum listeners, "The Supreme Court's decision is not the law of the land."[62] The Impeach Earl Warren campaign harmonized with the right-wing politicians who were sounding anti-communist alarms and stoking anti-statist resentments.[63]

Ultraconservatives rallied to the cause. Courtney distributed 70,000 "Impeach Earl Warren" pamphlets and implored CSA members to get involved. At the 1961 Christian Crusade convention in Tulsa, Oklahoma, far-right leaders—including Manion, Welch, Fred Koch, fundamentalist preacher Bob Jones Sr., and Liberty Lobby leader Willis Carto—stumped against the communist threat. Though Hargis did not discuss the Birch Society's campaign against the Supreme Court in his keynote address, "Impeach Earl Warren" bumper stickers permeated the convention parking lot. In Dallas, right-wingers held a "National Indignation Convention," which provided a vehicle for various ultraconservative platforms. Tom Anderson gave a rousing speech calling for Warren's removal before inviting J. Evetts Haley to the stage. "Tom Anderson here has turned moderate," quipped the wiry Texan. "All he wants to do is impeach Warren—I'm for hanging him."[64]

The Warren campaign illustrated the Birch Society's success at rousing grassroots activism and capitalizing on white racial anxieties, but it also revealed the limitations of Welch's visceral anti-communism. The failed attempt to remove Supreme Court justice Samuel Chase in 1805 set the precedent that impeachment proceedings would prove difficult, if not impossible. George Sokolsky of the *Washington Post* noted that Welch had "no conception of the procedure involved in impeachment," and, in a later version of the *Blue Book*, Welch acknowledged that his plan was ambitious, even foolhardy.[65] Though the campaign did not result in Warren's departure from the judiciary, it accomplished Welch's goal by stoking anger about "activist judges" and further mobilizing a grassroots constituency.[66]

However, the crusade against Warren coincided with the brewing controversy surrounding Welch's unpublished book, *The Politician*. Welch had worked on the manuscript throughout the 1950s, only sending it under cloak of secrecy to close friends and potential allies, including Stone, Buckley, and Goldwater. In the book's opening pages, Welch urged the reader to "keep the manuscript safeguarded" and wrote that it was "for your eyes only."[67] Welch's caution was warranted, because in *The Politician* he launched a cornucopia of conspiracy theories, most notoriously accusing former president Dwight Eisenhower of "consciously serving the Communist conspiracy, for all of his adult life."[68] But then the manuscript leaked to the press; someone sent a copy to Jack Mabley of the *Chicago Daily News*, which led to a media firestorm in 1961. Headlines across the country read "Welch Letters: 'Communists Have One of Their Own (Ike) in Presidency'" and "Reds Influence U.S. Decisions, Welch Charges." Without warning, undiluted far-right conspiracy theories had barreled into the political mainstream.[69]

For conservatives concerned about respectability, this was a bridge too far. General Wedemeyer lost confidence in Welch's judgment and severed ties with the Birch Society, though he still traveled within far-right circles. Buckley, who had privately disavowed *The Politician*, now publicly condemned Welch. Despite the fact that the far right constituted the base of the conservative movement, Buckley argued in *National Review* that Welch's conspiratorial rhetoric was "damaging the cause of anti-Communism."[70] Buckley's pragmatic denunciation of Welch signified his gradual maturation into the role of conservative gatekeeper. Buckley sought to make Welch an exemplar of irresponsible politics, even though his own ideologies and activities intersected with the far right. Some conservatives, including Eisenhower and Goldwater, believed Welch's deluded views did not represent the Birch Society's rank and file and hoped Welch would resign. However, many ultra-conservatives professed themselves unperturbed by Welch's allegations and refused to excommunicate the Birch leader. "He may exaggerate sometimes," admitted Spruille Braden, a Birch council member and former U.S. ambassador, "[but] when you're in a barroom brawl, no holds are barred. You don't fight by the Marquis of Queensbury rules."[71] The Senate Internal Security Subcommittee, chaired by James Eastland, cleared the Birch Society as a "patriotic organization." The controversy surrounding *The Politician* represented an early skirmish in the struggle over the ideological contours of modern conservatism that pitted elements of the far right against those of the "respectable" right.[72]

Despite the handwringing over Welch's conspiracy theories, the Birch Society's grassroots tactics brought the organization significant influence, a fact Richard Nixon discovered during his 1962 California gubernatorial campaign. Orange County, his home territory, boasted thirty-eight Birch Society chapters. In fact, 300 Birch Society chapters dotted the California countryside, and members wielded tangible political power through local public offices and within the California Republican Assembly (CRA). Aware of the tempest involving Welch, Nixon believed it was imperative for the Republican Party to "not carry the anchor of the reactionary right" and swore to "take on the lunatic fringe once and for all."[73] Nixon defeated hard-line conservative Joe Shell for the Republican nomination, but Shell refused to support Nixon because of the former vice president's moderate platform.

When Nixon urged CRA members "to once and for all renounce Robert Welch and those who accept his leadership," the far right declared war.[74] Santa Clara County Republican assemblyman George W. Milias told newspaperman Leonard Finder that "Birch groups throughout the state were instructed to vote for [Democrat] Pat Brown for Governor in order to prevent that important job from falling into the hands of a Republican moderate such as Dick Nixon."[75] Courtney's CSA encouraged California members to ignore the gubernatorial election entirely in favor of boosting conservatives in congressional races. "Please don't waste energy or votes on either Brown or Nixon," Poag advised, "let collectivists fight their own battles!"[76] These statements revealed the far right's long game to eradicate Republican moderates. "A Nixon victory would practically destroy any chance we might ever have to get Goldwater as a presidential nominee," Poag continued. "Victory by Nixon would re-establish his preeminence in the GOP and would appear to prove that the only way to win is by being a collectivist."[77] Nixon's repudiation of far-right conservatism cost him the election—he lost to Pat Brown by just under 300,000 votes.[78]

The Birch Society was not the only far-right group capitalizing on the dis-illusion of California conservatives—Willis Stone's National Committee for Economic Freedom stormed into the new decade. By 1960 four states had passed resolutions in favor of his amendment to repeal the income tax, and NCEF and *American Progress* remained the movement's central nexuses. How-ever, the passage of the actual Twenty-Third Amendment, which expanded electoral privileges in Washington, D.C., stole Stone's tagline and prompted a thorough organizational rebranding. The cover of the 1961 Winter-Spring issue of *American Progress* blared "Liberty Is the Issue" as Stone transformed his "Proposed 23rd Amendment" into the "Liberty Amendment."[79] Then, in 1963, Stone purged the word "progress," a word long associated with liberal-left reform, from his periodical's title—*American Progress* became *Freedom Magazine*, a name better suited, Stone argued, for a magazine "devoted to the job of securing freedom for all."[80] Companies that once purchased space in *American Progress* switched to *Freedom Magazine* and tailored their promo-tional materials to match Stone's new slogans. For example, an advertisement for A. G. Heinsohn's Spindale Textile Mills declared, "The proposed Liberty Amendment . . . will restore solvency, sanity, and freedom to America."[81] Stone's last modification changed the NCEF's name to better reflect its mis-sion. "We have unified the name of this organization with the name of our project," read a 1963 internal report. "The legal steps have been completed to adopt the new name: Liberty Amendment Committee of the U.S.A."[82]

The rebranding helped the Liberty Amendment movement expand during the early 1960s. Kent Courtney, still serving as a Louisiana state chairman, worked closely with Stone by making financial contributions, advising Liberty Amendment Committee (LAC) chapters on increasing their outreach, and publishing informational materials. Hargis echoed Stone's rhetoric, criticizing liberals as "foolish spenders" and publishing articles demonizing the "hoax" of "soaking the rich."[83] At one of Stone's conferences, Congressman Utt led a panel titled "Economic Freedom and the Liberty Amendment" and state chairs held discussions on topics such as "stimulating study groups" and "setting up letter writing clubs." The LAC reached its zenith in the early 1960s, topping out at around 17,200 dues-paying members. By mid-1964, seven states—Nevada, Wyoming, Texas, Louisiana, Georgia, Mississippi, and South Carolina—had adopted the Liberty Amendment, resolutions had been introduced in twenty-two additional states, and Stone expected roughly a dozen more states to con-sider Liberty Amendment proposals. Though he did not know it, Stone was watching his movement reach its crescendo. Growing societal affluence, a lack of new tax policy threats, President Kennedy's tax cuts, and a mainstream conservative pivot toward tax reductions and corporate subsidies all reduced Stone's proposal to a radical outlier over the next decade.[84]

While Stone obsessed over the Liberty Amendment, Hargis waged a much broader culture war through a transcontinental speaking tour in 1963. Dubbed "Operation: Midnight Ride!"—named after Paul Revere's famous dash through New England on the eve of the American Revolution—the tour featured Hargis and Major General Edwin A. Walker. A gruff Texan, West Point graduate, and war veteran, Walker disagreed with Eisenhower's use of federal power to force desegregation, and after the Cold War crystallized he created the Pro-Blue program to fight an ideological battle against communism. Walker gave his soldiers voting advice through Pro-Blue and recommended numerous right-wing tomes, including Robert Welch's *The Life of John Birch*. Pro-Blue went afoul of military regulations, leading the Texan to resign his commission after receiving an official military censure. The far right sprung to Walker's defense. Kent and Phoebe Courtney published a book, *The Case of General Edwin A. Walker*, and nearly a year's worth of editorials in the *Independent American*, arguing that the "muzzling of the generals" was part of a broad conspiracy "planned in Moscow" to "'soften up' America for ultimate surrender to the International Communist Conspiracy."[85] Mainstream outlets such as *National Review* kept Walker at more of an arm's length. Ever the pragmatist and right-wing translator, Buckley straddled the line, commending Walker's dedication to fighting communism but declining to ascribe the "muzzling" controversy to a grand communist plot. Nevertheless, the Pro-Blue scandal turned into a cause célèbre for ultraconservatives because it proved, to them at least, that liberal-communists were stifling right-wing views.[86]

After leaving the military, Walker embarked on a second career as a far-right hell-raiser. Billboards, each bearing Birch-inspired slogans, including "Impeach Earl Warren," welcomed visitors to his home in the posh Dallas neighborhood of Oak Lawn. One year after a 1961 *Newsweek* profile made Walker one of the most famous ultraconservatives in the country, the native Texan ran for the Democratic gubernatorial nomination, arguing that the "thunder on the right" and a single-issue platform of anti-communism would propel him to the governor's mansion. His reactionary campaign recalled J. Evetts Haley's narrow segregationist platform in 1956. Small wonder, then, that Haley supported Walker to the hilt. "We're going to elect him governor," enthused Haley.[87] The Courtneys supported Walker's candidacy, too, running editorials about "Why the Liberals Fear Gen. Walker." In the end, Walker came within striking distance in a few counties but received just under 10 percent of primary ballots, losing out to future governor and moderate conservative John Connally.[88]

A few months later, Walker again made national headlines for stoking a riot at the University of Mississippi. The potential enrollment of James Meredith, a black Air Force veteran, led to a hostile situation similar to the Little Rock violence in 1957. Walker pledged to lead "tens of thousands" in protest against the integration of Ole Miss. President Kennedy hoped Governor Ross Barnett, a dedicated segregationist, would maintain law and order, but Kennedy's faith was misplaced.[89] Mob violence swept across campus, and during the riot Walker guided a charge of white students and adults, roughly three hundred total, against U.S. Marshals. Kennedy sent in 10,000 troops to quell the violence, but the damage was done; two people were dead, twenty others sustained injuries, and the United States had experienced yet another embarrassing spectacle. Federal troops arrested Walker on four counts, including "insurrection against the United States," and, in a move that irked conservatives, flew him to the U.S. Medical Center for Federal Prisoners in Springfield, Missouri, for a psychiatric evaluation. Senator Wayne Morse, an Oregon Democrat, speculated, "Maybe he's a sick man. If he is, he ought to be committed—he ought not to be at large."[90] Senator Eastland, on the other hand, blamed the Justice Department and federal marshals for inciting the mobs and ordered a Senate Judiciary Committee inquiry. After being released on bail, Walker flew to Dallas aboard Haley's private plane and was greeted by throngs of cheering right-wingers. Haley acted as Walker's personal spokesman, offering reporters a counternarrative that Walker "did not in any way urge the students to violence."[91] Right-wingers closed ranks around Walker after a grand jury declined to issue an indictment, claiming him not only as one of their own, but as a victim of a liberal-communist smear campaign.[92]

Hargis hoped the "Midnight Ride" speaking tour would capitalize on Walker's rising star. The Christian Crusade was already a formidable, million-dollar-a-year organization, and Hargis believed Walker's status as "a symbol of freedom and resistance to the growing tyranny of dictatorial socialism and communism" could burnish his organization's reputation.[93] Noting that the "fate of the nation" hung in the balance, Hargis encouraged grassroots activists to promote the rallies by calling friends, notifying pastors, printing handbills, and enlisting "every local patriotic group and fundamentalist Bible-believing church."[94] However, citing concerns about respectability, he cautioned his supporters to ensure that attendees were "good patriotic Americans and not associated with rabid anti-Semitic or anti-Catholic activities."[95] The ultraconservative network helped get the word out—Courtney's *CSA Newsletter* advertised the tour, for example. Most importantly, Hargis informed his constituency, "something dramatic needs to be done in America today to get people interested in the anti-communist and conservative movements again."[96] That "something dramatic" evolved into a barnstorming tour through twenty-nine cities in nineteen states, roughly 6,000 miles in six weeks.[97]

At each stop the duo formed a far-right harmony. Hargis spoke first on the "ever-present threat of communism internally," bringing his "bawl and jump" preaching to a crescendo against the National Council of Churches or a stirring defense of HUAC. Walker, a much more wooden speaker, went second, discussing the "mechanisms and threats of communism internationally," which often entailed harangues against the United Nations, foreign aid, or Kennedy's Cuba policy.[98] An ice cream bucket passed from hand to hand, gradually filling with donations as Hargis and Walker spoke. On the stump both men attacked numerous institutions, political figures, and government programs, but at the very first stop in Miami they added a new enemy to the rotation: the media. At the morning's press conference, *Palm Beach Post* reporter Edith Haynie asked Walker a pointed question about his role in the Ole Miss riot. Walker angrily rebuked Haynie and stormed out of the presser. Later that evening, Hargis upbraided Haynie in front of 3,000 attendees. "We never get fair reporting in the newspapers," Hargis roared, much to the crowd's delight. "They never tell what we say. They tell how we take up donations, and sell books, and pass the ice cream bucket for money . . . but they don't tell what we say."[99] The crowd shouted their approval, and the night's donation haul approached $3,000. Accosting the media not only made good money, it allowed Hargis to portray conservatives as an aggrieved group victimized by liberal tyrants. This sort of bare-knuckle politicking appealed to disillusioned conservatives and foreshadowed a future where national politicians, such as Vice President Spiro Agnew and President Donald Trump, would use the media as a punching bag for political gain.[100]

Hargis and Walker employed this anti-media strategy throughout the tour. In West Palm Beach, Hargis raged that the press distorted the "news to make the anti-communists' voice ineffective," then a few days later he called the Tampa press "unfriendly." After a reporter in Jacksonville wrote that Walker callously described the Ole Miss riots as "a comedy, almost amusing," Hargis accused the journalist of publishing a "twisted, distorted account of a perfectly legitimate statement."[101] One week later in Louisville, Walker revised his Ole Miss story, claiming he went to Oxford to *stop* any potential violence. It was Robert Kennedy's Justice Department that stirred up trouble, Walker said, calling himself "America's first political prisoner." Hargis told members of the Christian Crusade that this "vital information" had been "suppressed by the majority of the Liberal press."[102] Perhaps the best illustration of the pair's antipathy toward the media was a picture from an Atlanta rally showing a stone-faced Walker thrusting his hand in a photographer's face.[103]

While rally attendees ate up the attacks on the Kennedys, the media, and liberals in general, numerous groups started picketing the "Midnight Rides." Roughly two weeks into the tour some audience members heckled Hargis and Walker, and then, at the very next stop in Columbus, Ohio, the first real demonstrations occurred. The National Association for the Advancement of Colored People organized a picket line, and it was soon joined by other civil rights and left-wing organizations, including the Congress of Racial Equality, the AFL-CIO, and the Committee for Non-Violent Action. Protesters voiced their displeasure throughout the latter half of the tour, appearing in Cincinnati, Wichita, Denver, Oklahoma City, San Diego, and Los Angeles. A letter to the editor of the *Chicago Daily Defender*, an African American newspaper, applauded the demonstrators. The writer, N. W. Holland, a black man from Cotton Plant, Arkansas, worried that the Midnight Rides might spur "ill thinking people to accept a reactive impression of our people."[104] Liberal groups were not the only organizations keeping an eye on Hargis's "Midnight Rides"—the FBI tracked the tour as a potential breeding ground for white supremacists. At first Hargis said that the protests "create excitement and emphasize the threat of liberalism," but as the picketers numbered into the hundreds Hargis retreated to conspiracy theories. He told the Denver crowd, "These pickets outside, intentionally or unintentionally, are marching to the call of Khrushchev," and he later wrote that a policeman told him that a mysterious person paid each protester $1.00 for participating.[105]

Despite the protests, "Midnight Ride" succeeded thanks to the efforts of far-right activists and organizations. Ultraconservative groups helped turn out thousands at nearly every stop as the tour snaked through the South, Midwest, and Southwest before landing on the West Coast. Courtney's CSA, the Birch Society, and a smattering of local fundamentalist churches and right-wing radio stations supported Hargis's stop in Tampa. Hargis invited John Birch's parents onto the stage in Atlanta, and "Bull" Connor joined him on the dais in Birmingham. In Greenville, South Carolina, Hargis spoke in the chapel of Bob Jones University alongside the university's namesake, fundamentalist minister

Bob Jones Sr. When the tour touched down in Nashville, Tom Anderson presided over the meeting. The local Birch Society sponsored the Cincinnati meeting. Harry Everingham, a close associate of Willis Stone and leader of We the People, officiated the Chicago gathering at the Flick-Reedy Auditorium, where Hargis thanked industrialist Frank Flick for supporting Stone's LAC. Hargis described Amarillo as "on fire for God and Country" and claimed that most of the city officials, including the meeting's officiant Mayor Jack Seale, were Birch Society members.[106] At the Los Angeles finale, businessman Dallas B. Lewis—the owner of Dr. Ross Pet Food Company, Birch Society sponsor, and frequent advertiser in *Freedom Magazine*—took the stage with Hargis. Ultimately, the "Midnight Ride" tour traced a star map of the ultraconservative network, illuminating the grassroots constituency and far-right institutions that would push Goldwater onto the Republican ticket one year later.[107]

Surprisingly, Hargis's tour did not wind through Dallas, the epicenter of Texas ultraconservatism. John F. Kennedy traveled to Dallas, though, as part of an early campaign swing in November 1963. A full-page advertisement in the *Dallas Morning News*, purchased by three Birch Society members, welcomed Kennedy by bragging about recently elected conservative politicians and accusing Kennedy of communist sympathies. Kennedy fretted about the visceral right-wing streak that coursed through Dallas, or "nut country" as he called it. Indeed, numerous high-profile right-wingers called Dallas home, including Walker, Republican congressman Bruce Alger, fundamentalist minister W. A. Criswell, and H. L. Hunt, an avid conspiracy theorist and oil tycoon who funded the *Life Line* radio show. On November 22, Lee Harvey Oswald shot Kennedy twice as the president's motorcade crawled past downtown's Dealey Plaza. Kennedy died within hours, leading to the swearing-in of a new president, Lyndon B. Johnson.[108]

A tall, gruff, ambitious, and dynamic man from central Texas, Johnson made a name for himself in Congress as a dedicated liberal foot soldier before eventually becoming one of the most powerful Senate majority leaders in history. He yearned for the presidency, however, joining Kennedy's ticket only after failing to secure the nomination himself in 1960. After assuming the presidency, Johnson sought to forge his own legacy by expanding Franklin Roosevelt's liberal tradition and completing Kennedy's unfulfilled platform. Within a year, Johnson started a war on poverty and proposed a vast liberal program called the Great Society. Perhaps most importantly, both for securing his legacy and stoking right-wing anger, Johnson shepherded the landmark Civil Rights Act through Congress in the summer of 1964.[109]

To ultraconservatives, Johnson epitomized the worst of big-spending, tyrannical, communist-adjacent liberalism. Rather than viewing the civil rights bill as salubrious social progress, far-right activists saw it as a Trojan horse for communist subversion and social upheaval. Kent Courtney derided the bill as "Socialist legislation" that underscored "how the United States is now being Communized."[110] In one interview, Phoebe Courtney made a ham-fisted attempt to conceal her racism beneath a brittle glaze of liberty-based rhetoric, stating, "We've got niggers living in the next block to us and that's all right but we're against the civil rights bill because it destroys property rights and freedom of choice."[111] An editorial in Stone's *Freedom Magazine* blamed the bill's passage on a nebulous "creeping socialism."[112] Additionally, conservatives considered Johnson too soft on North Vietnam, too lenient on civil rights protesters, and too loose with the budget. In the pages of *American Opinion*, Martin Dies Jr. even suggested that Johnson overstepped his power in creating a commission to investigate Kennedy's assassination, let alone one helmed by the far-right's *bête noire*, Chief Justice Earl Warren. With the 1964 presidential campaign looming, the far right thought it was imperative to nominate one of their own to challenge Johnson's liberalism.[113]

The obvious choice was Barry Goldwater. The pro-Goldwater groundswell had blossomed since 1960. All of the frustration, resentment, and excitement that appeared during the last election—even going back to Taft's defeat in 1952—fueled a Goldwater surge in 1964. However, some Republicans feared the Goldwater fanatics and worried that extremists were taking over the party, particularly after Welch openly published his conspiratorial opus, *The Politician*. California Senator Thomas H. Kuchel, a liberal Republican, captured this sentiment in a speech, calling far-right activists "fright peddlers," "apostles of hate and fear" who posed a danger to "reasonable, rational, free American citizens."[114] Eisenhower received so much mail regarding Welch's accusations in *The Politician* that his staff created form letters dismissing Welch's claims as unhinged and redirecting voters to other, less conspiratorial right-wing organizations such as the Freedom Foundation. National journalists, including Buckley, piled on, characterizing Welch's conspiratorial beliefs as out of touch with the American polity. The anti-Birch campaign influenced public opinion: only 5 percent of the 1,250 adults surveyed approved of the Birch Society in the summer of 1963. Even the FBI opened an investigation into the Birch Society's potential for subversive activity—one agent described Welch as "unbalanced" and concluded that his "hate for Communist [sic] has obscured his judgment."[115] However, Republican congressman James B. Utt, a hard-line conservative, represented the other side of the coin, denouncing Kuchel's address as "a brazen attempt to smear millions of patriotic Americans by innuendo."[116] Even though the far right remained controversial, activists had built a national movement dedicated to right-wing revanchism. Getting a conservative on a major party's presidential ballot seemed like a natural next step.[117]

Goldwater had to fend off numerous opponents during the primaries because the Republican establishment feared his insurgent candidacy. Rockefeller became Goldwater's main rival, but other Republicans joined the race, including Pennsylvania governor William W. Scranton and former Massachusetts senator Henry Cabot Lodge Jr. Scranton's campaign, in particular, coalesced late in the primaries to stymie Goldwater's momentum. "The Establishment is Goliath, and you are David," Elizabeth Brown wrote to Goldwater. "Our only chance is that David and we little Davids can hit the Goliath in the eye."[118] The analogy appeared fitting—Goldwater seemed like a long shot, but he could call on a deep reservoir of zealous supporters who wanted to rupture the perceived dominance of postwar liberalism. Goldwater wrote back with assurance, "There are more Davids in this country than you might imagine. If we could only get enough smooth, round stones."[119]

Ultraconservatives formed the vanguard of Goldwater "Davids." By 1964, the far right had mobilized a substantial grassroots force. The Birch Society boasted a five-million-dollar yearly budget and claimed roughly 100,000 members, though scholarly estimates trim that figure to around 50,000 to 60,000 at the society's height. Much of the Birch Society's membership was concentrated in the Sunbelt—California and Texas, in particular—a key battleground region for Goldwater. Hargis's radio show had spread to forty-six states, and his Christian Crusade piloted a youth organization (the Torchbearers), annual conferences, and numerous speaking tours. Clarence Manion hawked Goldwater's *Conscience* and promoted the Chance for a Choice campaign on his *Manion Forum* broadcast, framing the coming election as an ideological battle to avoid losing his tax exemption. Phyllis Schlafly agreed with Manion. She criticized eastern establishment "kingmakers" in her book *A Choice, Not an Echo*, arguing that voters deserved a choice between competing ideologies, not a consensus, me-too imitation. Stone's LAC had chapters in almost every state, while Kent and Phoebe Courtney controlled a significant publishing and activist empire through the Conservative Society of America. Despite believing that Goldwater betrayed conservatives by supporting Nixon in 1960, the Courtneys shelved their third-party aspirations to organize and propagandize on behalf of the Arizona senator. "Tell your States's [sic] GOP delegates that a 'me-too' Republican like Richard Nixon cannot defeat President Lyndon Johnson in November," Courtney demanded in a CSA pamphlet, "but that a pro-American, anti-Communist like Barry Goldwater CAN DEFEAT JOHNSON."[120]

Goldwater's primary campaign sparked a flurry of ultraconservative activity, perhaps none more notable than the Independent Americans for Goldwater campaign waged by Kent and Phoebe Courtney. Unlike the Birch Society or Christian Crusade, both of which led quiet, behind-the-scenes movements, the CSA had no tax exemption to lose by stumping for Goldwater. Courtney attacked liberal and moderate Republicans, smearing Rockefeller and Lodge as "socialists" who were "soft on communism."[121] One of Courtney's inflammatory newsletters took a line straight from Welch, arguing, "Eisenhower was one of the best friends that the Communists ever had!"[122] Scranton, in particular, received withering denunciations from Courtney because he led the GOP's "Stop Goldwater" faction. Courtney claimed his organization distributed over 108,000 anti-Scranton pamphlets during a pro-Goldwater rally and took partial credit for Scranton's inability to effectively challenge Goldwater's movement.[123]

Throughout the spring of 1964, Goldwater amassed a significant delegate advantage, mostly from Sunbelt, Midwestern, and Rocky Mountain states. Goldwater's advisors decided to skip Oregon in favor of focusing on the potentially decisive California primary. Rockefeller, on the other hand, mounted a half-a-million-dollar last-ditch effort to win Oregon and build momentum heading into California. Courtney took it upon himself to lead the conservative offensive after Goldwater's campaign abandoned the Beaver State. He distributed over 20,000 pro-Goldwater pamphlets and purchased CSA ads demonizing Goldwater's opponents in all of Oregon's daily newspapers. Courtney also hired attractive young women to stand outside of storefronts and pass out pro-Goldwater CSA pamphlets in downtown Portland. The models donned red, white, and blue aprons, each handmade by Phoebe and Kent's personal secretary, and wore "Uncle Sam hats with a 'Goldwater for President' bumper sticker wrapped around the crown."[124] He paid the models $100 total to distribute CSA propaganda, a cost he considered "well worthwhile" after his efforts received coverage in the *Oregonian* and two local Portland papers.[125] The strategy underscored women's complex role in the conservative movement. On one hand, activists such as Schlafly and Phoebe Courtney wrote right-wing treatises and operated as key organizers.

On the other hand, hiring models, soon to be known as "Goldwater Girls," to peddle propaganda reinforced derivative gender stereotypes, which potentially explained women's flagging support for Goldwater. Ultimately, Rockefeller's financial largesse bedeviled Courtney's efforts and put the final nail in Lodge's campaign. Goldwater lost the Oregon primary, earning only 17 percent of the vote; however, Goldwater's returns could have been far worse without the activity of Courtney and the CSA, and Courtney's efforts underscored the lengths to which ultraconservatives would go to support Goldwater.[126]

On May 30, 1964, three days before the California primary, over 20,000 avid supporters gathered for "An Evening With Barry" at Knott's Berry Farm. Just days earlier Goldwater had refused to disavow Birch Society members. Instead, Goldwater said he welcomed their votes and praised former Republican congressmen and Birch members John Rousselot and Edgar Hiestand. The rally, one of the final California stops during the grueling primary season, featured a coterie of prominent right-wingers. Goldwater Girls led the crowd in a ceremony honoring the American flag, while rising star Ronald Reagan and Hollywood legend John Wayne emceed the event. Speakers included Texas senator John Tower, California Republican Joe Shell, and General Wedemeyer. The entire program was taped and broadcast statewide so Californians could hear Wedemeyer laud Goldwater as a "statesman" who "puts the country's interest before political success."[127] A more apt framing might have been that Goldwater and his supporters valued ideological purity more than political pragmatism, effectively writing moderation and compromise out of the movement. Goldwater did not suffer from his no-holds-barred conservative agenda, squeezing out a victory in California, but the razor-thin margin—52 to 48 percent—foreshadowed Goldwater's struggle in the general election.[128]

Despite trailing in public opinion polls, Goldwater remained the favorite heading into the July convention because of his delegate lead and strength at the grassroots level. Ultraconservatives wanted to push him over the top. Kent Courtney established an Independent Americans for Goldwater headquarters in San Francisco—he planned to "work for the nomination of Barry Goldwater running on a conservative platform, and ... [to] see Goldwater select an anti-Communist as his Vice-Presidential running mate."[129] Wallace Turner of the *New York Times* noted Courtney's, and the broader far right's, intent to "create a movement of opposition to all liberal and moderate tendencies in platform, candidates and speeches."[130] However, establishment

Republicans wanted no part of a Goldwater candidacy. Scranton criticized Courtney by name and proclaimed that the Republican Party stood for "responsible Americans, not radical extremists."[131] Mainstream media outlets followed suit. Richard Wilson, a journalist for the *Los Angeles Times*, wondered why "respectable" conservatives such as Buckley were willing to share an ideological bed with "kooks" such as J. Bracken Lee, Tom Anderson, and Courtney, the latter of whom Wilson described as "so far right he comes within one degree of making a complete circle."[132] There were even murmurs that Courtney was an "enormous headache" for Goldwater's campaign strategists, who "privately wish he would get lost in the High Sierras."[133] Despite party concerns over propriety and respectability, the far-right vanguard buttressed Goldwater's momentum heading into the convention.[134]

The Republican National Convention, staged at the Cow Palace near San Francisco, opened with civil rights activists protesting under the shadow of a giant Goldwater banner. Moderate and liberal Republicans tried in vain to truncate far-right influence. The first keynote speaker, Oregon governor Mark Hatfield, excoriated the "bigots in this Nation who spew forth their venom of hate," linking together ideologically disparate groups such as the Communist Party, Ku Klux Klan, and the Birch Society.[135] Goldwater delegates skipped Hatfield's address, but the speech heralded the battle over the soul of the Republican Party that dominated the convention. Despite conservatives being a minority in the Republican Party, their attendance surpassed expectations. The Goldwater delegation was young (mostly under fifty), male, affluent, and white, and even the Birch Society boasted about a hundred members on the convention floor. Conservative delegates hammered out a platform that blamed moderation and "federal extremists" for America's descent into centralization. Republican moderates fought back. Michigan governor George Romney proposed motions that favored civil rights and rejected radicalism, while Scranton and Rockefeller put forth planks to rebuke the Birch Society. When Rockefeller took the stump and warned that "the Republican Party is in real danger of subversion by a radical, well-financed, and highly disciplined minority," Goldwater supporters shouted him down.[136] Rockefeller smirked as a chorus of "We Want Barry!" chants rippled through the auditorium. The Goldwater faction swept away every moderate proposal, and then Goldwater crushed his competition on the first ballot. He received 883 votes. The next closest candidate, Scranton, earned a paltry 214.[137]

After winning the nomination, Goldwater gave an acceptance speech that deepened the divisions within the Republican Party. Goldwater was no unifier—he made clear on which side of the ideological chasm he stood. "I would remind you that extremism in the defense of liberty is no vice," lectured the Republican candidate. "And let me remind you also that moderation in the pursuit of justice is no virtue." After Goldwater brazenly courted the far right, Rockefeller issued a statement calling Goldwater's speech "dangerous, irresponsible, and frightening."[138] On the other side of the political aisle, the Democratic National Convention shut out conservatives and passed a resolution condemning the Birchers. Incensed, Tom P. Brady, the Democratic National Committeeman and segregationist author of *Black Monday*, issued a prescient warning: "When November comes this thing which they have said is a backlash, white backlash, they will find is a white tornado and what the South is going to do in November will astound the world."[139] Nevertheless, it was clear that many mainstream politicians from both parties thought ultra-conservatives, especially Robert Welch and the Birch Society, crossed the line of political propriety. The GOP's divided response to the Birch Society reflected the national mood, but Goldwater's words endeared him to hard-line right-wingers. Wedemeyer praised Goldwater as "the dedicated leader of this conservative movement," and compared the "extremism in defense of liberty" phrase to Patrick Henry's revolutionary battle cry: "Give me liberty, or give me death."[140]

During the general election, far-right organizations mobilized behind Goldwater's campaign. At Welch's insistence, the Birch Society maintained a façade of neutrality, but Welch encouraged Birchers to get involved as individuals. Conservative journalist George Todt described Birchers as "zealous Republican workers" and marveled at the number of "Republican grass roots leaders" that attended Birch Society meetings.[141] The Christian Crusade bestowed its "Real Man of the Year" award upon Goldwater for his willingness to "risk [his] fame and fortune to fight political liberalism . . . and for becoming a symbol of freedom to all men everywhere."[142] Though he normally avoided overt political statements, Hargis told *Crusade* readers that Goldwater's victory would be "the greatest miracle of the 20th century." He further confided, "Personally I am praying to God for that miracle."[143] Stone's Liberty Amendment Committee published pamphlets noting that 1964 provided a choice "between the exponents of diametrically opposed philosophies—that of limited Government and free enterprise, versus that of bureaucratic collectivism."[144] "The choice has not come as a result of a sudden change," read the LAC pamphlet. "It is due to a constitutional renaissance that has been building for many years." The Liberty Lobby sold polemical anti-Johnson books,

including its own *LBJ: A Political Biography*, and pamphlets about "the conspiracy to Get-Goldwater and to discredit Conservatives."[145] The Conservative Society of America remained one of the most prolific ultraconservative
political action groups. The Courtneys claimed they printed and distributed
over one million pro-Goldwater pamphlets throughout the campaign with the
purpose of exposing "the Socialist, pro-Communist backgrounds of those
opposing Goldwater."[146]

Goldwater's ascendance created a path for conservative southerners, many
of whom were Democrats, to support a Republican candidate, and Goldwater
went to great lengths to woo those voters. "Being a Republican, or at least
voting Republican if you can't make the switch, is much better for you because
the Republican Party represents Jefferson and Jackson more than the hollow
shell of the once great Democratic Party now in Washington," Goldwater told
30,000 people at a Mississippi rally.[147] Goldwater kept some segregationists,
notably Alabama's George Wallace, at arm's length, but his support for states'
rights and opposition to civil rights legislation convinced southerners to reex-
amine their relationship with the Republican Party. When Goldwater attended
a campaign event in Longview, Texas, Martin Dies Jr., the aging former congressman and HUAC chairman, confided to the crowd that he was voting for
a Republican "for the first time in my life."[148] Not many southern Democratic
politicians defected to the Republican Party, but Goldwater's conservative
revolution convinced one of the most notorious Dixiecrats, South Carolina's
Strom Thurmond, to make the switch. The 61-year-old Thurmond argued that
the Democratic Party had "invaded the private lives of people" while encouraging "lawlessness, civil unrest, and mob actions."[149] After Thurmond's pro-
nouncement, Goldwater stopped by Knoxville to congratulate the senator and
encourage other southerners to follow Thurmond's example.[150]

Though not as famous as Thurmond, longtime Texas Democrat J. Evetts
Haley abandoned the Democratic Party and joined forces with the Republicans. Disillusioned by the Democratic Party's embrace of liberalism and
perceived threats to southern tradition, Haley had crossed party lines on
occasion. He flirted with the Republican Party while leading the Jeffersonian
Democrats and Texans For America, and he even ran an absentee congressional campaign as a Republican in 1948. By 1964, Haley made the change official. Goldwater's platforms convinced him that the GOP was now the party
of conservatism. "[Goldwater] would return us to fiscal sanity and return us
to observance of the Constitution," proclaimed an exuberant Haley.[151] Haley
advanced Goldwater's crusade by writing a polemical book, *A Texan Looks*

at Lyndon: A Study in Illegitimate Power, which catapulted Haley's brand of ultraconservatism into the national political discourse and symbolized the Democratic Party's internecine schism.

Self-published out of Haley's Palo Duro Press, *A Texan Looks at Lyndon* landed during the critical summer months before the election. Haley claimed his book accurately portrayed Lyndon Johnson's personal and political career, but, in reality, it was a hatchet job. The book depicted Johnson as a scheming criminal whose support for the 1964 Civil Rights Act was a "most extreme position" that would "end the American Republic."[152] Haley detested Johnson on a personal level. He once called Johnson "the slickest operator ever sent to Washington from Texas" and further declared, "There is nothing more significant in Johnson's career than the fact that he has never been known to take an unpopular position and resolutely go down the line for it."[153] This was a ludicrous portrayal considering Johnson's obstinate devotion to divisive civil rights and foreign policy platforms. Plus, Haley often relied extensively on hearsay and personal vendettas rather than factual evidence. Regardless, Haley spoke for many southerners when he called Lyndon Johnson a "traitor to the South," and he augured that Goldwater could restore America's integrity.[154]

Republican campaign headquarters around the nation proffered right-wing books, including Haley's, in an effort to bolster Goldwater's electoral chances. Many GOP offices stocked *A Texan* alongside Schlafly's *A Choice, Not an Echo* and John A. Stormer's *None Dare Call It Treason*. Bookstores and airports around the nation carried Haley's book, and M. Stanton Evans of *National Review* noted that readers will learn "more about Lyndon Johnson from Mr. Haley than from an army of authorized biographers."[155] Contemporary journalist Donald Janson marveled, "Never before . . . have paperback books of any category been printed and distributed in such volume in so short a time. Never before has such literature been used to such an extent in a Presidential campaign."[156]

The far-right grassroots effort that supported Goldwater's campaign amplified the distribution of Haley's book. The Birch Society lauded *A Texan* as a book "loaded with facts," and sent instructions to Birch members: "You need it in your field equipment."[157] American Opinion bookstores loaded up on Haley's book, and wealthy Birchers purchased the one-dollar paperback in bulk for distribution at political rallies. Wedemeyer called it a "thought-provoking account," Courtney sent free editions to new *Independent American* subscribers, and the Liberty Lobby shipped copies to its members.[158]

Hargis advertised Haley's book in *Christian Crusade*, encouraging crusaders to buy and circulate *A Texan* so people could read the "sordid details" of Johnson's life. The book received accolades from a legion of smaller far-right journals and organizations, such as the *Bulletin Board of Conservatives* and the Austin Anti-Communism League. Haley even traveled the far-right circuit to promote his book. He gave a keynote address at the Independent Americans for Goldwater rally in Atlanta, where Courtney billed Haley as "The man whom Lyndon B. Johnson fears most!"[159] All told, Haley reputedly moved over seven million copies of *A Texan* during the campaign.[160]

The groundswell of support for Haley's book—from individuals, far-right groups and journals, and GOP branches—illustrated that a significant amount of the population sought a conservative turn away from Johnson's liberalism. This constituency commended Haley for assailing liberalism and lauding Goldwater as a legitimate political challenger to LBJ. Indeed, Haley's book tapped into the resentment felt by hard-line conservatives, anti-communists, and other groups that felt ignored and mocked by liberals. *A Texan* added fuel to the national movement that propelled Goldwater conservatism into the political mainstream. "There is a real stirring at the grass roots," Haley said. "Otherwise, how could somebody like me, who is absolutely unknown, and with no sales organization at all and no promotion, bring out a book and have those millions of sales."[161] To Haley, Goldwater's nomination and the support for *A Texan* evinced the beginnings of the conservative revolution he and other far-right activists had spent their lives trying to foment.[162]

Despite the success of Haley's self-published book, politicians and reviewers excoriated *A Texan* as politically motivated and poorly researched. Governor Robert E. Smylie of Idaho, the chairman of the Republican Governors Association, referred to Haley's book as "smut," while Paul W. Wolf, the Republican chairman in Colorado, said his outfit would "try to produce votes by entirely different methods."[163] Texas governor and Democrat John Connally dismissed Haley's book as a "propaganda piece" in a White House press conference, highlighting the chasm between Haley's insurgent ultra-conservatism and the party-loyal, moderate conservatism that inhabited the governor's mansion.[164] Mainstream media outlets roasted *A Texan* as "propaganda," "stridently partisan," and "outrageously, surreptitiously wrong."[165] *A Texan* contained minor highlights, such as recounting LBJ's electoral chicanery in the 1948 senate primary against Coke Stevenson, but the narration remained skewed by rumor and Haley's personal grudges. Most importantly, the mass repudiation of Haley's work illustrated that far-right conservatism remained out of step with mainstream politics despite Goldwater's nomination and outspoken supporters.[166]

In fact, many Americans, especially the press, viewed Goldwater diehards with a mixture of horror and bewilderment. The senator's flirtations with far-right groups made him an easy target for liberal Republicans and Democrats. Opponents characterized the Republican nominee as a dangerous extremist, and Goldwater found himself caught between alienating either mainstream Americans or his most hard-core supporters. Political pressure forced Goldwater into a lukewarm denunciation of the far right in an attempt to unify the divided Republican Party, but he still refrained from directly criticizing the Birch Society. Todt worried that ostracizing the Birchers would damage Goldwater's chances. In a letter to Eisenhower, Todt wrote, "I don't like to have them read out of the Republican Party. I want our side to win, not lose, at the polls. Dick Nixon ordered these people to go in 1962—and they did—and he lost the race for governor."[167] Nevertheless, writers feasted on Goldwater's public miscues and outlandish supporters. Scorning the far right came easy when activists such as Courtney prophesied a coming "purge of liberals from the Republican Party."[168] Goldwater argued that the press cast him and his supporters in an unflattering light, but a deep well of conservative radicalism existed within Goldwater's camp. Regardless of the election's outcome, the push for Goldwater represented the culmination of decades of ultraconservative organizing.[169]

*   *   *

The Republican Party's ideological schism prohibited a unified front for Goldwater. Major GOP figures such as Rockefeller and Romney refused to endorse Goldwater, though Nixon campaigned on Goldwater's behalf. Incumbent president Lyndon Johnson portrayed Goldwater as a foreign policy extremist during a time when global events, such as China's first nuclear test, seemed to call for restraint rather than hawkishness. To make matters worse, Goldwater's connection to ultraconservative activists alienated many voters—an October poll showed a scant 16 percent approval rating, compared to 49 percent disapproval, for the Birch Society. Even though Goldwater tried to tamp down his far-right supporters, the stench of radicalism emanated from his campaign.[170]

On Election Day, November 3, 1964, Johnson overpowered Goldwater. "Landslide" Lyndon won the popular vote by a margin of around sixteen million votes, netting a 61 percent to 39 percent victory. The electoral college returns were even more devastating. Goldwater garnered a scant 52 electoral votes compared to Johnson's titanic 486. It was the biggest electoral avalanche since Franklin Roosevelt trounced Alfred Landon in 1936. Johnson's victory was a microcosm of Democratic gains across the nation. Republicans lost seats in the Senate and House and within state legislatures, though the GOP did gain a handful of governorships. "The decimation of the Republican Party in Congress will make life on Capitol Hill much easier for Lyndon B. Johnson," wrote journalist Philip W. McKinsey.[171] As groups such as Americans for Democratic Action moved to push Johnson further to the left, liberalism, it seemed, remained hegemonic.[172]

The election of 1964 prompted a flurry of autopsies on the state of conservatism. Many commentators announced that conservatism, as a viable political ideology, had breathed its last. Historian Richard Hofstadter argued that the Goldwater movement stemmed from "the animosities and passions of a small minority," a symptom of a "paranoid style" of American politics.[173] James Reston of the *New York Times* wrote, "Barry Goldwater not only lost the Presidential election yesterday but the conservative cause as well."[174] "Of all the lessons the election returns taught," suggested journalist Robert J. Donovan, "the clearest is that the Republican Party, if it is ever to win again, must nominate a candidate who can attract the votes of Democrats and independents as well as Republicans."[175] According to the postmortems, not only had conservatism been crushed, voters had exiled it to the political periphery. Goldwater blamed Johnson's "ruthless" behavior, an apathetic citizenry, GOP backstabbing, and a biased liberal media for his overwhelming defeat.[176] After the shock had worn off, the Republican Party took steps to empower moderates and unmoor itself from Goldwater. Roscoe Drummond of the *Los Angeles Times* put it bluntly, "Thus ends the Republican Party's experiment with extreme conservatism."[177]

However, Goldwater's campaign was a crucial moment for the ascent of modern conservatism, despite contemporary obituaries that relegated right-wing thought to the historical dustbin. Goldwater won his home state of Arizona, but he also notched victories in Louisiana, Mississippi, Alabama, Georgia, and South Carolina. As Brady predicted, the South shocked the country. It was the first time in eighty-eight years that a Republican carried multiple Deep South states, marking an inflection point in the American political landscape. Goldwater's states' rights libertarianism appealed to the politics of white racial protest in the Deep South and fostered a right-wing base waiting to be capitalized upon by future Republican conservatives. Additionally, Johnson's landslide masked the fact that conservatism was growing in ways not evidenced by electoral results. The election witnessed the emergence of a new generation of far-right activists who had now solidified their influence within the Republican base. Donald Janson of the *New York Times* noted that Goldwater conservatives "feel they have gained a grip on the Republican Party machinery, and they have no intention of relaxing it."[178] Polls indicated that the Republican rank and file preferred a conservative charting the GOP's course. To all the journalists and pundits keen on burying conservatism, William Buckley wrote, "The undertakers are premature, I believe."[179]

The election should have been a disaster for ultraconservatives because Goldwater's loss was attributed to his association with radicalism, but they considered the campaign a rousing success. Far-right groups such as the Birch Society and Liberty Lobby rejoiced because over 27 million voters pulled a ballot for a true conservative. Courtney's Conservative Society of America started selling bright-orange bumper stickers proclaiming "27,000,000 Americans Can't Be Wrong!" Rather than trying to chart a new party, Haley wrote to his For America colleagues, "It seems to me we should concentrate on training Conservative control of the Republican Party where we have it and capturing it where we do not."[180] Even in the aftermath of Goldwater's defeat, the GOP represented the future of right-wing politics. The election not only helped crystallize modern conservatism, it signaled the maturation of far-right activism. Goldwater's 1964 campaign represented the apex of the grassroots mobilization ultraconservatives had championed for decades, and they were determined to maintain the energy that sowed the seeds of a national conservative movement.

CHAPTER 6

The Aftershock

Goldwater's defeat in 1964, rather than sounding the death knell for conservatism, prompted a conservative surge. The far-right movement, in particular, seemed primed to capitalize on the energy that propelled Goldwater's candidacy. Ultraconservatives had flexed their muscles, getting a true right-winger on a major party's ballot. Louisiana publisher Kent Courtney crowed, "The conservatives demonstrated that they could exert enough pressure and they could work hard enough to do an education job thorough enough to capture control of the Republican nominating convention."[1] The election results indicated that millions of Americans were willing to vote for a principled conservative, and far-right organizations benefited from their connection to Goldwater's campaign. Membership rosters soared and more people subscribed to right-wing periodicals than ever before. As the far-right network expanded across the nation, radicals looked poised to stage an insurgency within the Republican Party.[2]

The post-Goldwater moment seemed like a coronation for the far right, but they soon found themselves on the defensive. Other conservatives blamed the radicals for Goldwater's loss, arguing that far-right activists epitomized what historian Richard Hofstadter was calling the "paranoid style" in American politics.[3] The John Birch Society and its leader, Robert Welch, became the poster children for irresponsible politics. Out of concern for mainstream respectability, conservative media figures and politicians sought to distance themselves from the movement's original base. William Buckley, once a far-right ally, increasingly viewed ultraconservatives as a clear and present danger to the nascent movement. Goldwater's loss convinced Buckley that, in order to achieve respectability, conservatives needed to establish more stringent ideological parameters by disentangling themselves from the kooks. In other words, he wanted to redefine the conservative movement's core by excommunicating the far right. To achieve this, Buckley took direct aim at the Bircher faithful in a series of articles: "One continues to wonder how it is that the membership of the John Birch Society tolerates such paranoid and unpatriotic drivel."[4] Buckley was not alone. In the mid-1960s, numerous ultraconservative allies transformed from far-right translators into ideological gatekeepers, hell-bent on clarifying and strengthening conservatism's hazy borders by limiting radical influence.[5]

Numerous Republicans joined Buckley in disavowing the far right's conspiratorial radicalism. Republican congressman Melvin Laird warned that "anyone associated with the society is automatically considered irresponsible and, thus, his effectiveness must necessarily be impaired. This is why the John Birch Society has harmed the conservative cause."[6] Politicians who traveled in far-right circles, such as right-wing darling Ronald Reagan, had to walk a political tightrope. Reagan's views often dovetailed with those of the far right—he once disparaged Kennedy's "tousled boyish hair cut" as a disguise for "old Karl Marx" and fretted that "by 1970 the world will be all slave or all free"—and Birch affiliates were among his earliest supporters.[7] Like many other conservative Republicans, Reagan never fully repudiated rank-and-file Birch members, but he did criticize Welch's more outlandish conspiracies. This was not a heartfelt disavowal—conservatives wanted to have their cake and eat it, too. They needed ultraconservative support but hoped to create the illusion of ideological separation by saying the right things to curry favor with moderates. But even a few far-right allies, such as Christian Anti-Communism Crusade leader Fred Schwarz, recalibrated their relationship with the Birch Society. Welch and Schwarz shared a similar constituency of anti-communist evangelicals, and Welch promoted Schwarz's anti-communist schools to Birch members. Yet, Schwarz demurred to the idea that his organization shared any commonalities with the Birch Society, indicating that the Birchers' conspiratorial views, and those of ultraconservatives more broadly, were being cast as a political liability.[8]

The aftershocks of 1964 thus created a period marked by growth and uncertainty for the far right. With the recent Goldwater nomination in mind, some ultraconservatives favored coalescing within the GOP and reforming the party from the inside. Because Buckley and company were trying to write them out of the movement, however, other far-right leaders continued to believe that a third party provided the only avenue for successfully challenging liberalism. Goldwater, the consummate Republican, cautioned against third-party action, noting, "Whether it is liberal or conservative, it won't work, and it does not have any part in our American scheme of things."[9] Nevertheless, analysts Rowland Evans and Robert Novak observed that a substantial portion of far-right agitators were growing "disillusioned with the Republican Party as a vehicle for super-conservatism."[10] Under siege and riven by internecine disagreements, the far right struggled to maintain its pole position within the conservative movement and chart a unified path forward. During these pivotal years, the far right struggled. While being ostracized from the political mainstream, ultraconservatives thrived in the margins, propelling one of the most successful third-party insurgencies in American history with the candidacy of Alabama governor George Wallace.

*   *   *

On May 1, 1965, Louisiana publisher Kent Courtney convened the Congress of Conservatives in Chicago, hoping to assess the state of conservatism and reignite his long-range plan to unite right-wingers under a third party. Goldwater's defeat, he wrote to CSA members, illustrated the need for a "new national, anti-Communist, pro-American political party."[11] Nearly one decade after forming the Constitution Party in 1956, Courtney was tapping back into his third-party roots. The congress attracted a broad swath of far-right activists; over five hundred individuals registered for the conference, with roughly 150 to 200 people in attendance on opening day. Keynote speaker Robert Welch, who had recently garnered an honorable mention in Gallup's "Most Admired Man" poll, focused on the racial tensions knifing through America. "Thousands of whites will be murdered in time by the few Negro criminals," Welch declared, "and tens of thousands of fine Negroes themselves will be killed by those seeking leadership of the Negro state."[12] Welch was projecting his fear of a coming "Negro Revolutionary Movement" led by violent black communists who intended to create a "Negro Soviet Republic" in the Old Confederacy.[13] Paul Gapp of the *Washington Post* observed the conference's conspiratorial tones, noting that many of the guests held "an overriding fear that the Communist conspiracy already has progressed so far that America may be doomed; that all may be destined to imprisonment behind barbed wire, or be slaughtered."[14] In other words, standard far-right fearmongering.[15]

The congress reflected the ultraconservative movement's strategic fractures. In keeping with the tradition of previous far-right conventions, delegates passed a declaration of principles featuring typical nostrums, such as calling for a withdrawal from all projects and organizations linked to "the establishment of a world government" and a break in diplomatic ties "with all governments that are openly creatures of the Communist Party."[16] However, just like Courtney's National States' Rights Conference in 1956, the Chicago congress failed to bridge the persistent schism between those who favored the formation of a third party and those who opposed it. David Halvorsen of the *Chicago Tribune* reported, "Many [attendees] feared that the liberals would benefit from the formation of a new party since it would weaken the [conservative] ranks of the Republican Party."[17] The other faction, led by Courtney, preferred forming a new party featuring George Wallace as the standard bearer. The Chicago congress ultimately tabled all third-party proposals. Instead, a committee was formed to explore future options, including creating a national confederation of independent third parties. Courtney called the delay "realistic" because, as he wrote to his subscribers, "there were not enough new party organizations established in a sufficient number of states."[18] The plan called for the development of state-level third parties until a national apparatus could be organized.[19]

The congress's failure to form a permanent third party must have been a bitter pill for Courtney, though he put on a brave public face. By 1965 he had spent a decade trying, and failing, to organize conservatives under a new banner. The congress *did* inspire grassroots third-party activism, however. Attendees returned home from the conference and fostered right-wing movements in their own backyards. Mark Andrews, who served on the congress's political action executive committee, held a similar meeting in Missouri. Following Courtney's blueprint, Andrews sent mass mailers to "Missouri Conservatives" and urged people to support the formation of a new political party based on the Chicago congress's declaration. The ensuing Missouri convention brought in roughly one hundred delegates from neighboring states and eventually led to the creation of a new right-wing party. Other far-right parties popped up around the nation. An anti-communist party formed in Florida and a conservative party appeared in La Grange, Illinois. Twenty Michigan activists created the Michigan American Party to break the "one-party" system and stymie the implementation of a state income tax. The Michigan American Party even invited Courtney to attend the founding meeting as the keynote speaker. Similar conservative parties were founded in Pennsylvania, Georgia, Colorado, and Massachusetts, all of which claimed direct lineage with Courtney's Chicago congress.[20]

The national third-party crusade blossomed just one year after the Chicago meeting. Courtney situated the CSA as the movement's central hub and told members, "As soon as parties are organized in 30 or more States, then it will be time to call a national organizing convention and . . . raise sufficient money to run their national committee and establish a Washington office."[21] The umbrella term "Conservative Party" came to encompass multiple parties with different names across the U.S., including Florida's Constitution Party and Michigan's American Party. Some of these parties siphoned members away from local GOP branches. For example, two executive committee members of the Manitowoc County Republican Party resigned and joined the newly created Wisconsin Congress of Conservatives. One of the men, Joseph J. Birkenstock, president of Formrite Tube Company, explained his reasoning in a letter to the editor, criticizing the Democratic Party's "rapid push toward socialism" and the "slower but also dangerous socializing program that appears to have become the policy of most Republicans in government."[22] The other defector, small business owner Robert A. MacDonald, argued that conservative voices were "muted" by "vocal bi-partisanship" and Republican "me tooism" which resulted in "virtual uniparty rule." As a result, he concluded, "I intend to work towards the success of a new party for Wisconsin." The ultimate goal, aside from fomenting a permanent conservative movement, was to nominate a right-wing candidate for the 1968 election under a third-party banner.

The insistence on creating an alternate party underscored the far right's lingering distrust with the GOP as a home for their movement. Even though Goldwater earned tens of millions of votes, some ultraconservatives believed the party remained beholden to the "Modern Republicanism" of the previous decade. Courtney scorned conservative Republicans for placating liberals in the name of "party unity," and he viewed Republican votes in favor of the 1965 Voting Rights Act, which curbed Jim Crow–era voter discrimination, as confirmation that the GOP was complicit in advancing the liberal agenda. There were indicators, however, pointing to a strengthening conservative coalition within the Republican Party. For example, Reagan's gubernatorial and John Tower's Senate victories in 1966 illustrated an ascendant Sunbelt conservatism supported by numerous far-right activists, including Texan J. Evetts Haley. Nevertheless, many ultraconservatives still contended that both major parties were irreversibly tainted by socialism. This not only reflected the continued tactical struggle between third-party diehards and major-party insurrectionaries, but also foreshadowed ultraconservative support for George Wallace in 1968.[23]

The expansion of a right-wing third-party movement coincided with the growth of other far-right outlets, including Willis Stone's Liberty Amendment Committee. "Our crusade for liberty is reaching maturity," Stone bragged in early 1965.[24] Two decades after formulating the Liberty Amendment, Stone believed Americans were finally rallying around libertarian anti-statism. Republican congressman James B. Utt continued to sponsor Stone's amendment in the House, and numerous press sources, including local CBS affiliates, covered the Liberty Amendment Committee's 1966 convention. The committee even dabbled in television programming, creating a series titled *It's Your Money* that was sponsored by Sand Steel Building Company and broadcast on a local channel in Fargo, North Dakota. Stone's collaboration with the broader far-right network continued to pay dividends as Courtney's CSA and the Birch Society distributed millions of Liberty Amendment tabloids. By the end of 1967, Stone's LAC had chapters in all fifty states and boasted a National Youth Council and National Women's Division.[25]

There were signs that Stone's crusade was waning, however. Between 1965 and 1968, no new states passed Liberty Amendment resolutions, though Arizona came close in 1966. The publication of *Freedom Magazine* grew more sporadic; by 1968 it appeared bimonthly and sometimes even trimonthly. To arrest any declining interest, Stone turned to increasingly ambitious gambits. He tried to enact a local strategy, similar to Courtney's CSA action units, because he believed the committee struggled "to overcome the glitter of personalities and the delirium of politics."[26] Then, in 1968, Stone entered the New Hampshire and Wisconsin Republican presidential primaries as a write-in candidate. Stone's single issue: the Liberty Amendment. A political neophyte, he fared poorly. Stone earned such a dismal number of votes in Wisconsin that his name did not even appear in newspaper tallies. The *Washington Post* combined Stone's results with other listless campaigns that, altogether, earned 1.2 percent of the vote. Nevertheless, Stone proclaimed victory: "We attained our purpose . . . we put the Liberty Amendment into the national campaign as a main issue."[27]

Stone's boasting masked his concerns about the Liberty Amendment Committee's longevity. In the summer of 1968, he tried to negotiate a merger between his organization and the Birch Society. Stone originally reached out to the Birch Society for help in setting up the LAC grassroots committees, but Welch declined. Birch organizers were stretched too thin already. Stone wrote back, suggesting that the Birch Society simply absorb the Liberty Amendment Committee. After all, Stone admired Welch, once telling him in a private letter,

"I have long regarded you as the Thomas Jefferson of our time, capable of rallying people to the cause of truth, justice and equity."[28] The idea of a far-right merger made sense from a strategic perspective. The Liberty Amendment Committee contained battle-hardened libertarians who already cooperated with the Birch Society. Welch saw the potential—he envisioned turning Stone's organization into a Bircher front group. However, the Birch Society's executive committee thought "anything resembling a formal 'merger' of any other organized group into the Society would be a mistake."[29] Welch informed a crestfallen Stone that his proposed merger was dead on arrival.[30]

Stone felt a creeping sense of desperation concerning the far right's legacy. Writing to Welch, Stone confessed to "feeling that somehow time is running out on me, and perhaps on you" and stressed that "the movements we have both started, built and made relatively effective will, unfortunately, be very short-lived after you and I let go." Stone concluded, "I am trying to find the means by which continuity can be developed and this is a pretty rough deal."[31] According to Stone, the far-right movement was hurtling toward its terminus, not because of ideological infirmity or listless institutions, but because of old age. Thirty years had passed since the demise of the Jeffersonian Democrats, and now Father Time was catching up with the Jeffersonians' midcentury successors. When he entered the Republican primaries, Stone was 68 years old—the same age as Welch. Stone resigned himself to accepting "close coordination and cooperation" with the Birch Society rather than a merger, but he never stopped trying to leave a concrete foundation for future anti-tax advocates.

While Stone fretted about the future, other organizations thrived in the Goldwater afterglow. Billy James Hargis's Christian Crusade had grown into a million-dollar-a-year operation, which lined Hargis's pockets and invigorated his religiously infused culture war. Acrimony over changes in public education gave Hargis a platform to defend ultraconservative social and religious values. Controversies over desegregation continued unabated, and the Supreme Court's *Engel v. Vitale* decision, which found that official school prayers violated the First Amendment's Establishment Clause, enraged social traditionalists. Hargis charged that the public education system, from grade school through college, was poisoned by federal overreach and communist influence. He fretted about "dictators" controlling schools and warned that federal aid implied "more and more brainwashing of your children."[32] States should control education, Hargis argued, which aligned him with southern segregationists while putting him at odds with the general *zeitgeist* of education reform that was a staple of liberal platforms, including Johnson's Great Society. He also attacked higher education, contending that professors "poisoned" the minds of students under a cloak of "academic freedom."[33] In a televised address, Hargis encouraged crusaders to be proactive by enrolling their children in "pro-American" schools and demanding legislation that would permit the investigation and ouster of "communist" teachers.[34] In short, Hargis advocated reactionary, censorial education policies based on his own stringent ideological parameters.[35]

Hargis protested the teaching of evolution and stumped for prayer in public schools, but it was his protracted battle against sex education that best exemplified the far right's campaign against the perceived moral degradation of American culture. Sex education in the public school system started at the turn of the twentieth century, existing in an *ad hoc* manner at the local level until the advent of formalized "sex ed" classes in the 1940s and 1950s. The creation of formal classes led to greater parental scrutiny that was often heavily influenced by religious, racial, and anti-communist anxieties. Far-right groups, including the Christian Crusade, formed the bleeding edge of this reactionary backlash. Hargis fashioned anti–sex education talking points that then filtered into the conservative mainstream. Sex education, Hargis told his radio listeners, is "part of a giant communist conspiracy to demoralize the youth, repudiate New Testament morality in the land, and drive a cleavage between students and parents."[36] Hargis and the Christian Crusade cynically wielded the Supreme Court's *Engel* decision as a weapon. If sex was a religious topic, as Hargis believed, and the Establishment Clause prohibited the government from creating a state religion, then, Hargis reasoned, teaching about sex in public schools was tantamount to teaching about religion. "Well, if teachers in the public schools are not qualified to teach religion, they are certainly not qualified to teach sex," Hargis told his radio listeners.[37] Hargis conjured images of the innocent "little red school house" in order to demonize sex education as perverted and un-American. The crusade's salaciously titled book, *Is the School House the Proper Place to Teach Raw Sex?*, soared to 250,000 in sales as the debate raged, which ensured Hargis's prominence within the culture war maelstrom.[38]

Hargis did not fight against sex education alone—the far-right network mobilized to defend traditional values and demonize the liberal state. George Wallace attacked federal education policies as a "blueprint devised by the Socialists which has as its objectives the capture and regimentation of our children and the destruction of our public education system."[39] Clarence Manion accused the Supreme Court and various leftist bogeymen of trying "to secu-larize and demoralize the government" while turning the nation into a "nihil-istic hell on earth."[40] The Birch Society joined the cause, too. Welch criticized sex education as a "communist plot" to "keep our high school youth obsessed with sex."[41] The Birch Society formed a front group, the Movement to Restore Decency (MOTOREDE), which became the first national group to lobby for local and parental controls over sex education rather than federal man-dates. One MOTOREDE chapter leader reasoned that sex education was "the major reason for the unrest among youth, who are growing up in a permis-sive society."[42] The campaign occasionally intertwined with the far right's racist underpinnings. Willis Carto's Liberty Lobby created a "Save Our Schools" cam-paign to protest everything from sex education to integration and interracial dating. According to the lobby, a nebulous cabal of "totalitarian Leftists" was waging a war of "anarchy and mind molding" against America's children.[43]

The far right's campaign against sex education represented a key skirmish within the larger culture war against liberalism. It encompassed the far right's religious moralism, political conservatism, and conspiratorial anti-communism. Ultraconservatives deployed their anti-statist rhetoric to challenge federal reg-ulations and advocate for a local, family-oriented social structure. Their efforts ultimately played a key role in the smear campaign against the Sexuality Infor-mation and Education Council of the United States (SIECUS) curriculum. Far-right traditionalists lambasted the curriculum creators as communists and spread false conspiracies that educators were actually demonstrating sex to young children. This fearmongering galvanized a constituency of social conser-vatives who believed parents should be society's cultural gatekeepers. The battle over sex education also signified that schools remained contested grounds, and conservative white Christians intended to maintain their cultural hegemony. The vanguard formed by ultraconservative traditionalists sought to erase the legacies of liberal reform, bequeathing a tradition of culture-war rhetoric that would be exploited by future generations of right-wing activists.[44]

Hargis's stature as a far-right culture warrior—particularly his inflamma-tory, politically driven radio broadcasts—made him a target for liberal detrac-tors and caught the attention of the Internal Revenue Service. At its founding in 1947, Hargis's Crusade applied for and received an IRS tax exemption as an "educational organization." However, concerns about the prevalence and influence of right-wing tax-exempt groups led John F. Kennedy's administra-tion to create the Ideological Organizations Project (IOP), a branch within the IRS that targeted political opposition groups. Using tax audits to obfuscate the project's true intentions, the IOP investigated numerous groups along the right-wing fringe, including Hargis's Christian Crusade, Welch's Birch Society, and Courtney's Conservative Society of America. The IOP reviewed and sustained the Christian Crusade's tax exemption multiple times in the early 1960s. But, as Hargis's notoriety grew, political pressures from the national IRS office led to the revocation of the Crusade's exempt status in 1964 on the grounds that Hargis's activities extended beyond education and into the realm of political activism. Hargis viewed this as politically motivated harassment and sued the agency. "This is clearly an attack upon religious liberty and free exercise of religion as guaranteed in the First Amendment," wrote an incensed Hargis. He concluded that the IRS provided "liberty for religious liberals but no religious liberty for conservatives or fundamentalists."[45] In other words, Hargis accused the government of playing favorites.[46]

The IRS indeed struggled to delineate the dividing line between political commentary and political activism, an issue at the heart of its accusations against Hargis's Christian Crusade, but its decision to revoke the Crusade's tax-exempt status was easily defensible. Hargis used the Crusade to attack liberal platforms and politicians and fostered a nationwide conservative movement through the Crusade's media outlets and activist base. In one radio address Hargis dissembled, "No matter how much I would want to endorse Gov. Wallace or Richard Nixon or Sen. Goldwater or any other candidate, I wouldn't dare subvert our present litigation against the Internal Revenue Service."[47] Such a statement amounted to an implicit endorsement of conservative candidates, not to mention the fact that the Crusade published fanatical pamphlets such as "These Liberals Are Allied to Destroy Your Christian Crusade" and "Liberalism's Latest Gestapo on the Left," all of which made Hargis's apolitical professions difficult to believe.[48] The IRS did probe right-wing groups at a higher rate than liberal organizations, but Hargis ignored the fact that ultraconservative groups, including his own, often violated IRS regulations. Hargis insisted that the Christian Crusade had done nothing to "justify the government's cruel and oppressive punishment," but it is beyond doubt that the Christian Crusade was an activist organization following a conservative political agenda.[49]

Nevertheless, Hargis's fight against the IRS became a cause célèbre for right-wing politicians. Speaking on the House floor in 1967, Kentucky Republican Gene Snyder observed, "I suspect the problem is that Dr. Hargis' [sic] organization is on the wrong side of the center line of the highway to suit the Federal Government."[50] One year later, Utt made a similar argument, noting that the IRS found Walter Knott of Knott's Berry Farm liable for tax deductions based upon contributions Knott made to the conservative California Free Enterprise Association. Utt considered the IRS's ruling against the Christian Crusade and Knott's Berry Farm blatant liberal hypocrisy that hinted at communist subversion. "It is amazing how easy it is to deduct money for . . . left-wing organizations which support the socialistic Communist ideology," Utt marveled, "but when you attempt to educate people on the free enterprise capitalist system, you are then dispensing political propaganda."[51] For the far right and their fellow-traveling politicians, the revocation of tax exemptions represented only the tip of the iceberg—untold magnitudes of federal tyranny lurked beneath the water.

In particular, ultraconservatives blamed the federal government for enabling, even stoking, urban unrest and cultural decay. After the passage of the Fair Housing Act, which prevented property owners from using race to discriminate against potential tenants, Kent Courtney offered thinly veiled racist warnings to his readers that "rioters and looters" could "wreck your property or neighborhood."[52] Phoebe Courtney wrote that Johnson's effort to relax immigration laws would allow "unlimited, non-quota Orientals and Negroes" to enter the country, threatening "American jobs, our cultural heritage, and national security."[53] Racial violence morphed into treasonous liberal conspiracies when viewed through the ultraconservative prism. During a radio interview with General Edwin Walker, Hargis alleged, "I think these riots [in Detroit] are part of a design." Walker, a committed conspiracy theorist himself, agreed: "They couldn't possibly be spontaneous at all. They are too large . . . [they] have to be planned."[54] Dan Smoot accused civil rights activists of trying to "establish a Soviet dictatorship," and Utt alleged that Democrats promoted "civil rights by riot, strife, and revolution" and were "doing much to implement the communist manifesto."[55] Even Willis Stone, who generally avoided racial issues, argued that guaranteeing civil rights "would deprive others of *their* freedom."[56] The far right's racial animosity fed into an undercurrent of conservative resentment, which in turn laid the groundwork for right-wing campaigns, both immediate and in the future, against minority and immigrant communities.

Ultraconservatives saw themselves as under attack from liberal bureaucrats, communist subversives, and milquetoast moderates, and this besieged mentality deepened when long-simmering tensions erupted in the late 1960s. Crime and leftist social movements appeared more prevalent, and ominous, than previous decades. Street violence received breathless media coverage.

The seemingly interminable Vietnam War, and especially the Tet Offensive, exacerbated the "credibility gap" and eroded public trust in the government. Hargis went so far as to label President Johnson "America's first dictator."[57] The far right were not the only critics of Johnson's liberalism—the student anti-war movement, led by Students for a Democratic Society, swelled and turned militant. Similarly, the civil rights movement entered a more radical phase, with groups such as the Black Panthers taking up arms in self-defense and the Student Non-Violent Coordinating Committee espousing Black Power. To the far right, these developments evinced a grand conspiracy. "Communists and their fellow-travelers are behind the cries of black power," Courtney wrote in his magazine. "They are behind the racial turmoil; they are behind the riots and the burnings of our cities."[58] The chaos in the streets, Johnson's support for civil rights, and the quagmire of Vietnam irreparably fractured the remnants of the New Deal coalition. Contemporary analyst Theodore H. White described the state of Democratic liberalism as "out of date as a Ptolemaic chart of the Mediterranean."[59]

With liberalism at its weakest point since Franklin Roosevelt's New Deal revolution, the far right searched for a politician who could carry the ultraconservative banner into the 1968 election. They found a kindred spirit in former Alabama governor George Wallace. Born into rural poverty in 1919, George Corley Wallace worked odd jobs as a boy and made a name for himself as a bantamweight Gold Glove champion in high school. Politics captured Wallace early. While enrolled at the University of Alabama he networked with local Alabama politicians and ran for half a dozen student government positions, serving as the freshmen class president. World War II briefly suspended Wallace's political ambitions. He joined the war effort as a flight engineer with the Twentieth Air Force group in Tuscaloosa, where he met and soon married Lurleen Burns. After the war he quickly returned to the political fray. His first big break came when he served as an assistant to the Alabama attorney general, and then Wallace struck out on his own, winning an election to become a member of the Alabama House of Representatives in 1946—he was only 26 years old.

Wallace made a name for himself as an ambitious young politician with a penchant for folksy populism and segregationist rhetoric. As an alternate delegate to the Democratic National Convention in 1948, Wallace disagreed with Truman's stance on civil rights but did not walk out with the rest of the Dixiecrats. Instead, he hitched himself to the party's loyalist faction in order to curry favor with Democratic leadership. In 1958, he barnstormed across

Alabama as a gubernatorial candidate but lost to the state's attorney general, John Patterson, a staunch segregationist who leaned on race-baiting tactics to whip up the white vote. It was a formative moment for Wallace. Before making his concession speech, Wallace told some of his closest advisors that "no son-of-a-bitch will ever out-nigger me again."[60] Wallace returned to the gubernatorial race in 1962 reborn as a hellfire segregationist. He soundly defeated his opposition, and then, during his inaugural address, solidified himself as the leading tribune of white rage. "We will tolerate [the federal government's] boot in our face no longer," he proclaimed before bringing the house down with his most indelible phrase: "I draw the line in the dust and toss the gauntlet before the feet of tyranny, and I say: Segregation now, segregation tomorrow, segregation forever."[61]

Despite not being a physically imposing man—he stood a mere 5'7" and weighed less than 150 pounds—Wallace cut a formidable figure. His slicked-back hair, dark eyes, cleft chin, and broad smile could quickly erupt into scathing denunciations of Washington or harangues about communist subversives. He built a career upon a foundation of white aggrievement and states' rights conservatism. As governor, he fought to maintain segregation, most famously during his "stand in the schoolhouse door" when he tried to prevent the integration of the University of Alabama. He encouraged Eugene "Bull" Connor's aggressive response to civil rights protesters in Birmingham, making Alabama the poster child of violent massive resistance. After Wallace reached his term limit in 1966, Lurleen ran and won the governor's seat. Everyone knew that George was the one running the show, but he already had his eyes on the White House.[62]

By 1967 it was an open secret that Wallace was going to run for president. But rather than trying to win the nomination of a major party, Wallace tapped into the far-right third-party movement by running as the American Independent Party candidate. After all, like the rest of the far right, Wallace saw little separating Republicans from Democrats. "We intend to give the people a choice," Wallace quipped. "The two national parties are Tweedledee and Tweedledum. There's not a dime's worth of difference between them."[63] Despite being an extreme long shot, Wallace believed he could throw the election to the House of Representatives by carrying the entire South and picking up a couple of industrial midwestern states. Such a scenario would have made Wallace the kingmaker—either the House would elect him outright or other presidential candidates would have to agree to Wallace's terms to secure his support, meaning a probable abandonment of civil rights platforms and a boost to states' rights philosophies. "Wallace has long contended that the nation is ripe for a cataclysmic realignment of politics which will mean the death of one of the national parties," observed Ray Jenkins of the *Christian Science Monitor*. "He envisions himself as a prime influence in this realignment of liberals and conservatives."[64] In short, Wallace's strategy threatened reactionary reform by taking the electoral system hostage.[65]

Ultraconservatives played a critical role from the beginning of Wallace's campaign. Sheriff Jim Clark, the man responsible for the police brutality during the Selma march, as well as Klansman and Wallace speechwriter Asa Carter organized a meeting to coordinate the far-right vanguard. Two dozen people representing a broad cross-section of the far right came to the meeting at Montgomery's Woodley Country Club. Prominent attendees included former Mississippi governor Ross Barnett and Leander H. Perez Jr., the segregationist millionaire who dominated Louisiana's Plaquemines Parish and became Wallace's official Louisiana state campaign manager. Floyd G. Kitchen, the chairman of the Missouri Conservative Party, and Kent Courtney represented the national third-party movement and the broader ultraconservative constellation. Courtney accompanied Wallace on his tour of California in early 1968, boasting that he found "members of the John Birch Society, of the Conservative Society of America, and subscribers of the Independent American working in the Wallace Headquarters everywhere we went."[66] The far right turned out to be both the campaign's stimulant and its primary support group.[67]

Wallace's campaign was a media spectacle that reflected his constituency's ultraconservative sensibilities. He traveled with a heavily armed entourage. At a campaign stop at the Orange County Fairgrounds, for example, Wallace strode to the rostrum flanked by sixteen Alabama state troopers. The podium covered him from three sides and was designed to withstand bullets from a would-be assassin. Wallace loved to tell stories, and one of his favorites involved committing violence against a hypothetical protester. "When I get to be President," Wallace regaled a Daytona Beach crowd, "if an anarchist lies down in front of my car that's the last one he'll ever want to lie down in front of." The crowd ate it up. "Run over them, George," someone shouted from the audience. "Kill the sonsabitches."[68] Journalist Thomas O'Neill noted that Wallace's show of force was "aimed at the titillation of his special audience type, running heavily to the John Birch Society persuasion."[69] Cars parked outside of Wallace's Long Beach rally bore Bircher-inspired bumper stickers: "SUPPORT YOUR LOCAL POLICE." "REGISTER COMMUNISTS, NOT FIREARMS."[70]

Part of Wallace's appeal was his outsider status—he was a political grenade thrower, a verbal pugilist, and with the country riven by racial strife in the late 1960s, he hoped to capitalize on white anxiety and deep-seated racism.[71]

Wallace did not paint an uplifting view of tomorrow but instead provided brimstone parables about a wayward country. Despite claiming that Vietnam was his number-one issue, Wallace deployed the language of "law and order," communist conspiracies, and culture wars. "Stand Up for America," his slogan demanded. Wallace demonized everyone from "briefcase-toting bureaucrats" and communistic "pseudo-intellectuals" to "bearded professors" and college "anarchists." Like the rest of the far right, Wallace loosely used the terms "communists" and "subversives" to slander opposing ideologies and hint at racial issues rather than raise serious questions about national security. The state, in Wallace's view, existed as a force for law and order, a maintainer of hierarchies through selective governance rather than a guarantor of civil rights or equality. His solutions included more police and more troops but, somehow, less government. Wallace mused in one speech, "If we could let the police run this country for two years, the streets would be safe." His anecdotes pandered to white fears of urban chaos and promoted violent vigilantism. "Bam, shoot 'em dead on the spot! Shoot to kill if anyone throws a rock at a policeman or throws a Molotov cocktail," Wallace told one audience. "That may not prevent the burning and looting," he intoned, "but it will sure stop it after it starts."[72] Wallace reveled in his authoritarian populism, juxtaposing the "common man" against the scourge of "lazy" welfare recipients and the tyranny of "big government," with an underlying message that only he could solve the problems.[73]

Despite actively exploiting racial anxieties, Wallace tried to separate himself from the overt racism that dominated his gubernatorial years. Wallace employed the more muted phrase "local government forever" rather than the fire-breathing "segregation forever."[74] When an ABC-TV film crew recorded Wallace shaking hands with Robert Shelton, the Imperial Wizard of the Ku Klux Klan, Wallace ordered a bodyguard to seize and destroy the footage. On CBS's *Face the Nation*, Wallace weaponized the very idea of being called a racist, stating, "I don't regard myself as a racist and I think the biggest racists in the world are those who call other folks racist."[75] Wallace argued that a belief in segregation did not connote racism. "The first thing I want to say is—and you tell this to Buckley—Buckley thinks I'm a racist you know—is that I'm not a racist," Wallace told James Kilpatrick of *National Review*. "Oh, I believe in segregation all right, but I believe in segregation here in Alabama. What

New York wants to do, that's New York's business."[76] Wallace was sending a message to his supporters: you are not a racist for demanding law and order or believing in segregation and states' rights.

Wallace's racial views resonated with many Americans. A Little Rock waitress told reporters, "I've got two young kids at home that will be going to school in a few years. I didn't go to school with niggers, but next year my kids will be going with them unless we elect George Wallace." For emphasis, she added, "He'll stop all that foolishness."[77] Roy Harris—president of the Citizens' Council of America and chairman of Georgia's Wallace for President organization—praised Wallace for speaking up about "states' rights and the right to run your own schools." But, Harris admitted, "when you get right down to it there's really going to be only one issue and you spell it n-i-g-g-e-r."[78] Even George Lincoln Rockwell, the American Nazi Party leader, said, "While not a 'Nazi,' [Wallace] is close enough as that, as President, he would probably preserve our nation and race."[79] Wallace supporters, in short, viewed the world through a lens of white anxiety and aggrievement. Wallace's folksy authoritarianism was a finely tuned racist dog whistle intended to drum up ultraconservative support, siphon voters away from the major parties, and realign the two-party system.

Even though red-baiting, racist demagoguery brought Wallace a great deal of support, his state-level fiscal liberalism threatened his conservative reputation. As governor, Wallace implemented regressive taxes on gasoline and monetary transactions and embraced deficit spending in order to expand Alabama's budget and boost welfare spending for his supporters. He protected New Deal legacies, such as farm subsidies and Social Security, and reinforced liberal spending measures such as highway construction, even though he despised the federal strings attached to government programs. As one journalist sarcastically wrote, "Wallace is a 'state's righter' who apparently wants the Federal government to continue to shovel disproportionate amounts of Federal funds to his state but to have no say as to how it is spent."[80] Wallace defended his liberal economic spending by calling it an investment "in our children's future" and an effort to "feed the economic stream of our growing industry."[81] These economic policies nevertheless ran contrary to the libertarianism pulsing throughout the broader conservative movement.[82]

Given Wallace's penchant for state-level tax-and-spend policies, far-right supporters looked for signs of fiscal conservatism. Wallace did not endorse the Liberty Amendment in public, but there was evidence of tacit approval. At a meeting of Alabama's chapter of Women for Constitutional

Government (WCG), Lurleen Wallace provided the opening remarks before Mary Cain, a segregationist newspaper editor, took the stage to declare that the Liberty Amendment would stop the "national evil" of federal overreach.[83] A few months later, George met with WCG advocates to discuss the proposed amendment. Alabama failed to pass a Liberty Amendment resolution in 1963, but he privately reassured one supporter, "I feel reasonably sure that stronger efforts will be made for the passage of this Amendment when the Alabama Legislature convenes in the next session."[84] Wallace's muted public response allowed ultraconservatives to use him as an empty vessel—they claimed Wallace supported the amendment to the hilt. Writing for the *Conservative Journal*, Courtney said that Wallace viewed the amendment as a positive move toward local governance and constitutional principles. Tom Anderson wrote in his widely syndicated "Straight Talk" series that Wallace favored the Liberty Amendment to oppose "centralized government and world government."[85] An article appeared in *Freedom Magazine* titled "Wallace for Liberty Amendment," in which Stone declared that the Liberty Amendment was "the best possible yardstick" to measure candidates.[86] Stone never formally endorsed Wallace, despite privately describing him as having "all the attributes of greatness." [87] However, Stone's words were clear enough: Wallace favored the Liberty Amendment; thus, he was the best candidate.[88]

Wallace's anti-communism, selective anti-statism, and segregationism held significant appeal for far-right activists looking for a home. Ultraconservatives such as Hargis, Smoot, and Walker all voiced support for Wallace's presidential aspirations. Manion brought Wallace onto his radio show to discuss the "prevailing unlawful disorder" afflicting the country.[89] Naturally, Wallace's support network was especially dense in the South. Georgia governor Lester Maddox stumped for Wallace around the country, while Arkansas Supreme Court justice Jim Johnson organized Wallace's campaign in Arkansas. At a Georgia Klan meeting, Shelton showed a Birch Society film that depicted urban riots as communist-inspired. After the video, Shelton urged the assembled Klansmen to support George Wallace: "I think he's our only salvation."[90] Wallace openly courted the militant, racist vote and refused to unequivocally condemn his own radical entourage, though he did disavow groups that openly advocated violence (militia groups such as the Klan and the Minutemen supported him anyway). Wallace knit together a motley coalition of conservative southern Democrats, reactionary West Coast Republicans, Citizens' Council members, disgruntled blue-collar laborers, and right-wing businessmen from across the nation.[91]

Out of Wallace's ultraconservative patchwork, one of the most dedicated advocates was Kent Courtney. The 1968 presidential election provided the opportunity, Courtney believed, for conservatives to illustrate their electoral strength. Courtney transformed the Conservative Society of America into the grassroots vanguard of the Wallace operation, dismantling parts of his own organization to support Wallace's campaign. The CSA shuttered its radio programming in order to fund "Wallace for President" clubs throughout the nation, and the organization started selling "Win with Wallace in 1968" buttons. Fellow Birch Society members, notably Tom Anderson of *Farm and Ranch*, were among Courtney's earliest boosters. Courtney used mass mailers and the *CSA Newsletter* to keep his members up to date regarding the minutiae of the election season, sending polls showing Wallace's favorable numbers in southern states and information regarding conventions that Courtney organized throughout Louisiana. Courtney also started publishing *Wallace for President News*, which became the semiofficial periodical of Wallace's campaign. Similarly, Roy Harris turned his newspaper, the *Augusta Courier*, into a pro-Wallace outlet. Wallace's campaign infrastructure itself became a critical hub within the far right's institutional network.[92]

Courtney's publications pandered to the undercurrent of racism that permeated Wallace's supporter groups. For example, when Wallace visited Richmond, Virginia, he was greeted by a jeering crowd of civil rights protesters. Courtney detailed the encounter in *Wallace for President News*, describing one of the activists as a "buxom Negress" with "her hair standing on end like a fuzzy wuzzy" and "her eyes popping in all directions, her body contorted with a rhythmic rage." Courtney tried to contrast the supposed uprightness of Wallace's campaign with the perceived subversion of the civil rights movement. "If you closed your eyes you could imagine yourself in deepest Africa far from any civilization," Courtney wrote. "These chanting puppets of the red-black plague in America may have been trained at the Communist camp in Midvale, New Jersey, the Highlander Folk School in Monteagle, Tennessee, or at some local temple of the fanatically anti-white Black Muslims."[93] None of the places Courtney listed were "communist camps," but the imagery convinced readers that the protests were somehow treasonable. In reality, Courtney's racist language highlighted the symbiosis between anti-communism and segregationism and appealed directly to the ultraconservatives undergirding Wallace's campaign.[94]

While much of the far right marshaled behind Wallace, other conservatives, especially party-line Republicans and those yearning for mainstream respectability, took a dim view of his candidacy. Buckley worried that Wallace might siphon support away from the Republican Party, particularly if the GOP put forth a moderate-liberal candidate. The Republicans could defuse Wallace by nominating a conservative, Buckley wrote, which would ensure that "some of the votes pried loose by Wallace from Democratic fastnesses might tumble down into Republican rather than Wallace ranks."[95] Some right-wingers wondered whether Wallace should even be classified as a conservative. "When it comes to civil rights and the state-federal relationship, George Wallace tents in the conservative camp," Kilpatrick concluded. "On other issues, contrary to widespread impression, he is moderate to populist."[96] Frank S. Meyer, *National Review*'s resident political philosopher, agreed that some of Wallace's positions ran "parallel" to conservatism, but he rejected Wallace's "nationalist and socialist appeals" as "radically alien to conservatism."[97] Despite the fact that ultraconservatives formed the base of the conservative movement and their ideas and activities overlapped substantially with the "respectable" right, Buckley and his cohort hoped to discredit Wallace's conservative bona fides. This was a battle over longevity, credibility, and institutional power. Buckley had transformed from a far-right translator into a conservative gatekeeper, hoping to convince his fellow right-wingers to ignore the third-party siren song in favor of fighting within, and hopefully transforming, the Republican Party.

Republicans certainly felt the pinch of Wallace's campaign. Evans and Novak observed that Republicans worried about "losing their right wing to Wallace," while Thomas O'Neill of Baltimore's *Sun* gauged that Wallace could be a "lethal blow for the Republican [nominee]."[98] Pollster George Gallup called Wallace "a greater threat to the Republicans than to the Democrats."[99] Despite his long history as a segregationist Democrat, Wallace appealed to the GOP's right wing. Republican politicians concurred. Goldwater offered a withering appraisal of Wallace: "He's a conservative, and he's a disaster."[100] At a Wallace function in Harrisburg, Pennsylvania, a Republican official looked upon the crowd and lamented, "I hate to say this, but I see some of our people out there—too many of them."[101] Ralph Greiten, a district manager of a Santa Barbara life insurance company, embodied the Wallace threat. After changing his registration to support Wallace, Greiten told reporters, "We Republican ultraconservatives had no home to go to until Wallace came along."[102] Despite the remonstrations from pragmatists such as Buckley, Wallace's insurgency threatened to outflank the GOP's budding conservative movement.

Not every ultraconservative joined Wallace's ranks, however. Cattleman and recent GOP transplant J. Evetts Haley called 1968 "the most critical year in our history," but warned that only the Republican Party, not Wallace's third-party gambit, could prevent the destruction of "all we hold dear."[103] In fact, Haley fought against Wallace supporters in Randall County, Texas, where he served as the Republican county chairman. Rather than supporting Wallace, Haley urged his compatriots to embrace the GOP. He was particularly fond of Ronald Reagan. But Haley was not a down-the-line Republican yet. Just two years earlier he had supported Democrat Jim Johnson's bid for Arkansas governor because of Johnson's segregationist values. Nevertheless, Haley remained unconvinced by Wallace. "A lot of my friends went into the Wallace movement years ago, but I wouldn't go," Haley said nearly a decade later. "I knew Wallace wasn't a real conservative."[104] Haley soon took a hiatus from politics, but his decision to spurn Wallace's campaign illustrated that the ultraconservative movement was fracturing. Much of the far right remained loyal to Wallace, but over the next two decades many ultraconservatives would follow in Haley's footsteps, being reborn as Republican conservatives.

The election of 1968 represented an identity crisis for the conservative movement. The far right's centrality to the movement, particularly its role in Goldwater's nomination and defeat, loomed like a dark star. Conservatives yearning for respectability, Buckley and other writers from *National Review* in particular, were trying to redefine the ideological parameters of conservatism by winnowing out the far right. According to their calculus, conspiratorial anti-communist groups were liabilities, embarrassments that eroded credibility. Buckley derided the Birch Society as a "drag on the conservative movement." But in the same breath he conceded that Welch's organization provided an "emotionally satisfactory means of serving many Americans concerned for their country's future."[105] Republican politicians felt this friction, too. The GOP wanted to capitalize on the far right's grassroots fervor but fretted that open collaboration would damage the party. For their part, many ultraconservatives were willing to work with the GOP only insofar as Republicans were dedicated to running strictly conservative candidates. The Republican Party faced a fork in the road. Moderate and liberal Republicans feared that nominating a conservative would beget smears of extremism and another landslide loss. Conservatives, on the other hand, believed nominating a moderate might steer energized voters toward Wallace's third-party insurgency.

The Republicans needed to find a candidate who could navigate this narrow channel. Richard Nixon endeared himself to the GOP rank and file and cemented his status as the front-runner by stumping for Goldwater and other Republican candidates in 1964 and 1966. Nixon borrowed Franklin

Roosevelt's terminology by focusing on the "forgotten Americans" of the sub-urban Sunbelt and embraced the anti-communist rhetoric that often doubled as a race-baiting code language for southerners. He stumped for "law and order" and railed against the perceived divisiveness of liberal policies. Nix-on's strategy entailed surrendering the Deep South to George Wallace while attacking Wallace's hold on the Upper South. Reagan challenged Nixon's can-didacy from the right while George Romney and Nelson Rockefeller charged from the left. Romney dropped out of the race early in 1968, and Rockefeller's late announcement left little time to rattle the sabers of the traditional eastern elite wing of the GOP. Reagan, on the other hand, charmed conservatives and made Nixon's campaign sweat through the summer.[106]

Nixon still had work to do as delegates arrived in Miami for the 1968 Republican National Convention. In particular, he needed to win over the conservative skeptics who soured on Nixon after the Republican "Munich" of 1960. Recent Republican transplant Strom Thurmond remained a well-respected voice in the South, and he helped Nixon pick up crucial southern votes. Thurmond arranged a preconvention meeting with southern delegates, where Nixon agreed to appoint right-wing Supreme Court justices and vetoed four potential vice-presidential candidates anathema to southerners. Though Thurmond did not laud Nixon's nomination of Maryland governor Spiro Agnew, he agreed that southerners would view Agnew more favorably than a northeastern liberal like Rockefeller. Nixon also secured support from other conservative leaders, including Goldwater, Texas senator John Tower, and grassroots activist Phyllis Schlafly. Eight years after kowtowing to the GOP's liberal faction and just three years after claiming that the "real menace to the Republican Party came from the Buckleyites," Nixon sided with the party's conservative future.[107]

The ideological disagreements within the Republican Party paled in com-parison to the Democratic Party's disarray. Under intense pressure due to the Vietnam War, Lyndon Johnson shocked the world by deciding not to stand for reelection. Multiple candidates had already emerged to contest Johnson for the nomination, including Minnesota congressman Eugene McCarthy and New York senator Robert F. Kennedy. They were soon joined on the cam-paign trail by Vice President Hubert Humphrey and Senator George McGov-ern of South Dakota. Many analysts penciled in Humphrey as the favorite, but his milquetoast liberalism failed to inspire the civil rights activists and anti-war advocates who marshaled behind Kennedy and McGovern. To make matters worse for Humphrey, he struggled to distance himself from the

Johnson presidency. Kennedy appeared to have the Democratic nomination sewn up after winning the California primary, but three bullets from the .22 revolver of Sirhan Sirhan ended his presidential aspirations in the kitchen of the Ambassador Hotel. Buoyed by the strength of labor unions and the lack of a true adversary after Kennedy's tragic demise, Humphrey received the Democratic nomination in Chicago. Yet the anti-war protests outside of the DNC wrought a spectacle of police brutality that diminished Humphrey's victory. An air of desperation plagued the Democratic Party as the election loomed.[108]

From the perspective of far-right activists, Nixon and Humphrey represented varying shades of liberalism. Ultraconservatives considered Nixon's nomination a regression from Goldwater. Nixon had a predilection for Machiavellian pragmatism, which fueled distrust. Additionally, many far-right activists still resented Nixon's actions during the "Munich of the Republican Party" and his previous disavowal of the Birch Society. Welch sent fundraising letters warning that a mysterious cabal of "insiders" wanted a Nixon presidency in order to further the communist conspiracy.[109] Kent Courtney printed pamphlets upbraiding the Republican candidate for facilitating big government, supporting civil rights, promoting "phony anti-communism," backing the United Nations, and for simply being too liberal.[110] "Under no circumstances should Nixon be considered a Conservative or of any value to the Conservative cause," Courtney wrote.[111] In the eyes of the far right, Nixon remained a creature of "Modern Republicanism." On the other hand, supporting the Democratic nominee was a nonstarter. Humphrey was a "flaming liberal," according to Courtney, who "spent his life promoting Socialism, promoting Communism, and dividing and destroying his party and his country."[112] Welch believed Humphrey's nomination itself was a conspiracy to "improve the image" and "increase the stature of Richard Nixon as a conservative."[113] The far right often homogenized the two parties—Stone accused both of eroding constitutional traditions by proposing "vast new political excursions into fields of private enterprise and state jurisdiction."[114] Many of the right-wingers who felt disenchanted with the two major parties, who considered the Democrats too liberal and questioned Nixon's conservative credentials, turned to Wallace's insurgency.[115]

The American Independent Party lacked a traditional structure, and Wallace relied heavily on local organizers to run his state-level campaigns, a decision which greatly empowered ultraconservatives. Birchers signed up in droves, fueling the drive to get Wallace on state ballots around the nation, a task they took up with "a missionary zeal."[116] As one man at the American

Party of Texas's state convention proclaimed, "It is the patriotic duty of every Bircher to work and vote for Mr. Wallace."[117] In Bakersfield, California, the Birch Society trained seventy special registrars to sign up voters while over 3,900 members canvassed the state. Bircher enthusiasm meant that many of the Wallace-pledged electors were society members. At least three electors in New York were Birchers, four in New Jersey, and three in Connecticut. Wallace offices in Connecticut sold Bircher paraphernalia such as "Support Your Local Police" bumper stickers and books found in American Opinion bookstores. When the Wallace campaign asked for additional help in Connecticut, Kent and Phoebe Courtney sent out a letter to subscribers of the *Independent American* with instructions on how to join and support Wallace's local campaign. Eleven of Massachusetts's fourteen electors were Birchers or had ties to the society. Out west, Birchers were equally visible. Of the six Wallace-pledged electors in Colorado, two were Birchers (two others were Citizens' Council members). All three of the Wallace electors from Nevada were Birchers. In the state of Washington, more than half of the 40-member Wallace campaign committee were Birch Society members. The *Wall Street Journal* described Bircher-led efforts as "impressively smooth," indicating that, aside from perhaps the southern Citizens' Councils, the Birch Society was the foremost group propelling Wallace's movement at the ground level.[118]

However, the Birch Society frequently downplayed any official role in the Wallace campaign and, as an organization, remained neutral on Wallace's candidacy. "Our job is to create a climate of knowledge and understanding so conservative candidates can be elected," Welch opined.[119] When Wallace won straw polls at a Bircher gathering, the organization denied any direct connection to Wallace's campaign, but noted that they both shared an interest in "real constitutional conservatism."[120] Individual Birchers strove to maintain this façade. For example, when Willard S. Voit signed up as an unpaid Wallace volunteer, he resigned as vice president of the Birch Society's publishing house to sever any linkages to the society (he also quit the Republican State Central Committee and the United Republicans of California). Another Wallace worker repeated Welch's line that "the society and the campaign operate independently," but he also added, "It's just that the two stand for a lot of the same things."[121] In fact, Welch later estimated that 80 percent of Birchers "not only voted for but worked for Wallace."[122] When rumors spread that the Birch Society had distributed its mailing lists to Wallace's campaign, Welch exploded, "There might be some members who give him lists of names of friends that include members of the society, but no self-respecting organization would release its mailing list."[123] However, Welch's disavowal betrayed an important truth: a significant amount of overlap existed between the Birch Society and Wallace's operation.[124]

Pennsylvania Birchers, for example, used society connections to build Wallace's campaign while ostensibly not involving the organization directly. Three Birch members ran Wallace's campaign in western Pennsylvania, centered on the city of Pittsburgh. They recruited twenty-nine Wallace-pledged electors, of whom seventeen admitted their Birch Society membership. To get Wallace on the state ballot, they organized a signature drive, collecting 7,000 of the necessary 10,500 signatures in two days around the Pittsburgh area, and created a network of twenty-five campaign offices. Investigators from the *Wall Street Journal* visited eleven of the offices and found that six were run by avowed Birchers. "We went to people we knew would be interested," remarked John W. Mehalic, a businessman and Birch chapter leader. "It just happens that most of your active workers in the conservative movement are Birchers. Who else works in a conservative movement?"[125]

Not only did the Pennsylvania operation indicate the Birch Society's centrality to Wallace's campaign, it also revealed how racism animated Wallace's constituency even outside of the South. One of the key Pittsburgh-area organizers, dentist Charles A. Provan, distributed Wallace literature to his patients and contributed to the "Let Freedom Ring" telephone operation, which robocalled citizens with recorded messages accusing civil rights leaders of advancing the cause of communism. Another Pennsylvania organizer, Robert J. Crow, occupied a leadership position in Truth About Civil Turmoil (TACT), a Bircher front which blamed civil rights disputes on communist subversion and sent "copies of the criminal records of black militants to local newspapers." Noxious forms of racism often combined with xenophobic fears of demographic change. J. Warren Keel, the Pennsylvania chairman of Citizens for Wallace, blamed "race riots" on Congress "illegally" passing the 14th Amendment and argued that black Americans should have to go through a naturalization process because they were not proper citizens. The racist, conspiratorial undercurrents that mobilized behind Goldwater in 1964 now formed the backbone of Wallace's machinery.[126]

The far-right network energized Wallace's campaign, but it also contributed a significant amount of friction. Journalists asked Wallace incessantly about the Birch Society. "I'm not going to denounce the John Birch Society," Wallace replied to one reporter, describing Birchers as "some of our finest citizens."[127] However, Bircher influence often brought bad press. In Texas, home to some 6,000 active Birchers, discord bedeviled Wallace's apparatus. Bard Logan, the 56-year-old chairman of the American Party of Texas, was an old hand third-party organizer and dedicated Society member. He had no patience for "pathological Birch haters" because, in his view, "People are only against the Birch Society because it has been a successful anti-Communist organization." This mindset led Logan to purge state-level American Party officeholders who remained cool toward the society. When the party's state secretary, Margaret Bacon, refused to distribute Bircher materials, Logan interpreted her actions as an "anti-Birch kick" and fired her for not toeing the line. She received anonymous menacing phone calls afterward. The final caller growled, "If you don't quit stirring the pot, you're going to take a swim in the Colorado River with concrete boots on."[128] Bacon distanced herself from the party—"I never want to go through that again"—but still claimed to be "one hundred percent" behind Wallace. Other chapter leaders who questioned the distribution of Bircher materials met the same fate: Logan replaced them with dedicated Birchers, and intimidating threats often followed.[129]

The Texas campaign highlighted both the Birch Society's influence at the grassroots level and the ongoing struggle to define conservatism. The threats of violence also showed that, at times, the line separating far-right activists from violent extremists blurred substantially. "Those Birchers were bent on destroying the American Party," complained one ousted worker. "They've gotten our people into a state of fear and confusion by the techniques of divide, conquer, and destroy. We were asleep and they were organized."[130] Chairman Logan took exception to these criticisms and fired back, "They looked to the John Birch Society to organize this party. Now they want us to get out. Well, we're not getting out."[131] Indeed, the Birch Society dominated the American Party of Texas. Bacon claimed that twenty-seven of the party's thirty-one executive committee members were Birchers. Another man said it was at least half. The turbulence in Texas received coverage in numerous national newspapers, but Wallace's national campaign director Tom Turnipseed downplayed the controversy as nothing more than a "personality quarrel." And yet, reports circulated that the Wallace campaign asked for Logan's resignation and sent an official representative to smooth things over in the Lone Star State.[132]

As evidenced by the Pennsylvania operation and the turmoil in Texas, the broad far-right coalition that fueled Wallace's campaign was both a blessing and a curse. Ultraconservatives certainly brought a crusading energy—grass-roots activists canvassed local areas, solicited signatures, and formed a network of Wallace headquarters across the country. Their efforts helped facilitate Wallace's rise in the polls. A Harris poll taken in mid-September showed Wallace cruising at 21 percent compared to the 39 percent and 31 percent earned by Nixon and Humphrey, respectively. From the vantage point of a Wallace supporter, it appeared that Wallace had a real opportunity to topple the two-party duopoly. However, many contemporary observers and fellow conservatives still believed that the far-right wing of Wallace's movement remained an immense liability. This fear seeped into Wallace's campaign; as analyst Jack Nelson reported, "[Wallace] fears the extremist label would kill him as a significant national figure."[133] Another seemingly insurmountable problem facing Wallace was the disadvantage of running as a third-party candidate in a two-party system. Without the activism on the right-wing fringe, however, Wallace's campaign might have stalled out before takeoff.[134]

Ultimately, multiple issues doomed Wallace's campaign. The resuscitation of Humphrey's campaign, Thurmond's support for Nixon, and the persistence of extremism all diminished Wallace's appeal. In late September, Humphrey finally broke away from the Democratic party line on Vietnam by inching toward advocating a peaceful resolution. This led to a flood of support from northeastern labor unions and won over some of the die-hard anti-war advocates. While Humphrey solidified his left flank, Nixon drifted rightward in order to pick up conservative swing voters. Nixon reiterated his opposition to "forced bussing" and promoted the "freedom-of-choice" education plan that reinforced de facto segregation.[135] Nixon's right turn peeled voters away from Wallace, but Strom Thurmond's continued loyalty to Nixon proved even more detrimental to Wallace's hopes. Thurmond canvassed southern states, detailing the similarities between Nixon and Wallace and, more importantly, warning that voting for Wallace might ensure a Humphrey victory. At a Georgia campaign stop, Thurmond cautioned, "I don't know of a state of the South the third-party candidate will carry."[136] In Mountville, South Carolina, Thurmond climbed aboard a flatbed truck and instructed the crowd, "Don't dissipate your votes on a third party candidate, even though he says what a lot of people believe." Thurmond's actions proved pivotal for Nixon. As one farmer said, "I'm not going to kick Strom Thurmond just to cast a ballot for George Wallace."[137]

Thurmond's advocacy helped shift the Upper South toward Nixon, but Wallace's declining popularity was partially self-inflicted. Wallace tapped

General Curtis LeMay as his running mate in early October, an intentional nod to his ultraconservative supporters. During his acceptance speech, LeMay said he did not think atomic weaponry was necessary to win the Vietnam War, but he refused to take the "nuclear option" off of the table. Far-right activists supported LeMay; Courtney had already provided positive coverage of LeMay's aggressive solutions for the Vietnam question. However, the press had a heyday portraying LeMay as an unhinged warmonger. His off-the-cuff speaking style and apparent hawkishness scared voters and earned the Wallace-LeMay ticket a pithy nickname from Humphrey: "the Bombsy twins."[138] Wallace rushed to clarify that LeMay was only pointing out the need for a military plan if negotiations failed, but the damage was already done. Theodore White thought that LeMay brought "no strength or eloquence to the Wallace ticket," and Buckley, though he complained that the nuclear comments were taken out of context, called LeMay "a damn fool for consenting to run with George Wallace."[139]

LeMay's gaffe crippled the campaign, and, when combined with all of the other issues, Wallace's support evaporated. Over the month of October, Wallace's poll numbers across the country plummeted from 21 to 13 percent. Republicans smelled blood in the water. Senator Goldwater wrote a column in *National Review* two weeks before the election urging conservatives to avoid Wallace. Repackaging Thurmond's argument, Goldwater told readers that a vote for Wallace was essentially a vote for Humphrey and four more years of liberalism. Not only did Wallace stand no chance of becoming president, Goldwater noted, his candidacy was a threat to the two-party system and the conservative effort to remake the Republican Party. "We conservatives have made great strides since 1960," Goldwater pleaded. "Let's not throw that progress down Governor Wallace's rathole."[140] In this moment, Goldwater turned away from his far-right boosters because they threatened the GOP's candidate *and* the party's growing conservative faction. Right-wing gatekeepers, such as Goldwater and Buckley, were sending a message to ultraconservatives: get in line or get written out of the movement.[141]

Wallace made it onto all fifty state ballots, listed either under the American Independent Party banner or under a variety of third-party titles such as the American Party, the Courage Party, and even the George Wallace Party. His popularity had cratered, however. On Election Day, November 5, roughly ten million Americans (13.5 percent) cast a ballot for George Wallace and the American Party. Nixon barely edged out Humphrey in the popular vote, but he earned enough electoral votes, 301 (56 percent), to win the presidency.

Despite the overwhelming electoral defeat, Wallace's numbers revealed that
his far-right ideologies were not fringe or sectional. He won five states in the
Deep South—Alabama, Arkansas, Georgia, Louisiana, and Mississippi—for
a total of forty-six electoral votes. Plus, more than four million of the votes
Wallace received came from outside of the South. It was the strongest third-
party result since Theodore Roosevelt's Progressive Party run in 1912, and
certainly more impressive than T. Coleman Andrews's poor performance in
1956. White concluded that one consequence of the 1968 election, exemplified
by Wallace's showing, was an undeniable "swing to the right, an expression
of a vague sentiment for a government oriented to caution and restraint."[142]
Nevertheless, Wallace's loss, despite foreshadowing future conservative gains
and popularizing a "politics of rage," must have been bitter fruit for his most
avid supporters.[143]

After the dust settled, ultraconservatives expressed a mixture of anger and
self-loathing. The far right distrusted Nixon and resented the GOP's campaign against Wallace. "The American people during the election were fed
THE BIG LIE," Courtney bemoaned in a CSA mailer. "They were told that a
vote for Wallace was a vote for Humphrey, when, as a matter of fact, a vote
for Nixon was a vote for the continuation of the Johnson-Humphrey Administration."[144] At the same time, the far right found reasons to blame Wallace.
Courtney lashed out at Wallace's campaign for ineffective organizing and
having "a lot of slogans, but no solutions," ignoring the fact that his own organization played a key role in Wallace's movement.[145] Smoot dismissed portions of Wallace's platform as "unconstitutional" while Courtney derided his
domestic policies as "too socialistic."[146] This sort of post-election autopsy, a
ritual of self-flagellation, was commonplace among the far right, and it fit a
notable pattern: ultraconservatives often shelved their own puritanical ideals
to back imperfect right-wing candidates but then repudiated those candidates' more liberal policies after their campaigns crumbled.

The reality was that Wallace's decision to court extremists, like Goldwater
before him, simultaneously energized and narrowed his base. The American
public knew that Wallace's support network ranged from the Birch Society
and Citizens' Councils to klaverns and extremist militias, a volatile political
cocktail with limited appeal. Contemporary analyst Nicholas C. Chriss noted
that Wallace's platforms were often superseded by "behind-the-scenes power
plays among right-wing extremists, and bickering over John Birch Society
issues."[147] Furthermore, Wallace was running on a third-party ticket in a two-
party system, hoping to accomplish something—diverting the election to the

House of Representatives—that had last occurred back in 1825. While Nixon's shift to the right and Humphrey's renaissance contributed to Wallace's defeat, the radicals that comprised Wallace's national constituency also had a hand in his failure.[148]

*　*　*

Despite the clear repudiation of far-right third-party politics, some ultraconservatives refused to make amends with Nixon and the Republicans. They assumed Nixon would disappoint them. When asked about Nixon's potential as president, Welch gave a tepid "Let's wait and see."[149] Jim Johnson grumbled, "If [Nixon] does what conservatives want him to do, then there'd be no place for a third-party conservative candidate four years from now."[150] Courtney remained loyal to Wallace and contended that Americans would "suffer" under Nixon's administration. Just weeks after the election, Courtney wrote to CSA members, "Nixon doesn't have a chance of getting re-elected in 1972 unless he adopts, or appears to adopt, the Conservative philosophy of George Wallace, and puts into action programs which will slow down the Communist conspiracy."[151] These misgivings about Nixon's, and thus the GOP's, conservative convictions led some ultraconservatives to continue down the path of third-party activism.

The movement that unified behind Wallace, however, splintered into competing factions after the election. In early 1969, roughly 250 people representing 44 states descended upon Dallas, Texas, for a meeting of the "Association of Wallace Voters." The group intended to create a permanent, ambitious American Independent Party. Courtney was elected to the party's national committee, and at the convention he could be found handing out pamphlets featuring an article titled "The Pro-Communist Administration of Richard Nixon." "I don't expect any radical change in the Nixon administration from the soft-on-communism policy of the past," Courtney told reporters. Some activists sought to capitalize on Wallace's southern popularity by focusing on local elections. Bard Logan, the Birch member and chairman of the American Party of Texas, wanted to target liberal Democrats such as Texas senator Ralph Yarborough. "They've gotten the idea that they can't be toppled," Logan remarked. "But they could be has-beens just as much as we could be also-rans." By the end of the conference, the gathering had laid out plans for a Wallace run in 1972.[152]

While the Dallas contingent sought to revitalize the American Independent Party, other right-wingers moved away from Wallace's machine. William

Shearer, the Los Angeles businessman who led a California Citizens' Council and coordinated the western region of Wallace's campaign, held a meeting in Louisville to create a separate third party. He wanted to implement one of Courtney's earlier blueprints by establishing a localized party structure that would decide platforms and candidates through national conventions. Shearer noted that this was a response to Wallace's domineering tactics—Wallace's confidants wrote the 1968 platform and picked his running mate without the input of local organizers. Essentially, Shearer argued that Wallace's folksy populism veered too close to an authoritarian cult of personality. "We're states [sic] rights and local control people," Shearer said, "and we're not interested in creating an institution that's dictatorial in nature." The disagreements between Shearer's camp and Courtney's group displayed the far right's increasing factionalism. The two sides did not trust or respect each other. Robert Walters, organizer of the Dallas conference, said there was "a pretty damn high nut content" among Shearer's associates. Shearer took a similarly dim view of Walters's gathering: "I don't think some of them are too savory characters." The right-wing disunity that shadowed Wallace's campaign metastasized in the election's aftermath, further fraying the far-right base.[153]

Ultimately, Nixon's ascent and Wallace's defeat marked a significant turning point for the far-right movement. As the GOP pivoted rightward, ultra-conservatives either melded into the conservative mainstream or lost traction altogether. Some longtime far-right activists, such as J. Evetts Haley, agreed with Goldwater's argument about continuing the conservative insurgency within the Republican Party. The GOP provided fertile ground for the conservative movement, and it seemed prudent to try and push the party further rightward. However, other far-right activists, such as Courtney, spun into increasingly isolated orbits outside of the political mainstream. The passing of time represented another problem—far-right leaders were growing old, prompting questions of who would lead the movement in the future. Ultraconservatives had failed to get a conservative purist into the White House, but by the end of the 1960s they had created strategies and built a grassroots network that would form a foundation for conservative activists in the later decades of the twentieth century.

The Influence of Far-Right Conservatism

In the summer of 1969, the *Boston Globe* sent analyst Gordon Hall to cover the John Birch Society's "God, Family, and Country" convention. Despite the fact that this was the rally's seventh consecutive year, Hall noted that an overwhelming sense of ennui dominated the proceedings. "The thunder on the extreme right has diminished to a distant rumble," Hall reported. Fewer people were present than in previous years and the gathering seemed listless, as if people were just going through the motions. Even the conference's controversial theme—sex education in public school!—failed to jolt the crowd. One attendee, a Chicago woman and far-right patron, disparaged the conference as a "national convention of booksellers." She wanted political action, not another right-wing "study group."[1] Her words offered a damning indictment of the once-potent vanguard of modern conservatism. Whether because of old age, ideological battles, or internecine divisions, by the end of the 1960s, the far-right movement was starting to resemble an aging pugilist struggling through his final bout.

The aftershocks of Wallace's defeat ripped through the far right. Not every ultraconservative aligned with the Alabama firebrand, but his loss marked a definitive turning point for the movement. No one felt the impact more than the Conservative Society of America and its leaders, Kent and Phoebe Courtney. Not only had their third-party aspirations foundered once again, but financial problems plagued their organization. The CSA spent thousands of dollars promoting, publishing, and organizing for Wallace, forcing the Courtneys to send urgent mass mailers begging for donations in the campaign's waning days. After the election, the organization was $34,000 in debt. Additionally, the Courtneys were dealing with their own personal struggles. The pair legally separated in 1967 but still worked together on Wallace's campaign. They could not mend their relationship, however, and officially divorced a few years later. Phoebe relocated to Littleton, Colorado, and continued producing right-wing literature in line with conservatism's widening culture war, including pamphlets such as "Is Abortion Murder?" and the book *Gun Control Means People Control*. Kent remained in Louisiana and pinned his hopes on another third-party Wallace run in 1972. Wallace decided, however, to run for the Democratic Party's nomination, but an assassination attempt severely injured him and dashed his campaign hopes. Kent briefly resurfaced as a fringe third-party candidate in a couple of Louisiana elections during the 1970s, but by that point his national influence had withered.[2]

Willis Stone, one of the Courtneys' closest collaborators, also struggled to keep his movement afloat. By the late 1960s, the Liberty Amendment Committee's membership plunged below 10,000, which prompted an aggressive, but ill-fated, membership drive. Flagging interest and funding woes led Stone to attempt another merger with Welch's Birch Society in 1971. Stone was also mourning the death of his wife Marion—his heart just was not in the fight anymore. When Stone convened the LAC's national committee to discuss the potential merger, he told his colleagues, "I am old, I am tired, and I just can't carry this workload. And there isn't anybody in our group that's going to."[3] Despite some misgivings about merging with the Birch Society, the committee voted in favor, and Welch tentatively agreed to subsume the LAC. But the proposal quickly unraveled. The Birch Society formed a "tax reform" front instead of absorbing Stone's committee, and the LAC lumbered forward, hemorrhaging members. By early 1973, the organization had lost state chairmen in Delaware, Maine, Montana, Vermont, and Virginia. In the summer of 1974, the last edition of *Freedom Magazine* rolled off the presses. The final issue explained the Liberty Amendment's history and Stone's personal journey, but it made no mention of the committee's struggles. From a certain perspective, it read like an obituary. Stone was seventy-five years old at the time, his signature pencil mustache now entirely white. Perhaps knowing that the end was near, Stone wanted to leave one last artifact for future right-wing activists to unearth when the time was right. The Liberty Amendment Committee ebbed out of existence, but Stone's radical libertarianism persevered within the broader conservative intellectual and activist tradition.[4]

With allies such as Stone and Courtney falling by the wayside, the outlook seemed dire for the John Birch Society, but it took much longer for the Birchers to fade from the American mainstream. By the end of the 1960s, the organization claimed between 60,000 and 100,000 members and boasted 4,000 chapters, 100 paid coordinators, and 450 American Opinion book-stores. Front groups organized the grass roots, and millions of dollars poured in through donations, dues, and publishing profits. Membership rosters experienced stagnation, however. Once hoping to reach one million members, Welch recalibrated: "We don't need a million. . . . We've found the power of concerted action is much greater than we thought."[5] While Welch convinced himself that less might actually be more, other signs of decay appeared. Rallies attracted fewer visitors and, worse yet, more conservative allies turned against the society. When Governor Lester Maddox was tapped as a keynote speaker for a 1970 Birch rally, Young Americans for Freedom boycotted the event because, according to one YAF leader, Maddox was "a racist."[6] The YAF had a turbulent history with the Birchers already, but the boycott signaled a deepening rift, or at least the perception of one, between "respectable" conservatives and the far right.

Nevertheless, the society clung to its conspiratorial ways. Birchers deemed Jimmy Carter a "second-echelon member" of the communist conspiracy, while Ronald Reagan was characterized as a "lackey" because, according to Bircher delusions, only water-carriers for the conspiracy could gain the nomination of a major party.[7] This language, a relic of the Red Scare, marginalized the Birch Society. One analyst wrote, "They're alive . . . but they're impotent," while another called the society's anti-communist conspiracies "an anachronism." Laurel Leff of the *Wall Street Journal* noted that the Birch Society "no longer grabs headlines—or even footnotes."[8] By the early 1980s, official membership estimates were down to 40,000. In 1983, at the age of eighty-three, Welch stepped down as chairman. The organization limped into the following decades—vestiges of the Birch Society still exist, now headquartered in Appleton, Wisconsin—but it failed to regain the influence it held in previous decades.[9]

While the Birch Society and LAC slowly receded from public consciousness, Billy James Hargis and the Christian Crusade experienced a meteoric fall from grace. Compared to his older far-right brethren, Hargis was a spry fifty-five years old at the dawn of the 1970s, his ministry ever-expanding. Years earlier Hargis had established the American Christian College in Tulsa, Oklahoma, which offered an education based on anti-communism and patriotic Americanism. Hargis was serving as the college's president when, in 1974, a male student revealed Hargis's sexual predation to the college's vice president, longtime Christian Crusade member David Noebel. According to Noebel, the student married another student in a wedding conducted by Hargis. Then, as *Time* magazine reported, "On the honeymoon, the groom and his bride discovered that both of them had slept with Hargis." Ultimately five students, including four men, accused Hargis of having sexual relations with them.[10]

Hargis resigned from his university post in disgrace, sealing his own fate and that of the Christian Crusade. Perhaps most scandalous was the revelation that Hargis used the Bible to support his secret homosexual acts. According to the students, Hargis detailed the "friendship between David and Jonathan" as biblical evidence supporting homosexuality, and he further "threatened to blacklist the youths for life if they talked." When pressed for a response by *Time* interviewers, he meekly replied, "I have made more than my share of mistakes. I'm not proud of them." Hargis's statement did not satisfy his contemporaries. When Noebel confronted him, Hargis admitted to his actions and nebulously blamed it on "genes and chromosomes." The Crusade stumbled into the 1980s, but Hargis lost his integrity as a crusader for fundamentalist morality and far-right conservatism.[11]

Even before the sex scandal destroyed Hargis's empire, he failed to reach the respectability of other conservative evangelists. When the religious right coalesced, Hargis was ostracized from the inner circle, despite the fact that he had pioneered many of the broadcasting and fundraising tactics later used by evangelical and political activists. One modern commentator quipped that "if Oral Roberts never quite achieved the respectability of Billy Graham, Billy Hargis never quite achieved the respectability of Oral Roberts."[12] This could partially be attributed to Hargis's reputation as a conspiratorial hard-liner or the lingering damage from the sex scandal, but it also signaled that the conservative movement was outgrowing the vehement anti-communism upon which it was built. Nevertheless, Hargis represented an early prototype of modern right-wing evangelicals, a man who championed coordination among conservatives and helped funnel hardened, ideological warriors into the religious right.[13]

Out of all the midcentury far-right leaders, J. Evetts Haley was one of the few to successfully navigate the rise of mainstream conservatism. In 1976, Haley came out of a self-imposed political retirement to support Reagan's insurgent candidacy. The former Democrat stumped for the GOP out in West Texas, converting old George Wallace supporters to the new conservatism of Reagan. At the state GOP convention, Haley defeated longtime national Republican leader Fred Agnich to serve as an at-large Texas delegate, illustrating the growing influence of far-right conservatism within the party. When

Reagan failed to earn the Republican nomination, an ornery Haley called the GOP's national convention "political suicide," barking that incumbent Gerald Ford "doesn't have a Chinaman's chance of beating Jimmy Carter."[14] Four years later, Haley helped bring the "Reagan Revolution" to the Lone Star State by serving as an organizer for the Reagan for President committee. At last, nestled within the GOP's right flank at the age of seventy-nine, Haley found a permanent political home.[15]

Haley's life provided a prism through which to examine the fluctuations of party politics. He connected anti–New Deal ultraconservatism to the mid-century conservative movement, and, recognizing the gradual leftward shift of the national Democratic Party, encouraged a conservative exodus to the Republican Party rather than doomed third-party crusades. His grassroots campaigns brought disillusioned conservatives together and strengthened bonds both within the radical right and between far-right activists and mainstream conservatives. Haley never received the acclaim of activists such as Phyllis Schlafly, or even Robert Welch, but his organizing strategies created constituencies attuned to the values of modern conservatism. In Texas, conservative Republicans such as Bruce Alger, John Tower, and George H. W. Bush benefitted from the anti-liberal environment fostered by agitators such as Haley. Haley's pivot from far-right Democrat to right-wing Republican exemplified the fracturing of the Democratic Party's traditional coalition, the rise of conservative southern Republicanism (particularly in Texas), and the appeal of grassroots populism.[16]

Ultimately, the far right's ideologies and organizational tactics significantly influenced the modern conservative movement. Ultraconservatives abhorred the centrist pragmatism which congealed around the remnants of New Deal liberalism, and their rhetoric about communists in government amplified, and at times served as a surrogate for, structural critiques of liberal governance. Though they demonized the liberal state as a destructive force, far-right activists and politicians came to view state power, when wielded by conservatives, as a skeleton key for unlocking right-wing political victories. The far right gained a foothold in party politics by helping to catalyze the nation's gradual political realignment, first through cross-party action and third-party organizing before eventually melding into the Republican Party's right-wing vanguard. By scorning moderation and demanding ideological purity, far-right leaders capitalized on right-wing aggrievement and built a zealous constituency, which pressured politicians to tack rightward. The success of the far-right movement, defined by the creation of a mainstream conservative party (the modern Republican Party), laid the groundwork for the rightward shift in late twentieth-century American politics.[17]

Ultraconservative activism, from the Jeffersonian Democrats through the Goldwater and Wallace campaigns, underscored the importance of institutional coordination, especially in terms of building a right-wing base for future elections. Far-right leaders focused on the grass roots as the key theater of political engagement and built a collaborative web of organizations to amplify their philosophies. These groups became critical nodes within a vast far-right network that stretched across the nation and provided points of convergence for right-wing businesspeople, politicians, and local activists. Their leaders, rallies, and media platforms became conduits for fighting liberalism and pushing American politics rightward. Moreover, ultraconservatives' organizing, campaigning, and fundraising strategies transferred over to a new generation of battle-hardened right-wing warriors. Though the far right had little success at the ballot box, their tactics were not only co-opted by mainstream conservatives, they catalyzed a puritanical culture that continues to reverberate within American conservatism.[18]

Indeed, mainstream conservatives did not entirely turn away from far-right ideals, despite the attempts by translators-turned-gatekeepers, such as William Buckley, to write ultraconservatives out of the movement. In fact, ultraconservatives precipitated and molded many of the themes of the coming New Right. Far-right agitators were often cast as villains, particularly after Goldwater's loss in 1964, but future conservatives inherited their intellectual tradition and simply smoothed out the rough edges: anti-statism, free-market economics, "family values" rhetoric, religious traditionalism, and anti-communism all remained fixtures of the modern conservative firmament. Furthermore, like Haley, ultraconservatives funneled into the Republican Party, sharpening the growing conservatism therein. Previously staunch segregationists such as Wallace and Thurmond attenuated their positions to reflect the right's shift away from segregationism, but conservatism nevertheless bore the roots of white supremacy. In short, modern conservatism was erected, at least in part, upon a foundation laid by the far right.[19]

Ronald Reagan's landslide victory in 1980 positioned conservatism as the dominant force in American politics and solidified the Republican Party as the conservative flagship. The GOP retained the libertarianism, social traditionalism, and anti-communism of the previous generation of conservatives while welcoming the religious right and neoconservatives. As this New Right ascended, ultraconservatism persisted as a subculture whose ideas percolated and gradually gained traction within the political mainstream. For example, new groups took up Stone's crusade against taxation. In the late 1970s, the National Taxpayers Union quoted Stone in its promotional materials as it battled for income-tax limitations and a balanced budget. Nine states had adopted the Liberty Amendment by 1981, though it was never passed by Congress nor voted on by the states. In 1995, *National Review*'s Stephen Moore crowed, "Abolishing the income tax is no longer a utopian fantasy," illustrating a growing commitment to an uncompromising conservative vision.[20] Despite the fact that the New Right absorbed the far right's obsession with ideological purity, many of the older far-right leaders witnessed only the earliest years of the conservative revolution they had helped foster. Welch had a stroke and passed away in 1985. Willis Stone died in 1989. Just a few years later, Haley passed on as well. The legacies left by these ultraconservative trailblazers, though, continued to permeate American politics.[21]

One of the far right's most significant innovations was their role in creating a right-wing media network. Media outlets, including periodicals, radio shows, and television programming, became key conduits for conservatives trying to build a movement. Richard Viguerie, the man credited with bringing direct-mail advertising to the conservative movement, drew a straight line from far-right publishers to the modern right-wing media sphere. Viguerie called the midcentury conservative publishing network "the beginning of a communications revolution."[22] This revolution, Viguerie wrote, "allowed conservatives to fly under the radar of the so-called mainstream media . . . and eventually [led] to conservatives' use of talk radio, cable news, and the Internet."[23] The right-wing media sphere established a space for conservative voices, promoted grassroots activism, and inspired an angry constituency eager to push American politics further rightward.[24]

A new generation of media activists built upon the far right's foundation. The 1987 repeal of the fairness doctrine, which stipulated that broadcasters must present both sides of an issue, created an environment primed for partisan media. Numerous right-wing outlets burst forth in the late twentieth and early twenty-first century, each bearing a conservatism laced with aggrievement and bitterness. Rush Limbaugh created a radio empire by selling a message that combined conservative purity with a mocking disdain for liberals. Limbaugh's influence grew so immense that President George H. W. Bush invited him to the White House during his embattled 1992 reelection campaign in order to curry favor with grassroots conservatives. Four years later Rupert Murdoch and Roger Ailes created Fox News, a twenty-four-hour conservative news network that featured a potent blend of entertainment and political commentary. Fox News represented the culmination of decades of right-wing media activism. These new partisan outlets had no interest in giving the other side a voice. Instead, they argued that right-wing outlets were necessary to "balance" out the dominance of the "liberal media."[25]

These media empires formed an echo chamber to stoke right-wing resentment, and the Republican Party capitalized on this invigorated, hyper-partisan constituency. Newt Gingrich, the Georgia Republican and House minority whip, made a name for himself through his no-holds-barred demagoguery. When President Bush broke his central campaign promise—"Read my lips: no new taxes"—by agreeing to a deficit-reducing tax increase, Gingrich led an open rebellion within the GOP. Years later Gingrich called the tax revolt a "major turning point" in American politics because it "deepened people's anger."[26] Weakened by Gingrich's attacks, a primary challenge from paleoconservative Pat Buchanan, and Ross Perot's third-party campaign, Bush lost to Arkansas's Democratic governor Bill Clinton in 1992. Clinton's victory opened the door for more aggression as Gingrich lobbed partisan haymakers at Democrats and waged ideological war on middle-of-the-road Republicans. When Clinton proposed a moderate health care bill that included market-based and government-based reforms, Gingrich lambasted the president as "a pleasant socialist, who believes government knows best."[27] His cohorts at Empower America, a conservative think tank, agreed, raising dark warnings about "central planning" and characterizing Clinton's proposal as "sinister" and "ominous." The very next year, Gingrich proposed the "Contract with America," a program containing numerous right-wing proposals, including a balanced-budget amendment, capital gains tax cuts, and vast welfare rollbacks. He circulated a memo encouraging his fellow Republicans to attack Democrats with scathing language. Democrats were now "sick" and "pathetic," members of a political party that embodied "stagnation" and "waste," perhaps even "traitors" that sought America's "decay."[28] Gingrich's rhetoric and platforms not only helped the Republicans dominate the 1994 midterms, they illustrated that the ideologies and tactics of the far right never truly disappeared from the conservative movement.[29]

The radical roots of modern conservatism did not wither, but blossomed as American politics turned increasingly rightward. Dormant far-right ideas began reappearing in the political mainstream. In particular, far-right ideologies flourished thanks to media democratization in the twenty-first century. Internet blogs, alternative news outlets, and social media websites obviated traditional sentinels such as *National Review*. As the pioneering historian of conservatism George Nash wrote, "In the ever-expanding universe of cyber-space, no one can be an effective gatekeeper because *there are no gates*."[30] The lack of ideological watchmen allowed far-right rhetoric to fester. Websites such as Breitbart, the Gateway Pundit, and WorldNetDaily pander to hard-line conservatives, while Infowars resembles an updated, internet-fueled John Birch Society. Run by pundit Alex Jones, Infowars proffers outrageous conspiracy theories. Much like his anti-communist forbears, Jones alleges that a "deep state" conspiracy threatens the United States and has described liberal politicians as "demons" who "smell like sulfur."[31] Infowars receives millions of unique hits every month despite, or perhaps because of, Jones's beliefs. While midcentury far-right literature circulated from hand-to-hand or through well-connected organizations and publishers, in the new millennium anyone can access the farthest fringes of the right-wing spectrum with just the click of a mouse.[32]

Perhaps no movement illustrated the continuation of far-right thought better than the Tea Party. Exploding into public consciousness after the inauguration of America's first black president, Democrat Barack Obama, the Tea Party was often depicted in popular media as a small-government, low-taxes movement loosely aligned with GOP principles. However, activists carried the same social and racial aggrievements as the midcentury far right. In fact, there are many connections between the two movements: both claimed an affluent, educated, middle-aged or older, majority white membership; both found a great deal of support in the South; both held anti-statist, libertarian beliefs; both viewed nonwhites and immigrant groups as a latent threat to American society; both proffered conspiratorial views; and both utilized media strategies to promote their ideas. Birch Society members were some of the Tea Party's earliest proponents, and extremist groups, including militias such as the paramilitary Oath Keepers, collaborated with Tea Party "patri-ots." After storming the 2010 midterm elections, politicians aligned with the Tea Party filed a deluge of far-right proposals. One bill put forth by Republican congressmen Steve King of Iowa and Rob Woodall of Georgia sought to repeal the Sixteenth Amendment with a single sentence. Congressman Ron Paul, a libertarian Republican from Texas, filed a separate bill that introduced Stone's exact 1956 Liberty Amendment. Paul could not recall how he discovered the Liberty Amendment, but the fact that he filed it at all illustrated the endurance of far-right ideas.[33] Similar to the midcentury far right's institutional network, the Tea Party served as a point of convergence for zealous conservatives who networked with, and eventually radicalized, the Republican Party.[34]

The confluence of Tea Party activism and right-wing news media pushed conservatism further rightward, priming the political environment for a renascence of xenophobic nativism and reactionary anger. Donald Trump, a New York real estate mogul and reality television star, transformed into a right-wing demagogue by capitalizing on the growing sense of aggrievement within conservative ranks. "I think the people of the Tea Party like me," Trump mused during a Fox News interview, "because I represent a lot of the ingredients of the Tea Party."[35] Trump tapped into the government mistrust, racial resentment, and conspiratorial beliefs that had festered within conservatism for decades. He accused Obama of being a Kenyan-born Muslim and refused to back down even when proved wrong, a saga that constituted the origin story of Trump's political career and has come to represent his political oeuvre. At the beginning of his 2015 presidential campaign, Trump referred to Mexican immigrants as "rapists" and "criminals" and promised to build a wall along the Mexican border. He later appeared on Infowars and gushed to Jones, "Your reputation is amazing. I will not let you down."[36] Similar to George Wallace, Trump ran as a right-wing populist, someone from outside Washington who claimed to speak for the little people—ironic, considering his claim to fame as a billionaire playboy—and would ensure that government benefits went to the "right" kind of people. As a result, his base skewed whiter, less educated, and more affluent. Trump rode the wave of anti-establishment, nativist populism, and, despite losing the popular vote by three million, shocked the nation by defeating Democrat Hillary Clinton in the Electoral College.[37]

As president, Trump continued to exploit visceral xenophobia and conspiratorial language. He tried unilaterally to implement a "Muslim ban" on foreign travel to the United States and declared a "national emergency" to build a border wall, revealing the malleability (or hypocrisy) of the GOP's "small government" language. His administration exacerbated the plight of Latin American refugees by concentrating them in internment camps along the border. At times, as Adam Serwer of the *Atlantic* noted, the cruelty seems to be the point.[38] His Manichean view of the political spectrum is an indication that far-right ideals hold significant purchase within the modern Republican Party. Trump's myriad conspiracies—he calls all unflattering media coverage "fake news" and has made unsubstantiated claims about voter fraud, immigrant crime rates, and Muslims cheering on 9/11, to name just a few—led numerous media outlets to dub him the "conspiracy theorist in chief."[39]

He even embraced the delusional QAnon movement. In a previous era, these actions would have earned strong rebukes from mainstream conservatives, but in the modern era, as scholar George Hawley observed, "That is what ordinary Republicans want to see."[40] During the mid-twentieth century, right-wing translators laundered far-right messages for the general public, but the far right no longer needs translators because their views are mainstream and their intellectual heir inhabits the White House. Indeed, Trump and the modern Republican Party represent the culmination of the long ultraconservative movement.[41]

Another critical, and troubling, development during the Trump era is the explosion of right-wing extremism, the militia movement in particular. What started as a fringe white power movement in the aftershock of Vietnam had, by the end of the twentieth century, metastasized into a widespread network of militant organizations. The militia movement unified behind a conspiratorial mistrust of government but never fully separated from its white supremacist roots. The election of Barack Obama further galvanized the right-wing extremities. By the end of Obama's first term the number of militia and antigovernment organizations tallied nearly 1,400, an eight-fold increase since 2008. The militia movement provides a big tent for extremist views, housing groups such as the Three Percenters, who "will not disarm, will not compromise" on gun control; the nihilistic Boogaloo Boys, who yearn for a second civil war and the collapse of American society; and the Proud Boys, street toughs who converge in Democratic cities to intimidate liberals.[42] Prowling the streets in paramilitary uniforms and bearing assault rifles, these groups claim to defend "law and order," but their associates have committed acts of violence against the government and their fellow citizens. Making matters worse, Trump's authoritarian inclinations have fostered a permissive environment for right-wing extremism. He referred to impeachment proceedings as a "coup," disparaged protesters as "anarchists," and claimed that Democratic victories will spark a civil war. And the militias are listening. "We ARE on the verge of a HOT civil war. Like in 1859. That's where we are," read a tweet by the Oath Keepers. "And the Right has zero trust or respect for anything the left is doing. We see THEM as illegitimate too."[43] The militia movement reflects conservatism's history of white supremacy, conspiracies, and vigilantism, a history that Trump has tapped into again and again.[44]

With the Republican Party increasingly moored to Trump, conservatism seems to be skewing further rightward. While the Democratic Party grows younger, more diverse, and more progressive, conservatives have returned to their roots, lobbing conspiracies about perceived left-wing tyranny. A fund-raising e-mail from Trump-Pence 2020 portrayed Democratic policies as a "big government SOCIALIST agenda" that would "rip up the Constitution to appease their radical socialist base."[45] However, numerous right-wing skeptics have voiced concerns about Trump's effect on conservatism. David Frum, a speechwriter for President George W. Bush and noted Never Trumper, opined, "Trump is changing conservatism into something different."[46] In writing Trump out of the movement, Frum donned the mantle of conservative gatekeeper, reflecting Buckley's attempt to sideline the Birchers sixty years prior. But Frum repeated Buckley's mistake by ignoring that "respectable" and radical conservatives draw from the same ideological well. The only difference is that now ultraconservatives wield legitimate power, and they show little interest in relinquishing their grip. After losing the 2020 presidential election to Democrat Joe Biden, Trump touted debunked conspiracies about voter fraud and filed lawsuits and threatened officials in numerous states in an effort to overturn the election results. His actions were not an aberration or those of an autocratic lone wolf—as this book goes to press, twelve senators and over one hundred members of the U.S. House, all Republicans, have joined Trump's attempt to undermine democracy by disputing the Electoral College results. Former president Barack Obama summarized the radicalization of modern conservatism and the Republican Party by stating, "This is not normal. These are extraordinary times. And they're dangerous times."[47] Whether or not America's illiberal turn is an ephemeral shock or a sign of dark times ahead, one thing is certain: the midcentury far right laid the foundation for the acerbic conservatism coursing throughout the country today.[48]

NOTES

Introduction

1. Letter from Kent Courtney to Friend, January 12, 1967, in Folder 38, Box 6, Kent Courtney Collection, Cammie G. Henry Research Center, Northwestern State University, Natchitoches, La. (hereafter shortened to "Courtney Papers"). Benjamin R. Epstein and Arnold Forster, *The Radical Right: Report on the John Birch Society and Its Allies* (New York: Random House, 1967), 11.

2. CNN, "Transcript: Donald Trump's RNC Speech," August 28, 2020, accessed on September 11, 2020, https://www.cnn.com/2020/08/28/politics/donald-trump-speech-transcript/index.html.

3. Scott Adams (@ScottAdamsSays), Twitter post, July 1, 2020, https://twitter.com/Scott AdamsSays/status/1278309835453284357.

4. David Smith and Julie Carrie Wong, "Trump Tacitly Endorses Baseless QAnon Conspiracy Theory Linked to Violence," *Guardian*, August 19, 2020, accessed on September 11, 2020, https://www.theguardian.com/us-news/2020/aug/19/trump-qanon-praise-conspiracy-theory-believers.

5. David Frum, "How to Build an Autocracy," *Atlantic* (March 2017), accessed on September 11, 2020, https://www.theatlantic.com/magazine/archive/2017/03/how-to-build-an-autocracy/513872.

6. Mike Madrid, "Donald Trump Isn't a Conservative, He's a Big Spending Nationalist," *Orange County Register*, January 11, 2020, accessed on September 11, 2020, https://www.ocregister.com/2020/01/11/donald-trump-isnt-a-conservative-hes-a-big-spending-nationalist.

7. Clinton Rossiter, *Conservatism in America* (New York: Knopf, 1955), 5.

8. Russell Kirk, *The Conservative Mind*, 7th revised edition (Washington, D.C.: Regnery Publishing, 2001), vx.

9. William F. Buckley Jr., "Our Mission Statement," *National Review* (November 19, 1955).

10. George H. Nash, "The Conservative Intellectual Movement in America: Then and Now," *National Review* (April 26, 2016).

11. Rossiter, *Conservatism in America*, 11–15. George H. Nash referred to the general terms used by Rossiter as "inadequate and tendentious," instead arguing for the emergence of post–World War II conservatism bearing similar themes with more nuanced divisions (libertarianism, evangelical anti-communism, and traditionalism), in George H. Nash, *The Conservative Intellectual Movement in America Since 1945* (New York: Basic Books, 1976), xiv-xv. However, by underappreciating the influence of the far right, Nash constructed a narrow definition of conservatism. George Hawley, *Right-Wing Critics of American Conservatism* (Lawrence: University Press of Kansas, 2016), 12.

12. Scholars focusing on political culture and grassroots activism have highlighted the influence of far-right activists, the John Birch Society in particular. For examples, see: Lisa McGirr, *Suburban Warriors: The Origins of the New American Right* (Princeton: Princeton University Press, 2001); Jonathan M. Schoenwald, *A Time for Choosing: The Rise of Modern American Conservatism* (New York: Oxford University Press, 2001).

13. Kim Phillips-Fein, *Invisible Hands: The Making of the Conservative Movement from the New Deal to Reagan* (New York: W. W. Norton, 2009), xi–xii. Lawrence B. Glickman, *Free Enterprise: An American History* (New Haven: Yale University Press, 2019), 2–6. Since the late 2000s, numerous scholars have analyzed the business conservative movement. A few choice examples include Angus Burgin, *The Great Persuasion: Reinventing Free Markets Since the Great Depression* (Cambridge, Mass.: Harvard University Press, 2012); Darren E. Grem, *The Blessings of Business: How Corporations Shaped Conservative Christianity* (New York: Oxford University Press, 2016); Bethany Moreton, *To Serve God and Wal-Mart: The Making of Christian Free Enterprise* (New York: Cambridge University Press, 2009); Kathryn S. Olmsted, *Right Out of California: The 1930s and The Big Business Roots of Modern Conservatism* (New York: The New Press, 2015).

14. Robert H. W. Welch Jr., "Through All the Days to Be," in *The New Americanism and Other Speeches and Essays*, ed. Robert H. W. Welch Jr. (Boston: Western Islands, 1966), 58.

15. Billy James Hargis, "Racial Strife . . . and America's Future," p. 17, in Folder 36, Box 2, Billy James Hargis Papers, Special Collections, University of Arkansas, Fayetteville, Ark. (hereafter shortened to "Hargis Papers").

16. "J. Evetts Haley: Candidate for Governor of Texas," in Wallet 1, Box 1, Series 3-C, J. Evetts Haley Collection, Haley Memorial Library and History Center, Midland, Tex. (hereafter shortened to "Haley Papers"). Statement by J. Evetts Haley to the State Democratic Executive Committee, June 11, 1956, in Folder—Speeches and Material, Box 4, Series 3-C, Haley Papers.

17. For more on how conservatives weaponized anti-communism, see Landon R. Y. Storrs, *The Second Red Scare and the Unmaking of the New Deal Left* (Princeton: Princeton University Press, 2013).

18. My network analysis framework was influenced by Jana Elford Smith's description of periodical readers as "nodes" in "Recovering Women's History with Network Analysis: A Case Study of the Fabian News," *Journal of Modern Periodical Studies* 6, no. 2 (2015): 200.

19. Much of the early historiography on modern conservatism highlighted Barry Goldwater's candidacy and the 1964 presidential election as the pivotal moment for the ascendance of modern conservatism. For examples, see Mary C. Brennan, *Turning Right in the Sixties: The Conservative Capture of the GOP* (Chapel Hill: University of North Carolina Press, 1995); Robert Alan Goldberg, *Barry Goldwater* (New Haven: Yale University Press, 1997); Rick Perlstein, *Before the Storm: Barry Goldwater and the Unmaking of the American Consensus* (New York: Hill and Wang, 2001). For scholarly accounts of the 1968 election, see: Dan T. Carter, *The Politics of Rage: George Wallace, the Origins of The New Conservatism, and the Transformation of American Politics* (Baton Rouge: Louisiana State University Press, 1995); Lewis Gould, *1968: The Election That Changed America* (Chicago: Ivan R. Dee, 1993); Michael Nelson, *Resilient America: Electing Nixon in 1968, Channeling Dissent, and Dividing Government* (Lawrence: University Press of Kansas, 2014); Rick Perlstein, *Nixonland: The Rise of a President and the Fracturing of America* (New York: Scribner, 2008).

20. Robert C. Albright, "GOP Leaders Lash Out at Birch Society," *Washington Post*, October 1, 1965. Samuel Lubell, "Republicans Divided on John Birch Issue," *Los Angeles Times*, September 20, 1965.

21. Political histories from the mid-twentieth century shortchanged the importance of the radical right. For examples, see Daniel Bell, *The New American Right* (New York: Criterion Books, 1955); Richard Hofstadter, "The Pseudo-Conservative Revolt," *American Scholar*, 24, no. 1 (Winter 1954–1955): 9–27; Rossiter, *Conservatism*; Arthur M. Schlesinger, *The Vital Center: The Politics of Freedom* (Boston: Houghton Mifflin, 1949). However, contemporary analysts from the Anti-Defamation League produced numerous books about the "radical right," such as Arnold Forster and Benjamin R. Epstein's *Danger on the Right* (New York: Random House, 1964). I agree with scholar Nick Fischer's assessment that "effective political crusades can be waged by very small numbers of people," in *Spider Web: The Birth of American Anticommunism* (Urbana: University of Illinois Press, 2016), xviii.

22. Rick Perlstein, "I Thought I Understood the American Right. Trump Proved Me Wrong." *New York Times*, April 11, 2017, accessed on November 26, 2019, https://www.nytimes.com/2017/04/11/magazine/i-thought-i-understood-the-american-right-trump-proved-me-wrong.html.

23. Nicole Hemmer, *Messengers of the Right: Conservative Media and the Transformation of American Politics* (Philadelphia: University of Pennsylvania Press, 2016), 95–97. Jennifer Burns, "What Was Conservatism?," *Chronicle Review* 63, no. 13 (November 18, 2016); George H. Nash, "Populism, I: American Conservatism and the Problem of Populism," *New Criterion* 36, no. 6 (February 2018). Since the Tea Party movement in 2010, scholars have started reassessing the foundational elements of modern conservatism. Kim Phillips-Fein encouraged historians to probe the "philosophical and political connections" linking far-right groups with mainstream conservatism and the "animating spirit of disappointment and fury" that fueled far-right activism, in "Conservatism: A State of the Field," *Journal of American History* 98, no. 3 (December 2011): 727, 736. For studies examining the Republican Party's internecine conflicts and the rise of hard-line conservatism, see: Geoffrey Kabaservice, *Rule and Ruin: The Downfall of Moderation and the Destruction of the Republican Party, From Eisenhower to the Tea Party* (New York: Oxford University Press, 2012) and Edward H. Miller's *Nut Country: Right-Wing Dallas and the Birth of the Southern Strategy* (Chicago: University of Chicago Press, 2015). Two key studies of the ultrawealthy libertarian movement are Nancy MacLean's *Democracy in Chains: The Deep History of the Radical Right's Stealth Plan for America* (New York: Viking, 2017) and Jane Mayer's *Dark Money: The Hidden History of the Billionaires Behind the Rise of the Radical Right* (New York: Doubleday, 2016). For examinations of ideological or institutional subsections of the radical right, see: Kathleen Belew, *Bring the War Home: The White Power Movement and Paramilitary America* (Cambridge, Mass.: Harvard University Press, 2018); Hawley, *Right-Wing Critics*; D. J. Mulloy, *The World of the John Birch Society: Conspiracy, Conservatism, and the Cold War* (Nashville: Vanderbilt University Press, 2014); Colin E. Reynolds, "The Not-So-Far Right: Radical Right-Wing Politics in the United States, 1941–1977" (PhD diss., Emory University, 2016); David Austin Walsh, "The Right-Wing Popular Front: The Far Right and the American Conservative Movement from the New Deal to the 1960s" (PhD diss., Princeton University, 2020).

24. Forster and Epstein, *Danger on the Right*, 175.

25. Benjamin R. Epstein and Arnold Forster viewed conspiracy theories as the separational boundary between far-right and mainstream conservatives in *Danger on the Right*, 176. Sean P. Cunningham called the far right's electoral efforts a "miserable failure" in his study of Texas ultraconservatism, but focusing solely on electoral victories ignores the far right's substantial cultural and political influence. Sean P. Cunningham, "The Paranoid Style and Its Limits: The Power, Influence, and Failure of the Postwar Texas Far Right," in *The Texas Right: The Radical*

Roots of Lone Star Conservatism, ed. David O'Donald Cullen and Kyle G. Wilkison (College Station: Texas A&M University Press, 2014), 113–115. Hawley, *Right-Wing Critics*, 44.

26. Goldberg, *Goldwater*, 139, 150.

27. For scholarship on the influence of the Dixiecrat Revolt, see: Joseph Crespino, *Strom Thurmond's America* (New York: Hill and Wang, 2012), 172. Kari Frederickson, *The Dixiecrat Revolt: States' Rights Democrats and the end of the Solid South, 1932–1968* (Chapel Hill: University of North Carolina Press, 2001), 4. Earl Black and Merle Black, *The Rise of Southern Republicans* (Cambridge, Mass.: Belknap Press of Harvard University Press, 2002), 32–33. Sean P. Cunningham, *Cowboy Conservatism: Texas and the Rise of the Modern Right* (Lexington: University Press of Kentucky, 2010), 34, 60.

28. Epstein and Forster referred to this group as "extreme conservatives" that were "fellow travelers of today's Radical Right," in *Danger on the Right*, 176. The idea of William F. Buckley Jr. serving as a conservative gatekeeper, a theory first put forth by John Judis, has permeated analyses of conservatism; see John Judis, *William F. Buckley, Jr.: Patron Saint of the Conservatives* (New York: Simon and Schuster, 1988), 200. D. J. Mulloy notes that, despite Buckley's disavowal, the Birch Society still fit within the conservative movement in *John Birch Society*, 82. Kevin M. Schultz, *Buckley and Mailer: The Difficult Friendship That Shaped the Sixties* (New York: W. W. Norton, 2015), 22, 52. Hemmer, *Messengers of the Right*, 106.

29. Lee Roy Chapman, "The Strangelove of Dr. Billy James Hargis: How a Tulsa Preacher and an Army General Created America's Religious Right" *This Land* 3, no. 21 (November 1, 2012).

30. Schoenwald, *Time for Choosing*, 105–106.

31. For analyses of right-wing extremism, see: Belew, *Bring the War Home*, 8–9, 34; Martin Durham, *White Rage: The Extreme Right and American Politics* (New York: Routledge, 2007). D. J. Mulloy, *American Extremism: History, Politics, and the Militia Movement* (New York: Routledge, 2005).

Chapter 1

1. Uncredited, "Jim Reed Charges Roosevelt Made an 'Unholy and Ungodly Alliance With Communism,'" *St. Louis Globe-Democrat*, October 20, 1936.

2. Speech, James A. Reed before the National Jeffersonian Democratic Committee, St. Louis, Missouri, October 19, 1936, in Folder 4A, Phonograph Box 001, James Alexander Reed Papers, Kansas City Research Center, University of Missouri-Kansas City, State Historical Society of Missouri, Kansas City, Mo. (hereafter shortened to "Reed Papers").

3. Robert Dallek, *Franklin D. Roosevelt: A Political Life* (New York: Viking, 2017), 113.

4. William E. Leuchtenburg, *Franklin D. Roosevelt and the New Deal* (New York: Harper and Row, 1963), 165. Eric Rauchway, *Winter War: Hoover, Roosevelt, and the First Clash over the New Deal* (New York: Basic Books, 2018), 7–8.

5. "Real Democrats on the New Deal," *New York Herald Tribune*, October 31, 1936. Douglas B. Craig, *After Wilson: The Struggle for the Democratic Party* (Chapel Hill: University of North Carolina Press, 1992), 11.

6. Heather Cox Richardson, *To Make Men Free: A History of the Republican Party* (New York: Basic Books, 2014), 204–205. Joseph Scotchie, *Revolt from the Heartland: The Struggle for an Authentic Conservatism* (New Brunswick: Transaction Publishers, 2002), 19.

7. George Wolfskill, *The Revolt of the Conservatives: A History of the American Liberty League, 1934–1940* (Westport, Conn.: Greenwood Press, 1962). Paul V. Murphy, *The Rebuke of*

History: The Southern Agrarians and American Conservative Thought (Chapel Hill: University of North Carolina Press, 2001).

8. Patrick Allitt, *The Conservatives: Ideas and Personalities Throughout American History* (New Haven: Yale University Press, 2009), 97–116, 124. Lewis L. Gould, *Grand Old Party: A History of the Republicans* (New York: Random House, 2003), 105, 109, 117. Richardson, *To Make Men Free*, 122.

9. Elaine Frantz Parsons, *Ku-Klux: The Birth of the Klan During Reconstruction* (Chapel Hill: University of North Carolina Press, 2016), 1–7. Glenda Gilmore, *Defying Dixie: The Radical Roots of Civil Rights, 1919–1950* (New York: Norton, 2008), 15–16. George C. Rable, *But There Was No Peace: The Role of Violence in the Politics of Reconstruction* (Athens: University of Georgia Press, 1984), 188.

10. Meriwether's biography of Reed is hagiographic, so I verified his claims and found his excerpts using contemporary newspapers, when possible. Lee Meriwether, *Jim Reed, Senatorial Immortal* (Webster Groves, Mo.: International Mark Twain Society, 1948), 3. Allitt, *Conservatives*, 116–123. John Higham, *Strangers in the Land: Patterns of American Nativism, 1860–1925* (New York: Atheneum, 1963), 4. Kristin L. Hoganson, *Fighting for American Manhood: How Gender Politics Provoked the Spanish-American and Philippine-American Wars* (New Haven: Yale University Press, 1998), 138–139. Mae M. Ngai, *Impossible Subjects: Illegal Aliens and the Making of Modern America* (Princeton: Princeton University Press, 2004), 99. Richardson, *To Make Men Free*, 178–179. Ronald Schaffer, *America in the Great War: The Rise of the War Welfare State* (New York: Oxford University Press, 1991), xii.

11. James R. Green, *Death in Haymarket: A Story of Chicago, the First Labor Movement, and the Bombing that Divided Gilded Age America* (New York: Pantheon Books, 2006); Scott Miller, *The President and the Assassin: McKinley, Terror, and Empire at the Dawn of the American Century* (New York: Random House, 2011); Robert K. Murray, *Red Scare: A Study in National Hysteria, 1919–1920* (Minneapolis: University of Minnesota Press, 1955), 12, 129; Beverly Gage, *The Day Wall Street Exploded: A Story of America in Its First Age of Terror* (New York: Oxford University Press, 2009), 2. John Reed, *Ten Days That Shook the World* (New York: Modern Library, 1935). Fischer, *Spider Web*, xiv. For more on the broader history of anti-communism in the United States, see M. J. Heale, *American Anticommunism: Combatting the Enemy Within, 1830–1970* (Baltimore: Johns Hopkins University Press, 1990); Richard Gid Powers, *Not Without Honor: The History of American Anticommunism* (New York: Free Press, 1995).

12. Clarence E. Wunderlin, *Robert A. Taft: Ideas, Tradition, and Party in U.S. Foreign Policy* (Lanham, Md.: SR Books, 2005), 152.

13. Letter from Kent Courtney to All Members of Congress, in Folder 30, Box 5, Courtney Papers.

14. Murray, *Red Scare*, 4. Richardson, *To Make Men Free*, 184.

15. Robert Welch, "The New Americanism," in *New Americanism*, 10.

16. Willis E. Stone, "A Look at 1955," *American Progress* 1, no. 1 (January 1955): 8.

17. Craig, *After Wilson*, 10. Brian Doherty, *Radicals for Capitalism: A Freewheeling History of the Modern Libertarian Movement* (New York: Public Affairs, 2007), 52–56. Glickman, *Free Enterprise*, 68–69. Charles H. Hamilton, "*Freeman*, 1920–1924" in *The Conservative Press in Twentieth-Century America*, ed. Ronald Lora and William Henry Longton (Westport, Conn.: Greenwood Press, 1999), 310–315. Ellis W. Hawley, "Herbert Hoover, the Commerce Secretariat, and the Vision of an 'Associative State,' 1921–1928," *Journal of American History* 61, no. 1 (June 1974): 117, 118, 127. Hemmer, *Messengers of the Right*, 35. Robert R. Keller, "The Role

of the State in the U.S. Economy During the 1920s," *Journal of Economic Issues* 21, no. 2 (June 1987): 882. Ellis W. Hawley, "Herbert Hoover and American Corporatism, 1929–1933," in *The Hoover Presidency: A Reappraisal*, ed. Martin Fausold and George Mazuzan (Albany: State University of New York Press, 1974), 101–119. Olmsted, *Right Out of California*, 3. Richardson, *To Make Men Free*, 186–188, Joan Hoff Wilson, *Herbert Hoover: Forgotten Progressive* (Boston: Little, Brown, and Company, 1975), 70.

18. Pamphlet, Billy James Hargis, "The Cross or the Sickle?: Christianity vs. Communism in a Changing World," undated, in Folder 27, Box 2, Hargis Papers.

19. Darren Dochuk, *From Bible Belt to Sunbelt: Plain-Folk Religion, Grassroots Politics, and the Rise of Evangelical Conservatism* (New York: W. W. Norton, 2011), xvii, 15–16. Frances Fitzgerald, *The Evangelicals: The Struggle to Shape America* (New York: Simon and Schuster, 2017), 117. Allan J. Lichtman, *White Protestant Nation: The Rise of the American Conservative Movement* (New York: Atlantic Monthly Press, 2008), 9. George S. Marsden, *Fundamentalism and American Culture: The Shaping of Twentieth-Century Evangelicalism, 1870–1925* (New York: Oxford University Press, 1980), 141, 189, 208. Leo P. Ribuffo, *The Old Christian Right: The Protestant Far Right from the Great Depression to the Cold War* (Philadelphia: Temple University Press, 1983), 80.

20. Allitt, *Conservatives*, 136–141. Alfred L. Brophy, *Reconstructing the Dreamland: The Tulsa Riot of 1921: Race, Reparations and Reconciliation* (New York: Oxford University Press, 2002), ix, 24–62. Adam Fairclough, *Better Day Coming: Blacks and Equality, 1890–2000* (New York: Viking, 2001), 102. Jacquelin Dowd Hall, *Revolt Against Chivalry: Jessie Daniel Ames and the Women's Campaign Against Lynching* (New York: Columbia University Press, 1993), 78–80, 134. Murphy, *Rebuke of History*, 1–10. Erin Aubry Kaplan, "The 'Red Summer' of 1919 Reverberates 100 Years Later," *Los Angeles Times*, August 8, 2019. Jonathan Yardley, "After WWI, a Burst of Race Riots," *Washington Post*, July 17, 2011.

21. There are no reliable figures for Klan membership, but estimates range from one to ten million. Linda Gordon, *The Second Coming of the KKK: The Ku Klux Klan of the 1920s and the American Political Tradition* (New York: Liveright, 2017), 2–3, 6, 217n. Charles C. Alexander, *The Ku Klux Klan in the Southwest* (Lexington: University of Kentucky Press, 1965), 21, 27. Kenneth T. Jackson, *The Ku Klux Klan in the City, 1915–1930* (New York: Oxford University Press, 1967), 235–249.

22. Hiram Evans, *The Rising Storm: An Analysis of the Growing Conflict over the Political Dilemma of Roman Catholics in America* (Atlanta: Buckhead Publishing Company, 1930), vii.

23. Gordon, *Second Coming of the KKK*, 40.

24. Alexander, *Ku Klux Klan in the Southwest*, xvi. Gordon, *Second Coming of the KKK*, 15, 41. Nash, *Conservative Intellectual Movement*, xv.

25. Staff Correspondent, "Convention Throng Hails Roosevelt," *New York Times*, July 3, 1932. Alan Brinkley, "The New Deal and the Idea of the State," in *The Rise and Fall of the New Deal Order, 1930–1980*, ed. Steve Fraser and Gary Gerstle (Princeton: Princeton University Press, 1989), 86. Jefferson Cowie, *The Great Exception: The New Deal and the Limits of American Politics* (Princeton: Princeton University Press, 2016), 9. Lizabeth Cohen, *Making a New Deal: Industrial Workers in Chicago, 1919–1939* (New York: Cambridge University Press, 1990), 2. David M. Kennedy, *Freedom from Fear: The American People in Depression and War, 1929–1945* (New York: Oxford University Press, 1999), 365. Leuchtenburg, *Franklin D. Roosevelt*, 47. Jason Scott Smith, *Building New Deal Liberalism: The Political Economy of Public Works, 1933–1956* (New York: Cambridge University Press, 2006), 1–6. Doug Rossinow, *Visions of Progress:*

The Left-Liberal Tradition in America (Philadelphia: University of Pennsylvania Press, 2008), 136–137.

26. Dallek, *Franklin D. Roosevelt*, 154; Ira Katznelson, *When Affirmative Action Was White: An Untold History of Racial Inequality in Twentieth-Century America* (New York: W. W. Norton, 2005), 26–27; Ibram X. Kendi, *Stamped from the Beginning: The Definitive History of Racist Ideas in America* (New York: Nation Books, 2016), 337–338; Robert Mason, *The Republican Party and American Politics from Hoover to Reagan* (New York: Cambridge University Press, 2012), 43, 58. Olmsted, *Right Out of California*, 4, 76, 168. Phillips-Fein, *Invisible Hands*, 27. Mary Poole, *The Segregated Origins of Social Security: African Americans and the Welfare State* (Chapel Hill: University of North Carolina Press, 2006), 6. Richardson, *To Make Men Free*, 204–205. John Weber, *From South Texas to the Nation: The Exploitation of Mexican Labor in the Twentieth Century* (Chapel Hill: University of North Carolina Press, 2015), 130. Wunderlin, *Robert A. Taft*, 25–26.

27. Albert Jay Nock, *Our Enemy, The State* (New York: W. Morrow & Co., 1935), 10–11, 26.

28. George Wolfskill and John A. Hudson, *All but the People: Franklin D. Roosevelt and His Critics, 1933–1939* (London: Collier-Macmillan, 1969), 70.

29. Craig, *After Wilson*, 11. Leuchtenburg, *Franklin D. Roosevelt*, 165. Marquis Childs, "Why They Hate Roosevelt," in *The New Deal and the American People*, ed. Frank Freidel (Englewood Cliffs, N.J.: Prentice-Hall, 1964), 100. Kennedy, *Freedom from Fear*, 275–276, 372. Phillips-Fein, *Invisible Hands*, xii, 9, 15, 27; Frederick Rudolph, "The American Liberty League, 1934–1940," *American Historical Review* 56, no. 1 (October 1950): 19. Wolfskill and Hudson, *All but the People*, 65–92.

30. Richardson, *To Make Men Free*, 203. Mason, *Republican Party*, 45–46, 48. James T. Patterson, *Mr. Republican: A Biography of Robert A. Taft* (Boston: Houghton Mifflin, 1972), 152.

31. Patterson, *Mr. Republican*, 152.

32. Meriwether, *Jim Reed*, 28. J. Michael Cronan, a Missouri-based lawyer, self-published a biography of Reed, titled *James A. Reed: Legendary Lawyer; Marplot in the United States Senate* (Bloomington, Ind.: iUniverse, 2018). To my knowledge, there are no full-length, scholarly biographies of Reed.

33. James A. Reed, "The March of Monopoly-The Radio Trust-Democracy's Duty," June 7, 1930, in Folder—Speeches ptd, Box 43, Reed Papers.

34. Reprinted Radio Address, James A. Reed in Toledo, Ohio, October 29, 1936, in Folder 8, Box 43, Reed Papers.

35. James A. Reed, "Word About Taxation," in Folder—Unmarked Mss (1), Box 45, Reed Papers.

36. *Christian Science Monitor* Washington News Office, "Racial Question in Senate Debate on Nation League," *Christian Science Monitor*, May 27, 1919.

37. Associated Press, "Wilson Labels Reed 'Marplot,'" *Detroit Free Press*, May 9, 1922.

38. James A. Reed, "The Jew," February 27, 1916, in Folder 11, Box 41, Reed Papers.

39. Quote from Carlisle Bargeron, "Reed Will Combat Al Smith to Obtain Party Nomination," *Washington Post*, January 26, 1928. Special to the *Herald Tribune*, "Reed Demands Platform Party Can Agree Upon," *New York Herald Tribune*, February 23, 1928.

40. Meriwether, *Jim Reed*, 185. For an accounting of Reed's role in the libel trial of Henry Ford, see Leo P. Ribuffo, "Henry Ford and 'The International Jew,'" *American Jewish History* 69, no. 4 (June 1980): 437–477. For a defense of Reed, see Sam W. Small, "Jim Reed and the Jews," *Atlanta Constitution*, September 23, 1927. Washington Bureau of *New York Herald Tribune*,

"Coolidge Vetoes Bonus as Extravagant and Wrong; Japanese Ban Before Him," *New York Herald Tribune*, May 16, 1924.

41. Associated Press, "J. A. Reed Assails Hoover for 'Capitalist Socialism,'" *New York Herald Tribune*, September 30, 1932.

42. James A. Reed, "New Deal Taxes 'Robbery by Government,'" *Chicago Herald-Examiner*, August 4, 1935, in Folder—New Deal Statements to Press by Sen. Reed, Box 43, Reed Papers.

43. James A. Reed, "States Control Own Affairs," in Folder—Misc Mss (1), Box 45, Reed Papers.

44. Associated Press, "James A. Reed Lays Vote Buy to New Deal," *Washington Post*, October 25, 1934. Associated Press, "Vote Plot Is Laid to New Dealers," *Baltimore Sun*, October 25, 1934.

45. "Reed Sees Peril," *Kansas City Times*, October 25, 1934, in Folder—Anti–New Deal Materials, Box 51, Reed Papers.

46. Letter from Lee Meriwether to James A. Reed, October 16, 1934, in Folder 9, Box 13, Reed Papers.

47. Letter from Lee Meriwether to James A. Reed, November 7, 1934, in Folder 9, Box 13, Reed Papers.

48. Letter from Lee Meriwether to James M. Beck, November 7, 1934, in Folder 9, Box 13, Reed Papers.

49. Letter from James A. Reed to Lee Meriwether, December 20, 1934, in Folder 9, Box 13, Reed Papers.

50. Rudolph, "American Liberty League," 19.

51. Phillips-Fein, *Invisible Hands*, 9. Wolfskill, *Revolt of the Conservatives*, 24–25.

52. "Jouett Shouse," in *Dictionary of American Biography* (Farmington Hills, Mich.: Gale, 1988).

53. "Jouett Shouse."

54. "Bi-Partisan Group Formed for Battle on 'Radicalism,'" *Atlanta Constitution*, August 23, 1934.

55. Glickman, *Free Enterprise*, 4.

56. "Conservatives Unite to Test New Deal Under Construction," *Christian Science Monitor*, August 23, 1934.

57. "Conservatives Unite."

58. "Shouse Confers with Smith on Liberty League," *New York Herald Tribune*, August 29, 1934. Wolfskill, *Revolt of the Conservatives*, 61.

59. Letter from Raul F. Desvernine to James A. Reed, September 3, 1935, in Folder—American Liberty League Corr 1935–1937, Box 18, Reed Papers.

60. Letter from James A. Reed to Jouett Shouse, September 29, 1934, in Folder 20, Box 13, Reed Papers.

61. "Liberty League Letter Assails Roosevelt Talk," *Washington Post*, August 13, 1936.

62. James A. Reed Speech in Maine, September 5, 1936, in Folder—Misc Mss (4), Box 42, Reed Papers.

63. Arthur C. Wimer, "AAA Called 'Fascist' by Opponents," *Hartford Courant*, December 2, 1935.

64. Wolfskill, *Revolt of the Conservatives*, 109.

65. "Complete Text of Al Smith's Address Before American Liberty League," *Los Angeles Times*, January 26, 1936. Dallek, *Franklin D. Roosevelt*, 179.

66. Associated Press, "Gov' Talmadge Issues Call to the South," *New York Times*, January 5, 1936.

67. Glen Jeansonne, *Gerald L. K. Smith: Minister of Hate* (New Haven: Yale University Press, 1988), 47.

68. Associated Press, "Text of the Address by Governor Talmadge as Delivered Before the Macon Convention," *New York Times*, January 29, 1936.

69. Wolfskill, *Revolt of the Conservatives*, 178.

70. James A. Reed, "Shall We Have Constitutional Liberty or Dictatorship," April 14, 1936, in Folder—Const Liberty or Dictatorship 4-14-36, Box 42, Reed Papers.

71. Letter from James A. Reed to Sterling E. Edmunds, April 30, 1936, in Folder 22, Box 12, Reed Papers.

72. Letter from Sterling E. Edmunds to James A. Reed, April 20, 1936, in Folder 22, Box 12, Reed Papers.

73. Gould, *Grand Old Party*, 272. Mason, *Republican Party*, 60.

74. Form letter from Sterling E. Edmunds, July 23, 1936, in Folder 16, Box 13, Reed Papers.

75. Report of the National Jeffersonian Democrats on the Detroit Conference, August 7–8, 1936, in Folder 16, Box 13, Reed Papers. "The Jeffersonian Party Platform," *Chicago Daily Tribune*, August 9, 1936.

76. Turner Catledge, "Bolters Assemble to Map Campaign to Beat President," *New York Times*, August 7, 1936. Summary of Detroit Jeffersonian Democrat Conference, August 8, 1936, in Folder—Haley, J. Evetts, Wallet 11, Box 2, Series 3-A, Haley Papers.

77. Associated Press, "Gov. Talmadge."

78. Merrill D. Peterson, *The Jefferson Image in the American Mind* (New York: Oxford University Press, 1960), 368–369. Harry L. Watson, *Liberty and Power: The Politics of Jacksonian America* (New York: Hill and Wang, 1990), 6.

79. Letter from Hopewell L. Rogers to James A. Reed, September 23, 1936, in Folder 16, Box 13, Reed Papers.

80. Allitt, *Conservatives*, 279.

81. Dallek, *Franklin D. Roosevelt*, 280–281. Peterson, *Jefferson Image*, 355–356. Gordon S. Wood, *The Radicalism of the American Revolution* (New York: Knopf, 1992), 179.

82. Letter from Lafon Allen to James A. Reed, October 24, 1936, in Folder 16, Box 13, Reed Papers.

83. Letter from Gleason L. Archer to Sterling E. Edmunds, August 14, 1936, in Folder 22, Box 12, Reed Papers.

84. Letter from Sterling E. Edmunds to James A. Reed, August 14, 1936, in Folder 22, Box 12, Reed Papers. Felix Bruner, "Figures Show 1936 Campaign May Cost Most," *Washington Post*, October 31, 1936. Wolfskill, *Revolt of the Conservatives*, 197.

85. Letter from Sterling E. Edmunds to James A. Reed, August 26, 1936, in Folder 22, Box 12, Reed Papers.

86. Letter from Sterling E. Edmunds to Conference Attendees, August 11, 1936, in Folder 21, Box 12, Reed Papers.

87. Letter from Sterling E. Edwards to Fellow Democrat, undated, in Folder 22, Box 12, Reed Papers. Letter from Robert S. Bright to Sterling E. Edmunds, August 26, 1936, in Folder 21, Box 12, Reed Papers.

88. Letter from Sterling E. Edmunds to James A. Reed, September 29, 1936, in Folder 22, Box 2, Reed Papers. "The Jeffersonian Democrats," *New Journal and Guide*, September 12, 1936. Wolfskill, *Revolt of the Conservatives*, 197.

89. William Curry Holden, "J. Evetts Haley, The Man," undated, pp. 4–5, in Folder 8, Series 4-K, Haley Papers.

90. George Norris Green, *The Establishment in Texas Politics: The Primitive Years, 1938–1957* (Westport, Conn.: Greenwood Press, 1979), 7.

91. J. Evetts Haley, "Crystal Gazing in the Dust Bowl," undated, p. 1, in Folder—JD MSS Unpublished, Wallet 22, Box 4, Series 3-A, Haley Papers.

92. For more on Haley's political life, see John S. Huntington, "'The Voice of Many Hatreds:' J. Evetts Haley and Texas Ultraconservatism," *Western Historical Quarterly* 49, no. 1 (Spring 2018): 65–89; Stacey Sprague, "James Evetts Haley and the New Deal: Laying the Foundations for the Modern Republican Party in Texas" (master's thesis, University of North Texas, 2004). Journalist Bill Modisett self-published a hagiographic biography of Haley, *J. Evetts Haley: A True Texas Legend* (Midland, Tex.: Staked Plains Press, 1996). B. Byron Price, "J. Evetts Haley: Southwestern Historian," undated, in Folder 4, Series 4-K, Haley Papers.

93. J. Evetts Haley, *Men of Fiber* (El Paso, Tex.: Carl Hertzog, 1963), p. 6, in Folder—Literary Productions 1932–1964, Wallet 1, J. Evetts Haley Papers, Southwest Collection, Texas Tech University, Lubbock, Tex.

94. Haley wrote numerous histories about the western frontier, including the seminal work on Charles Goodnight, *Charles Goodnight: Cowman and Plainsman* (Norman: University of Oklahoma Press, 1949). J. Evetts Haley, "A Survey of Texas Cattle Drives to the North, 1877–1895" (master's thesis, University of Texas, 1926). Norman D. Brown, *Hood, Bonnet, and Little Brown Jug: Texas Politics, 1921–1928* (College Station: Texas A&M University Press, 1984), 6–7. Cunningham, *Cowboy Conservatism*, 59; Keith Volanto, "The Far Right in Texas Politics During the Roosevelt Era," in *Texas Right*, 74–76. Modisett, *Haley*, 31, 34.

95. Corporate Charter of the Jeffersonian Democrats of Texas, undated, in Folder—Jeff Dems of Texas, Wallet 13, Box 2, Series 3-A, Haley Papers.

96. Letter from W. P. Hamblen to Editor of *The Cherokeean*, August 8, 1936, in Folder 3, Wallet 1, Box 1, Series 3-A, Haley Papers. Volanto, "Far Right," 74.

97. Pamphlet, J. Evetts Haley, "The New Deal and the Negro Vote" (Austin: The Jeffersonian Democrats of Texas, 1936), p. 4 in Wallet 20, Box 3, Series 3-A, Haley Papers.

98. J. Evetts Haley, "Labor and the New Deal," undated, p. 2, in Folder—Advertising #2, Wallet 11, Box 2, Series 3-A, Haley Papers. Katznelson, *Affirmative Action*, 55–57.

99. Volanto, "Far Right," 76.

100. Green, *Establishment*, 237n. Volanto, "Far Right," 74–77. Robert Wuthnow, *Rough Country: How Texas Became America's Most Powerful Bible Belt State* (Princeton: Princeton University Press, 2014), 33.

101. "A Hopeless Undertaking," *Morning Avalanche*, August 26, 1936, in Wallet 14, Box 4, Series 3-A, Haley Papers.

102. Volanto, "Far Right," 76.

103. Prospective Advertisement for the Jeffersonian Democrats of Texas, undated, in Folder—Advertising #2, Wallet 11, Box 2, Series 3-A, Haley Papers.

104. Letter from J. Evetts Haley to Mr. L. R. Atkins, October 15, 1936, and Letter from J. Evetts Haley to Mr. E. Lee Tucker, September 22, 1936, both in Folder 1, Wallet 1, Box 1, Series 3-A, Haley Papers. E. Paul Jones, "Anti-New Dealers Plan Campaigns Will Organize Campaigns

Covering Entire State of Texas," October 1936, in Folder—Advertising Rates, Wallet 10, Box 2, Series 3-A, Haley Papers. Cunningham, *Cowboy Conservatism*, 19–20. Sean P. Cunningham, "The Political Culture of West Texas" in *West Texas: A History of the Giant Side of Texas*, ed. Paul H. Carlson and Bruce A. Glasrud (Norman: University of Oklahoma Press, 2014), 174. Ricky F. Dobbs, *Yellow Dogs and Republicans: Allan Shivers and Texas Two-Party Politics* (College Station: Texas A&M University Press, 2005), 3. Green, *Establishment*, 6–7. Volanto, "Far Right," 69, 74–75. Keith Volanto, *Texas, Cotton, and the New Deal* (College Station: Texas A&M University Press, 2005), 143–144.

105. Letter from H. L. Mencken to James A. Reed, September 30, 1936, in Folder 7, Box 13, Reed Papers.

106. Letter from James A. Reed to Jouett Shouse, May 2, 1936, in Folder 20, Box 13, Reed Papers.

107. Form Letter from Sterling E. Edmunds, October 28, 1936, in Folder 22, Box 12, Reed Papers.

108. Letter from J. Evetts Haley to Mr. R. F. Evans, October 1, 1936, in Folder 1, Wallet 1, Box 1, Series 3-A, Haley Papers.

109. Letter from Fannie B. Campbell to J. Evetts Haley, September 24, 1936, in Folder—Harris Co. Club, Wallet 31, Box 5, Series 3-A, Haley Papers.

110. Letter from James W. Mellen to Sterling E. Edmunds, October 29, 1936, in Folder 3, Box 13, Reed Papers.

111. Pamphlet, Lee Meriwether, "The New Deal is a Raw Deal," in Folder 12, Box 13, Reed Papers.

112. James A. Reed's Speech Before the National Jeffersonian Democratic Committee, St. Louis, Mo., October 19, 1936, in Folder 4A, Phonograph Box 001, Reed Papers.

113. James A. Reed's Speech Before the National Association of Jeffersonian Democrats, Cincinnati, Ohio, October 20, 1936, in Folder 4A, Phonograph Box 001, Reed Papers.

114. James A. Reed's Speech Before the National Jeffersonian Democratic Committee, St. Louis, Mo., October 19, 1936, in Folder 4A, Phonograph Box 001, Reed Papers. Associated Press, "Roosevelt Foes Map Tour," *New York Times*, September 27, 1936. Wolfskill, *Revolt of the Conservatives*, 220.

115. Booklet, Lee Meriwether, "American Institutions: They Must and Shall Be Preserved," February 1936, in Folder 12, Box 13, Reed Papers.

116. Haley, "New Deal and the Negro Vote," 3.

117. Mason, *Republican Party*, 63–64.

118. Letter from Fred Moore to J. Evetts Haley, October 9, 1936, in Folder—Harris Co. Club, Wallet 31, Box 4, Series 3-A, Haley Papers. Mason, *Republican Party*, 65.

119. Associated Press, "Coughlin Attacks Roosevelt as Red," *New York Times*, August 3, 1936.

120. Jeansonne, *Gerald L. K. Smith*, 55.

121. Dallek, *Franklin D. Roosevelt*, 251.

122. Jeansonne, *Gerald L. K. Smith*, 57. Ribuffo, *Old Christian Right*, 140. For more on Huey Long, see Alan Brinkley, "Huey Long, the Share Our Wealth Movement, and the Limits of Depression Dissidence," *Louisiana History: The Journal of the Louisiana Historical Association* 22, no. 2 (Spring 1981).

123. Sheldon Marcus, *Father Coughlin: The Tumultuous Life of the Priest of the Little Flower* (New York: Little, Brown, and Company, 1973), 115.

124. Jeansonne, *Gerald L. K. Smith*, 59.

125. Dallek, *Franklin D. Roosevelt*, 252. Jeansonne, *Gerald L. K. Smith*, 58, 60. Leuchtenburg, *Franklin D. Roosevelt*, 182.

126. D. J. Mulloy, *Enemies of the State: The Radical Right in America from FDR to Trump* (Lanham, Md.: Rowman & Littlefield, 2018), 14. Ribuffo, *Old Christian Right*, 49, 53, 67, 69, 70, 72.

127. Letter from Joseph C. Borden Jr., *Hartford Courant*, November 18, 1935.

128. Alice V. McGillivray, Richard M. Scammon, and Rhodes Cook, *America at the Polls, 1920–1956, Harding to Eisenhower: A Handbook of American Presidential Election Statistics* (Washington, D.C.: CQ Press, 2005), 12, 19.

129. Wolfskill, *Revolt of the Conservatives*, 215.

130. Letter from Sterling E. Edmunds to James A. Reed, February 1, 1937, in Folder 23, Box 12, Reed Papers.

131. Letter from J. Evetts Haley to W. P. Hamblen, November 2, 1936, in Folder—Committee, Wallet 11, Box 2, Series 3-A, Haley Papers.

132. Emphasis in the original document. Letter from Lee Meriwether to James A. Reed, December 17, 1936, in Folder 9, Box 13, Reed Papers.

133. Letter from Sterling E. Edmunds to James A. Reed, February 1, 1937, in Folder 23, Box 12, Reed Papers.

134. Letter from James A. Reed to Lee Meriwether, May 19, 1937, in Folder 9, Box 13, Reed Papers.

135. "Glass to Attack Court Plan in Radio Address Tonight," *Washington Post*, March 29, 1937. Robert C. Albright, "House to Get Two Bills Today for Changes in U.S. Court," *Washington Post*, February 10, 1937. "Court Bill's Foes Charge Cummings Tries to Gag Them," *New York Times*, April 4, 1937. Dallek, *Franklin D. Roosevelt*, 275. Leuchtenburg, *Franklin D. Roosevelt*, 237–238. Wolfskill, *Revolt of the Conservatives*, 249.

136. Wolfskill, *Revolt of the Conservatives*, 251.

137. Letter from Sterling E. Edmunds to John J. Raskob, March 27, 1937, in Folder 23, Box 12, Reed Papers.

138. Wolfskill, *Revolt of the Conservatives*, 252–253.

139. "Roosevelt Upset by Senate," *Chicago Daily Tribune*, July 23, 1937. Wolfskill, *Revolt of the Conservatives*, 252.

140. Dobbs, *Yellow Dogs and Republicans*, 115–120. Green, *Establishment*, 198. Phillips-Fein, *Invisible Hands*, 25. Volanto, "Far Right," 77, 84.

141. Black and Black, *Southern Republicans*, 15. James T. Patterson, *Congressional Conservatism and the New Deal: The Growth of the Conservative Coalition in Congress, 1933–1939* (Lexington: University of Kentucky Press, 1967), 9, 225, 337.

Chapter 2

1. Kennedy, *Freedom from Fear*, 642.

2. Associated Press, "Troops Used to Take Over Ward Plant," *Baltimore Sun*, April 27, 1944.

3. Ben W. Gilbert, "Troops Seize Montgomery Ward Plant," *Washington Post*, April 27, 1944. Lisa Phillips, "When CEOs Were Removable: The Montgomery Ward Strikes, Public Outcry, and the Corporate Problem in U.S. History," *Journal of Labor and Society* 21, no. 1 (March 2018): 88.

4. Uncredited, "President's Defense of Ward Seizure a Thin One," *Los Angeles Times*, December 29, 1944.

5. Uncredited, "Rule at Machine-Gun Point," *Los Angeles Times*, April 28, 1944.

6. Westbrook Pegler, "Fair Enough," *Los Angeles Times*, April 29, 1944.

7. Numerous scholars have noted Dies's importance to Cold War conservatism. For examples, see Nancy Lynn Lopez, "'Allowing Our Fears to Overwhelm Us': A Re-Examination of the House Special Committee on Un-American Activities, 1938–1944" (PhD diss., Rice University, 2002), 715–721; Powers, *Not Without Honor*, 125. Nancy Beck Young, *Why We Fight: Congress and the Politics of World War II* (Lawrence: University Press of Kansas, 2013), 222. Walter Goodman, *The Committee: The Extraordinary Career of the House Committee on Un-American Activities* (New York: Farrar, Straus & Giroux, 1968).

8. James T. Sparrow, *Warfare State: World War II Americans and the Age of Big Government* (New York: Oxford University Press, 2011). Glickman, *Free Enterprise*, 91–94.

9. John W. Dower, *War Without Mercy: Race and Power in the Pacific War* (New York: Pantheon Books, 1986), 22. John Arch Getty, *Origins of the Great Purges: The Soviet Communist Party Reconsidered, 1933–1938* (New York: Cambridge University Press, 1985), 6. Richard Pipes, *A Concise History of the Russian Revolution* (New York: Knopf, 1995), 224. Robert Service, *Stalin: A Biography* (Cambridge, Mass.: Belknap Press of Harvard University Press, 2005), 351. James L. Stokesbury, *A Short History of World War II* (New York: HarperCollins, 1980), 49. Richard J. Evans, *The Third Reich at War* (New York: Penguin, 2009), 9–10.

10. Excerpt from Report No. 1476, "Nazi-Fascist Organizations," January 3, 1940, p. 15 in File 10, Box 16, Papers of U.S. Representative Martin Dies Jr., Sam Houston Regional Library & Research Center, Liberty, Tex. (hereafter shortened to "Dies Papers").

11. Excerpt from Report No. 1476, "Nazi-Fascist Organizations," pp. 3, 6, 8.

12. For additional information on the German American Bund, see Leland V. Bell, "The Failure of Nazism in America: The German American Bund, 1936–1941," *Political Science Quarterly* 85, no. 4 (December 1970); Geoffrey S. Smith, *To Save a Nation: American Countersubversives, the New Deal, and the Coming of World War II* (New York: Basic Books, 1973). For more on Elizabeth Dilling and the Mothers' Movement, see: Glen Jeansonne, *Women of the Far Right: The Mothers' Movement and World War II* (Chicago: University of Chicago Press, 1996). For more on the America First movement, see Wayne S. Cole, *America First: The Battle Against Intervention, 1940–1941* (Madison: University of Wisconsin Press, 1953); Sarah Churchwell, *Behold, America: The Entangled History of "America First" and "The American Dream"* (New York: Basic Books, 2018). Ribuffo, *Old Christian Right*, 64, 71, 76.

13. Christian Mobilizers Membership Application Form in File 21, Box 15, Dies Papers.

14. Smith, *Save a Nation*, 87.

15. Washington Bureau of *The Sun*, "Dies Turns Probe to Other Groups," *Baltimore Sun*, April 3, 1940.

16. Goodman, *Committee*, 5–9. Powers, *Not Without Honor*, 124. Lopez, "'Allowing Our Fears,'" 56. Special to the *New York Times*, "Dickstein to Fight 'Hate' Propaganda," *New York Times*, November 15, 1936.

17. Lopez, "'Allowing Our Fears,'" 39. For an overview of the McCormack-Dickstein Committee, see Goodman, *Committee*, 3–23.

18. Lopez, "'Allowing Our Fears,'" 39.

19. Letter from Martin Dies Jr. to J. V. Berglund, June 29, 1935, in File 31, Box 2, Dies Papers.

20. Lopez, "'Allowing Our Fears,'" 40, 420–422. Goodman, *Committee*, 20.

21. H.R. 12044, May 13, 1932, in File 31, Box 1, Dies Papers. Letter from Martin Dies Jr. to J. V. Berglund, June 29, 1935, in File 31, Box 2, Dies Papers.

22. Letter from Martin Dies Jr. to J. V. Berglund, June 29, 1935, in File 31, Box 2, Dies Papers.

23. Ira Katznelson, *Fear Itself: The New Deal and the Origins of Our Time* (New York: Liveright, 2013), 329. Lopez, "'Allowing Our Fears,'" 44.

24. Sidney Fine, "The General Motors Sit-Down Strike: A Re-Examination," *American Historical Review* 70, no. 3 (April 1965): 692.

25. For more on Reuther, Lewis, and the CIO, see Nelson Lichtenstein, *Walter Reuther: The Most Dangerous Man in Detroit* (Urbana-Champaign: University of Illinois Press, 1997); Robert Zieger, *The CIO, 1935–1955* (Chapel Hill: University of North Carolina Press, 1995). Nelson Lichtenstein, *State of the Union: A Century of American Labor* (Princeton: Princeton University Press, 2002), 48–49. Kennedy, *Freedom from Fear*, 309. Fine, "General Motors Sit-Down Strike," 709.

26. Staff Correspondent, "President's Silence Is Criticized," *Christian Science Monitor*, March 24, 1937.

27. Letter from Matt [L. Love] to Martin Dies Jr., March 24, 1937, in File 39, Box 6, Dies Papers.

28. Letter from Martin Dies Jr. to C. T. Duff, March 29, 1937, in File 39, Box 6, Dies Papers.

29. Katznelson, *Fear Itself*, 173.

30. Westbrook Pegler, "Fair Enough: Communist Device," *Atlanta Constitution*, March 20, 1937.

31. Letter from John Caffrey to Martin Dies Jr., March 22, 1937, in File 38, Box 6, Dies Papers.

32. Letter from Mr. Hustmyre to Martin Dies Jr., March 27, 1937; Letter from Herman Weber to Martin Dies Jr., March 27, 1937; Letter from C. T. Duff to Martin Dies Jr., March 25, 1937; Letter from C. M. Wells to Martin Dies Jr., March 24, 1937, all in File 39, Box 6, Dies Papers. Letter from Tom (J. T.) Booth to Martin Dies Jr., March 24, 1937, in File 41, Box 6, Dies Papers. Letter from Martin Dies Jr. to United Brotherhood of Carpenters and Joiners, April 2, 1937, in File 40, Box 6, Dies Papers. Telegram from H. M. Fredrichesen to Martin Dies Jr., March 30, 1937, in File 38, Box 6, Dies Papers. Fine, "General Motors Sit-Down Strike," 697. Lichtenstein, *State of the Union*, 45–49. Kennedy, *Freedom from Fear*, 311. George Gallup, "Public Sympathizes with General Motors," *Washington Post*, February 7, 1937. George Gallup, "67% Demand States Ban New Tactic," *Washington Post*, March 21, 1937.

33. Charles Groves, "U.S. Won't Act on Sit-Downs," *Daily Boston Globe*, March 28, 1937.

34. Robert C. Albright, "Dies Proposal Is Tabled After Stormy Debate," *Washington Post*, April 9, 1937. Robert C. Albright, "Senate Votes Condemnation of Sit-Downs," *Washington Post*, April 8, 1937.

35. Associated Press, "Hostile Propaganda Aimed at U.S. Due for House Probing," *Christian Science Monitor*, May 27, 1938.

36. Letter from John W. McCormack to William B. Bankhead, June 2, 1938, in File 3, Box 15, Dies Papers.

37. Martin Dies Jr. Statement, Principles and Rules of Procedure for Committee on Un-American Activities, August 12, 1938, in File 5, Box 16, Dies Papers.

38. Frederick R. Barkley, "The Dies Inquiry Likely to Go On," *New York Times*, January 8, 1939. Katznelson, *Fear Itself*, 604n. Young, *Why We Fight*, 199.

39. Letter from Peter J. Nolan to Rhea Whitley, August 24, 1939, in File 21, Box 15, Dies Papers.

40. Ribuffo, *Old Christian Right*, 74.

41. Ribuffo, *Old Christian Right*, 64, 71, 184.

42. Associated Press, "Will Investigate Sit-Down Strikers," *Daily Boston Globe*, October 13, 1938. Goodman, *Committee*, 28. Nelson Lichtenstein, *Labor's War at Home: The CIO in World War II* (Philadelphia: Temple University Press, 2003), 213. Goodman, *Committee*, 31–33. Leuchtenburg, *Franklin D. Roosevelt*, 282. Lopez, "'Allowing Our Fears,'" 415. Ribuffo, *Old Christian Right*, xii, 187.

43. Goodman, *Committee*, 39–40. Associated Press, "Reply of Dies to President," *New York Times*, October 27, 1938.

44. Special to the *New York Times*, "Says Reds Started Sit-Down Strikes," *New York Times*, October 12, 1938.

45. Lopez, "'Allowing Our Fears,'" 191, 202, 243–244. Goodman, *Committee*, 27. Young, *Why We Fight*, 205–206.

46. Uncredited, "Dies Tells Perils of Bureaucracy," *Daily Boston Globe*, April 7, 1939.

47. Goodman, *Committee*, 43.

48. Goodman, *Committee*, 45. Lopez, "'Allowing Our Fears,'" 187–244, 712–718.

49. Goodman, *Committee*, 30. Young, *Why We Fight*, 205–206. Barkley, "Dies Inquiry."

50. Letter from John B. Trevor to Martin Dies Jr., April 25, 1940, in File 31, Box 1, Dies Papers.

51. Letter from Paul B. Matlock to Martin Dies Jr., June 7, 1940, in File 10, Box 15, Papers.

52. Letter from Newton W. Powers to Martin Dies Jr., April 24, 1941, in File 11, Box 15, Dies Papers. Letter from Curtis Beaty to Martin Dies Jr., April 18, 1940, in File 9, Box 15, Dies Papers.

53. Letter from Adolph J. Sabath to Martin Dies Jr., September 21, 1938, in File 7, Box 15, Dies Papers.

54. Associated Press, "Ickes Sees Congress Irked By Dies' 'Despicable Tactics,'" *Washington Post*, February 13, 1943.

55. Letter from A. D. Covin to Martin Dies Jr., August 30, 1938, in File 6, Box 15, Dies Papers.

56. Barkley, "Dies Inquiry." Marquis Childs, "Washington Calling: Wasteful Duplicating Committees," *Washington Post*, May 18, 1944.

57. Goodman, *Committee*, 49.

58. John Fisher, "Class Murphy, La Follette as Agitators' Aids," *Chicago Daily Tribune*, October 22, 1938.

59. Alan Brinkley, *The End of Reform: New Deal Liberalism in Recession and War* (New York: Knopf, 1995), 141; Leuchtenburg, *Franklin D. Roosevelt*, 281; Young, *Why We Fight*, 201. Goodman, *Committee*, 51.

60. Turner Catledge, "10 Points Draft," *New York Times*, December 16, 1937.

61. Catledge, "10 Points Draft."

62. John Robert Moore, "Josiah W. Bailey and the 'Conservative Manifesto' of 1937," *Journal of Southern History* 31, no. 1 (February 1965): 29–32.

63. Robert C. Albright, "Senators Give Coalition Plea Wide Publicity," *Washington Post*, January 19, 1938.

64. Dewey L. Fleming, "Bailey Openly Urges Bloc of Conservatives," *Baltimore Sun*, December 21, 1937. Historian John Robert Moore argued that Bailey's "Conservative Manifesto"

sought to crystallize opposition to liberal spending policies rather than arrange a bipartisan anti-Roosevelt bloc, in "Josiah W. Bailey," 38.

65. Associated Press, "Coalition Plea Given Setback," *Daily Boston Globe*, December 17, 1937. Washington Bureau of *The Sun*, "Bailey Admits Manifesto His," *Baltimore Sun*, December 17, 1937.

66. Washington Bureau of *The Sun*, "Publicity and Ridicule Kill Move for Conservative Bloc," *Baltimore Sun*, December 16, 1937. Moore, "Josiah W. Bailey," 32.

67. Uncredited, "Sobering Defeat," *Baltimore Sun*, December 19, 1937.

68. Chicago Tribune Press Service, "Tydings Blasts Purge in Words off Roosevelt," *Chicago Daily Tribune*, September 10, 1938.

69. Uncredited, "Dies Twits Roosevelt on 'Purge,'" *Washington Post*, October 27, 1938.

70. Turner Catledge, "Final 'Purge' Showdown at Hand for Roosevelt," *New York Times*, September 11, 1938.

71. Mason, *Republican Party*, 77.

72. Mark Sullivan, "What Will Roosevelt Do Now?," *Washington Post*, December 25, 1938.

73. Institute of Public Opinion, "Trend to G.O.P. Began in 1936, Polls Show," *Washington Post*, November 13, 1938. John W. Jeffries, *A Third Term for FDR: The Election of 1940* (Lawrence: University Press of Kansas, 2017), 33, 35.

74. Patterson, *Mr. Republican*, 217–218.

75. Jeffries, *Third Term for FDR*, 52, 136–137.

76. Letter from James A. Reed to Lee Meriwether, February 1, 1940, in Folder 10, Box 13, Reed Papers. Letter from James A. Reed to Alice Moss Ferris, January 25, 1939, in Folder 27, Box 12, Reed Papers.

77. Letter from Lee Meriwether to James A. Reed, January 29, 1940, in Folder 10, Box 13, Reed Papers.

78. Letter from Sterling E. Edmunds to James A. Reed, February 2, 1940, in Folder 25, Box 12, Reed Papers.

79. Letter from Sterling E. Edmunds to James A. Reed, February 19, 1940, in Folder 25, Box 12, Reed Papers.

80. George Gallup, "Gallup Poll Shows Close Race Between Dewey, Hull, F.D.R.," *Atlanta Constitution*, May 12, 1940.

81. Letter from James A. Reed to Al Smith, July 18, 1940, in Folder 20, Box 13, Reed Papers.

82. Jeffries, *Third Term for FDR*, 31, 107, 118. Dallek, *Franklin D. Roosevelt*, 364. Kennedy, *Freedom from Fear*, 454–455.

83. Letter from James A. Reed to Sterling E. Edmunds, April 24, 1940, in Folder 25, Box 12, Reed Papers.

84. Letter from Sterling E. Edmunds to James A. Reed, April 25, 1940, in Folder 25, Box 12, Reed Papers.

85. Jeffries, *Third Term for FDR*, 55–57. Mason, *Republican Party*, 80. Susan Dunn, *1940: FDR, Willkie, Lindbergh, Hitler—the Election and the Storm* (New Haven: Yale University Press, 2014), 80–82, 89.

86. Dunn, *1940*, 84.

87. Jeffries, *Third Term for FDR*, 60. Dunn, *1940*, 84.

88. Letter from Joe Bailey to Sterling E. Edmunds, May 30, 1940, in Folder 25, Box 12, Reed Papers.

89. Letter from James A. Reed to Joseph W. Bailey, June 5, 1940, in Folder 25, Box 12, Reed Papers.

90. Letter from James A. Reed to Lee Meriwether, June 17, 1940, in Folder 10, Box 13, Reed Papers.

91. Letter from Lee Meriwether to James A. Reed, June 29, 1940, in Folder 10, Box 13, Reed Papers.

92. Lee Meriwether, Plank for the Republican Party's 1940 Platform, in Folder 10, Box 13, Reed Papers. Letter from Lee Meriwether to James A. Reed, June 29, 1940, in Folder 10, Box 13, Reed Papers.

93. George Gallup, "Willkie and Roosevelt Shown Close in Popular Strength," *Los Angeles Times*, July 12, 1940.

94. Letter from James A. Reed to Sterling E. Edmunds, July 5, 1940, in Folder 25, Box 12, Reed Papers.

95. Letter from Sterling E. Edmunds to James A. Reed, September 13, 1939, in Folder 24, Box 12, Reed Papers.

96. Letter from James A. Reed to Alice Moss Ferris, August 11, 1936, in Folder 27, Box 12, Reed Papers.

97. Letter from James A. Reed to Al Smith, July 27, 1940, in Folder 20, Box 13, Reed Papers. Letter from Lee Meriwether to James A. Reed, July 27, 1940, in Folder 10, Box 13, Reed Papers.

98. Press Release by Al Smith, July 31, 1940, in Folder 20, Box 13, Reed Papers.

99. Letter from Lee Meriwether to James A. Reed, September 28, 1940, in Folder 10, Box 13, Reed Papers. Letter from Sterling E. Edmunds to James A. Reed, September 19, 1940, in Folder 24, Box 12, Reed Papers. Press Statement of Former Senator James A. Reed, August 26, 1940, in Folder 16, Box 13, Reed Papers. Mason, *Republican Party*, 88.

100. Letter from the National Jeffersonian Democrats, August 31, 1940, in Folder 24, Box 12, Reed Papers. National Jeffersonian Democrats Form Letter, September 5, 1940, in Folder 16, Box 13, Reed Papers. Mason, *Republican Party*, 88.

101. Wolfskill, *Revolt of the Conservatives*, 64, 247–248. Special to the *New York Times*, "New Deal Foe Folds Up," *New York Times*, September 24, 1940. Associated Press, "Three Families Gave $276,725 to Republicans," *New York Herald Tribune*, January 18, 1941.

102. Letter from James A. Reed to Al Smith, November 9, 1940, in Folder 20, Box 13, Reed Papers.

103. McGillivray, Scammon, and Cook, *America at the Polls, 1920–1956*, 10–11. Jeffries, *Third Term for FDR*, 180–181, 195.

104. Patterson, *Mr. Republican*, 242.

105. Patterson, *Mr. Republican*, 243.

106. Julian E. Zelizer, *Arsenal of Democracy: The Politics of National Security–From World War II to the War on Terrorism* (New York: Basic Books, 2012), 50–51. Stokesbury, *World War II*, 119.

107. Wayne S. Cole, "The America First Committee," *Journal of the Illinois State Historical Society* 44, no. 4 (Winter 1951): 308.

108. Cole, "America First Committee," 310.

109. Cole, "America First Committee," 312–314.

110. Smith, *Save a Nation*, 172, 173.

111. Associated Press, "Lindbergh Hits Jewish, British 'War Agitators,'" *Daily Boston Globe*, September 12, 1941.

112. Washington Bureau of *The Sun*, "Willkie Terms Lindbergh's Des Moines Talk Un-American," *Baltimore Sun*, September 14, 1941.

113. Louis Lyons, "Speech of Lindbergh Upheld Here by Many America First Leaders," *Daily Boston Globe*, September 16, 1941.

114. For more on World War II mobilization and foreign policy, see Robert Dallek, *Franklin D. Roosevelt and American Foreign Policy, 1932–1945* (New York: Oxford University Press, 1979); Paul A. Koistinen, *Arsenal of World War II: The Political Economy of American Warfare* (Lawrence: University Press of Kansas, 2004); Mark R. Wilson, *Destructive Creation: American Business and the Winning of World War II* (Philadelphia: University of Pennsylvania Press, 2016). Sparrow, *Warfare State*, 68–69, 76, 123. W. Elliot Brownlee, *Federal Taxation in America: A History*, Third Edition (New York: Cambridge University Press, 2016), 139–146.

115. For more on what Leo Ribuffo called "the Brown Scare," see Ribuffo, *Old Christian Right*, 178–224. Associated Press, "War Labor Board to Prevent Strikes Created by F.D.R.," *Atlanta Constitution*, January 13, 1942. John P. Frank, "All's Fair: The Battle over the Wartime Seizure Power," *Litigation* 28, no. 3 (Spring 2002): 51. Sparrow, *Warfare State*, 196. Kennedy, *Freedom from Fear*, 644. Phillips, "CEOs Were Removable," 82. Elizabeth Tandy Shermer, *Sunbelt Capitalism: Phoenix and the Transformation of American Politics* (Philadelphia: University of Pennsylvania Press, 2013), 94–98.

116. For more on the labor-capital backdrop to the Montgomery Ward strike, see Lisa Phillips's "CEOs Were Removable," 82–83, 87. Associated Press, "Troops Used to Take Over Ward Plant," *Baltimore Sun*, April 27, 1944.

117. Ben W. Gilbert, "Troops Seize Montgomery Ward Plant," *Washington Post*, April 27, 1944.

118. On April 27 and 28, 1944, the Avery story featured in the *Daily Boston Globe*, *Hartford Courant*, *Baltimore Sun*, *Wall Street Journal*, *Atlanta Constitution*, *Chicago Daily Tribune*, *Christian Science Monitor*, *Los Angeles Times*, *New York Times*, and *Washington Post*. The story made the front page of the majority of these newspapers.

119. Associated Press, "Montgomery Ward's Chief Ejected Bodily by Troops," *Los Angeles Times*, April 28, 1944.

120. Associated Press, "Montgomery Ward's Chief."

121. Phil S. Hanna, "Avery Describes How Soldiers Carried Him Out," *Los Angeles Times*, April 28, 1944.

122. Phillips, "CEOs Were Removable," 88–89.

123. Childs, "Wasteful Duplicating Committees."

124. Childs, "Wasteful Duplicating Committees."

125. Telegram from Frank W. Boykin to Editor of *Beaumont Enterprise*, May 13, 1944, in File 4, Box 15, Dies Papers. Drew Pearson, "The Washington Merry-Go-Round," *Washington Post*, May 19, 1944. Drew Pearson, "The Washington Merry-Go-Round," *Washington Post*, September 1, 1944. Robert De Vore, "'Kickback' Quiz Reveals Many Relatives Are on U.S. Payroll," *Washington Post*, March 1, 1942. Mason, *Republican Party*, 107.

126. Racism and class conflict played critical roles in the Philadelphia seizure. For more information, see Alexander Gourse, "'Such Power Spells Tyranny': Business Opposition to Administrative Governance and the Transformation of Fair Employment Policy in Illinois, 1945–1964," in *The Right and Labor in America: Politics, Ideology, and Imagination*, ed. Nelson Lichtenstein and Elizabeth Tandy Shermer (Philadelphia: University of Pennsylvania Press, 2012), 189; Lichtenstein, *State of the Union*, 86; Allan M. Winkler, "The Philadelphia Transit

Strike of 1944," *Journal of American History* 59, no. 1 (June 1972): 73–89. Associated Press, "Labor News: Montgomery Ward Properties Seized by Army Under Roosevelt's Order," *Wall Street Journal*, December 29, 1944. Associated Press, "Sewell Avery's Statement," *New York Times*, December 29, 1944. Phillips, "CEOs Were Removable," 78, 90.

127. Arthur Sears Henning, "U.S. Seething in Anger over Ward Seizure," *Chicago Daily Tribune*, May 8, 1944.

128. Uncredited, "3,465 Cheers and 172 Boos in Avery's Mail; Big and Little Business See Common Peril," *Chicago Daily Tribune*, May 6, 1944.

129. Letter from Lee Meriwether to James A. Reed, May 6, 1944, in Folder 12, Box 13, Reed Papers.

130. Uncredited, "Reed Declares Ward's Seizure Is Bayonet Rule," *Chicago Daily Tribune*, April 30, 1944.

131. Willis E. Stone, "This Curious World," *Sherman Oaks Citizen-Tribune*, June 2, 1944, reprinted in *American Progress* 6, no. 1 (Winter-Spring 1961): 9.

132. Willis E. Stone, "The Cost of Socialism," undated, in Folder—Stone, Willis E. Speeches, Box 1, Willis E. Stone Papers, Special Collections and University Archives, University of Oregon, Eugene, Ore. (hereafter shortened to "Stone Papers").

133. Uncredited, "Progress Report," *American Progress* 4, no. 3 (Summer 1958): 67. Frank Chodorov, *The Income Tax: Root of All Evil* (New York: Devin-Adair Company, 1954), vii. Charles H. Hamilton, "*Freeman*, 1950–" in *Conservative Press*, 323. House Joint Resolution 355, June 10, 1957, in Folder—Amendment Revision, Box 1, Stone Papers.

134. Green, *Establishment*, 50.

135. Cunningham, *Cowboy Conservatism*, 25. Green, *Establishment*, 49–57. Volanto, "Far Right," 82.

136. Associated Press, "Dies Tells 'Texas Regulars' New Deal Against Democracy," *Los Angeles Times*, October 11, 1944.

137. Green, *Establishment*, 55.

138. Associated Press, "Communists Run New Deal, Bricker Says," *Washington Post*, October 31, 1944.

139. "Republicans Get Money in Fight in the Campaign," *Canyon News*, September 28, 1944.

140. Michael Bowen, *The Roots of Modern Conservatism: Dewey, Taft, and the Battle for the Soul of the Republican Party* (Chapel Hill: University of North Carolina Press, 2011), 21. McGillivray, Scammon, and Cook, *America at the Polls, 1920–1956*, 8–9.

141. Numerous historians have written about the modulation of liberalism as a consequence of World War II. Choice examples include Brinkley, *End of Reform*, 265–268; Fraser and Gerstle, *New Deal Order*; Sparrow, *Warfare State*, 242–260; Young, *Why We Fight*, 223–246.

142. Letter from Lee Meriwether to James A. Reed, July 19, 1944, in Folder 12, Box 13, Reed Papers.

143. Powers, *Not Without Honor*, 125. Young, *Why We Fight*, 222.

Chapter 3

1. Uncredited, "Communism in America Exposed," *Seminole Producer*, September 21, 1951.

2. For more on Carl McIntire, see Heather Hendershot, *What's Fair on the Air?: Cold War Right-Wing Broadcasting and the Public Interest* (Chicago: University of Chicago Press, 2011), 102-136. Associated Press, "Bible Balloon Barrage Out," *Baltimore Sun*, August 31, 1953. Billy

James Hargis, "Challenge of the Sky," in "The Bible Balloon Story," ed. Richard Briley III, undated, in Folder 14, Box 1, Hargis Papers.

3. United Press, "2,000 Balloons Waft Message of Hope to Iron Curtain Nations," *New York Herald Tribune*, August 14, 1951.

4. Uncredited, "To Drop Bibles Behind Iron Curtain," *Joplin Globe*, June 10, 1953.

5. Booklet, "The Christian Way to Conquer Communism," undated, in Folder 14, Box 1, Hargis Papers.

6. Associated Press, "Department Isn't Opposed to Ballooning Bibles," *Hartford Courant*, September 1, 1953.

7. Briley, "Bible Balloon Story."

8. Associated Press, "Bible Balloons up over Iron Curtain," *Baltimore Sun*, September 4, 1953. "Christian Way."

9. Associated Press, "Bibles Due to Float over Iron Curtain," *Christian Science Monitor*, June 10, 1953; "Russia Faces Bombardment with Bibles: Evangelist Will Send Books via Balloons," *Chicago Daily Tribune*, April 15, 1957; "Balloon-Lift Set for 10,000 Bibles to Soviet World," *Washington Post*, September 10, 1953; "Balloons to Carry Bibles to Reds," *New York Times*, April 25, 1955. Stanton Doyle, "The Watchman on the Wall," *This Land*, 3, no. 21 (November 1, 2012).

10. The historiography on Senator Joseph McCarthy is immense. For choice readings, see David M. Oshinsky, *A Conspiracy So Immense: The World of Joe McCarthy* (New York: Free Press, 1983); Ellen Schrecker, *Many Are the Crimes: McCarthyism in America* (Princeton: Princeton University Press, 1998); Storrs, *Second Red Scare*. For more on Senator John W. Bricker, see Richard O. Davies, *Defender of the Old Guard: John Bricker and American Politics* (Columbus: Ohio State University Press, 1993).

11. For select readings on the Second Red Scare and the civil rights movement, see Jeff Woods, *Black Struggle, Red Scare: Segregation and Anti-Communism in the South, 1948–1968* (Baton Rouge: Louisiana State University, 2004); Clive Webb, *Rabble Rousers: The American Far Right in the Civil Rights Era* (Athens: University of Georgia Press, 2010). Powers, *Not Without Honor*, 191–192. Daniel K. Williams, *God's Own Party: The Making of the Christian Right* (New York: Oxford University Press, 2010), 13, 19, 23.

12. Robert H. W. Welch Jr., *The Blue Book of the John Birch Society* (Belmont, Mass.: Western Islands, 1959), 2. Melvyn P. Leffler, *For the Soul of Mankind: The United States, the Soviet Union, and the Cold War* (New York: Hill and Wang, 2007), 65, 71, 82. Melvyn P. Leffler, *A Preponderance of Power: National Security, the Truman Administration, and the Cold War* (Stanford, Calif.: Stanford University Press, 1992), 291–298, 332. William Appleman Williams, *The Tragedy of American Diplomacy* (New York: World Publishing, 1959), 258.

13. Stone, "Look at 1955."

14. Nash, *Conservative Intellectual Movement*, xv–xvi. Hawley, *Right-Wing Critics*, 145–178. Powers, *Not Without Honor*, 191. Leffler, *Soul of Mankind*, 72.

15. Bowen, *Modern Conservatism*, 43. Matthew Dallek, *The Right Moment: Ronald Reagan's First Victory and the Decisive Turning Point in American Politics* (New York: Oxford University Press, 2004), 33–34; Powers, *Not Without Honor*, 218; Goodman, *Committee*, 167, 207–225. Storrs, *Second Red Scare*, 2–3.

16. Associated Press, "Rep. Cox Brands Walter Reuther 'A Violent Red,'" *Washington Post*, January 17, 1941.

17. Booklet, "Walter Reuther's Secret Memorandum," in Folder 10, Box 2, Hargis Papers.

18. For more on Walter Reuther, see Lichtenstein, *Most Dangerous Man*. Sparrow, *Warfare State*, 248. David Farber, *The Rise and Fall of Modern American Conservatism: A Short History*

(Princeton: Princeton University Press, 2010), 32–33. Lichtenstein, *Labor's War at Home*, 234–240. Lichtenstein, *State of the Union*, 103–104. Robert Rodgers Korstad, *Civil Rights Unionism: Tobacco Workers and the Struggle for Democracy in the Mid-Twentieth-Century South* (Chapel Hill: University of North Carolina Press, 2003), 290–300.

19. For more on how the Cold War influenced the civil rights movement and the U.S. government, see Mary L. Dudziak, *Cold War Civil Rights: Race and the Image of American Democracy* (Princeton: Princeton University Press, 2000); Gerald Horne, *Black and Red: W.E.B. Du Bois and the Afro-American Response to the Cold War, 1944–1963* (Albany: State University of New York Press, 1986); Azza Salama Layton, *International Politics and Civil Rights Policies in the United States, 1941–1960* (New York: Cambridge University Press, 2000). Mary L. Dudziak, "Desegregation as a Cold War Imperative," *Stanford Law Review* 41, no. 1 (November 1988): 66, 118. Fairclough, *Better Day Coming*, 185–186, 206–209.

20. Carol Anderson, *Eyes off the Prize: The United Nations and the African American Struggle for Human Rights, 1944–1955* (New York: Cambridge University Press, 2003), 124. Frederickson, *Dixiecrat Revolt*, 129.

21. Fairclough, *Better Day Coming*, 206–209. Frederickson, *Dixiecrat Revolt*, 118–119. James T. Patterson, *Grand Expectations: The United States, 1945–1974* (New York: Oxford University Press, 1996), 149.

22. Lee McCardell, "South Nominates Thurmond to Run Against Truman," *Baltimore Sun*, July 18, 1948. Frederickson, *Dixiecrat Revolt*, 137.

23. United Press, "Dixie Rebels Nominate Thurmond and Wright," *Washington Post*, July 18, 1948.

24. For more on Strom Thurmond's role within the Dixiecrat Revolt, see Nadine Cohodas, *Strom Thurmond and the Politics of Southern Change* (New York: Simon and Schuster, 1993); Crespino, *Strom Thurmond's America*; Joseph E. Lowndes, *From New Deal to the New Right: Race and the Southern Origins of Modern Conservatism* (New York: W. W. Norton, 2007).

25. Black and Black, *Southern Republicans*, 43–49. Mason, *Republican Party*, 14–15.

26. Bowen, *Modern Conservatism*, 6–7, 24, 67–69. Farber, *American Conservatism*, 28. Mason, *Republican Party*, 124.

27. Associated Press, "Thurmond Sees Cover-Up," *New York Times*, August 22, 1948.

28. Associated Press, "Thurmond Hits Truman, Dewey, Wallace as Leading U.S. to 'Rocks of Totalitarianism,'" *New York Times*, August 12, 1948.

29. United Press, "Text of Address by Reece Formally Opening Convention," *New York Times*, June 22, 1948.

30. Mason, *Republican Party*, 118. William Moore, "Dems' Record Hit by Dewey," *Chicago Daily Tribune*, October 27, 1948.

31. Transcribed by the *New York Times*, "Text of President's Speech in Boston Attacking GOP and Communism," *New York Times*, October 28, 1948.

32. George Gallup, "Final Poll Gives Dewey 49.5%, Truman 44.5% of Popular Vote," *Washington Post*, November 1, 1948. McGillivray, Scammon, and Cook, *America at the Polls, 1920–1956*, 6–7.

33. Frederickson, *Dixiecrat Revolt*, 4, 5–9.

34. David M. Oshinsky noted that Senator McCarthy spoke extemporaneously, despite having written notes, and that there is no recording of his speech, so no record exists of his exact statement. As a result, the statement about a communist infestation in the State Department varies slightly by source. Oshinsky, *Conspiracy So Immense*, 109. My version of McCarthy's quote comes from Mulloy, *Enemies of the State*, 27–28.

35. Oshinsky, *Conspiracy So Immense*, 30–33. Mulloy, *Enemies of the State*, 37–38.

36. Gerald Griffin, "McCarthy Puts Jessup at Top of 26 Named," *Baltimore Sun*, August 10, 1951.

37. Mason, *Republican Party*, 132.

38. Patterson, *Mr. Conservative*, 446.

39. For more on the relationship between the Old Left and the New Left, see Maurice Isserman, *If I Had a Hammer: The Death of the Old Left and the Birth of the New Left* (New York: Basic Books, 1987); Van Gosse, *Rethinking the New Left: An Interpretative History* (New York: Palgrave Macmillan, 2005). Schrecker, *Many Are the Crimes*, 369.

40. Phillips-Fein, *Invisible Hands*, 58.

41. Associated Press, "Eastland Leads Fight to Keep Jim Crow Ways," *Boston Globe*, February 5, 1956. Woods, *Black Struggle*, 42–43.

42. For more on the Rosenberg Trial, see Marjorie B. Garber and Rebecca L. Walkowitz, *Secret Agents: The Rosenberg Case, McCarthyism, and Fifties America* (New York: Routledge, 1995); Ronald Radosh and Joyce Milton, *The Rosenberg File: A Search for Truth* (New York: Holt, Rinehart, and Winston, 1983). Robert Alan Goldberg, *Enemies Within: The Culture of Conspiracy in Modern America* (New Haven: Yale University Press, 2012), 30–31. Mulloy, *Enemies of the State*, 40.

43. Associated Press, "Nixon Calls Stevenson Appeaser of Communism," *Los Angeles Times*, October 17, 1952. Mulloy, *Enemies of the State*, 42. Robert A. Rutland, *The Democrats: From Jefferson to Carter* (Baton Rouge: Louisiana State University Press, 1979), 210.

44. Uncredited, "Adlai Stevenson," *Wall Street Journal*, July 28, 1952.

45. Holmes Alexander, "Stevenson's Rivals Slowly Fading Away," *Los Angeles Times*, July 23, 1952.

46. Mulloy, *John Birch Society*, 177; Welch, *Blue Book*, 112.

47. Mason, *Republican Party*, 143. Wunderlin, *Robert A. Taft*, 3. Farber, *American Conservatism*, 12–13. Welch, *Blue Book*, 103. Oshinsky, *Conspiracy So Immense*, 229. Patterson, *Mr. Republican*, 547–558. McGillivray, Scammon, and Cook, *America at the Polls, 1920–1956*, 2–3.

48. Welch, *Blue Book*, 105, 106, 112.

49. Uncredited, "Urges a Third Party to Stop Liberal Trend," *Chicago Daily Tribune*, April 16, 1961.

50. For more on the relationship between conservatives and Eisenhower's "Modern Republicanism," see Kabaservice, *Rule and Ruin*; Gary W. Reichard, *Politics as Usual: The Age of Truman and Eisenhower* (Arlington Heights, Ill.: Harlan Davidson, 1988); Schoenwald, *Time for Choosing*. Mason, *Republican Party*, 156. Robert R. McCormick, "The American Party," *Chicago Daily Tribune*, August 24, 1952. Robert Griffith, "The General and the Senator: Republican Politics and the 1952 Campaign in Wisconsin," *Wisconsin Magazine of History* 54, no. 1 (Autumn 1970): 23. Allen Yarnell, "Eisenhower and McCarthy: An Appraisal of Presidential Strategy," *Presidential Studies Quarterly* 10, no. 1 (Winter 1980): 91–92. Mulloy, *John Birch Society*, 177.

51. Schrecker, *Many Are the Crimes*, 145.

52. Dochuk, *Bible Belt to Sunbelt*, xxiii. Gary K. Clabaugh, *Thunder on the Right: The Protestant Fundamentalists* (Chicago: Nelson-Hall Publishers, 1974), 126. Lichtman, *White Protestant Nation*, 29. Grant Wacker, *America's Pastor: Billy Graham and the Shaping of a Nation* (Cambridge, Mass.: Belknap Press of Harvard University Press, 2014), 21–22. Williams, *God's Own Party*, 23.

53. Few books have been written exclusively on Billy James Hargis, but many historians have devoted pages to Hargis's radicalism: John Harold Redekop wrote an analysis of Hargis's

religious and political ideologies in *The American Far Right: A Case Study of Billy James Hargis and Christian Crusade* (Grand Rapids, Mich.: W. B. Eerdmans Publishing Co., 1968). Daniel K. Williams and Darren Dochuk contended that Hargis represented a symptom of the religious fundamentalism that permeated the Sunbelt in *God's Own Party*, 40–43, and *Bible Belt to Sunbelt*, 151, respectively. Heather Hendershot wrote a chapter on Hargis's influence as a media strategist, organizer, and fundraiser in *What's Fair*, 170–205.

54. "Hargis, Billy James," *Current Biography 1972*, p. 202, in Folder 1, Box 1, Hargis Papers.

55. Fernando Penabaz, *"Crusading Preacher from the West": The Story of Billy James Hargis* (Tulsa, Okla.: Christian Crusade Publishing, 1965), 40. Penabaz's biography is a friendly account written by a fellow conspiratorial anti-communist. Most of the biographical information in Penabaz's account comes from interviews with Hargis or Hargis's sermons.

56. Penabaz, *Crusading Preacher*, 40–42.

57. Penabaz, *Crusading Preacher*, 42.

58. Penabaz, *Crusading Preacher*, 41.

59. Billy James Hargis, "Souvenir Booklet of the Billy James Hargis Revival!" (Sapulpa, Okla.: Christian Echoes National Ministry), p. 7, in Folder 13, Box 1, Hargis Papers.

60. "Hargis, Billy James," 203.

61. Penabaz, *Crusading Preacher*, 55.

62. Radio Script #1, "God Says Warn Them for Me," undated, p. 2, in Folder 24, Box 1, Hargis Papers.

63. "Hargis, Billy James," 202. "God Says Warn Them for Me," 2. Penabaz, *Crusading Preacher*, 49.

64. Penabaz, *Crusading Preacher*, 56. "Hargis, Billy James," 202.

65. "Hargis, Billy James," 204.

66. Hendershot, *What's Fair*, 172.

67. Dochuk, *Bible Belt to Sunbelt*, xx. Billy James Hargis, "Plans for Organizing Christian Crusade Chapters," undated, in Folder 19, Box 1, Hargis Papers.

68. Newsletter, Billy James Hargis, "The Truth About Peaceful Coexistence," February 1, 1960, p. 2, in Folder 18, Box 1, Hargis Papers.

69. Pamphlet, Billy James Hargis, "The Cross or the Sickle?: Christianity vs. Communism in a Changing World," undated, in Folder 27, Box 2, Hargis Papers.

70. "Hargis, Billy James," 202.

71. Hendershot, *What's Fair*, 172.

72. Pamphlet, Billy James Hargis, "Integration by Force Is Not a Christian Crusade!," 1956, in Folder 36, Box 2, Hargis Papers.

73. Newsletter, Billy James Hargis, "Usurpation—A Weapon Against American Freedom," February 14, 1960, in Folder 18, Box 1, Hargis Papers.

74. Pamphlet, Billy James Hargis, "Racial Strife . . . and America's Future," undated, in Folder 36, Box 2, Hargis Papers.

75. Hargis, "Racial Strife." Hargis, "Integration by Force."

76. FBI Agent Gordon, "Report No. 10—The Christian Crusade: Billy James Hargis," undated, p. 2, in Folder 4, Box 1, Hargis Papers.

77. Gordon, "Report No. 10," 2.

78. Heather Hendershot estimated that Hargis's zealous adherence to conspiratorial anti-communism restricted his success in *What's Fair*, 187. Reese Cleghorn, "Turn Ye Radio On! Old Elixirs Are Selling Better Now," *South Today: A Digest of Southern Affairs* 1, no. 1 (July 1969): 3,

in Folder 16, Box 1, Hargis Papers. Billy James Hargis, "Plans for Organizing Christian Crusade Chapters," in Folder 19, Box 1, Hargis Papers.

79. Billy James Hargis, "The Amarillo Story," *Christian Crusade* 13, no. 10 (November 1961): 4. Billy James Hargis, "'Operation Mississippi' Great Success!," *Christian Crusade* 13, no. 1 (January 1961): 5. "Christian Crusade Convention Resolution: Reaffirmation of the U.S. as a Christian Nation," August 5, 1964; "Resolution from Christian Crusade Convention: The Fairness Doctrine," August 7, 1964; "Resolution of Christian Crusade Convention: Support the House Committee on Un-American Activities," August 5, 1962, all in Folder 3, Box 3, Hargis Papers.

80. James B. Utt, "Who Are the Real Fright Peddlers?," (Tulsa, Okla.: Christian Crusade Publication), p. 16, in Folder 50, Box 4, Hargis Papers.

81. Epstein and Forster, *Radical Right*, 7. Hemmer, *Messengers of the Right*, 112–113. Redekop, *Far Right*, 25–26.

82. Radio Script, Billy James Hargis, untitled, 1968, in Folder 25, Box 1, Hargis Papers. Hendershot, *What's Fair*, 186.

83. Cleghorn, "Radio On," 3. Gordon, "Report No. 10," 2. Epstein and Forster, *Danger on the Right*, 72, 86. Richard V. Pierard, "Christian Crusade, 1948–1969," in *Conservative Press*, 474.

84. For more on the broader ecumenical movement, see Thomas E. Fitzgerald, *The Ecumenical Movement: An Introductory History* (Westport, Conn.: Praeger, 2004); John Nurser, *For All Peoples and All Nations: The Ecumenical Church and Human Rights* (Washington, D.C.: Georgetown University Press, 2005). Schrecker, *Many Are the Crimes*, 350. Uncredited, "Hargis Discloses He Wrote McCarthy Attack on Oxnam," *Sunday Times*, March 18, 1967, in Folder 16, Box 1, Hargis Papers. Goodman, *Committee*, 334, 337–341. John Harris, "Bishop Oxnam Cleared by House Red Probers," *Daily Boston Globe*, July 22, 1953.

85. Lucille Cardin Crain, "Atomic Energy: Socialism or Free Enterprise?," *American Progress* 1, no. 1 (January 1955): 3.

86. Rossinow, *Visions of Progress*, 1–12. Brownlee, *Federal Taxation*, 149. B. H. McCormack, "Looking Leftward," *Wall Street Journal*, July 27, 1935.

87. Willis E. Stone, "Legislation vs. Economic Laws," undated, in Folder—Stone, Willis E. Speeches, Box 1, Stone Papers.

88. "Honorable Discharge from the United States Army," undated, in Folder—Stone, Willis Emerson, Box 1, Stone Papers. Fact Sheet, "Who Is Willis E. Stone," undated, in Folder—Stone, Willis Emerson, Box 1, Stone Papers. Isaac William Martin, *Rich People's Movements: Grassroots Campaigns to Untax the One Percent* (New York: Oxford University Press, 2013), 141. Shermer, *Sunbelt Capitalism*, 2.

89. Corinne Griffith, "Why the Income Tax Must Go," *Human Events* 14, no. 2 (January 12, 1957).

90. Here I am repurposing Mary L. Dudziak's argument that dealing with civil rights became imperative to winning the Cold War, in "Cold War Imperative." For more on free-market economics as a defense against communism, see Burgin, *Great Persuasion*, 106; Jennifer Burns, *Goddess of the Market: Ayn Rand and the American Right* (New York: Oxford University Press, 2009), 2–4; Glickman, *Free Enterprise*, 230–231; Nash, *Conservative Intellectual Movement*, 115; Phillips-Fein, *Invisible Hands*, 58–60; Jason Stahl, *Right Moves: The Conservative Think Tank in American Political Culture Since 1945* (Chapel Hill: University of North Carolina Press, 2016), 11. For overviews of *National Review*, *Human Events*, and *Freeman*, see Lora and Longton, *Conservative Press*, 321–330, 449–460, 515–530. MacLean, *Democracy in Chains*, xviii–xxvi. Hemmer, *Messengers of the Right*, xii–xiv, 28–48. Carter, *Politics of Rage*, 10–11.

George Lewis, *Massive Resistance: The White Response to the Civil Rights Movement* (New York: Hodder Arnold, 2006), 12–13. Webb, *Rabble Rousers*, 4.

91. Info Sheet—"The 'American Progress' Magazine," October 15, 1954, in Folder—California Coalition for Freedom, Box 1, Stone Papers.

92. Uncredited, "Volume One, Number One," *American Progress* 1, no. 1 (January 1955): 2.

93. Isaac William Martin referred to Stone as a "movement entrepreneur," "a leader who initiates a new campaign, organization or tactic," in *Rich People's Movements*, 14, 141. For an analysis of *American Progress* and the centrality of periodicals to Stone's far-right movement, see John S. Huntington, "Taxation as Tyranny: *American Progress* and the Ultraconservative Movement," *Radical Americas* 3, no. 1 (November 2018). Letter from Willis E. Stone to Frank Flick, December 5, 1958, in Folder—Flick, Frank, Box 5, Stone Papers.

94. J. L. Doenges, "Social Security System . . . An Immoral, Fraudulent Scheme," *American Progress* 1, no. 1 (January 1955): 4.

95. Stone, "Look at 1955."

96. Ralph W. Gwinn, "TVA-Socialist Planning Drains Nation's Economy," *American Progress* 1, no. 1 (January 1955): 6. George Peck, "Tax on Your Big Brown Eyes," *American Progress* 1, no. 1 (January 1955): 7. Eunice Davy Dean, "Bridges We Cross," *American Progress* 1, no. 1 (January 1955): 12.

97. John K. Crippen, "Censorship—And How!," *American Progress* 1, no. 1 (January 1955): 14. Brinkley, *End of Reform*, 6. Kennedy, *Freedom from Fear*, 148–149. Leuchtenburg, *Franklin D. Roosevelt*, 165. Smith, *New Deal Liberalism*, 19.

98. American Progress Foundation Annual Report, January 1952, and American Progress Foundation Annual Report, Fiscal Year 1952–53, August 27, 1953, both in Folder—American Progress Foundation Annual Reports, Box 1, Stone Papers. Uncredited, "A Special Report in answer to Senate Document No. 5," *American Progress* 6, no. 1 (Winter–Spring 1961): 10.

99. Frank Hughes, "Bricker Issue Arouses Hope of New Party," *Chicago Daily Tribune*, March 3, 1954.

100. Frank Hughes, "Many Demand Pro-American Party," *Chicago Daily Tribune*, March 5, 1954.

101. Hughes, "Pro-American Party." Frank Hughes, "Birth of G.O.P. Shows Way for 3rd Party," *Chicago Daily Tribune*, March 8, 1954.

102. Frank Hughes, "Wire Pour in on Leaders of 'For America,'" *Chicago Daily Tribune*, May 9, 1954.

103. James Morgan, "First Round for Control of G.O.P.," *Daily Boston Globe*, June 20, 1954.

104. Frank Hughes, "'For America' Group Formed by 14 Leaders," *Chicago Daily Tribune*, May 8, 1954.

105. For America, Conference of National Policy Committee, March 19, 1955, p. 3 and Letter from Thomas M. McNicholas to J. Evetts Haley, March 29, 1955, both in Folder—For America, Box 3, Series 3-C, Haley Papers.

106. Frank Hughes, "Reds Endanger U.S. Freedoms Manion Warns," *Chicago Daily Tribune*, June 17, 1954.

107. Guardian Correspondent, "Third Force in U.S.: Against One-Worldism," *Manchester Guardian*, June 22, 1954.

108. Perlstein, *Before the Storm*, 10–11.

109. Hughes, "'For America.'"

110. Max K. Gilstrap, "McCormick Takes Lead," *Christian Science Monitor*, May 10, 1954.

111. William H. Stringer, "The Washington Scene: Critical Moment," *Washington Post*, May 10, 1954.

112. Guardian Correspondent, "Third Force in U.S."

113. Hughes, "'For America.'" For more on the political concept of a "silent majority," see Matthew D. Lassiter, *The Silent Majority: Suburban Politics in the Sunbelt South* (Princeton: Princeton University Press, 2006).

114. Associated Press, "'For America' Gifts Are Not Tax Exempt," *New York Times*, October 6, 1955.

115. Uncredited, "Fish Plans 'States' Rights' Political Unit; Denounces For America Group as 'Useless,'" *New York Times*, September 22, 1954.

116. Chicago Tribune Press Service, "Tax Exemption Denied Manion 'For America,'" *Chicago Daily Tribune*, October 5, 1955.

117. Russell Baker, "President Target of G. O. P. Attacks," *New York Times*, February 13, 1955.

118. Robert Howard, "G. O. P. Rallies Hear Leaders Hail Lincoln," *Chicago Daily Tribune*, February 13, 1955.

119. Baker, "President Target."

120. Associated Press, "Right-Wing G. O. P. Rallies Saturday," *New York Times*, February 6, 1955.

121. Baker, "President Target."

122. Uncredited, "Californians Urge Political 'For America,'" *Chicago Daily Tribune*, March 19, 1955.

123. Uncredited, "For America Reorganizes as Political Action Group," *Chicago Daily Tribune*, November 16, 1955.

124. John A. Andrew III revealed that numerous administrations used the IRS for partisan gain, in *Power to Destroy: The Political Uses of the IRS from Kennedy to Nixon* (Chicago: Ivan R. Dee, 2002), 8–9. Chicago Tribune Press Service, "Tax Exemption Denied." Hemmer, *Messengers of the Right*, 37.

125. For America Draft and Platform Revision, March 14, 1957, in Folder—For America, Box 2, Series 3-B, Haley Papers.

126. Walter Trohan, "For America's Program: Back Constitution!," *Chicago Daily Tribune*, November 28, 1955.

127. Hemmer, *Messengers of the Right*, 134.

128. Oshinsky, *Conspiracy So Immense*, 491. Powers, *Not Without Honor*, 265.

129. Welch, "All the Days," 73.

130. Radio Script, Billy James Hargis, "Guilt by Association," undated, p. 1, in Folder 24, Box 1, Hargis Papers.

131. Conservative Society of America, "Organizational Manual of The Conservative Society of America," May 1962, in Folder 33, Box 5, Courtney Papers.

132. William F. Buckley Jr. and L. Brent Bozell, *McCarthy and His Enemies: The Record and Its Meaning* (Chicago: Regnery Publishing, 1954), 245. For an in-depth look at the relationship between Buckley and McCarthy, see Samuel Bennett, "'A Critic Friendly to McCarthy:' How William F. Buckley Jr. Brought Senator Joseph R. McCarthy into the American Conservative Movement between 1951 and 1959" (2019), *MSSA Kaplan Prize for Use of MSSA Collections*. https://elischolar.library.yale.edu/mssa_collections/20.

133. Lewis, *Massive Resistance*, 62. Fairclough, *Better Day Coming*, 220.

134. "Interview with Noah M. Mason," Citizens Council Radio Forum Tape #597-5802, undated in Citizens' Council Radio Forum Digital Collection, Special Collections Department, Mississippi State University, Starkville, Miss. (hereafter shortened to "CCRFDC"). https://msstate.contentdm.oclc.org/digital/collection/p16631coll22/id/419.

135. Robert Welch, "A Letter to the South: On Segregation," in Folder 3, Box 85, Radical Right Collection, Hoover Institution Archives, Palo Alto, Calif. (hereafter shortened to "Radical Right Collection").

136. Proposed Newspaper Column, Billy James Hargis, "For and Against: Communists Intensify War on South," April 1961, p. 1, in Folder 21, Box 1, Hargis Papers.

137. Robin D. G. Kelley, *Hammer and Hoe: Alabama Communists During the Great Depression* (Chapel Hill: University of North Carolina Press, 1990), xiii. Woods, *Black Struggle*, 254, 257.

Chapter 4

1. Kent Courtney, Letter to the Editor, "Seeks Support of a Third Party," *Hartford Courant*, August 9, 1955.

2. Chicago Tribune Press Service, "Conservatives Map Plans for New U.S. Party," *Chicago Daily Tribune*, January 18, 1956.

3. Uncredited, "Open State's Rights Office Here: Work of 21 Parties Is Co-Ordinated," *Chicago Daily Tribune*, August 13, 1956.

4. United Press, "Constitution Party Proposes Own Ticket," *Los Angeles Times*, August 29, 1956.

5. Associated Press, "'Third Party' Groups to Pick '56 Candidates," *Chicago Daily Tribune*, September 9, 1956.

6. Nancy MacLean, "Getting New Deal History Wrong," *International Labor and Working-Class History*, no. 74 (Fall 2008): 51.

7. Welch, *Blue Book*, 60.

8. Richardson, *To Make Men Free*, 234.

9. Brownlee, *Federal Taxation*, 154–155. Alonzo Hamby, *Liberalism and Its Challengers from F.D.R. to Bush* (New York: Oxford University Press, 1985), 121–125. Kabaservice, *Rule and Ruin*, 14–15; Mason, *Republican Party*, 156; Gary W. Reichard, *The Reaffirmation of Republicanism: Eisenhower and the Eighty-Third Congress* (Knoxville: University of Tennessee Press, 1975), 13. Richardson, *To Make Men Free*, 236–237. Schoenwald, *Time for Choosing*, 5.

10. Associated Press, "Andrews Eyes Bid by States Rights Group," *Baltimore Sun*, August 17, 1956.

11. T. Coleman Andrews, "Let's Get Rid of the Income Tax," *Washington Post*, April 22, 1956. Associated Press, "Humphrey Gives Go-Ahead to Andrews' Retirement," *Hartford Courant*, October 21, 1955.

12. Willis E. Stone, "Repealing Income Taxes," *American Progress* 2, no. 3 (Summer 1956): 7.

13. Associated Press, "Ex-Tax Chief Boomed for Presidency," *Washington Post*, August 5, 1956.

14. Associated Press, "Urge Andrews as Candidate for President," *Chicago Daily Tribune*, August 17, 1956. Robert E. Baker, "3d Party Opens Battle Monday," *Washington Post*, October 14, 1956.

15. Associated Press, "Andrews Eyes Bid."

16. International News Service, "'For America' to Draft Andrews as Nominee," *Washington Post*, August 30, 1956.

17. Pamphlet, "Independent Candidates," in Folder 4, Box 43, Bonner Fellers Papers, Hoover Institution Archives, Palo Alto, Calif. (hereafter shortened to "Fellers Papers").

18. International News Service, "'For America' to Draft Andrews." Associated Press, "Andrews Eyes Bid."

19. United Press, "New Party." Uncredited, "Plans for New Party Drawn," *Chicago Daily Tribune*, September 1, 1956.

20. "New Membership Secretary on Duty," *Chamber of Commerce News Bulletin* 32, no. 9 (March 1, 1951), in Folder 109, Box 6, Courtney Papers. Pamphlet, "Meet Kent Courtney," in Folder 34, Box 5, Courtney Papers.

21. Uncredited, "Bircher Would Post Ike as Berlin Wall Sentry," *Boston Globe*, July 13, 1964.

22. Special to the *New York Times*, "Unsuccessful Causes," *New York Times*, April 15, 1961. Schoenwald, *Time for Choosing*, 109. Epstein and Forster, *Radical Right*, 79. CSA Flyer, "Meet Kent Courtney," undated, in Folder 37, Box 6, Courtney Papers.

23. Kent Courtney and John A. Gustafson, "Graduated Income Tax Repeal Moves Backed," *Los Angeles Times*, September 9, 1959.

24. Kent Courtney, "Buckley vs. Walker," *CSA Newsletter* 2, no. 1 (March 2, 1962), in Folder 40, Box 6, Courtney Papers.

25. Kent Courtney, "Let's Try Capitalism: Freedom and Private Enterprise," *CSA Handbook* (May 16, 1967), in Folder 33, Box 5, Courtney Papers. Uncredited, "Parley Backs Goldwater in Election of '64," *Chicago Tribune*, September 21, 1963. Letter from Willis E. Stone to Kent Courtney, August 3, 1964, in Folder 164, Box 19, Courtney Papers. Letter from Kent Courtney to Willis E. Stone, November 5, 1959, in Folder 166, Box 19, Courtney Papers. Kent Courtney, "How Congress Is Carrying Out the Aims of the Communist Party, U.S.A.," *CSA Info Memo*, no. 28 (undated): 2, in Folder 31, Box 5, Courtney Papers.

26. Letter from Kent Courtney to Subscriber of *The Independent American*, January 19, 1962, in Folder 30, Box 5, Courtney Papers.

27. Hemmer, *Messengers of the Right*, 136. "Third Party to Stop Liberal Trend." "Plans for New Party." International News Service, "'For America' to Draft Andrews."

28. John N. Popham, "States Righters Shun a 3D Party," *New York Times*, September 16, 1956.

29. Popham, "States Righters."

30. Mulloy, *John Birch Society*, 77.

31. John Fischer, "Why Is the Conservative Voice So Hoarse?," *Harper's Magazine* (March 1956).

32. Hemmer, *Messengers of the Right*, 136.

33. John Van Camp, "GOP to Outspend Democrats 2-to-1 for TV-Radio Time," *Baltimore Sun*, October 9, 1956. Pamphlet, "Independent Candidates," in Folder 4, Box 43, Fellers Papers.

34. Robert E. Baker, "Income Tax Is Assailed by Andrews," *Washington Post*, October 16, 1956.

35. Robert E. Baker, "3d Party Opens Battle Monday," *Washington Post*, October 14, 1956.

36. Associated Press, "Open 3D Party Group Meeting by Ripping Ike," *Chicago Daily Tribune*, September 30, 1956. Associated Press, "Third Party So Far Has 118,000," *Washington Post*, November 9, 1956.

37. George Peck, "We Are Here to Stay," *American Progress* 3, no. 1 (Fall–Winter 1956): 5. "Total 1956 Vote Exceeds 1952 Record by 473,658: Ike Majority 2d to Roosevelt's," *Chicago Daily Tribune*, December 16, 1956. McGillivray, Scammon, and Cook, *America at the Polls, 1920–1956*, 26. Associated Press, "Third Party So Far Has 118,000."

38. Ronald B. Rapaport and Walter J. Stone, *Three's a Crowd: The Dynamic of Third Parties, Ross Perot, and Republican Resurgence* (Ann Arbor: University of Michigan Press, 2005), 5.

39. Peck, "Here to Stay," 5.

40. Timothy B. Tyson, *The Blood of Emmett Till* (New York: Simon & Schuster, 2017), 211. Robert A. Caro, "Autherine Lucy at the University of Alabama: How the Mob Won," *Journal of Blacks in Higher Education*, no. 37 (Autumn 2002): 124–125. David M. Chalmers, *Hooded Americanism: The History of the Ku Klux Klan* (Durham, N.C.: Duke University Press, 1965), 345. Dudziak, *Cold War Civil Rights*, 13–14. Fairclough, *Better Day Coming*, 216. Layton, *Civil Rights Policies*, 7–8. James Zeigler, *Red Scare Racism and Cold War Black Radicalism* (Jackson: University Press of Mississippi, 2017), 3–6.

41. "Interview with John Bell Williams," Tape #597-1922, undated, in CCRFDC. https://msstate.contentdm.oclc.org/digital/collection/p16631coll22/id/535.

42. William F. Buckley, "Why the South Must Prevail," *National Review* (August 24, 1957).

43. "Interview with Noah M. Mason," Tape #597-5802, undated, in CCRFDC. https://msstate.contentdm.oclc.org/digital/collection/p16631coll22/id/419.

44. For an overview of Richard Weaver's ideologies, see Murphy, *Rebuke of History*, 151–178. Richard M. Weaver, "Integration Is Communization," *National Review* (July 13, 1957): 67.

45. Joseph Crespino, *In Search of Another Country: Mississippi and the Conservative Counterrevolution* (Princeton: Princeton University Press, 2007), 49–54. Frederickson, *Dixiecrat Revolt*, 47. Kevin M. Kruse, *White Flight: Atlanta and the Making of Modern Conservatism* (Princeton: Princeton University Press, 2005), 23–24; Lewis, *Massive Resistance*, 33–35, 65–67. George Lewis, *The White South and the Red Menace: Segregationists, Anticommunism, and Massive Resistance* (Gainesville: University Press of Florida, 2004), 40, 47. Woods, *Black Struggle*, 5. Webb, *Rabble Rousers*, 137, 145.

46. Chalmers, *Hooded Americanism*, 322, 325, 329, 337, 340.

47. Chalmers, *Hooded Americanism*, 345, 356–365. Fairclough, *Better Day Coming*, 239. David Cunningham, *Klansville, U.S.A.: The Rise and Fall of the Civil Rights-Era Ku Klux Klan* (New York: Oxford University Press, 2013), 101.

48. Tom P. Brady, *Black Monday: Segregation or Amalgamation . . . America Has Its Choice* (Winona, Miss.: Association of Citizens' Councils, 1954).

49. Lewis, *Massive Resistance*, 43. Neil R. McMillen, *The Citizens' Council: Organized Resistance to the Second Reconstruction, 1954–64* (Urbana: University of Illinois Press, 1971), 17, 19.

50. Lewis, *Massive Resistance*, 41. McMillen, *Citizens' Council*, 11. Elizabeth Gillespie McRae, *Mothers of Massive Resistance: White Women and the Politics of White Supremacy* (New York: Oxford University Press, 2018), 177.

51. Thomas P. Brady, "A Review of Black Monday" in Pamphlets and Broadsides, Citizens' Council Collection, University of Mississippi eGrove Digital Archive.

52. Fairclough, *Better Day Coming*, 221. Lewis, *Massive Resistance*, 39. McMillen, *Citizens' Council*, 314–315, 360, 360n. Charles M. Payne, *I've Got the Light of Freedom: The Organizing Tradition and the Mississippi Freedom Struggle* (Berkeley: University of California Press, 1995), 290–291.

53. McMillen, *Citizens' Council*, 197.

54. "Unsuccessful Causes," *New York Times*, April 15, 1961. Crespino, *Another Country*, 50. Lewis, *Massive Resistance*, 46. McMillen, *Citizens' Council*, 191, 202–203, 329. Sprague, "James Evetts Haley," 81. Woods, *Black Struggle*, 33, 143.

55. Booklet, Billy James Hargis, "Communism Exposed!," undated, p. 14, in Folder 2, Box 2, Hargis Papers. Billy James Hargis, "The Truth About Segregation: A Resume of the Best on the Subject," undated, p. 2, in Folder 10, Box 2, Hargis Papers.

56. Kent Courtney, "Letter to the Editor," January 30, 1963, in Folder 35, Box 6, Courtney Papers.

57. "Status of Bills to Restrict the Court to Its Proper Jurisdiction," *TFA Newsletter* 1, no. 5 (June–July 1958), in Folder—Texans For America Newsletters, Wallet—TFA Newsletters Late 1950s, Box 3, Series 3-B, Haley Papers.

58. Willis E. Stone, "Spenders Grab for More Power," *American Progress* 1, no. 7 (July, August, September 1955): 52.

59. John T. Flynn, "What About This Civil Right?," *American Progress* 3, no. 2 (Spring 1957): 23.

60. Martin, *Rich People's Movements*, 148–149.

61. J. Evetts Haley, "States Rights—The Issue! Announcement for Governor of Texas," February 29, 1956, in Folder—Pamphlets, Wallet 6, Box 2, Series 3-C, Haley Papers.

62. Letter from J. B. McMillan to J. Evetts Haley, June 9, 1956, and Letter from J. B. McMillan to J. Evetts Haley, June 23, 1956, both in Folder—N (Nacodoches, Navarro, Nueces), Wallet 6, Box 2, Series 3-C, Haley Papers. Letter from Miss Mary Bosworth to J. Evetts Haley, March 29, 1956, in Folder—H, A-M, Wallet 4, Box 1, Series 3-C, Haley Papers.

63. Letter from Dan Smoot to Mr. J. C. Phillips, May 13, 1956, in Folder—D, Wallet 2, Box 1, Series 3-C, Haley Papers.

64. For more on Haley's gubernatorial campaign, see Huntington, "'Voice of Many Hatreds,'" 77–80. Green, *Establishment*, 175. Texas 1956 Gubernatorial Election Results, *Texas Almanac, 1958-1959* (Dallas: A. H. Belo Corporation, 1957), 460–463. Woods, *Black Struggle*, 5.

65. Frank Hughes, "'For America' Leaders Deny It Splits G.O.P.," *Chicago Daily Tribune*, May 12, 1954.

66. Van Camp, "GOP to Outspend Democrats." Associated Press, "Urge Andrews." Hemmer, *Messengers of the Right*, 137–138.

67. Speech Transcript, J. Evetts Haley, "Americanism—and the Cowman's Part," Program of the 58th Convention of the American National Cattlemen's Association, 1955, in Folder—Jan. 10, 1955, Series 4-F, Haley Papers.

68. "Summary of Proceedings at a Meeting of Certain Members of the For America Policy and Finance Committees," May 23, 1955, in Folder—'For America,' Box 3, Series 3-C, Haley Papers. J. Evetts Haley, "Special Report to the Committees of Correspondence," October 1, 1959, in Folder—Committees of Correspondence, Box 1, Series 3-B, Haley Papers.

69. Emphasis in the original document. Haley, "Special Report," 1–2.

70. Uncredited, "Daniel Asks Aid of Schoolteachers," *Dallas Morning News*, March 23, 1959. Allen Duckworth, "Writers to Papers Organize," *Dallas Morning News*, December 3, 1959. Jimmy Banks, "Teacher Pay Bill Passed by House, Sent to Governor," *Dallas Morning News*, August 8, 1961. Pauline Maier, *From Resistance to Revolution: Colonial Radicals and the Development of American Opposition to Britain, 1765-1776* (New York: W. W. Norton, 1972), 89–90, 224. Sprague, "James Evetts Haley," 89.

71. TFA Newsletter, "Report to Texans for America, Committees of Correspondence," undated, in Wallet—TFA Form Letters (Copies), Box 3, Series 3-B, Haley Papers; Billy James Hargis, "Uncle Sam M.D.?," in Folder 19, Box 1, Hargis Papers.

72. Wilbur J. Cohen rejected Haley and Hargis's arguments in "The Forand Bill: Hospital Insurance for the Aged," *American Journal of Nursing* 58, no. 5 (May 1958): 698–702. Lenore A. Epstein and James C. Callison, "Financing Health Care for the Aged," *Law and Contemporary Problems* 27, no. 1 (Winter 1962): 106–107. "Court Impeachment Petition Growing," *Ft. Worth Star Telegram*, January 7, 1958, in Folder—TFA Newsletter Jan 1958 Issue, Wallet—TFA Newsletters late 1950s, Box 3, Series 3-B, Haley Papers. Mulloy, *John Birch Society*, 109–117.

73. Newsletter, "For America—Our Urgent and Immediate Problems," December 31, 1958, in Folder—Notes on 1958 Campaign, Box 3, Series 3-B, Haley Papers.

74. TFA Financial Statement, November 30, 1958, in Wallet—Notes on 1958 Campaign, Correspondence-General, 1958, Box 3, Series 3-B, Haley Papers. Sean P. Cunningham, *American Politics in the Postwar Sunbelt: Conservative Growth in a Battleground Region* (New York: Cambridge University Press, 2014), 34. Cunningham, "Paranoid Style," 105, 111, 115. Green, *Establishment*, 186. Phillips-Fein, *Invisible Hands*, ix–xi.

75. Testimony of Willis E. Stone Before the Ways and Means Committee, February 7, 1958, p. 9, in Folder—Hearings–Ways & Means–House, Box 1, Stone Papers.

76. Testimony of Willis E. Stone Before the Ways and Means Committee, February 7, 1958, p. 6.

77. H.Res. 475, February 10, 1958, in Folder—Hiestand, Edgar W., Box 6, Stone Papers.

78. H.R. 3177, January 22, 1959, in Folder—Hiestand, Edgar W., Box 6, Stone Papers. House Joint Resolution 355, June 10, 1957, in Folder—Amendment Revision, Box 1, Stone Papers. List of Witnesses Appearing Before the Committee on Ways and Means, February 7, 1958, in Folder—Ways and Means Comm. Hearings, Box 1, Stone Papers. Stone, "A Special Report," 10–11. Glickman, *Free Enterprise*, 3. Powers, *Not Without Honor*, 183–185.

79. Special to the *New York Times*, "G.O.P. Juniors Put on Key House Units," *New York Times*, January 15, 1953.

80. Radio Edition of the *Independent American*, undated, in Folder—American Progress Magazine Summer Edition 58 Adv. Copy Contracts, Box 1, Stone Papers.

81. Letter from Willis E. Stone to Edgar W. Hiestand, April 15, 1959, in Folder—Hiestand, Edgar W., Box 6, Stone Papers.

82. H.R. 3177 and H.R. 3012, January 22, 1959, in Folder—Hiestand, Edgar W., Box 6, Stone Papers. Stone, "A Special Report," 10–11.

83. Ernest E. Anthony Jr., "The Texas Story," *American Progress* 5, no. 2 (Spring–Summer 1959): 28.

84. Letter from Willis E. Stone to A. G. Heinsohn, December 5, 1958, in Folder—Heinsohn, A. G., Box 6, Stone Papers. Newsletter, Gordon Winrod, "N.S.R.P. Chaplain Named," March 19, 1962, in Folder 2.2, Box 002, Radical Right Collection. Letter from Willis E. Stone to Kent Courtney, May 8, 1959, in Folder—Courtney, Kent, Box 3, Stone Papers. Letter from Willis E. Stone to Garland Embry Jr., June 9, 1959, in Folder—American Progress Magazine Spring 1959, Box 1, Stone Papers. Dan Hanson, "The Wyoming Story," *American Progress* 5, no. 2 (Spring–Summer 1959): 27. Stone, "A Special Report." Dochuk, *Bible Belt to Sunbelt*, xix–xxiv, 37. Ribuffo, *Old Christian Right*, xi. Williams, *God's Own Party*, 33–34.

85. Letter from Edgar W. Hiestand to Willis E. Stone, June 2, 1958, in Folder—Hiestand, Edgar W., Box 6, Stone Papers.

86. Info Sheet, "The 'American Progress' Magazine." Form Letter from Dwight Claar, undated, in Folder—California Coalition for Freedom, Box 1, Stone Papers.

87. Info Sheet, "The 'American Progress' Magazine." Amy Erdman Farrell, "From a Tarantula on a Banana Boat to a Canary in a Mine: *Ms. Magazine* as a Cautionary Tale in a Neoliberal Age," *Tulsa Studies in Women's Literature* 30, no. 2 (Fall 2011): 394, 401. Hemmer, *Messengers of the Right*, 60. Sean Latham and Robert Scholes, "The Rise of Periodical Studies," *PMLA* 121, no. 2 (March 2006): 520.

88. The "Fall–Winter Advertisers List" revealed that F. Gano Chance paid for the advertisement, in Folder—American Progress Magazine Fall–Winter 57–58 Adv. Schedule, Box 1, Stone Papers. Advertisement, *American Progress* 4, no. 1 (Fall–Winter 1957–1958): 22. Epstein and Forster, *Danger on the Right*, 168.

89. Memo to Taxpayers from Joseph S. Kimmel Sr., *American Progress* 4, no. 1 (Fall–Winter 1957–1958): 30.

90. Kevin M. Kruse, *One Nation Under God: How Corporate America Invented Christian America* (New York: Basic Books, 2019), 131.

91. The list of paid advertisers did not include *National Review*, in "Fall–Winter Advertisers List." *National Review* Advertisement, *American Progress* 4, no. 1 (Fall–Winter 1957–1958): 12. Epstein and Forster, *Danger on the Right*, 170, 278. Kennametal Advertisement, *National Review* (April 5, 1958): inside back cover. Timken Roller Bearing Company Advertisement, *National Review* (May 17, 1958): inside back cover.

92. "The Proposed 23rd Amendment to the Constitution of the United States," undated, in Folder—American Progress Magazine Fall Edition 1958, Box 1, Stone Papers.

93. Subscription Order Blank, *American Progress* 1, no. 1 (January 1955): 17.

94. "Fall–Winter Advertisers List." Letter from Willis E. Stone to Bill Yeager, undated, in Folder—American Progress Winter Edition 1960–1961, Box 1, Stone Papers.

95. Letter from Willis E. Stone to F. Gano Chance, December 15, 1959, in Folder—Chance, F. Gano, Box 3, Stone Papers. The merger was first acknowledged in *American Progress* 3, no. 1 (Fall–Winter 1957). Letter from Willis E. Stone to Finance Committee, July 5, 1958, and Letter from Willis E. Stone to Max A. Koffman, undated, both in Folder—Joint Operating Committee APF and ORFIT Correspondence & Memos, Box 1, Stone Papers. Trial Balance of Joint Operating Committee–ORFIT & American Progress Foundation, April 30, 1958, in Folder—American Progress Foundation Treasurer's Reports, Box 1, Stone Papers.

96. Letter from Willis E. Stone to Frank Flick, June 26, 1959, in Folder—Flick, Frank, Box 5, Stone Papers. Letter from Willis E. Stone to F. Gano Chance, December 15, 1959, in Folder—Chance, F. Gano, Box 3, Stone Papers. Letter from Kent Courtney to Willis E. Stone, May 11, 1959, in Folder—Courtney, Kent, Box 3, Stone Papers.

97. Welch, *Blue Book*, 24.

98. The eleven attendees were: T. Coleman Andrews, Colonel Laurence E. Bunker, William J. Grede, William R. Kent, Fred C. Koch, W. B. McMillan, Revilo P. Oliver, Louis Ruthenburg, Fitzhugh Scott Jr., Robert W. Stoddard, and Ernest G. Swigert. G. Edward Griffin, *Life and Words of Robert Welch: Founder of the John Birch Society* (Thousand Oaks, Calif.: American Media, 1975), 258. Griffin's hagiographic account was sanctioned by Welch himself. Schoenwald, *Time for Choosing*, 62–63. Phillips-Fein, *Invisible Hands*, 59.

99. Welch, *Blue Book*, xiv.

100. Welch, *Blue Book*, 156.

101. Welch, *Blue Book*, 148.

102. Robert H. W. Welch Jr., *The Life of John Birch* (Chicago: Regnery Publishing, 1954), 100–101. For more on John Birch, see Terry Lautz, *John Birch: A Life* (New York: Oxford University Press, 2016). Schoenwald, *Time for Choosing*, 63.

103. Griffin, *Robert Welch*, ix–x, 30, 67–68. Heale, *American Anticommunism*, 60–78. Murray, *Red Scare*, 17. Michael E. Parrish, *Felix Frankfurter and His Times: The Reform Years* (New York: Free Press, 1982), 3, 121.

104. Griffin, *Robert Welch*, 92, 111, 165. J. Allen Broyles, *The John Birch Society: Anatomy of a Protest* (Boston: Beacon Press, 1966), 28. Phillips-Fein, *Invisible Hands*, 13, 14. Mulloy, *John Birch Society*, 177. Reichard, *Politics as Usual*, 79–80. Wunderlin, *Robert A. Taft*, 145, 177, 181.

105. Welch, *Blue Book*, 44, 123. Robert H. W. Welch Jr., "Republics and Democracies" in *New Americanism*, 105. Robert H. W. Welch Jr., *The Politician*, in Cable from Acting Chief, Security Division to SAC Boston, Massachusetts, February 11, 1959, FBI File 62-104401-8, pp. 122, 123, 127.

106. Cable from Acting Chief, Security Division to SAC Boston, Massachusetts, February 11, 1959, FBI File 62-104401-8, p. 18.

107. Robert H. W. Welch Jr., "A Letter to Khrushchev" in *New Americanism*, 37–38. Welch, *Blue Book*, 105, 106. Welch, *Politician*, 115, 118–120. Aaron Wildavsky, "TVA and Power Politics," *American Political Science Review* 55, no. 3 (September 1961): 583. Phillips-Fein, *Invisible Hands*, ix, xi, 15. Rossinow, *Visions of Progress*, 22–23.

108. Welch, "Letter to Khrushchev," 45.

109. Welch, *Blue Book*, 19.

110. Robert H. W. Welch Jr., "Two Revolutions at Once" in *New Americanism*, 186. Fairclough, *Better Day Coming*, 143, 215. Gilmore, *Defying Dixie*, 6. Wilson Record, *The Negro and the Communist Party* (Chapel Hill: University of North Carolina Press, 1951), 285–286.

111. Leonard V. Finder, "Extremism: Historically and the John Birch Society," *Sacramento Union*, October–November 1964, in Folder—AP-1 Finder, Leonard V., 4-19-65, Box 1, Principal File 1965, Eisenhower Post-Presidential Papers, Dwight D. Eisenhower Presidential Library, Abilene, Kan. (hereafter shortened to "Eisenhower Post-Presidential Papers"). Schoenwald, *Time for Choosing*, 93.

112. Robert H. W. Welch Jr., "More Stately Mansions" in *New Americanism*, 147. Robert O. Self, *All in the Family: The Realignment of American Democracy Since the 1960s* (New York: Hill and Wang, 2012), 10.

113. Griffin, *Robert Welch*, 139.

114. Broyles, *John Birch Society*, 27. Epstein and Forster, *Radical Right*, 74. Griffin, *Robert Welch*, 267, 270.

115. Benjamin R. Epstein and Arnold Forster, *Report on the John Birch Society, 1966* (New York: Random House, 1967), 89.

116. Broyles, *John Birch Society*, 37, 85.

117. Letter from Robert H. W. Welch Jr. to General A. C. Wedemeyer, May 14, 1957, in Folder 13, Box 68, Albert C. Wedemeyer Papers, Hoover Institution Archives, Palo Alto, Calif. (hereafter shortened to "Wedemeyer Papers"). Griffin, *Robert Welch*, 193. Epstein and Forster, *John Birch Society*, 15.

118. Finder, "Extremism," 15–16, 19.

119. McGirr, *Suburban Warriors*, 114. Welch, *Blue Book*, 94.

120. Advertisement, "The John Birch Book—'A World Gone Crazy,'" *Christian Crusade* 13, no. 5 (May 1961): 16. McGirr, *Suburban Warriors*, 114. Mulloy, *John Birch Society*, 96.

121. Letter from Douglas C. Morse to Willis E. Stone, December 28, 1961, in Folder—Morse, Douglas C., American Opinion Speakers Bureau, Box 9, Stone Papers.

122. Letter from W. C. Lemly to Robert Welch, July 14, 1968, in Folder—John Birch Society 1967–71, Box 30, Stone Papers.

123. Letter from Robert W. Welch to Kent Courtney, March 30, 1960, in Folder 153, Box 18, Courtney Papers.

124. Letter from Willis E. Stone to Douglas C. Morse, January 8, 1962, in Folder—Morse, Douglas C. American Opinion Speakers Bureau, Box 9, Stone Papers. Letter from Francis X. Gannon to Willis E. Stone, November 8, 1960, in Folder—Birch, John (Society), Box 3, Stone Papers. Letter from Pierre F. Goodrich to Robert Welch, December 29, 1960; Letter from Robert Welch to Willis E. Stone, August 21, 1959; and Letter from Robert Welch to Willis E. Stone, October 27, 1959, all in Folder—Welch, Robert, Box 13, Stone Papers. Welch, *Politician*, 287. Letter from Kent Courtney to Pearl Adams, June 24, 1969, in Folder 110, Box 14, Courtney Papers. Letter from Kent Courtney to All Members and Friends of the John Birch Society in the City of New Orleans, March 23, 1961, in Folder 153, Box 18, Courtney Papers. Anti-Defamation League, "Rev. Billy James Hargis: The Christian Crusade," *Facts* 14, no. 6 (April 1962): 234, in Folder 19, Box 1, Hargis Papers. Donald Janson, "Right-Wing Leaders Shape Secret Fraternity," *New York Times*, September 16, 1961. Mulloy, *John Birch Society*, 18–19, 77, 84.

125. Welch, "Letter to Khrushchev," 19. Mulloy, *John Birch Society*, 145.

126. Welch, *Blue Book*, 79, 98n. Advertisement, "Please, President Eisenhower, Don't!," *New York Herald Tribune*, August 24, 1959. Advertisement, "Please, President Eisenhower, Don't!," *New York Times*, August 30, 1959.

127. Mulloy, *John Birch Society*, 147. Welch, *Blue Book*, 98n. Uncredited, "Goldwater Aided Birch Unit, Rousselot Says," *Los Angeles Times*, October 10, 1964.

128. "Goldwater Aided Birch Unit." Leadership List of Committee Against Summit Entanglements, undated, and Letter from Elizabeth Churchill Brown to Robert "Bob" Welch, May 11, 1959, both in Folder 7, Box 4, Elizabeth Churchill Brown Papers, Hoover Institution Archives, Palo Alto, Calif. (hereafter shortened to "Brown Papers"). Mulloy, *John Birch Society*, 147–148.

129. Kara Hart, TFA Newsletter, undated, in Folder—Committees of Correspondence, Box 2, Series 3-B, Haley Papers.

130. Tom Anderson, "Straight Talk," *American Progress* 5, no. 2 (Spring–Summer 1959): 38.

131. Clarence E. Manion, "Red Traps Are Set for Ike at 'Summit' Conference," April 10, 1960, in Folder 8, Box 16, Wedemeyer Papers.

132. Albert C. Wedemeyer, "Manion Forum" Speech, May 1, 1960, in Folder 8, Box 16, Wedemeyer Papers.

133. Manion, "Red Traps."

134. Welch, *Blue Book*, 98n. Stephen E. Ambrose, *Eisenhower: Soldier and President, The Renowned One-Volume Life* (New York: Simon and Schuster, 1990), 500–517. Mulloy, *John Birch Society*, 150–151.

135. Uncredited, "Plan Political Party to Repeal Income Tax," *Chicago Daily Tribune*, October 24, 1959.

136. Uncredited, "Third Party Federation Formed at Parley Here," *Chicago Daily Tribune*, October 25, 1959. Special to the *New York Times*, "3D Party Mapped by Conservatives," *New York Times*, October 25, 1959. Associated Press, "Rightwing Tide Claimed by 2 Groups," *Baltimore Sun*, October 24, 1959.

137. Associated Press, "Rightwing Tide."

138. An article in *Texans For America* listed a slightly different name, the Federation for Autonomous State Parties, for the third-party federation. "New Party Proposed by Patriots in Chicago," *Texans For America* 2, no. 2 (October–November 1959) in Wallet—Notes on 58

Campaign, Box 3, Series 3-B, Haley Papers. Associated Press, "Rightwing Tide." Special to the *New York Times*, "3D Party."

139. Associated Press, "Rightwing Tide."

140. Uncredited, "Lincoln G.O.P., Third Party Rivals Gather," *Chicago Daily Tribune*, October 23, 1959.

141. "Lincoln G.O.P."

Chapter 5

1. "Interview with Barry Goldwater," Citizens' Council Radio Forum Tape #597-5926, undated, in CCRFDC. https://msstate.contentdm.oclc.org/digital/collection/p16631coll22/id/52.

2. "Interview with Barry Goldwater."

3. For more on Goldwater and 1964, see Brennan, *Turning Right*; Goldberg, *Goldwater*; McGirr, *Suburban Warriors*; Perlstein, *Before the Storm*; Schoenwald, *Time for Choosing*; Nancy Beck Young, *Two Suns of the Southwest: Lyndon Johnson, Barry Goldwater, and the 1964 Battle Between Liberalism and Conservatism* (Lawrence: University Press of Kansas, 2019). Bernard von Bothmer, *Framing the Sixties: The Use and Abuse of a Decade from Ronald Reagan to George W. Bush* (Amherst: University of Massachusetts Press, 2010), 11–12.

4. Cover Image, *Life* Magazine (November 1, 1963). Peterson, *Jefferson Image*, 368–369. Goldberg, *Goldwater*, 3–24. Perlstein, *Before the Storm*, 17–19. Shermer, *Sunbelt Capitalism*, 33–34.

5. Goldberg, *Goldwater*, 31.

6. Cunningham, *American Politics*, 24–30. Shermer, *Sunbelt Capitalism*, 4–5. Elizabeth Tandy Shermer, "Sunbelt Boosterism: Industrial Recruitment, Economic Development, and Growth Politics in the Developing Sunbelt," in *Sunbelt Rising: The Politics of Place, Space, and Region*, ed. Michelle M. Nickerson and Darren Dochuk (Philadelphia: University of Pennsylvania Press, 2011), 34–37. Barry Goldwater, *With No Apologies* (New York: Penguin, 1979), 44.

7. Cunningham, *American Politics*, 27–41. Goldberg, *Goldwater*, 59–62, 64, 92–99, 134. Perlstein, *Before the Storm*, 23.

8. Welch, *Blue Book*, 108–109. "Interview with Barry Goldwater." Barry Goldwater, *The Conscience of a Conservative* (Shepherdsville, Ky.: Victor Publishing Company, 1960), 37. Brennan, *Turning Right*, 30, 32. Goldberg, *Goldwater*, 106–108, 137–140, 143. Hemmer, *Messengers of the Right*, 139. Perlstein, *Before the Storm*, 59.

9. Theodore H. White, *The Making of the President 1960* (New York: Atheneum Publishers, 1961), 68.

10. "Party to Repeal Income Tax." Goldberg, *Goldwater*, 142–143. Hemmer, *Messengers of the Right*, 140. W. J. Rorabaugh, *The Real Making of the President: Kennedy, Nixon, and the 1960 Election* (Lawrence: University Press of Kansas, 2009), 101.

11. Goldberg, *Goldwater*, 138–139. Hemmer, *Messengers of the Right*, 141. Perlstein, *Before the Storm*, 51–52.

12. Goldwater, *Conscience*, 111–112, 114.

13. Goldwater, *Conscience*, 24.

14. Goldwater, *Conscience*, 16.

15. Goldwater, *Conscience*, 26.

16. Goldwater, *Conscience*, 70.

17. For more on the importance of *Conscience of a Conservative*, see Brennan, *Turning Right*, 30; Hemmer, *Messengers of the Right*, 142; Perlstein, *Before the Storm*, 65. Schoenwald, *Time for Choosing*, 126.

18. Brennan, *Turning Right*, 31.

19. Alfred Regnery, "Goldwater's 'The Conscience of a Conservative' Transformed American Politics," *Washington Times*, November 17, 2014. Accessed on April 21, 2019. https://www.washingtontimes.com/news/2014/nov/17/goldwaters-the-conscience-of-a-conservative-transf/. Goldberg, *Goldwater*, 139. Hemmer, *Messengers of the Right*, 143. Perlstein, *Before the Storm*, 61–62. Schoenwald, *Time for Choosing*, 126.

20. Perlstein, *Before the Storm*, 53.

21. Letter from Robert W. Welch to Kent Courtney, March 30, 1960, in Folder 153, Box 18, Courtney Papers.

22. Pamphlet, "Goldwater for President," Tax Fax Pamphlet No. 18, 1960, in Folder 34, Box 5, Courtney Papers. Goldberg, *Goldwater*, 143–144.

23. "Gen. Albert C. Wedemeyer Suggests New Political Party," *Texans For America* 2, no. 1 (June 1959), in Folder—Texans For America Newsletters, Wallet—TFA Newsletters Late 1950s, Box 3, Series 3-B, Haley Papers.

24. United Press International, "Johnson Raps 'Stampede' Tactics of Kennedy Camp," *Washington Post*, July 8, 1960. Goldberg, *Goldwater*, 143–144. Perlstein, *Before the Storm*, 76.

25. Letter from Elizabeth Churchill Brown to Barry Goldwater, July 25, 1960, in Folder 2.4, Box 02, Brown Papers.

26. Perlstein, *Before the Storm*, 83.

27. Letter from Elizabeth Churchill Brown to Barry Goldwater, August 9, 1960, in Folder 2.4, Box 02, Brown Papers. Letter from J. Evetts Haley and Kara Hart to Committees of Correspondence, undated, in Folder—Committees of Correspondence, Box 1, Series 3-B, Haley Papers. Letter from Willis Stone to Kent Courtney, July 27, 1960, in Folder—Courtney, Kent, Box 3, Stone Papers. CSA Press Release, March 13, 1964, in Folder 36, Box 6, Courtney Papers. Associated Press, Photo, Untitled, *Los Angeles Times*, July 25, 1960. Howard H. Boyle Jr., "Proposed Repeal of Connally Reservation–A Matter for Concern," *Marquette Law Review* 43, no. 3 (Winter 1960): 317–324.

28. Richard L. Lyons, "Big Night at GOP Convention Is a Nixon Show All the Way," *Washington Post*, July 28, 1960. Felix Belair Jr., "President Shuns Goldwater View," *New York Times*, July 25, 1960. Brennan, *Turning Right*, 33–36. Kabaservice, *Rule and Ruin*, 30. Mason, *Republican Party*, 178. Perlstein, *Before the Storm*, 85–86.

29. Letter from Elizabeth Churchill Brown to Barry Goldwater August 9, 1960, in Folder 2.4, Box 02, Brown Papers.

30. Letter from Barry Goldwater to Mrs. Constantine Brown, September 1, 1960, in Folder 2.4, Box 02, Brown Papers.

31. Letter from Barry Goldwater to Mrs. Constantine Brown, December 13, 1960, in Folder 2.4, Box 02, Brown Papers.

32. Stephen Shadegg, *Barry Goldwater: Freedom Is His Flight Plan* (New York: Fleet Publishing, 1962), 250. Brennan, *Turning Right*, 38.

33. Shadegg, *Goldwater*, 250.

34. Associated Press, "Goldwater Nominated, but Quickly Withdraws: Sen. Goldwater," *Los Angeles Times*, July 28, 1960. United Press International, "Conservative Group to Map Third Party," *Los Angeles Times*, April 13, 1961.

35. Letter from Elizabeth and Constantine Brown to Barry and Peggy Goldwater, July 28, 1960, in Folder 2.4, Box 02, Brown Papers.

36. Uncredited, "Right Wingers Call for End to Income Tax," *Chicago Daily Tribune*, April 17, 1961. United Press International, "Bircher Leads Parley to Form Third Party," *Los Angeles Times*, April 14, 1961.

37. Associated Press, "Third Party Is Deplored," *Baltimore Sun*, April 15, 1961. Uncredited, "Birch Member Says 3D Party Can Not Win," *Chicago Daily Tribune*, April 15, 1961.

38. For more on anti-Catholicism during the 1960 election, see Shaun A. Casey, *The Making of a Catholic President: Kennedy vs. Nixon 1960* (New York: Oxford University Press, 2009).

39. Robert Dallek, *An Unfinished Life: John F. Kennedy, 1917–1963* (Boston: Little, Brown, 2003), 594–602. Fairclough, *Better Day Coming*, 241–244, 253–256. Gosse, *Rethinking the New Left*, 40. Iwan Morgan and Philip Davies, eds., *From Sit-Ins to SNCC: The Student Civil Rights Movement in the 1960s* (Gainesville: University of Florida Press, 2013), 1–6.

40. "Interview with Strom Thurmond," Citizens' Council Radio Forum Tape #597-56328, undated, in CCRFDC. https://msstate.contentdm.oclc.org/digital/collection/p16631coll22/id /267.

41. "Interview with Strom Thurmond." Billy James Hargis, "For and Against: Communists Intensify War on South," April 1961, p. 1, in Folder 21, Box 1, Hargis Papers. Benjamin Gitlow, "The Negro Question—Communist Civil War Policy," *Christian Crusade* 14, no. 8 (December 1962): 5.

42. Julian Williams, "In Defense of the South," *Christian Crusade* 13, no. 5 (May 1961): 12.

43. Letter from Elizabeth Churchill Brown to Barry Goldwater, July 13, 1963, Letter from Barry Goldwater to Mrs. Constantine Brown, July 19, 1963, and Letter from Barry Goldwater to Mrs. Constantine Brown, July 27, 1963, all in Folder 2.4, Box 02, Brown Papers.

44. Kelley, *Hammer and Hoe*, xiii, 221. Record, *Negro and the Communist Party*, 285–286.

45. "Meet Kent Courtney." Letter from Kent Courtney to Member, April 9, 1965, in Folder 30, Box 5, Courtney Papers.

46. Pamphlet, "The Conservative Society of America: An Invitation to Patriotic Political Action," in Folder 34, Box 5, Courtney Papers.

47. Letter from Kent Courtney to Members, undated, in Folder 30, Box 5, Courtney Papers.

48. Both pamphlets located in Folder 41, Box 6, Courtney Papers. Thomas O'Neill, "Politics and People: Restless Right," *Baltimore Sun*, April 21, 1961. Letter from Kent Courtney to Carl Prussian, February 15, 1965, in Folder 30, Box 5, Courtney Papers. Bill Coppenbarger, "Mayor Thompson (Jackson, Miss.) Suggests National Third Party," *Jackson Daily News,* and "Why Alabama Was Chosen," *Lynchburg News,* both in *CSA Info Memo,* no. 3, in Folder 31, Box 5, Courtney Papers. Kent Courtney, "Constitutional Party of Penna.," *CSA Newsletter* in the *CSA Handbook,* October 3, 1966, p. 4, in Folder 33, Box 5, Courtney Papers. Receipts and Expense, July 1961 through October 31, 1962, in Folder 32, Box 5, Courtney Papers.

49. Kent Courtney, "Needed: A Shadow Government," *CSA Info Memo,* no. 13 (undated): 1, in Folder 31, Box 5, Courtney Papers.

50. Letter from Kent Courtney to Alice Mills Creveling, November 14, 1962, in Folder 30, Box 5, Courtney Papers. It is difficult to assess the success of Kent Courtney's electoral approach because his papers detail strategies rather than results or sponsored candidates. Ward Poag, "What Not to Do!," *CSA Political Action Bulletin,* no. 1 (April 11, 1963), in Folder 35, Box 6, Courtney Papers. Ward Poag, "Notes on California," June 14, 1962, p. 2, in Folder 192, Box 22, Courtney Papers. Letter from Kent Courtney to Members, undated, and Letter from Kent Courtney to Members of the CSA, Subscribers of the *Independent American* in the State of California,

undated, both in Folder 30, Box 5, Courtney Papers. "How to Write Your Congressman" and "How to Write Letters-to-the-Editor," *CSA Handbook* (undated), in Folder 33, Box 5, Courtney Papers.

51. Durham, *White Rage*, 20.

52. Durham, *White Rage*, 21.

53. Walsh, "Right-Wing Popular Front," 236–241.

54. CSA Memo, "Leadership Security Measures," undated, in Folder 37, Box 6, Courtney Papers.

55. Letter from Kent Courtney, November 27, 1961, in Folder 30, Box 5, Courtney Papers. Poag, "Notes on California," 1–13. Green, *Establishment*, 7. Letter from Kent Courtney to Subscriber of *The Independent American*, January 19, 1962; Letter from Kent Courtney to All Newspapers in the State of Missouri, undated; and Letter from Kent Courtney to Walter Wetzel, November 1, 1965, all in Folder 30, Box 5, Courtney Papers. Special to the *New York Times*, "Rockefeller Stirs Rightists' Wrath," *New York Times*, April 14, 1963. Cunningham, "Political Culture of West Texas," 165–180. Durham, *White Rage*, 13–14.

56. Letter from Kent Courtney to Robert W. Welch (Bob), July 27, 1965, in Folder 152, Box 18, Courtney Papers. Letter from Donald R. Gray to Kent Courtney, March 8, 1965, and Letter from Kent Courtney to Robert W. Welch (Bob), February 24, 1965, both in Folder 153, Box 18, Courtney Papers. Letter from Kent Courtney to Billy James Hargis, August 17, 1962; Letter from Billy James Hargis to Kent Courtney, February 24, 1964; Letter from Billy James Hargis to Kent Courtney, October 9, 1962; and Letter from Billy James Hargis to Kent Courtney, January 6, 1962, all in Folder 117, Box 15, Courtney Papers. Letter from Kent Courtney to Willis E. Stone, November 5, 1959, in Folder 166, Box 19, Courtney Papers. George Tagge, "Conservative Leader Backs Birch Society," *Chicago Daily Tribune*, April 4, 1961.

57. Welch, "Letter to the South." Welch, *Politician*, 225–226, 256.

58. George Sokolsky, "These Days: Jumping Jupiter!," *Washington Times*, January 14, 1961.

59. Robert W. Welch, *The John Birch Society Bulletin*, August 1964, p. 7, in Folder—Political Correspondence and Clippings 1964, Wallet—Correspondence, clippings and campaign material—1964, Box 1, Series 3-E, Haley Papers. John Wicklein, "Birch Society Will Offer $2,300 for Impeach-Warren Essays," *New York Times*, August 5, 1961. Maurice Isserman and Michael Kazin, *America Divided: The Civil War of the 1960s* (New York: Oxford University Press, 2000), 214. Mulloy, *John Birch Society*, 109–117.

60. Woods, *Black Struggle*, 67.

61. "Interview with James O. Eastland," Citizens' Council Radio Forum Tape #597-5929, 1959, in CCRFDC. https://msstate.contentdm.oclc.org/digital/collection/p16631coll22/id/276.

62. "Interview with Congressman Noah M. Mason," Citizens' Council Radio Forum Tape #597-5802, 1958, in CCRFDC. https://msstate.contentdm.oclc.org/digital/collection/p16631coll22/id/419.

63. Ward Just, "Birch vs. Warren," *Washington Post*, November 28, 1965. Crespino, *Another Country*, 9. Lewis, *Massive Resistance*, 25. Mulloy, *John Birch Society*, 116–117. Welch, *Blue Book*, 100n. G. Edward White, "Earl Warren as Jurist," *Virginia Law Review* 67, no. 3 (April 1981): 473–474.

64. "Thunder on the Right," *Newsweek* (December 4, 1961): 18. Tagge, "Conservative Leader." Virginia Wilson, "How U.S. Government Supports the Communist Revolution," *CSA Info Memo*, no. 23 (undated), in Folder 31, Box 5, Courtney Papers. "American Conservative Leaders to Address Third Annual Crusade Convention August 4–6," *Christian Crusade* 13, no. 7

(July 1961): 1. "Background Analysis: Facts You Should Know About the Christian Crusade and Its Leader," *North Dakota Union Farmer*, December 6, 1961, in Folder 16, Box 1, Hargis Papers.

65. Welch, *Blue Book*, 100n.

66. Richard B. Lillich, "The Chase Impeachment," *American Journal of Legal History* 4, no. 1 (January 1960): 49.

67. Welch, *Politician*, 1.

68. Welch, *Blue Book*, 87. Welch, *Politician*, 287.

69. James E. Clayton, "John Birch 'Antis' Point Unwelcome Spotlight," *Washington Post*, March 26, 1961. Uncredited, "Welch Letters: 'Communists Have One of Their Own (Ike) in Presidency,'" *Boston Globe*, April 2, 1961. Gene Blake, "Reds Influence U.S. Decisions, Welch Charges," *Los Angeles Times*, April 12, 1961. Mulloy, *John Birch Society*, 15. Schoenwald, *Time for Choosing*, 72.

70. William F. Buckley Jr., "The Question of Robert Welch," *National Review* 12 (February 13, 1962). Lee Edwards, *William F. Buckley Jr.: The Maker of a Movement* (Wilmington, Del.: ISI Books, 2010), 80–81. Mulloy, *John Birch Society*, 79. Schoenwald, *Time for Choosing*, 74, 177–178.

71. Barbara Bundschu, "Blue Book Gives Goals," *Boston Globe*, March 31, 1961.

72. Letter from A. C. Wedemeyer to Robert Welch, September 5, 1961, in Folder 9, Box 115, Wedemeyer Papers. Carl T. Bogus, *Buckley: William F. Buckley and the Rise of American Conservatism* (New York: Bloomsbury Press, 2011), 12–13, 194, 334. Mulloy, *John Birch Society*, 82. Nash, *Conservative Intellectual Movement*, 275. Schultz, *Buckley and Mailer*, 22, 287.

73. Letter from Richard Nixon to Dwight D. Eisenhower, March 5, 1962, in Folder—Nixon, Richard M., 1962, Box 14, Special Name Series, Eisenhower Post-Presidential Papers.

74. Attached Statement of Richard Nixon, Letter from Richard Nixon to Dwight D. Eisenhower, March 5, 1962, p. 2, in Folder—Nixon, Richard M., 1962, Box 14, Special Name Series, Eisenhower Post-Presidential Papers.

75. Letter from George W. Milias to Leonard V. Finder, March 25, 1964, pp. 1–2, in Folder—Extremist Associations: John Birch Society (2), Box 16, Papers of Leonard V. Finder, Dwight D. Eisenhower Presidential Library, Abilene, Kan.

76. "Poag Suggestions to the Members of California," undated, in Folder 192, Box 22, Courtney Papers.

77. "Poag Suggestions."

78. Isserman and Kazin, *America Divided*, 212. McGirr, *Suburban Warriors*, 63, 120, 127. Perlstein, *Before the Storm*, 60.

79. "Liberty Is the Issue," *American Progress* 6, no. 1 (Winter–Spring 1961): Front Cover.

80. Rossinow, *Visions of Progress*, 233. Uncredited, "*American Progress* Magazine to Become," *American Progress* 8, no. 1 (January–February 1963): 3.

81. Spindale Textile Mills Advertisement, *Freedom Magazine* 8, no. 2 (March–April 1963): 22.

82. Liberty Amendment Committee Progress Report, January–August, 1963, in Folder—Annual Reports 1963, Box 22, Stone Papers.

83. Billy James Hargis, "The Foolish Spenders," August 10, 1960, p. 1, in Folder 18, Box 1, Hargis Papers. Julian Williams, "The 'Soak the Rich' Hoax," *Christian Crusade*, 13, no. 8 (September 1961): 14.

84. Letter from Kent Courtney to Willis E. Stone, July 28, 1964; Letter from Kent Courtney to Mr. M. J. Giese, November 5, 1963; Letter from Kent Courtney to Willis E. Stone, August 6, 1964, all in Folder 164, Box 19, Courtney Papers. Advertisement for Leadership Conference for

the Liberty Amendment, *American Progress* 6, no. 2 (September 1961): 12–13. "1963: Year of Opportunity," *Freedom Magazine* 8, no. 2 (March–April 1963): Front Cover. "Approval by Mississippi," *Freedom Magazine* 9, no. 3 (May–June 1964): Front Cover. Brownlee, *Federal Taxation*, 174–175. Laura Kalman, *Right Star Rising: A New Politics, 1974–1980* (New York: W. W. Norton, 2010), 227–232. Martin, *Rich People's Movements*, 132, 133, 151.

85. Advertisement, "Special Announcement: The Case of General Edwin A. Walker," in Folder 30, Box 5, Courtney Papers.

86. Associated Press, "Walker Joins Speaking Tour on Red Peril," *Los Angeles Times*, February 25, 1963. Schoenwald, *Time for Choosing*, 100–104, 112, 121–123.

87. Richard M. Morehead, "Connally Slates Dallas Tour; Uniformed Girls to Aid Drive," *Dallas Morning News*, February 24, 1962.

88. Sasha Issenberg, "The Wild Road Trip That Launched the Populist Conservative Movement," *Smithsonian Magazine* (September 2018). "Thunder on the Right," 18–21. United Press International, "Walker Says Thunder on Right Will Elect Him Texas Governor," *Boston Globe*, February 4, 1962. Elections of Texas Governors, *Texas Almanac, 1964–1965* (Dallas: A. H. Belo Corporation, 1963), 512. Schoenwald, *Time for Choosing*, 110.

89. Fairclough, *Better Day Coming*, 266.

90. Michael Dorman, "Walker Arrested, Is Held at Hospital," *Newsday*, October 2, 1962.

91. Tom Barrett, "Walker Psychiatric Test Called Fantastic, Mystifying by Lawyer," *New York Herald Tribune*, October 9, 1962.

92. Associated Press, "Army Takes Over," *Los Angeles Times*, October 2, 1962. United Press International, "Walker Is Cheered on Return," *Washington Post*, October 8, 1962. Associated Press, "Walker Put in Hospital after Arrest," *Boston Globe*, October 2, 1962.

93. Billy James Hargis, "Why I Must Make This Coast to Coast Tour with General Walker!," *Christian Crusade* 15, no. 2 (February 1963): 8.

94. Uncredited, "What You Can Do to Help the Midnight Ride Tour!," *Christian Crusade* 15, no. 2 (February 1963): 2. Letter from Billy James Hargis to Mrs. Gerald Tanner, February 18, 1963, in Folder 13, Box 4, Hargis Papers. Hargis, "Coast to Coast Tour," 8.

95. Issenberg, "Wild Road Trip."

96. Letter from Billy James Hargis to Mrs. Gerald Tanner, February 18, 1963, in Folder 13, Box 4, Hargis Papers. Kent Courtney, "The Midnight Ride," *CSA Newsletter* (February 22, 1963), in Folder 40, Box 6, Courtney Papers.

97. Hargis, "Coast to Coast Tour," 8. Billy James Hargis, "Our First Report on Operation: Midnight Ride Rallies!," *Christian Crusade* 15, no. 3 (March 1963): 1.

98. United Press International, "Walker Opens 'Midnight Ride,'" *Washington Post*, March 1, 1963. Hargis, "Coast to Coast Tour," 8.

99. Issenberg, "Wild Road Trip."

100. Hemmer, *Messengers of the Right*, xiv. Issenberg, "Wild Road Trip."

101. United Press International, "Ole Miss Riots 'Most Amusing,' Says Walker," *Los Angeles Times*, March 7, 1963. Hargis, "Our First Report," 4.

102. Hargis, "Our First Report," 6.

103. Issenberg noted this anti-media strategy in "Wild Road Trip." Photograph, "Shields Preacher," *Hartford Courant*, March 9, 1963.

104. Letter to the Editor from N. W. Holland, *Chicago Daily Defender*, April 2, 1963.

105. Billy James Hargis, "Concluding 'Operation: Midnight Ride' Report," *Christian Crusade* 15, no. 5 (May 1963): 33. Mark Boulton, "Sending the Extremists to the Cornfield: Rod

Serling's Crusade Against Radical Conservatism," *Journal of Popular Culture* 47, no. 6 (January 2015): 1226. Issenberg, "Wild Road Trip."

106. Hargis, "Amarillo Story," 4.

107. Hargis, "Our First Report," 2–3. Uncredited, "Cincy Groups Picket John Birch Meeting," *Call and Post*, March 23, 1963. Hargis, "Concluding 'Operation: Midnight Ride,'" 35. Issenberg, "Wild Road Trip."

108. "Advertisement, "Welcome Mr. Kennedy to Dallas," *Dallas Morning News*, November 22, 1963. Miller, *Nut Country*, 3–5, 7. Bill Minutaglio and Steven L. Davis, *Dallas, 1963* (New York: Twelve, 2013), 312.

109. Randall B. Woods, *LBJ: Architect of American Ambition* (New York: Free Press, 2006), 468–478.

110. Kent and Phoebe Courtney, "Johnson's Republicans," 1965, in Box 40, Courtney Papers. Pamphlet, "How the U.S. Is Being Communized," in Folder 35, Box 6, Courtney Papers.

111. Donald Janson, "Rightists Buoyed by the Election," *New York Times*, November 23, 1964.

112. Harry Browne, "You Made the 'Civil Rights' Bill Possible," *Freedom Magazine* 9, no. 4 (July–August 1964): 15.

113. Martin Dies Jr., "Assassination and Its Aftermath," *American Opinion* (March 1964): 1–7. Robert Dallek, *Flawed Giant: Lyndon Johnson and His Times, 1961–1973* (New York: Oxford University Press, 1998), 3, 6, 58–60, 111–120.

114. Thomas H. Kuchel, "The Fright Peddlers," *Cleveland State Law Review* 13, no. 4 (1964): 4–6.

115. Cable from Acting Chief, Security Division to SAC Boston, Massachusetts, February 11, 1959, FBI File 62-104401-8. Schoenwald, *Time for Choosing*, 94–96.

116. Anthony Lewis, "Kuchel Scores Birch Society as 'Fright Peddlers,'" *New York Times*, May 3, 1963.

117. Form Letter signed by Robert L. Schulz in reply to queries on Robert Welch's book, *The Politician*, and other pertinent correspondence in Folder—Memoranda (1), Box 25, Principal File 1963, Office of Dwight D. Eisenhower, Eisenhower Presidential Library, Abilene, Kan. (hereafter shortened to "Office of Eisenhower"). Letter from Dwight D. Eisenhower to Congressman Ralph R. Harding, October 7, 1963, in Folder—Ha (6), Box 48, Principal File 1963, Office of Eisenhower. William F. Buckley Jr., "Goldwater and the Birch Society," *Los Angeles Times*, November 4, 1963. Finder, "Extremism." Louis Harris & Associates, Harris Survey, July 1963, "On the whole do you approve or disapprove of the John Birch Society?," USHARRIS.072963.R1, accessed via iPOLL on March 27, 2016.

118. Letter from Elizabeth Churchill Brown to Barry Goldwater, December 10, 1963, in Folder 2.4, Box 02, Brown Papers.

119. Letter from Barry Goldwater to Mr. and Mrs. Constantine Brown, December 18, 1963, in Folder 2.4, Box 02, Brown Papers. Hemmer, *Messengers of the Right*, 161. Mason, *Republican Party*, 193.

120. Kent and Phoebe Courtney, "The Soft-on-Communism Record of Richard Nixon," Tax Fax Pamphlet No. 52, 1964, in Folder 36, Box 6, Courtney Papers. No exact figures for Birch Society membership exist. Mulloy, *John Birch Society*, 213n. Epstein and Forster, *John Birch Society*, 11, 195. Broyles, *John Birch Society*, 3. Perlstein, *Before the Storm*, 476. Hemmer, *Messengers of the Right*, 160. Donald T. Critchlow, *Phyllis Schlafly and Grassroots Conservatism: A Woman's Crusade* (Princeton: Princeton University Press, 2005), 119–120. Mason, *Republican Party*, 191. Phyllis Schlafly, *A Choice, Not an Echo* (Alton, Ill.: Pere Marquette Press, 1964).

121. Letter from Kent Courtney to Members of the Board of Advisors and All Political Action Unit Chairmen of The Conservative Society of America, April 12, 1963, in Folder 35, Box 6, Courtney Papers. Special to the *New York Times*, "Rockefeller Stirs Rightists' Wrath." Lawrence E. Davies, "Lodge Son Denies A Campaign 'Plot,'" *New York Times*, May 14, 1964. Chesly Manly, "Scranton Charges 'Smear' Plot: Television Address Slaps at Goldwater," *Chicago Tribune*, July 8, 1964.

122. Kent Courtney, "Special Report to CSA Members," *CSA Newsletter* 3, no. 3 (March 20, 1964), in Folder 36, Box 6, Courtney Papers.

123. Chalmers M. Roberts, "Barry's Arrival Stirs San Francisco Today," *Washington Post*, July 9, 1964. "Bircher Would Post Ike." Andrew, *Power to Destroy*, 29–30.

124. Kent Courtney, "Inside Oregon: A First-Hand Political Action Report," *CSA Newsletter* (April 29, 1964): 3, in Folder 36, Box 6, Courtney Papers.

125. Courtney, "Inside Oregon," 4.

126. Courtney, "Inside Oregon," 5–6. Goldberg, *Goldwater*, 187, 189, 194. Robert David Johnson, *All the Way with LBJ: The 1964 Presidential Election* (New York: Cambridge University Press, 2009), 108, 110–111. Catherine E. Rymph, *Republican Women: Feminism and Conservatism from Suffrage Through the Rise of the New Right* (Chapel Hill: University of North Carolina Press, 2006), 162–163, 172. Critchlow, *Schlafly*, 132–136.

127. Wedemeyer Address in Buena Park, California, May 30, 1964; Letter from Frank H. White to A. C. Wedemeyer, May 19, 1964; "An Evening With Barry" Flyer, all in Folder 2, Box 19, Wedemeyer Papers.

128. Mary McGrory, "Appeals to His Own: Goldwater Depends on Old Supporters," in Folder 2, Box 19, Wedemeyer Papers. Richard Bergholz, "State Primary Tactics Blasted by Goldwater," *Los Angeles Times*, May 24, 1964.

129. Wallace Turner, "Rightist Sets Up Convention Shop," *New York Times*, July 8, 1964.

130. Turner, "Rightist Sets Up."

131. Ernest B. Furgurson, "Is Cheered by Crowd as He Takes Attack into San Francisco," *Baltimore Sun*, July 9, 1964.

132. Richard Wilson, "These Are Strange Bedfellows," *Los Angeles Times*, July 16, 1964.

133. Robert Schulz, "Barry Wants One Backer to Get Lost," *Boston Globe*, July 12, 1964.

134. Goldberg, *Goldwater*, 201–204; Johnson, *All the Way*, 128. Mason, *Republican Party*, 193–194.

135. Perlstein, *Before the Storm*, 380.

136. Stan Hinden, "Inside Politics: Rockefeller Welcomes Boos," *Newsday*, July 16, 1964.

137. Robert J. Donovan, "Goldwater Wins on First Ballot," *Los Angeles Times*, July 16, 1964. Goldberg, *Goldwater*, 202. Perlstein, *Before the Storm*, 379.

138. Associated Press, "Statement of Rockefeller on 'Extremism,'" *Los Angeles Times*, July 18, 1964. Goldberg, *Goldwater*, 190.

139. "Interview with Tom P. Brady," Citizens' Council Radio Forum Tape #597-6435R, 1964, in CCRFDC. https://msstate.contentdm.oclc.org/digital/collection/p16631coll22/id/253.

140. A July 1964 Gallup poll asked voters if the Republicans should or should not have condemned the Birch Society by name. Thirty-three percent condoned censuring the Birch Society, 35 percent disagreed, and 30 percent were unsure. Gallup Poll (AIPO), July 1964, "Do you think that the (1964) Republican platform should or should not have condemned the John Birch Society by name?," USGALLUP.64-695.R15C, accessed via iPOLL on March 27, 2016.

A. C. Wedemeyer Speech at Bohemian Grove, August 1, 1964, in Folder 6, Box 19, Wedemeyer Papers. Finder, "Extremism," 27.

141. Letter from George Todt to Dwight D. Eisenhower, October 3, 1964, in Folder— To (1), Box 55, Principal File 1964, Office of Eisenhower.

142. "Real Man of the Year Award," *Christian Crusade* 6, no. 9 (October 1964): 8.

143. Pierard, *"Christian Crusade,"* 474.

144. Liberty Amendment Committee Pamphlet, September 1964, in Folder—Liberty Amendment Committee of the U.S.A 1964-1975, Box 29, Norman Allderdice Papers, Hoover Institution Archives, Palo Alto, Calif. (hereafter shortened to "Allderdice Papers").

145. Advertisement, "Goldwater MUST Be Destroyed," *Liberty Letter*, no. 46 (August 1964), in Folder 1, Box 33, Radical Right Collection.

146. Letter from Kent Courtney to Subscriber of the *Independent American*, August 2, 1965, in Folder 30, Box 5, Courtney Papers.

147. Robert E. Baker, "Goldwater Woos Dixie Democrats," *Washington Post*, September 17, 1964.

148. Robert J. Donovan, "Goldwater Denounces Anti-Poverty Campaign," *Los Angeles Times*, September 19, 1964. United Press International, "Barry Calls LBJ Wildest Spender Yet," *Hartford Courant*, September 19, 1964.

149. Lewis Lord, "Thurmond Switches to Goldwater Party," *Washington Post*, September 17, 1964. Black and Black, *Southern Republicans*, 140, 205. Joseph Crespino, "Strom Thurmond's Sunbelt: Rethinking Regional Politics and the Rise of the Right," in *Sunbelt Rising*, 61. Lowndes, *From New Deal to New Right*, 76.

150. Crespino, *Strom Thurmond's America*, 3, 166–167.

151. Chicago Tribune Press Service, "Haley Says Sale of Book Points Goldwater Victory," *Houston Post*, August 19, 1964, in Folder—Political Printed Material 1964, Wallet—Correspondence and Clippings LBJ 1964 and undated, Box 1, Series 3-E, Haley Papers.

152. J. Evetts Haley, *A Texan Looks at Lyndon: A Study in Illegitimate Power* (Canyon, Tex.: Palo Duro Press, 1964), 172.

153. TFA Newsletter, "Special Report to the Committees of Correspondence," November 12, 1959, in Folder—Committee of Correspondence Letters, Box 1, Series 3-B, Haley Papers. Haley, *Texan Looks at Lyndon*, 172.

154. Irving Bernstein, *Guns or Butter: The Presidency of Lyndon Johnson* (New York: Oxford University Press, 1996), 65–66, 379, 537. Cunningham, *American Politics*, 101, 105. Dallek, *Flawed Giant*, 111–112. Haley, *Texan Looks at Lyndon*, 178.

155. Perlstein, *Before the Storm*, 478. M. Stanton Evans, "The Pamphleteers Return," *National Review* (November 3, 1964): 981.

156. Donald Janson, "Extremist Book Sales Soar Despite Criticism in G. O. P.," *New York Times*, October 4, 1964. Dallek, *Flawed Giant*, 177.

157. "Your Own Reading," *John Birch Society Bulletin* (August 1964): 21, in Folder—Political Correspondence 1964, Wallet—Correspondence, clippings and campaign material—1964, Box 1, Series 3-E, Haley Papers.

158. Letter from A. C. Wedemeyer to Citizens of Hartland, Wisconsin, October 6, 1964, in Folder 14, Box 19, Wedemeyer Papers.

159. Independent Americans for Goldwater Rally Flyer, October 17, 1964, in Folder—Political Correspondence and Clippings 1964, Wallet—Correspondence, clippings and campaign material—1964, Box 1, Series 3-E, Haley Papers.

160. Mrs. J. Milton Lent, "We Recommend," *Bulletin Board of Conservatives* (July 24, 1964); "The Bookshelf," *Freedom Views* 4, no. 43 (Austin, Tex.: June 30, 1964), both in Folder—Political Printed Material 1964, Wallet—Correspondence and Clippings LBJ 1964 and undated, Box 1, Series 3-E, Haley Papers. Janson, "Rightists Buoyed." Janson, "Extremist Book Sales." Uncredited, "About Some Books," *Liberty Letter*, no. 47 (September 1964), in Folder 1, Box 33, Radical Right Collection. Advertisement, *Christian Crusade* 6, no. 9 (October 1964): 23. Chesly Manly, "Texan Looks Again at L.B.J.—Scathingly," *Chicago Tribune*, January 16, 1966. Perlstein, *Before the Storm*, 478.

161. Chicago Tribune Press Service, "Haley Says Sale of Book."

162. J. Evetts Haley, "A Texan Still Looks at Lyndon," January 6, 1967, p. 18, in Folder—6 Jan 1967, Series 4-F, Haley Papers. Evans, "Pamphleteers Return," 981. Johnson, *All the Way*, 229–230.

163. Janson, "Extremist Book Sales."

164. "Connally Says Texan's Book on Johnson Just Propaganda," *Times-Herald*, September 25, 1964, in Folder—1964 II, Wallet—Correspondence and Clippings LBJ 1964 and undated, Box 1, Series 3-E, Haley Papers. Robert Dallek, *Lone Star Rising: Lyndon Johnson and His Times, 1908–1960* (New York: Oxford University Press, 1991), 186–187.

165. "Anti-LBJ Propaganda Flowing in Texas," *Denver Post*, August 2, 1964; "Texan's Look at Lyndon Is Through Biased Eyes," *Corpus Christi Caller-Times*, July 19, 1964; "J. Evetts Haley Doesn't Play by Any Rules," *Houston Post*, October 13, 1964, all in Folder—Political Printed Material 1964, Wallet—Correspondence and Clippings LBJ 1964 and undated, Box 1, Series 3-E, Haley Papers.

166. Dallek, *Flawed Giant*, 177. Dallek, *Lone Star Rising*, 347–348. Ronnie Dugger, *The Politician: The Life and Times of Lyndon Johnson* (Old Saybrook, Conn.: Konecky & Konecky, 1982), 322–339. Perlstein, *Before the Storm*, 477.

167. Letter from George Todt to Dwight D. Eisenhower, October 3, 1964, in Folder—To (1), Box 55, Principal File 1964, Office of Eisenhower.

168. Robert J. Donovan, "Convention May Be Political Landmark," *Washington Post*, July 13, 1964.

169. Claude Sittons, "Goldwater Gets Backing in the South," *New York Times*, August 16, 1964. Charles Mohrs, "Goldwater, in a Unity Bid, Rejects Extremists' Aid; Eisenhower Is 'Satisfied,'" *New York Times*, August 13, 1964. Goldberg, *Goldwater*, 190, 224.

170. Goldberg, *Goldwater*, 196, 221, 234, 231. Johnson, *All the Way*, 143. Anti-Defamation League of B'nai B'rith, Anti-Semitism in the United States Survey, October 1964, USNORC.64BNAI.R09A, accessed via iPOLL on March 28, 2016.

171. Philip W. McKinsey, "Johnson Faces 'Go-Ahead' in Congress: Senate Already Strong," *Christian Science Monitor*, November 7, 1964.

172. "The Nation: Presidency: Johnson Wins It on His Own," *Los Angeles Times*, November 8, 1964. Alice V. McGillivray, Richard M. Scammon, and Rhodes Cook, *America at the Polls, 1960–2004, John F. Kennedy to George W. Bush: A Handbook of American Presidential Election Statistics*, (Washington, D.C.: CQ Press, 2005), 22.

173. Richard Hofstadter, "The Paranoid Style in American Politics," *Harper's* (November 1964): 77.

174. James Reston, "What Goldwater Lost," *New York Times*, November 4, 1964.

175. Robert J. Donovan, "GOP Learned Lesson in Vote Attraction," *Los Angeles Times*, November 12, 1964.

176. Philip Potter, "Goldwater Gives Views on Defeat," *Baltimore Sun*, December 15, 1964.

177. Roscoe Drummond, "GOP's Experiment with Extreme Conservatism Has Come to an End," *Los Angeles Times*, January 18, 1965.

178. Janson, "Rightists Buoyed."

179. William F. Buckley Jr., "Please Omit the Flowers," *Boston Globe*, November 8, 1964. Louis Harris, "GOPers Want Conservative, but Not Barry," *Newsday*, November 9, 1964. Black and Black, *Southern Republicans*, 149–150. Lowndes, *From New Deal to New Right*, 76. McGirr, *Suburban Warriors*, 143. Goldberg, *Goldwater*, 235.

180. Letter from J. Evetts Haley to J. S. Kimmel Sr., January 26, 1965, in Folder—For America, Box 2, Series 3-B, Haley Papers.

Chapter 6

1. Janson, "Rightists Buoyed."

2. Edward McGrath, "New Birch Goal," *Boston Globe*, May 29, 1967. Epstein and Forster, *John Birch Society*, 11, 91.

3. Hofstadter, "Paranoid Style."

4. William F. Buckley Jr., "Birch Society Drivel," *Boston Globe*, August 5, 1965.

5. Jeffrey Hart, *The Making of the American Conservative Mind: National Review and Its Times* (Wilmington, Del.: ISI Books, 2005), 154. Hemmer, *Messengers of the Right*, 196. Hendershot, *What's Fair*, 215. McGirr, *Suburban Warriors*, 218–223. Mulloy, *John Birch Society*, 78, 102, 189. Nash, *Conservative Intellectual Movement*, 276. Perlstein, *Before the Storm*, 156–157. Schoenwald, *Time for Choosing*, 98, 257, 260. Williams, *God's Own Party*, 4–7.

6. Rowland Evans and Robert Novak, "Conservatives in a Dilemma," *Boston Globe*, August 23, 1965.

7. Perlstein, *Before the Storm*, 123–124. Dallek, *Right Moment*, 106–108, 125–126. Schoenwald, *Time for Choosing*, 209–210.

8. Dallek, *Right Moment*, 124–125. Kruse, *One Nation Under God*, 155–156.

9. Joseph R. L. Strene, "Goldwater Says His Viet Plan Is Being Followed," *Baltimore Sun*, January 22, 1965.

10. Rowland Evans and Robert Novak, "Inside Report: Third Party Epidemic," *Washington Post*, November 23, 1965.

11. Letter from Kent Courtney to Member, March 12, 1965, in Folder 30, Box 5, Courtney Papers.

12. David Halvorsen, "Robert Welch Hits Foreign Policy of the U.S.," *Chicago Tribune*, May 1, 1965.

13. Welch, "Two Revolutions," 186.

14. Paul Gapp, "Radical Right Lets Off Its Steam but Fails to Launch Third Party," *Washington Post*, May 6, 1965.

15. Austin C. Wehrwein, "Conservatives Decide to Put Off the Formation of a Third Party," *New York Times*, May 1, 1965. Associated Press, "Anti-Red Party Planned by Conservative Group," *Los Angeles Times*, May 2, 1965. George Gallup, "'Most Admired Man' a Third Time," *Boston Globe*, January 2, 1966.

16. David Halvorsen, "Right Wingers Resolution on 3d Party Mild," *Chicago Tribune*, May 2, 1965.

17. Halvorsen, "Right Wingers Resolution."

18. Letter from Kent Courtney to Subscriber of the *Independent American*, August 2, 1965, p. 5, in Folder 30, Box 5, Courtney Papers. Wehrwein, "Conservatives Decide."

19. Halvorsen, "Robert Welch Hits."

20. Kent Courtney, "Anti-Communist Party Launched in Florida," *CSA Newsletter* (June 18, 1965); Kent Courtney, "Illinois Party Being Organized," *CSA Newsletter* (July 1, 1965); "Conservatives Map New Party In Michigan," *CSA Newsletter* (August 30, 1965); "3rd U.S. Party Planned," *Pacific Stars and Stripes*, reprinted in *CSA Newsletter* (October 8, 1965): 2; "Pennsylvania New Party Meeting—Dec 11," *CSA Newsletter* (October 8, 1965): 1; "Georgia New Party Underway," *CSA Newsletter* (November 1, 1965); "State-Wide Organization Established by Colorado Conservative Group," *Gazette-Telegraph*, November 19, 1965, in *CSA Newsletter* (December 7, 1965); "Mass. Conservatives Form Party," *Boston Globe*, December 18, 1965, reprinted in *CSA Newsletter* (January 15, 1966), all in Folder 40, Box 6, Courtney Papers.

21. Letter from Kent Courtney to CSA Member, June 15, 1966, p. 5, in Folder 37, Box 6, Courtney Papers.

22. "Wisconsin GOP Leaders Resign from Party, Join Conservative Forces," *CSA Newsletter* (May 20, 1966): 1, in Folder 40, Box 6, Courtney Papers. Uncredited, "Fair Housing at Manitowoc Set as Topic," *Manitowoc Herald-Times*, October 30, 1968.

23. Pamphlet, "G.O.P. Now Under Liberal Control," CSA Pamphlet No. 4, in Folder 34, Box 5, Courtney Papers. Letter from Kent Courtney to Subscriber of the *Independent American*, August 2, 1965, in Folder 30, Box 5, Courtney Papers. Cunningham, *American Politics*, 112–116. Fairclough, *Better Day Coming*, 293.

24. Willis E. Stone, "From the Publisher's Desk," *Freedom Magazine* 10, no. 1 (January–February 1965): 1.

25. Uncredited, "1966 Annual Liberty Amendment Conference," *Freedom Magazine* 11, no. 2 (March–April 1966): 2. William D. Graff, "The Liberty Amendment Comes to America's Living Rooms," *Freedom Magazine* 12, no. 3 (May–June 1967): 23. Letter from Willis E. Stone to Robert Welch, April 21, 1966, in Folder—John Birch Society 1964–66, Box 30, Stone Papers.

26. Willis E. Stone, "Major Effort Now Underway to Build in All Local Areas," *Freedom Magazine* 12, no. 6 (November–December 1967): 14–15. Willis E. Stone, "Politics, Personalities and Principles," *Freedom Magazine* 13, no. 2 (March–April 1968): 2.

27. Edward Clancy, "What Happened in Arizona?," *Freedom Magazine* 11, no. 3 (May–June 1966): 9. News Dispatches, "Primary Results in Wisconsin," *Washington Post*, April 4, 1968.

28. Letter from Willis E. Stone to Robert Welch, December 21, 1966, in Folder—John Birch Society 1964–66, Box 30, Stone Papers.

29. Letter from Robert Welch to Willis Stone, July 10, 1968, in Folder—John Birch Society 1967–71, Box 30, Stone Papers.

30. Letter from Robert Welch to Brig. Gen. W. C. Lemly, July 10, 1968, in Folder—John Birch Society 1967–71, Box 30, Stone Papers. Mulloy, *John Birch Society*, 133.

31. Letter from Willis E. Stone to Robert Welch, July 25, 1968, in Folder—John Birch Society 1967–71, Box 30, Stone Papers.

32. Newsletter, Billy James Hargis, "The Federal Government and Your Schools," August 13, 1961, p. 4, in Folder 24, Box 2, Hargis Papers.

33. Billy James Hargis, "Words Are a Weapon," August 31, 1960, p. 2, in Folder 18, Box 1, Hargis Papers.

34. Newsletter, Billy James Hargis, "Our Youth—Their Enemies and Their Friends" from "Christian Crusade TV-25," undated, p. 3, in Folder 18, Box 1, Hargis Papers.

35. Dallek, *Flawed Giant*, 330.

36. Radio Broadcast, Radio Script #2, Sept. 24, 1968, in Folder 24, Box 1, Hargis Papers.

37. Radio Script #2, Sept. 24, 1968.

38. Gordon V. Drake, *Is the School House the Proper Place to Teach Raw Sex?* (Tulsa, Okla.: Christian Crusade, 1968). Susan K. Freeman, *Sex Goes to School: Girls and Sex Education Before the 1960s* (Chicago: University of Chicago Press, 2008), x, 147. Kristin Luker, *When Sex Goes to School: Warring Views on Sex—and Sex Education—Since the Sixties* (New York: W. W. Norton, 2007), 8–9, 220. Bruce J. Dierenfield, *The Battle over School Prayer: How* Engel v. Vitale *Changed America* (Lawrence: University Press of Kansas, 2007), 4. "The Sins of Billy James" *Time* 107, no. 7 (February 16, 1976): 68.

39. George C. Wallace, "Guidelines: A Socialist Blueprint for Federal Control of Education," CSA Pamphlet No. 13, in Folder 34, Box 5, Courtney Papers.

40. James Stack, "High Court Hit at Rally," *Boston Globe*, July 5, 1968.

41. Associated Press, "Birch Head Sees Sex Education as Red Plot," *Washington Post*, January 19, 1969.

42. William J. McCance, "Birch Society Embroiled in Sex Education Battle," *Los Angeles Times*, May 18, 1969.

43. Pamphlet, "Save Our Schools," in Folder—Liberty Lobby 1960s 1970s, Box 29, Allderdice Papers. Luker, *Sex Goes to School*, 220.

44. Hendershot, *What's Fair*, 195. Dierenfield, *School Prayer*, 4. Luker, *Sex Goes to School*, 243.

45. Billy James Hargis, "Internal Revenue Service Package" (Tulsa, Okla.: Christian Crusade, 1966), p. 4, in Folder 7, Box 4, Hargis Papers. Andrew, *Power to Destroy*, 51.

46. Andrew, *Power to Destroy*, 27, 48–49. Elizabeth MacDonald, "The Kennedys and the IRS," *Wall Street Journal*, January 28, 1997.

47. Hargis, "Guilt by Association."

48. Both pamphlets found in Folder 1, Box 105, Radical Right Collection.

49. Billy James Hargis, *Why I Fight for a Christian America* (New York: Thomas Nelson, Inc., 1974), 98. Hendershot, *What's Fair*, 193. Andrew, *Power to Destroy*, 28, 30, 50.

50. Congressional Record—Appendix, "The Double Standard of Tax Exemption," Hon. M. G. (Gene) Snyder of Kentucky, October 18, 1967, p. A5140, in Folder 46, Box 2, Hargis Papers.

51. Congressional Record—Extension of Remarks, "Double Standard: U.S. Style," Hon. James B. Utt of California, April 24, 1968, p. E3262, in Folder 46, Box 2, Hargis Papers.

52. Kent Courtney, "The 'Open Housing' Law Must Be Repealed!," CSA Pamphlet No. 22, 1968, in Folder 34, Box 5, Courtney Papers.

53. Phoebe Courtney, "Our Immigration Law Under Attack," Tax Fax Pamphlet No. 62, in Folder 41, Box 6, Courtney Papers.

54. Radio Broadcast, "Christian Crusade Broadcast," Sunday, August 27, 1968, in Folder 24, Box 1, Hargis Papers. For more on the civil unrest in Detroit, see Thomas J. Sugrue, *The Origins of the Urban Crisis: Race and Inequality in Postwar Detroit* (Princeton: Princeton University Press, 1996).

55. Dan Smoot, "Civil Rights or Civil War?," *Dan Smoot Report* 11, no. 8 (February 22, 1965): 57, in Folder 6, Box 97, Radical Right Collection. Utt, "Real Fright Peddlers," p. 15, in Folder 50, Box 4, Hargis Papers.

56. Emphasis in the original document. Uncredited, "Let's Get Freedom For ALL!," *Freedom Magazine* 11, no. 2 (March–April 1966): 28.

57. Radio Script, Billy James Hargis, "Free Speech for Conservatives Is Dying in LBJ's U.S.A.," 1968, p. 1, in Folder 16, Box 1, Hargis Papers.

58. Kent Courtney, "Kent Courtney Comments on the News: The Real Causes of the Riots and Revolution in America," *CSA Handbook*, undated, in Folder 33, Box 5, Courtney Papers.

59. Theodore H. White, *The Making of the President 1968* (New York: Atheneum Publishers, 1969), 76. For in-depth analysis of the tumult in 1968, see Isserman and Kazin, *America Divided*, 221–240; Kyle Longley, *LBJ's 1968: Power, Politics, and the Presidency in America's Year of Upheaval* (New York: Cambridge University Press, 2018). For a broad overview of the New Left in the 1960s, see Gosse, *New Left*. For an examination of mass incarceration's roots in the 1960s, see Elizabeth Hinton, *From the War on Poverty to the War on Crime: The Making of Mass Incarceration in America* (Cambridge, Mass.: Harvard University Press, 2016). For more on the radicalization of the civil rights movement, see Clayborne Carson, *In Struggle: SNCC and the Black Awakening of the 1960s* (Cambridge, Mass.: Harvard University Press, 1981); Gerald Horne, *Fire This Time: The Watts Uprising and the 1960s* (Charlottesville: University Press of Virginia, 1995); Jeffrey Ogbonna Green Ogbar, *Black Power: Radical Politics and African American Identity* (Baltimore: Johns Hopkins University Press, 2004). Robert Buzzanco, *Vietnam and the Transformation of American Life* (Malden, Mass.: Blackwell Publishers, 1999), 85. Allen J. Matusow, *The Unraveling of America: A History of Liberalism in the 1960s* (New York: Harper & Row, 1984), 437–439; Nelson, *Resilient America*, 223–224.

60. Carter, *Politics of Rage*, 96.

61. Hal Steward, "The Wallace Phenomenon," *Boston Globe*, March 10, 1968. Carter, *Politics of Rage*, 17–44, 49–50, 88, 108–109. James Jackson Kilpatrick, "What Makes Wallace Run?," *National Review* (April 18, 1967): 404.

62. Carter, *Politics of Rage*, 116–117. Lewis, *Massive Resistance*, 153–155.

63. Ray Jenkins, "George Wallace Figures to Win Even If He Loses," *New York Times*, April 7, 1968.

64. Jenkins, "George Wallace."

65. Carter, *Politics of Rage*, 338.

66. Letter from Kent Courtney to Member of the CSA, January 15, 1968, in Folder 39, Box 6, Courtney Papers.

67. Uncredited, "Peddlers of Race Hatred a Threat," *Chicago Daily Defender*, September 28, 1968. Jules Witcover, "George Wallace Isn't Kidding," *Reporter*, February 23, 1967. Carter, *Politics of Rage*, 295.

68. Charles Whiteford, "Who Inhabits 'Wallace Country'?," *Baltimore Sun*, October 3, 1968.

69. Thomas O'Neill, "Cautious Candidate," *Baltimore Sun*, November 12, 1967.

70. Kenneth Lamott, "'It Isn't a Mirage They're Seeing,' Says George Wallace," *New York Times*, September 22, 1968.

71. Jenkins, "George Wallace."

72. Steward, "Wallace Phenomenon."

73. Carter, *Politics of Rage*, 297.

74. Jenkins, "George Wallace."

75. Jane Coasten, "A Question for Conservatives: What If the Left was Right on Race?," *Vox Media*, July 23, 2019, accessed on July 25, 2019, https://www.vox.com/2019/7/23/20697636/trump-race-gop-conservatism-racism. Video of Wallace's full comments can be found here: https://www.c-span.org/video/?443769-2/face-nation-george-wallace.

76. Kilpatrick, "Wallace Run," 402.

77. Whiteford, "'Wallace Country.'"

78. Jack Nelson, "A Profile of Electors Who Back Wallace," *Los Angeles Times*, October 27, 1968.

79. Jack Nelson and Nicholas C. Chriss, "Radical Rightists Play Key Roles in Wallace Drive," *Los Angeles Times*, September 17, 1968.

80. A. A. Michelson, "Carpets Out for Wallace; Don't Take Him Lightly," *Boston Globe*, July 7, 1968.

81. "Wallace for President: Join in Freedom's Cause," CSA Pamphlet No. 12, in Folder 34, Box 5, Courtney Papers.

82. Carter, *Politics of Rage*, 352. Jack Nelson, "Alabamian Ponders the Presidency: Wallace Could Be a 'Chaotic' Factor in 1968," *Los Angeles Times*, October 2, 1966. Kilpatrick, "Wallace Run."

83. Uncredited, "Butler Countian Named Officer in State WCG," *Greenville Advocate*, April 25, 1963.

84. Letter from George Wallace to T. L. Lauderdale, September 13, 1963, in Folder—Anthony, Ernest E., Box 21, Stone Papers.

85. Tom Anderson, "George Wallace—Why He Should Be President," *Southern Utah Free Press*, October 31, 1968.

86. Uncredited, "Wallace For Liberty Amendment," *Freedom Magazine* 13, no. 4 (July–August–September 1968): 22.

87. Letter from Willis E. Stone to George B. Fowler, June 17, 1969, in Folder—Fowler, George B. 1965–69, Box 29, Stone Papers.

88. Uncredited, "WCG Confers with Governor Wallace," *Selma Times-Journal*, August 8, 1963. Nelson, "Alabamian Ponders."

89. Hemmer, *Messengers of the Right*, 209.

90. Associated Press, "Riots, Black Power Militants Seen Helping Push Klan Membership Up," *Hartford Courant*, January 2, 1968.

91. Ray Jenkins, "Candidate Wallace," *Christian Science Monitor*, February 19, 1968. Nelson and Chriss, "Radical Rightists."

92. Nelson, "Alabamian Ponders." Nelson and Chriss, "Radical Rightists." Letter from Kent Courtney to Subscribers to Radio Edition, November 15, 1966, in Folder 37, Box 6, Courtney Papers. Kent Courtney, "Wallace Leads in 13 Southern States Over LBJ and Romney," *CSA Newsletter* in the *CSA Handbook*, May 16, 1967; Kent Courtney, "Gov. Wallace Hits Campaign Trail: C.S.A. Members Urged to Attend Events," *Wallace for President News* in the *CSA Handbook*, April 24, 1967, both in Folder 33, Box 5, Courtney Papers. CSA Press Release, March 27, 1967, in Folder 38, Box 6, Courtney Papers. *Wall Street Journal* News Roundup, "Wallace's Workers," *Wall Street Journal*, October 24, 1968.

93. Kent Courtney, "On the Campaign Trail: Wallace Defines Treason," *Wallace for President News* in the *CSA Handbook*, May 16, 1967, in Folder 33, Box 5, Courtney Papers.

94. Carter, *Politics of Rage*, 158. Orion A. Teal, "The Moral Economy of Postwar Radical Interracial Summer Camping," in *The Economic Civil Rights Movement: African Americans and the Struggle for Economic Power*, ed. Michael Ezra (New York: Routledge, 2013), 60–61. Bobbie Barbee, "Negroes Help Smash Plot of White Hate Group," *Jet* (November 17, 1966): 17.

95. William F. Buckley Jr., "Wallace Presidential Candidacy Could Have a Critical Impact," *Los Angeles Times*, April 24, 1967.

96. Kilpatrick, "Wallace Run."

97. Frank S. Meyer, "The Populism of George Wallace," *National Review* (May 16, 1967): 527.

98. Thomas O'Neill, "Vote Splitter," *Baltimore Sun*, February 25, 1968.

99. Steward, "Wallace Phenomenon."

100. Kilpatrick, "Wallace Run."

101. Rowland Evans and Robert Novak, "Wallace Is Roughening the Road for the GOP," *Los Angeles Times*, February 23, 1968.

102. Lamott, "Mirage."

103. Uncredited, "GOP in Hassle at Convention," *Canyon News*, May 16, 1968.

104. Roland Lindsey, "'Texan Looks at Lyndon' Author Backing Reagan," *Monitor*, July 18, 1976, in Folder 14, Series 4-K, Haley Papers.

105. William F. Buckley Jr., "Decline of the Birch Society Has Lessons for Conservatives," *Los Angeles Times*, November 15, 1967.

106. Nelson, *Resilient America*, 110. White, *President 1968*, 160, 379, 385.

107. Drew Pearson, "Thurmond, Nixon's Agent," *Los Angeles Times*, August 13, 1968. Nelson, *Resilient America*, 118–119. Perlstein, *Nixonland*, 130.

108. For more on the Democratic National Convention of 1968, see Frank Kusch, *Battleground Chicago: The Police and the 1968 Democratic National Convention* (Westport, Conn.: Praeger, 2004). Nelson, *Resilient America*, 106–107.

109. Uncredited, "Birch Society Chief Asks Contributions in Attack on Nixon," *Los Angeles Times*, October 10, 1968.

110. Pamphlet, "Nixon in '68?," CSA Pamphlet No. 5, in Folder 34, Box 5, Courtney Papers. Kent and Phoebe Courtney, Pamphlet Reprint, "Nix on Nixon," Tax Fax Pamphlet No. 53, in Folder 35, Box 6, Courtney Papers.

111. Kent Courtney, "Nixon Selectively Rejected by Conservatives," *CSA Newsletter* in the *CSA Handbook*, August 26, 1966, in Folder 33, Box 5, Courtney Papers.

112. Kent Courtney, "Who Is Hubert Humphrey?," *CSA Info Memo*, no. 24 (undated): 1, in Folder 31, Box 5, Courtney Papers.

113. Ralph McGill, "'What's Wrong with the Birchers?,'" *Boston Globe*, November 10, 1968.

114. Willis E. Stone, "On Elections," *Freedom Magazine* 13, no. 4 (July–August–September 1968): 2.

115. Mason, *Republican Party*, 158. Perlstein, *Nixonland*, 29–33, 44–45. Schoenwald, *Time for Choosing*, 219. White, *President 1968*, 167.

116. Michelson, "Carpets Out for Wallace."

117. Whiteford, "'Wallace Country.'"

118. *Wall Street Journal* News Roundup, "Wallace's Workers." Wallace Turner, "Rightists Strong in Wallace Drive," *New York Times*, September 29, 1968. Nelson and Chriss, "Radical Rightists." Thomas O'Neill, "Strange Company," *Baltimore Sun*, September 25, 1968. William Borders, "Wallace Forces in Connecticut Hold Candidate Can Win State," *Hartford Courant*, September 22, 1968. Letter from Phoebe and Kent Courtney to Friend, April 18, 1968, in Folder 39, Box 6, Courtney Papers. Jenkins, "George Wallace." Nelson, *Resilient America*, 205. Carter, *Politics of Rage*, 300.

119. Edward McGrath, "New Birch Goal," *Boston Globe*, May 29, 1967.

120. Gordon D. Hall, "The Far Right on the Fourth," *Boston Globe*, July 15, 1967. Bill Dickinson, "Wallace's Bay State Electors Mostly Birch Society Members," *Boston Globe*, June 25, 1968.

121. Borders, "Wallace Forces."

122. Douglas E. Kneeland, "Birch Society, Age 10, Vows Red Rout," *New York Times*, December 8, 1968.

123. Nelson and Chriss, "Radical Rightists."

124. Uncredited, "Voit Quits Birch Society Job to Join in Wallace Campaign," *Los Angeles Times*, November 21, 1967.

125. *Wall Street Journal* News Roundup, "Wallace's Workers."

126. Martin Waldron, "Citrus Growers Backing Wallace," *New York Times*, October 6, 1968. Carter, *Politics of Rage*, 362–363. Evans and Novak, "Wallace Is Roughening the Road."

127. Nelson and Chriss, "Radical Rightists."

128. Uncredited, "Texas Birchers Take Over Race," *Washington Post*, October 21, 1968.

129. Jon Ford, "Birchers' Role Roils Wallace State Drive," *Christian Science Monitor*, October 24, 1968. "Texas Birchers."

130. "Texas Birchers."

131. Ford, "Birchers' Role."

132. Nelson and Chriss, "Radical Rightists." George Lardner Jr., "Wallace Is Nominated by 3rd Party in Texas," *Washington Post*, September 18, 1968.

133. Nelson, "Alabamian Ponders."

134. Louis Harris, "Wallace Gains," *Boston Globe*, September 23, 1968. Rowland Evans and Robert Novak, "Inside Report: George Wallace Points North," *Washington Post*, February 3, 1967.

135. Carter, *Politics of Rage*, 363.

136. Associated Press, "Thurmond Says Wallace Cannot Win," *Hartford Courant*, October 20, 1968.

137. Don Oberdorfer, "Ex-Democrat, Ex-Dixiecrat, Today's 'Nixiecrat,'" *New York Times*, October 6, 1968. United Press International, "Thurmond: Nixon's View Like Wallace's," *Boston Globe*, September 15, 1968. White, *President 1968*, 414–416.

138. Carter, *Politics of Rage*, 360.

139. White, *President 1968*, 428–429; William F. Buckley Jr., "LeMay's Mistake Was in Joining Up with Wallace," *Los Angeles Times*, October 14, 1968. "Tell the North Vietnamese: 'Get out of town, we're going to drop the bomb' says Retired Gen. Curtis LeMay," *CSA Info Memo*, No. 11 (February 8, 1967): 1, in Folder 31, Box 5, Courtney Papers. S. J. Micciche, "LeMay, Named Wallace's VP, Might A-Bomb Vietnam," *Boston Globe*, October 4, 1968. George Lardner Jr., "Wallace Scores 'No Win' Policy of U.S.: Alabamian Meets Press," *Washington Post*, October 8, 1968.

140. Barry Goldwater, "Don't Waste a Vote on Wallace," *National Review* (October 22, 1968): 1079.

141. Lou Harris, "Harris Survey Puts HH in 3-Point Lead," *Boston Globe*, November 5, 1968. White, *President 1968*, 425. Nelson, *Resilient America*, xvi.

142. White, *President 1968*, 465.

143. Arlene J. Large, "Wallace's Loyalists Meet to Shape Plans for Another Try in '72," *Wall Street Journal*, February 3, 1969. McGillivray, Scammon, and Cook, *America at the Polls, 1960–2004*, 21. White, *President 1968*, 430. Carter, *Politics of Rage*, 466, 468.

144. Mass Letter from Kent Courtney to Friend, November 15, 1968, in Folder 39, Box 6, Courtney Papers.

145. George Lardner Jr., "Wallace on Political Future: 'We'll Have to Play It by Ear,'" *Washington Post*, November 7, 1968; Mass Letter from Kent Courtney to Friends, "Put None but Americans on Guard," December 23, 1968, in Folder 39, Box 6, Courtney Papers.

146. Nicholas C. Chriss, "Wallace Backers Balk at Leader's Principles," *Los Angeles Times*, February 2, 1969. Large, "Wallace's Loyalists."

147. Nicholas C. Chriss, "Members in Free-for-All at Wallace Convention," *Los Angeles Times*, February 3, 1969.

148. Nelson, *Resilient America*, 205.

149. Kneeland, "Birch Society."

150. Large, "Wallace's Loyalists."

151. Mass Letter from Kent Courtney to Subscriber, November 25, 1968, in Folder 39, Box 6, Courtney Papers.

152. Large, "Wallace's Loyalists."

153. Large, "Wallace's Loyalists."

Epilogue

1. Gordon Hall, "Thunder on the Right Dies to a Dull Rumble," *Boston Globe*, July 7, 1969.

2. Letter from Kent Courtney to Friend, September 23, 1968, and Mass Letter from Kent Courtney to Friends, "Put None but Americans On Guard," December 23, 1968, in Folder 39, Box 6, Courtney Papers. Biographical Data Sheet, in Folder 109, Box 6, Courtney Papers. Phoebe Courtney, "Is Abortion Murder?," Tax Fax Pamphlet No. 203, in Folder 41, Box 6, Courtney Papers. Phoebe Courtney, *Gun Control Means People Control* (Littleton, CO: The Independent American Newspaper, 1974). Carter, *Politics of Rage*, 446–448.

3. Martin, *Rich People's Movements*, 153.

4. Information about the dissolution of the merger can be found in Letter from Mark Andrews to Bill (Stone), October 31, 1971, in Folder—Andrews, Mark 1967–71, Box 28, Stone Papers. Liberty Amendment Committee, "Prospectus: Organizational Plan of Local Liberty Amendment Committees," October 9, 1967, in Folder 162, Box 19, Courtney Papers. Obituary, "Marion Travis Stone," *Freedom Magazine* 16, no. 2 (Summer 1971): 9. Letter from Willis E. Stone to Robert Welch, August 27, 1971, in Folder—John Birch Society 1967–71, Box 1, Stone Papers. *Freedom Magazine* 18, no. 2 (Summer 1974). Martin, *Rich People's Movements*, 155.

5. Kneeland, "Birch Society."

6. William Davis, "John Birch Society Still Going Strong but at the Same Time It's in Trouble," *Boston Globe*, August 9, 1970.

7. Associated Press, "John Birch Society Ignores Elections, Sees Plot by Soviets," *Hartford Courant*, October 26, 1980.

8. Laurel Leff, "Whatever Happened to the John Birch Society?," *Wall Street Journal*, August 29, 1979.

9. Michael Seiler, "Robert Welch, Birch Society Founder, Ex-Chairman, Dies," *Los Angeles Times*, January 8, 1985.

10. "Sins of Billy James," 68.

11. "Sins of Billy James," 68.

12. Doyle, "Watchman on the Wall."

13. Dochuk, *Bible Belt to Sunbelt*, 230. Hendershot, *What's Fair*, 173, 174, 186–187.

14. Uncredited, "Haley Labels Convention GOP 'Political Suicide,'" *Dallas Morning News*, August 21, 1976.

15. Magazine Clipping, "Names in the News," *Conservative Digest* (July 1976): 23, and Lindsey, "'Texan Looks at Lyndon,'" both in Folder 14, Series 4-K, Haley Papers. Carolyn Barta,

"Reagan Wins 'Em All in Texas GOP," *Dallas Morning News*, June 20, 1976. Carolyn Barta, "Texas Panel Planned," *Dallas Morning News*, March 8, 1980.

16. Cunningham, *American Politics*, 51, 113; Sprague, "James Evetts Haley," 103–104. Dominic Sandbrook, *Mad as Hell: The Crisis of the 1970s and the Rise of the Populist Right* (New York: Knopf, 2011), xiii. Black and Black, *Southern Republicans*, 211–221.

17. John S. Huntington, "How Conservatives Learned to Love Big Government," *Washington Post*, January 25, 2019, accessed on August 31, 2019, https://www.washingtonpost.com /outlook/2019/01/25/how-conservatives-learned-love-big-government.

18. McGirr, *Suburban Warriors*, 223; Mulloy, *John Birch Society*, 189; Schoenwald, *Time for Choosing*, 98, 260.

19. My argument expands upon Carter's in *Politics of Rage*, 466. For select scholarship that examines post-1968 conservatism, see Critchlow, *Phyllis Schlafly*; Kalman, *Right Star Rising*; Kevin M. Kruse and Julian E. Zelizer, *Fault Lines: A History of the United States Since 1974* (New York: W. W. Norton, 2019); Self, *All in the Family*. Sean Wilentz, *The Age of Reagan: A History, 1974–2008* (New York: Harper, 2008). Sandbrook, *Mad as Hell*, 134.

20. Stephen Moore, "Ax the Tax," *National Review* (April 17, 1995): 38.

21. Nash, *Conservative Intellectual Movement*, 332. Martin, *Rich People's Movements*, 166.

22. Richard A. Viguerie, *The New Right: We're Ready to Lead* (Falls Church, Va.: Viguerie Company, 1981), 91–96.

23. Richard A. Viguerie, "The Show Must Not Go On," *Washington Monthly* 38, no. 10 (October 2006): 42–43.

24. Hemmer, *Messengers of the Right*, xii–xv, 254. Hendershot, *What's Fair*, 215.

25. For a thorough examination of the fairness doctrine and right-wing media, see Hendershot's *What's Fair*, 16–20. For more on Rush Limbaugh and the influence of right-wing talk radio, see Brian Rosenwald, *Talk Radio's America: How an Industry Took Over a Political Party That Took Over the United States* (Cambridge, Mass.: Harvard University Press, 2019). Hemmer, *Messengers of the Right*, xii–xiii, 260–273.

26. Bob Woodward, "In His Debut in Washington's Power Struggles, Gingrich Threw a Bomb," *Washington Post*, December 24, 2011.

27. Mary McGrory, "Gingrich's Buzzword Pudding," *Washington Post*, December 16, 1993.

28. Thomas B. Rosensteil, "Gingrich's Plan for Power 10 Years in the Making," *Los Angeles Times*, December 19, 1994. Kruse and Zelizer, *Fault Lines*, 216.

29. For more on Newt Gingrich and Republican conservatism, see Julian E. Zelizer, *Burning Down the House: Newt Gingrich, the Fall of a Speaker, and the Rise of the New Republican Party* (New York: Penguin, 2020). For more on the health care debate, see Theda Skocpol, "The Rise and Resounding Demise of the Clinton Plan," *Health Affairs* 14, no. 1 (Spring 1995): 66–85. Theda Skocpol and Vanessa Williamson, *The Tea Party and the Remaking of Republican Conservatism* (New York: Oxford University Press, 2012), 123–125. Kathleen Hall Jamieson and Joseph N. Cappella, *Echo Chamber: Rush Limbaugh and the Conservative Media Establishment* (New York: Oxford University Press, 2010), x. Kruse and Zelizer, *Fault Lines*, 190, 212, 216. Kabaservice, *Rule and Ruin*, 376–377.

30. George H. Nash, "Populism, I: American Conservatism and the Problem of Populism," *New Criterion* 35, no. 1 (September 2016).

31. Jason Wilson, "Crisis Actors, Deep State, False Flag: The Rise of Conspiracy Theory Code Words," *Guardian*, February 21, 2018, accessed on September 12, 2019, https://

www.theguardian.com/us-news/2018/feb/21/crisis-actors-deep-state-false-flag-the-rise-of
-conspiracy-theory-code-words.

32. For more information, see "Alex Jones," Southern Poverty Law Center, accessed on September 8, 2020, https://www.splcenter.org/fighting-hate/extremist-files/individual/alex-jones.

33. Interview with former Republican congressman Ron Paul of Texas, May 8, 2018, author's papers.

34. Martin, *Rich People's Movements*, 195. Skocpol and Williamson, *Tea Party*, 23, 31, 33, 68–71, 122. Joshua Green, "Ron Paul: The Tea Party's Brain," *Atlantic* (November 2010). David Neiwert, *Alt-America: The Rise of the Radical Right in the Age of Donald Trump* (New York: Verso, 2017), 4.

35. Neiwert, *Alt-America*, 5.

36. Eric Bradner, "Trump Praises 9/11 Truther's 'Amazing' Reputation," *CNN*, December 2, 2015, accessed on August 29, 2019, https://www.cnn.com/2015/12/02/politics/donald-trump
-praises-9-11-truther-alex-jones/index.html.

37. Scotchie, *Revolt*, 74. George Hawley, "How Donald Trump Can Change Conservatism," *New York Times*, January 19, 2017, accessed on February 7, 2018, https://www.nytimes.com
/2017/01/19/opinion/how-donald-trump-can-change-conservatism.html. Thomas B. Edsall, "We Aren't Seeing White Support for Trump for What It Is," *Washington Post*, August 28, 2019, accessed on August 30, 2019, https://www.nytimes.com/2019/08/28/opinion/trump-white-voters.html.

38. Adam Serwer, "The Cruelty Is the Point," *Atlantic*, October 3, 2018, accessed on August 30, 2019, https://www.theatlantic.com/ideas/archive/2018/10/the-cruelty-is-the-point/572104.

39. Editorial Board, "Conspiracy Theorist in Chief," *Los Angeles Times*, April 6, 2017, accessed on August 27, 2019, https://www.latimes.com/projects/la-ed-conspiracy-theorist-in
-chief. Tim Murphy, "How Donald Trump Became the Conspiracy Theorist in Chief," *Mother Jones* (November-December 2016).

40. Hawley, "Donald Trump."

41. Huntington, "How Conservatives Learned to Love Big Government." Geoffrey Kabaservice, "Trump Has Failed the QAnon Test," *New York Times*, August 25, 2020, accessed on September 9, 2020, https://www.nytimes.com/2020/08/25/opinion/trump-qanon-birchers
.html. Charlotte Alter, "How Conspiracy Theories Are Shaping the 2020 Election—and Shaking the Foundation of American Democracy," *Time*, September 10, 2020, accessed on September 10, 2020, https://time.com/5887437/conspiracy-theories-2020-election.

42. Anti-Defamation League, "Three Percenters," accessed on August 9, 2020, https://www
.adl.org/resources/backgrounders/three-percenters. Leah Sottile, "The Chaos Agents," *New York Times Magazine* (August 19, 2020).

43. Oath Keepers (@Oathkeepers), Twitter post, September 30, 2019, https://twitter.com
/Oathkeepers/status/1178549790847590400.

44. Belew, *Bring the War Home*, 3–15. Mulloy, *American Extremism*, 1–16. Dana Leinwand Leger, "Record Number of Anti-Government Militias in USA," *USA Today*, March 5, 2013, accessed on September 23, 2020, https://www.usatoday.com/story/news/nation/2013/03/05
/southern-poverty-law-center-militias-gun-control/1964411.

45. Seth Cotlar (@sethcotlar), Twitter post, August 27, 2019, https://twitter.com/SethCotlar
/status/1166479581848559616.

46. David Frum, "Conservatism Can't Survive Donald Trump Intact," *Atlantic* (December 19, 2017), accessed on September 23, 2020, https://www.theatlantic.com/politics/archive
/2017/12/conservatism-is-what-conservatives-think-say-and-do/548738.

47. Politico Staff, "Transcript: Former President Obama's Speech at the University of Illinois," *Politico*, September 7, 2018, accessed on November 21, 2019. https://www.politico.com /story/2018/09/07/obama-university-of-illinois-speech-811130.

48. Amy Gardner, "'I Just Want to Find 11,780 Votes,'" *Washington Post*, January 3, 2021, accessed on January 3, 2021, https://www.washingtonpost.com/politics/trump-raffensperger-call -georgia-vote/2021/01/03/d45acb92-4dc4-11eb-bda4-615aaefd0555_story.html. Burgess Everett, "At Least 12 Senators to Challenge Biden's Win," *Politico*, January 2, 2021, accessed on January 3, 2021, https://www.politico.com/news/2021/01/02/ted-cruz-electoral-college-challenge-453430.

INDEX

ACKNOWLEDGMENTS

This book is the result of numerous research trips around the country, and I am deeply indebted to the staff of each archive and library I visited. My research started at Texas Tech University's Southwest Collection where manager Randy Vance helped me peruse J. Evetts Haley's papers. I am particularly thankful for Vance's suggestion that I visit the more expansive Haley collection down in Midland which proved instrumental to my research. I used a research grant from the East Texas Historical Association to travel to the Haley Memorial Library and History Center in Midland, where library director J. P. "Pat" McDaniel and assistant Cathy Smith helped me navigate Haley's extensive personal papers. When I visited the Special Collections at the University of Arkansas to examine Billy James Hargis's papers, Geoffrey Stark pulled countless boxes and, perhaps even more valuable on my long research trip, recommended local coffee shops and bookstores. I appreciate the help provided by Mary Burtzloff and Sydney Soderberg with Dwight Eisenhower's papers at his presidential library in Abilene, Kansas, and Becky Bronson guided me through the process of obtaining FBI files on Robert H. W. Welch Jr. through Freedom of Information Act requests.

My research also took me to the Cammie G. Henry Research Center at Northwestern State University of Louisiana in Natchitoches, where archivist Mary Linn Wernet and library associate Nolan Eller helped me sift through the Kent Courtney Collection. I was particularly grateful for their invitation to attend the St. Patrick's Day cookout with the rest of the library staff. The peerless Bruce Tabb, the Special Collections librarian at the University of Oregon, pulled dozens of boxes from Willis E. Stone's papers, and Alana Inman, the manager of the Sam Houston Regional Library and Research Center in Liberty, Texas, helped focus my dive into Congressman Martin Dies Jr.'s papers. I was honored to receive a Silas Palmer Research Fellowship from the Hoover Institution, which allowed me to investigate the voluminous Radical Right Collection with the help of assistant archivist Jean McElwee Cannon and program manager Bronweyn Coleman. The State Historical Society of Missouri in Kansas City was the last archive I visited, and archivists Rachel Forester, Whitney A. Heinzmann, and Michele Loran aided my research into Congressman James A. Reed's papers. All told, I feel fortunate and privileged to have met, been helped by, and worked alongside such a wonderful group of librarians and archivists.

Some of the research in *Far-Right Vanguard* has already appeared in academic journals. In 2018 I published "'The Voice of Many Hatreds:' J. Evetts Haley and Texas Ultraconservatism," in *Western Historical Quarterly*. Editor Anne Hyde and the anonymous reviewers provided invaluable feedback, and I am also indebted to Brenda Frink and Abigail M. Gibson for their editorial guidance. I also published an article, "Taxation as Tyranny: *American Progress* and the Ultraconservative Movement," on Willis E. Stone and his magazine *American Progress* for a special edition of *Radical Americas*. The *Radical Americas* editors and staff—including William A. Booth, James West, Sue Currell, Katherine La Mantia, and Jaimee Biggin—and the anonymous readers all helped sharpen my argument about the importance of print culture and grassroots networks. I would also like to thank Aiden M. Bettine, a Ph.D. candidate at the University of Iowa, for helping me photograph bound editions of *American Progress* and *Freedom Magazine*. Both the *Western Historical Quarterly* and *Radical Americas* were gracious enough to let me reprint portions of these articles in *Far-Right Vanguard*.

I am grateful to the many educators and scholars who nurtured my inquisitive nature and love for history during my lifelong academic journey. I would like to thank Mrs. Wieland, my third-grade teacher, for fueling my passion for reading. My high school history teachers—Mrs. Smith, Mrs. Voss, and Mr. Thomas—fostered a creative, engaging classroom environment, and my memory of their passion continues to influence my teaching. When I got to Texas Tech University as an undergraduate, I forged a strong relationship with Gary Bell, a history professor and then dean of the Honors College. I spent hours in Dr. Bell's office discussing my academic and personal goals, and I can unequivocally say that without his sage advice and guidance, in particular his encouragement that I follow my heart and switch majors, I would not be a historian today. I would also like to thank Randy McBee, a history professor and former chair of the Texas Tech History Department, for giving me the opportunity to work as a teaching assistant and grow as an instructor. At the time I was a graduate student in search of direction, and I found my calling in teaching. I had the privilege of working for and learning from excellent professors at Texas Tech, including Justin Hart, Miguel Levario, Ethan Schmidt, Aliza Wong, and McBee himself. I am incredibly thankful for the advice and encouragement professors Justin Hart (my thesis advisor) and Sean P. Cunningham (the outside reader on my dissertation committee) have offered over the years.

Numerous people at the University of Houston had a deep influence upon my development as a scholar. I had the fortune of working with Gerald Horne, Martin V. Melosi, Nancy Beck Young, and Leandra Ruth Zarnow, all of whom provided intellectual guidance during the dissertation phase and beyond. I am especially grateful for the scholarly example my dissertation advisor, Nancy Beck Young, set for me to follow. I would also like to thank professors Todd Romero, Mark Allan Goldberg, Kairn Klieman, Monica Perales, Kelly Hopkins, Matthew Clavin, and Lawrence Curry for enriching my graduate school experience. I would be remiss if I did not acknowledge my wonderful graduate student cohort, including Kristen Williams, Sandra I. Enríquez, Stephanie Weiss Calvert, Alex LaRotta, Andrew Gustafson, Allison Robinson, Chris Haight, Savannah Williamson, and Lindsay Amaral. All of these amazing individuals read my work, offered feedback, and helped commiserate over setbacks and celebrate victories.

After receiving my Ph.D., I taught U.S. history at Langham Creek High School, where my educational and academic vision was supported by principal David Hughes, director of instruction Tamara Meldahl, assistant principal Tim Silvey, history department chairwoman Rebecca Sliman, and fellow history teacher John Reed. I am likewise grateful to every student who entered my classroom, whether during my high school teaching stints at Harmony School of Advancement and Langham Creek or during my time as a college professor. Each of you influenced my academic journey, and I appreciate the support you all showed for my teaching and my random stories. I hope you learned as much from me as I learned from all of you.

Over the years I have had the opportunity to network, often through history conferences and academic Twitter, with numerous scholars, many of whom have read and critiqued my work. In particular I would like to thank Jennifer Burns, N. D. B. Connolly, Christopher Deutsch, Robin L. Einhorn, Michelle Nickerson, Elizabeth Gillespie McRae, Kathryn S. Olmstead, and other scholars whom I am surely forgetting for asking questions about my research at various history conferences. In equal measure, I am grateful to David Austin Walsh, Michael Koncewicz, Timothy J. Lombardo, Joel Zapata, Seth Cotlar, Edward H. Miller, Elizabeth Tandy Shermer, Rick Perlstein, Cari

S. Babitzke and many others for making the conference circuit a less daunting experience by welcoming me into their circles. I have also had the privilege of publishing in public-facing outlets like the *Washington Post* and *Politico* where editors Nicole Hemmer, Kathryn Cramer Brownell, Brian Rosenwald, Carly Beth Goodman, and Bill Duryea helped sharpen my ideas and writing. David Walsh merits a special thanks because we co-authored a piece on the idea of "entitlement conservatism" for the *Washington Post*'s "Made by History" series.

I feel incredibly fortunate to be publishing with the University of Pennsylvania Press. I am particularly indebted to my amazing editor Robert Lockhart. I was once told that a "fatigue" had congealed around the history of conservatism, but Bob shared my vision that considerable room remained to interrogate the ideas and boundaries of modern conservatism. He has helped sharpen my thoughts, provided a wonderful sounding board, and guided me through the entire process, from writing through publication. I am likewise grateful to Noreen O'Connor-Abel, the managing editor for *Far-Right Vanguard*, for her critical comments and revisions, and Gigi Lamm, one of Penn Press's publicists, who made the publishing experience a bit less intimidating for a first-time author. Thanks to Julie Ehlers's copy editing and fact checking, this book has far fewer mistakes, and any that remain are mine alone. I would also like to thank the two anonymous reviewers for their thoughtful feedback, which strengthened my arguments and pushed me to embrace my writerly instincts.

I could not have asked for a better academic home to finish my manuscript than Houston Community College. Gisela Ables, the chair of the History Department, has been incredibly supportive of my publishing goals, and fellow history professor Nicholas Cox has patiently answered all of my inquiries as I settled in at HCC. I am likewise grateful to my history department colleagues for creating such a welcoming environment. My office mates—professors Marjorie Brown, Angela Holder, Natalie Garza, Jacob Mills, and Genevieve Stevens—are a constant fount of enlightenment and humor, and I always look forward to debating the topics of the day with them.

I relied on the kindness of numerous people while working on *Far-Right Vanguard*. My fellow Red Raiders Nick Davis, Bryan Kitchens, and Sam Thompson gave me places to stay in Midland and Lubbock while I visited the Haley Library and the Southwest Collection, respectively. Thanks to my cousins Steve and Marla Sheeley, I had a roof over my head in Fayetteville when I went to the Special Collections at the University of Arkansas. Sandra I.

Enríquez and Andrew Gustafson graciously let me stay with them while I was researching at the University of Missouri–Kansas City. I would also like to thank fellow writers Brantley Hargrove and Michael J. Mooney for pushing me out of my academic comfort zone and encouraging me to tell a good story. Brantley is like an older brother to me, he's one of my oldest friends, and I look forward to eating enchiladas and chatting about the craft of writing with both of them every time I go to Dallas.

I would also like to thank my parents, Scott and Libby Huntington, for their constant encouragement and support. Ever since I was young, my parents preached the importance of education. My mother, a wonderful educator herself, was the guiding force behind my academic journey. She encouraged me to apply for scholarships, join honors societies, and befriend people along the way. She even put up with my rebellious spirit when I refused to take certain classes seriously (i.e., math). My father fostered my intellectual curiosity and taught me the necessity of pondering difficult, uncomfortable questions. It is impossible to list every way that my parents are amazing, but I try to live up to their patience, dedication, and kindness every single day. Without their example and support, this book certainly would not have been possible. I also want to thank my sister Mary Claire for being an incredible person. She might be the most popular person I know. For my entire life I have always been "Mary Claire's brother," which would probably make a suitable nom de plume. Her smile lights up the room, and I am grateful to have her steady, loving presence in my life.

My uncle Don merits a mention here, too, because he told me life was too short to study a subject I did not enjoy, which helped give me the confidence to pursue history. I am also grateful to my grandfather Bill Huntington, fondly known in the family as Paw-Paw. Listening to his stories about the Great Depression and World War II undoubtedly shaped my eventual career path, and he helped support me financially during one of the leanest times of my life. Unfortunately, Paw-Paw passed away in 2016 at the age of ninety-six, so he will not witness the publication of this book, but I know he would have been proud of the fact that his grandson became a history professor. I would regret not acknowledging my wonderful dogs, Hendrix (known to his friends as "Big Man") and Shadow. They have been excellent companions on this journey. Hendrix is no longer with us, but Shadow provides enough youthful exuberance for one household.

Kristen Williams has been with me on this journey since its inception. She has heard me talk about the people in this book so much she could probably give you a biography of each one. Our conversations over coffee, at dinner, or while walking the dog helped me organize my thoughts and hone my ideas. She has the patience of a saint. I cannot even begin to count the number of times I swiveled my chair around and asked, "Hey, will you read this?" just to see if what I had written made any sense. She has a knack for seeing the forest whereas I tend to focus on the trees, and I remain grateful for her ability to help me see the bigger picture. I am also thankful that she encourages me to step away from my work every once in a while, and I get excited for every opportunity we get to travel together. Kristen is a burgeoning scholar in her own right, and I look forward to supporting her as she writes her dissertation in the same way she supported me during this project. Above all, I am thankful every day to be married to such a caring, compassionate woman, and it is for all of these reasons that I dedicate this book to her.

Printed in the USA
CPSIA information can be obtained
at www.ICGtesting.com
JSHW021104290824
69014JS00004B/66